DISTANCE EDUCATION

STRATEGIES AND TOOLS

DISTANCE EDUCATION

STRATEGIES AND TOOLS

BARRY WILLIS
EDITOR
UNIVERSITY OF ALASKA SYSTEM

EDUCATIONAL TECHNOLOGY PUBLICATIONS
ENGLEWOOD CLIFFS, NEW JERSEY 07632

Library of Congress Cataloging-in-Publication Data

Distance education : strategies and tools / Barry Willis, editor
    p. cm.
    Includes bibliographical references and indexes.
    ISBN 0-87778-268-7
    1. Distance education. 2. Educational technology. 3. Audio
-visual education. 4. Computer-assisted instruction.   I. Willis,
Barry Donald, 1952–
LC5800.D575   1994
371.3'078--dc20   93-23229
                                                       CIP

Printed in the United States of America.

Library of Congress Catalog Card Number:
93-23229.

International Standard Book Number:
0-87778-268-7.

First Printing: January, 1994.

PREFACE

Never before in education have the increased demands for program access contrasted so sharply with the reduced financial and human resources available to meet those demands. In one breath, school districts and universities are told by governing boards, funding agencies, and legislatures to plan for reduced budgets. In the next, they are asked to expand programs to meet the needs of previously under-served learners.

The reaction to this dilemma has been predictable. Some educators have run for cover, while others have sought technological "quick fixes," without adequate preparation and planning. Still others have taken a more measured approach, examining lessons of the past in hopes of finding solutions for the present, and a vision for the future. In recent years, this visionary exploration has encouraged educators to consider the potential role of *distance education*. That is the focus of this book.

Like most educational innovations that have stood the test of time, growth in the area of distance education has been more evolutionary than revolutionary. Although much has changed since the early 1800s when distance education meant "correspondence study" and mail delivery was measured in months, not days, much has stayed the same. Student needs remain diverse, administrators still grapple with tight budgets and growing expectations, and teachers continue to balance expanding content requirements with contracting resources and limited time.

As the field of distance education has evolved, so has the terminology used to describe the organizational framework it represents and the anticipated instructional outcomes that result. Terms and phrases including "distance education," "distance learning," "outreach," "tele-work," "tele-teaching," and "tele-learning," and others, have been used interchangeably to describe the same basic process and outcomes. For consistency, "distance education" will be used here to describe the organizational framework and process of providing education at a distance. The phrase "distance learning" will be used to identify the intended instructional outcome, i.e., learning that takes place at a distance.

At its most basic level, *distance education takes place when a teacher and student(s) are separated by physical distance, and technology (i.e., audio, video, data, and print) is used to bridge the instructional gap.*

Although this definition notes the key role played by technology in the delivery of instruction, the most effective technical tools remain transparent, subtle servants to instructional goals and content demands. In fact, if educators are to avoid "technological solutions in search of instructional problems," they must remain firmly focused on instructional outcomes, not the technology of delivery. At the same time, effective distance educators will remember the critical and irreplaceable role played by face-to-face communication. In these days of "virtual" everything, some are seduced by the notion that electronic wizardry can replace the importance of actually "being there." In reality, the opposite is more often the case. Those who are educators first and technologists second are finding that the importance of personal contact and relationship building remains a critical component of most effective distance education programs and is likely to increase as technical capabilities expand.

Without exception, effective distance education programs begin with careful planning and a focused understanding of course requirements and student needs. Appropriate technology can only be selected once these elements are understood in detail. There is no mystery to the way effective distance education programs develop. They don't happen spontaneously; they evolve through the hard work and dedicated efforts of many individuals and organizations. In fact, successful distance education programs rely on the consistent and integrated efforts of students, faculty, facilitators, support staff, and administrators. The following briefly describes roles of these key players in the distance education enterprise and the challenges they face.

Students

Meeting the instructional needs of students is the cornerstone of every effective distance education program, and the test by which all efforts in the field are judged. Regardless of the educational context, the primary role of the student is to learn. This is a daunting task under the best of circumstances, requiring motivation, planning, and an ability to analyze and apply the instructional content being taught. When instruction is delivered at a distance, additional challenges result because students are often separated from others sharing their backgrounds and interests, have few if any opportunities to interact with teachers outside of class, and must rely on technical linkages to bridge the gap separating class participants.

Faculty

To a great extent, the success of any distance education effort rests squarely on the shoulders of the faculty. In a traditional classroom setting, the instructor's responsibility includes assembling course content and developing an understanding of student needs. Special challenges confront those teaching at a distance. For example, the instructor must:

- Develop an understanding of the characteristics and needs of distant students with little first-hand experience and limited, if any, face-to-face contact.
- Adapt teaching styles and course content to take into consideration the needs and expectations of multiple, often diverse, audiences.

- Develop a working understanding of delivery technology, while remaining focused on their teaching role.
- Function effectively as a skilled facilitator as well as content provider.

Facilitators

The instructor often finds it beneficial to rely on a site facilitator to act as a bridge between the students and instructor. To be effective, a facilitator must understand the students being served and the instructor's expectations. Most importantly, the facilitator must be willing to follow the directives established by the teacher.

Where budget and logistics permit, the role of on-site facilitators has increased even in classes in which they have little, if any, content expertise. At the very least, they set up equipment, collect assignments, proctor tests, and act as the instructor's on-site eyes and ears.

Support Staff

These individuals are the silent heroes of the distance education enterprise and the detail people who ensure that the myriad details required for program success are dealt with effectively. Most successful distance education programs consolidate support service functions to include materials duplication and distribution, textbook ordering, securing of copyright clearances, facilities scheduling, sending and receiving grade reports, operating and troubleshooting technical resources, etc. Support personnel are truly the glue that keeps the distance education effort together and on track.

Administrators

Although administrators are typically influential in planning an institution's distance education program, they often lose contact or relinquish control to technical managers once the program is up and running. Effective distance education administrators are more than idea people. They are consensus builders, decision makers, and referees. They maintain control of technical and facility managers, ensuring that technological resources are effectively deployed to further the institution's academic mission. Most importantly, they maintain an academic focus, realizing that meeting the instructional needs of distant students is their ultimate responsibility.

If those involved in the distance education enterprise are to be successful, they must look beyond traditional solutions in their quest to solve non-traditional problems. They must become comfortable and competent in addressing a wide range of issues, options, and concerns that didn't exist until recently.

In meeting these new challenges, the information that follows can serve as a guide and reference tool for veteran distance educators as well as those administrators, faculty, and staff who are approaching the challenge of distance education for the first time.

Chapter One explores the historical roots of distance education around the world and provides an overview of current national and international efforts to make innovative use of distant teaching methods and technology.

Chapter Two reviews distance education-related research and evaluation, including comparative studies of various media, characteristics of successful instructors, and examination of the variables that impact instructional success.

Chapter Three explores the basic tenets of strategic planning for distance education and their application to elementary, secondary, and higher education environments. Fundamental principles of strategic planning are set forth, and case study examples illustrate the application of these principles to conditions typically encountered in the distance education environment.

Chapter Four details the processes and products of needs assessment in the context of distance education. Procedures for program development and evaluation are also covered, including strategies for effective implementation.

Chapter Five examines the critical role of print, distance education's "unsung hero." Advantages and limitations are explored, as are utilization strategies, layout and design considerations, as well as strategies for integrating text with other instructional technologies.

Chapter Six examines audio's critical role in distance education focusing on strengths, limitations, utilization strategies, and different audio delivery options. Emphasis is placed on practical approaches for enhancing the effectiveness of audio interaction.

Chapter Seven surveys video technologies and discusses effective utilization ideas with emphasis on increasing the cost effectiveness of video applications. Special emphasis is placed on enhancing the interactive capabilities of video in the context of distance delivery.

Chapter Eight looks at the wide range of computer-based delivery options available to the distance educator. Areas of coverage include computer conferencing, electronic mail, hypermedia, and potential uses for personal computers and peripheral hardware.

Chapter Nine takes a look at future distance delivery technologies, with emphasis on tools that will enhance participant interaction. The potential impacts of various delivery systems are explored including videodisc, CD-ROM, compressed audio and video, multimedia systems, speech synthesis, and virtual reality.

Chapter Ten makes sense of the often confusing world of copyright regulation as it specifically relates to the process and products of distance education. Effort is made to simplify existing regulations and provide practical advice for maximizing the utilization of distance education resources within the confines of existing Federal law.

Chapter Eleven presents an overview of the telecommunications regulatory environment and related public policy issues. The discussion includes landmark regulatory decisions and describes strategies for enhancing participation in regulatory debates and public policy discussions.

Chapter Twelve explores the growing role and importance of regional planning and distance education cooperatives. Different models for regional cooperation are examined as are the educational and political realities of planning and implementing effective programs.

Chapter Thirteen details the importance of faculty development and in-service training, with emphasis on the unique instructional challenges and pressures facing the distance educator. Strategies for organizing successful faculty development workshops and issues related to institutional reward structures are also explored.

Distance education can be instrumental in addressing many of the dilemmas facing education today. At the same time, its inherent flexibility presents a potentially chaotic mix of possibilities that can just as easily lead to confusion as enlightenment. This book is intended to assist academic leaders, administrators, and faculty in effectively navigating this new world of challenging opportunity in a practical and straightforward manner.

In addition to those who contributed chapters, completion of this book relied upon the help and cooperation of a great many individuals. In particular, I would like to thank Maureen Clark, Stevan DeSoer, Scott Carter, Jay Massey, Martha Hogan, Grant Sims, Joan McMillen, Steve Fishback, Jan Messick, Dona McLean, Ali Bowles, Suzanne Tryck, and my parents, Virginia and William R. Willis.

Barry Willis
Lake Clark, Alaska

ABOUT THE AUTHORS

Chapter One: Distance Education Around the World

Barry Brown is Professor of Educational Communications in the College of Education, University of Saskatchewan in Canada. Dr. Brown is a worldwide consultant in the areas of distance learning and interactive televised instruction. Recently Dr. Brown has been assisting the New Zealand Polytechnic Institutes in the area of distance education.

Yvonne Brown is Dean of the College of Nursing at the University of Saskatchewan. In addition to her interests in distance education, Dean Brown's professional specialty is perinatal crisis support. She has consulted widely with nursing institutions in Australia, New Zealand, and Hawaii.

Chapter Two: Research in Distance Education

Robert Threlkeld is Director of the Distance Learning Center and a Professor in the School of Education at California State Polytechnic University, Pomona. Dr. Threlkeld has spent the last eight years in distance education using a variety of technologies. He is co-founder of the Alliance for Distance Education in California, an organization that promotes the use of technology at all levels of instruction. Dr. Threlkeld recently produced the monograph, "Rural Voices: Conversations about Distance Learning with Four Rural California Schools."

Karen Brzoska is an instructional designer for the Distance Learning Center at California State Polytechnic University, Pomona. She assists university instructors in adapting courses for delivery on a live, interactive instructional television system called PolyNet. Under a grant from the U.S. Department of Education, Ms. Brzoska recently produced a series of parent education broadcasts for the local community.

Chapter Three: Strategic Planning and Academic Planning in Distance Education

Robert Albrecht is Associate Vice President of the University of Colorado. Dr. Albrecht has taught in Minnesota, Chicago, and Oregon and held administrative posts at a number of institutions. He has chaired the steering committee of the Western Cooperative for Educational Telecommunications, Western Interstate Commission for Higher Education (WICHE). Dr. Albrecht currently heads the Cooperative's Policy Committee and directs the University of Colorado fiber-optic network.

Gary Bardsley is the Associate Director of the Interdisciplinary Telecommunications Graduate Program at the University of Colorado at Boulder. In this role he is active in the usage of ITFS, satellite, and video-based distance educational processes used in the telecommunications curriculum.

Chapter Four: Assessing Needs, Developing Instruction, and Evaluating Results in Distance Education

Nick Eastmond is Professor of Instructional Technology at Utah State University. For three years, Dr. Eastmond coordinated the Master Resource Teacher Program delivered over the University's COM-NET system. Prior to that, he was the Director of Instructional Development at Utah State University and Director of the Northern Rockies Consortium for Higher Education. He is co-author with Robert Brien of *Cognitive Science and Instruction* (1994, Educational Technology Publications).

Chapter Five: Print Tools for Distance Education

Earl R. Misanchuk is a Professor in the Extension Division at the University of Saskatchewan. Dr. Misanchuk has a background in instructional systems technology and has been involved in the instructional design of primarily print-based materials for distance education for 15 years. He has been using desktop publishing procedures since 1985. Dr. Misanchuk is author of *Preparing Instructional Text: Document Design Using Desktop Publishing* (1992, Educational Technology Publications) and co-author with Richard Schwier of *Interactive Multimedia Instruction* (1993, Educational Technology Publications).

Chapter Six: Audio Tools for Distance Education

Linda Lachance Wolcott is an Assistant Professor of Instructional Technology at Utah State University. Dr. Wolcott has been active in distance education as a program administrator, instructional developer, and as a distance teacher. In completing this chapter, Dr. Wolcott was assisted by **Robert E. Lindsay**, a graduate student in Instructional Technology at Utah State University, and **Vicki S. Napper**, a research analyst for the Southwest Research Institute and a doctoral student in Instructional Technology at Utah State University.

Chapter Seven: Video Tools for Distance Education

E. Lynne Oliver is Executive Director of Programming for the Saskatchewan Communications Network in Canada. Dr. Oliver's primary research interests include the adult distant learner and mediated communication in the distance education environment. Dr. Oliver is a specialist in the role and importance of interaction in instructional television.

Chapter Eight: Computer Tools for Distance Education

Richard A. Markwood is an English educator, evaluator, writer, and editor. Dr. Markwood recently served as project director for NorthWestNet, a high-speed regional network whose initial funding came from the National Science Foundation.

Chapter Nine: Contemporary and Emerging Interactive Technologies for Distance Education

Richard Schwier is a Professor of Educational Communications at the University of Saskatchewan and was Editor of the *Canadian Journal of Educational Communication*. Dr. Schwier has developed several interactive multimedia productions, is the author of *Interactive Video* (1987, Educational Technology Publications), and co-author with Earl R. Misanchuk of *Interactive Multimedia Instruction* (1993, Educational Technology Publications).

Chapter Ten: Copyright Issues in Distance Education

Janis H. Bruwelheide is an Associate Professor in the College of Education at Montana State University where she teaches and assists faculty in using telecommunications and adapting courses to distance delivery. Dr. Bruwelheide is a recognized consultant concerning copyright as applied to education and is currently revising *The Copyright Primer* for the American Library Association. She regularly presents national sessions and conducts workshops concerning copyright.

Chapter Eleven: Regulatory Issues in Distance Education

Ellen D. Wagner is a project consultant with the WICHE Western Cooperative for Educational Telecommunications. Dr. Wagner has a background in educational psychology and is an Associate Professor of Educational Technology with the Division of Research, Evaluation, and Development, University of Northern Colorado. She is a Contributing Editor of *Educational Technology* magazine.

Chapter Twelve: Distance Education: An Opportunity for Cooperation and Resource Sharing

Mollie A. McGill is the Assistant Director of the WICHE Western Cooperative for Educational Telecommunications. Ms. McGill has been involved in the development of a number of regional cooperative activities through her work with WICHE and was co-editor of *State Higher Education Policies in the Information Age.*

Sally M. Johnstone is Director of the WICHE Western Cooperative for Educational Telecommunications. Dr. Johnstone has a background in experimental psychology and has served in faculty positions on the East Coast and in Europe, as an academic administrator, and director of a university's instructional telecommunications office.

Chapter Thirteen: Enhancing Faculty Effectiveness in Distance Education

Barry Willis (Editor) currently directs outreach for the University of Idaho's College of Engineering. In addition, he is a professor of teacher education through an affiliate appointment with the College of Education. When completing this text, Dr. Willis was Statewide Director of Distance Education for the University of Alaska System, where he previously served as Associate Vice Chancellor for Distance Education and Academic Planning, and Director of Instructional Development. He has taught at Boston University, Alaska Pacific University, Utah State University, and the University of Alaska Fairbanks. Dr. Willis is a Contributing Editor of *Educational Technology* magazine and recently authored *Distance Education: A Practical Guide* (1993, Educational Technology Publications).

TABLE OF CONTENTS

DISTANCE EDUCATION

STRATEGIES AND TOOLS

Chapter One

Distance Education
Around the World

F. Barry Brown and Yvonne Brown

The early 90s have spawned technological breakthroughs that will come of age by the mid-90s and will provide a virtually seamless world communications network capable of reaching every inhabitant on earth. The challenge facing distance educators during this decade is daunting, because a means must be found to create infrastructures that will harness this network's power to provide education, training, information, and cultural programming in developed and developing countries. The concluding decade of the 20th century will be a time of change from the institutional based learning structures of the past few centuries to open architecture education that will occur at a time, place, and in a configuration suitable to the learner rather than to the teacher or administrator. Distance education and its variants have potential to provide equity of access on a world basis by the millennium.

Buckminster Fuller—architect, engineer, designer, teacher, and author, inventor of the geodesic dome, one of the world's most respected visionaries— directed his forward thinking to education of the future. In an April, 1961 speech he commented: "Much of the educational system today is aimed at answering: 'How am I going to get a job? I must earn a living.' That is the priority item under which we are working all the time — the idea of having to earn a living" (cited in Thorvaldsen, 1980, p. 2). Fuller proposed that traditional muscle and reflex jobs are going to go out the historical window forever and that our educational processes are the upcoming world industry. He pointed out that:

> Education is going to be number one amongst the great world industries, within which will flourish an educational machine technology that will provide tools such as the individually selected and articulated two-way TV

and an inter-continentally net-worked, documentaries call-up system, operative over any home two-way TV set. (Thorvaldsen, 1980, p. 3)

McLuhan and Leonard (cited in Thorvaldsen, 1980) foresaw that "the student of the future will truly be an explorer, a researcher, a huntsman who ranges through the new educational world of electrical circuitry and heightened human interaction just as the tribal huntsman ranged the wilds" (p. 7). They pointed out that the main "work" of the future is education, and that "people will not so much earn a living as learn a living" (p. 8). A final comment portends a future that has been more than realized during the 25 years since it was penned:

> The world communications net, the all-involved linkage of electric circuitry, will grow and become more sensitive. It will also develop new modes of feedback so that communication can become dialogue instead of monologue. It will breach the wall between "in" and "out" of school. It will join all people everywhere. When this has happened, we may at last realize that our place of learning is the world itself, the entire planet we live on. The little red schoolhouse is already well on its way toward becoming the little round schoolhouse. Some day, all of us will spend our lives in our own school, the world. (Thorvaldsen, 1980, p. 8)

Information explosion and information society are commonly used terms that reflect the nature of today's educational processes. Satellites, fiber optic cable, telephone, computers, and multimedia are but a few of the technologies that are now lending truth to early predictions for a world communications net. James Martin (cited in Thorvaldsen, 1980) mused that:

> Education used to be regarded as something that ended when one's working life began. In the electronic era it will go on throughout life: *adult* education is of vital importance. The decades ahead will be characterized by an extremely rapid rate of change in which work and leisure activities will change. Many persons will learn two, three, or four careers in a lifetime as telecommunications, automation and, later, machine intelligence will cause entirely different work patterns. Electronics will create both the need and the tools for lifelong learning. (Thorvaldsen, 1980, p. 9)

Current literature leaves little doubt concerning the need for or availability of the tools to engage in learning processes that extend beyond present institutional settings. *Technologies for Learning Outside the Classroom* (Niemi & Gooler, 1987) is illustrative of a trend by many educators to examine traditional educational practice and process in the context of burgeoning technological advances. Development of effective global distance education programs, as described by visionaries, remains an elusive goal, but thousands of hot spots world-wide continue to fuel the vision.

Beginnings

Itinerant wanderers delivering information by word of mouth were perhaps the world's first distance educators bringing information from afar to eager recipients encountered during their travels. This centuries old practice was irrevocably changed by the invention of writing and later, print. Print was first put to use in distance education with development of correspondence courses created by universities during the middle 1800s to disseminate learning beyond the walls of existing institutions. Electronic technology, beginning with radio broadcasting, brought a mass quality to learning at a distance in the early 1930s. Technology of information transfer has now outstripped the ability of educators and trainers to develop programs to serve the exponential increase in learners who wish to be educated outside traditional place-bound learning sites.

Present day distance education has its roots in early university correspondence and extension programs designed primarily to educate students via paper based processes. Media and communications technology were quickly incorporated to enhance these methods. Radio, television, and other emerging communications technologies, such as computers, often assume the role of primary carrier. Bates (1982) of the British Open University was commissioned in 1980 by the International Institute of Educational Planning to survey 12 distance learning systems and identify trends in the use of audio-visual media. He reported two distinct trends, finding that the "*number* of different audio-visual media suitable for distance education is increasing rapidly" and that the "*boundaries* between different media are breaking down" (p. 10).

From a global stand-point distance education has evolved quietly over the past quarter century. Evolution is an appropriate descriptor because distance education describes learning occurring within the constraint of Holmberg's (1981) essential elements (separation of teacher and learner, and structuring of learning materials, linked to the student in a planned educational organization) and appears to have infiltrated the process of education by reverse osmosis. Notable examples, such as the British Open University, may have bordered on revolutionary, but even this pivotal development in distance learning proceeded quietly and effectively, creating only a modicum of excitement within largely academic circles. Distance education evolved from traditional educational practice and process in reaction to specific access problems. Daniel, Stroud, and Thompson (1982) commented in the preface to *Learning at a Distance: A World Perspective*, which featured 120 papers by authors from 25 countries, that "Learning at a distance is becoming an increasingly common form of education in many countries of the world." They also pointed out that "A theme of international dimensions common to many papers is the prospect of distance education becoming a major shaping force in societies all over the world" (p. 5).

Writing in 1982, Hilary Perraton (1982) summed up the achievements of distance education in the world:

> Distance teaching has been taken more seriously in the south than in the north. That is the most striking difference between the two. In the west, it

has been used mainly to help small minorities of students beyond the reach of ordinary schools and colleges; from a national point of view the minorities were never particularly important. In the east, distance teaching had been more important: Stalin chose it as a way of increasing production of the technicians and technologists needed for Soviet society between the wars. But it was never at the centre of the educational system. In the south, it has come far nearer that centre, and has been used, for example, for the vital task of training teachers in a dozen or more countries. In Tanzania distance education using radio campaigns has played a central role in adult education, teaching people about political issues, about health, and about the environment. In a number of countries in Africa, distance teaching has been used on a scale that is proportionally far greater than in Europe or America. (p. 16)

Analysis of past, present, and future thought regarding distance education leads one to believe that, as a field of endeavor, distance education remains at a beginning stage. This bold statement is reinforced when one considers funds spent on traditional institution-based education versus funds expended on education at a distance and then juxtaposes comments by today's writers concerning the problematic state of traditional education versus the potential of emerging distance education and related technologies. It appears that the future of distance learning can only expand at an exponential rate if it is to fulfil the promise voiced by today's educators and technologists for the 90s and beyond.

Literature: World View

Review of the distance education literature from 1960 to 1980 reveals an impressive growth curve attesting to an increasing body of knowledge throughout the world. Literature during this period was primarily descriptive, providing a balanced world view of problems and solutions in correspondence programs and the emerging area of distance education. The general consensus of authors of the time (Bååth, 1978; Childs, 1971; Coldeway, 1982; Holmberg, 1977; Mathieson, 1971) was that a database sufficient for establishing and directing research was just evolving. Since 1980 the literature on distance education, open learning, and interactive technological learning interventions has burgeoned and has shown a bias toward the new and emerging technologies of distance learning with heavy emphasis on telecommunications driven advances in delivery methods. The trend in the literature has been to place emphasis on post-secondary distance education; however, this seems to be giving way to a broader "cradle-to-grave" outlook directed toward credit, non-credit, and training at all levels.

Early Initiatives

To classify agencies engaged in modern distance education, one would have to look back at the early open learning institutions as forerunners of the current distance education movement. Daniel Granger (1990) commented:

From Britain to Thailand, Japan to South Africa, distance learning is an important part of national strategies to educate large numbers rapidly and efficiently. In the U.S., educators are finding distance learning not only efficient for outreach to new populations, but an effective medium for new instructional models. ... "Distance learning," as a term associated with new technologies offering a full-fledged alternative to classroom education, got its biggest boost internationally with the founding of the British Open University (BOU) in 1969. The BOU gained rapid visibility and recognition by broadcasting its video course components weekly throughout the United Kingdom on the BBC network. ... Since then, new government-supported "open universities" in other countries have been established at a rate of about one every two years, with at least three more in the planning stages. (p. 45)

Table 1 illustrates that a significant number of learners receive university education by distance programming. The addition of learners who receive distance programming in elementary, secondary, training, and non-credit areas would perhaps quadruple these numbers.

Institution	Date established	Enrollment
University of South Africa	1951	50,000
Open University, U.K.	1969	50,000
Universidad Nacional, Spain	1972	83,000
Fernuniversitat, Germany	1974	37,000
Open University of Israel	1974	12,000
Allama Iqbal Open University, Pakistan	1974	150,000
Athabasca University, Canada	1975	10,000
University Nacional Abierta, Venezuela	1977	29,000
University Est A Distancia, Costa Rica	1977	11,000
Sukhothai Thammathirat OU, Thailand	1978	200,000
Central Radio and TV University, China	1978	1,000,000
Open University of Sri Lanka	1981	18,000
Open Universiteit, Netherlands	1981	33,000
Andrha Pradesh Open University, India	1981	41,000
Korean Air and Correspondence University	1982	300,000
University of the Air of Japan	1983	22,000
Universitas Terbuka, Indonesia	1984	70,000
Indira Gandhi National Open University, India	1986	30,000
National Open University of Taiwan	1986	48,000
Al-Quds (Palestinian) Open University, Jordan	1986	not available
Universidade Aberta, Portugal	1988	3,800
Open University of Bangladesh	1992	not available
Open University of Poland	Proposed	
Open University of France	Proposed	

Table 1. *Major open universities in the world (from Granger, 1990, updated by Brown, 1992)*

Sewart (cited in Keegan, 1986) stated:

> The last decade has seen a phenomenal growth in distance education and the integration of this method of education into the standard educational provision in a large number of countries to such an extent that it is now no longer possible to think solely in the traditional sense of the face-to-face contact. (p. 3)

Keegan (1986) speaks of the history and promise of distance education:

> For long the Cinderella of the educational spectrum, distance education emerged in the 1970s with a changed image. It has come of age after a chequered and often criticized first one hundred years. Furthermore, its future seems assured because of the growing privatization of life in many developed Western societies and the incapacity of on-campus programmes to cope with even minimal educational opportunity elsewhere. (pp. 3–4)

He goes on to point out that improvement of distance education during the 70s can be attributed to:
- the development of new communications technology;
- sophistication in the use of print materials;
- improved design of instructional materials;
- better support services for students;
- the founding of the Open University at Milton Keynes and similar structures in developed and developing countries.

Scale of operation of the British Open University proved to be the engine driving a renaissance of theoretical, foundational, and practical endeavor during the 70s. A critical examination of institutions undertaking early distance education initiatives provided insight to hundreds of educational, business, and industrial agencies throughout the world during the 80s. Education and business experienced an unprecedented increase in learners needing basic education, training, and re-training. A large number of institutions responded to enrollment pressure and educational and training demands by going outside the classroom walls. Rumble and Keegan (1982) developed seven major classifications describing the organization structures associated with autonomous, centralized, decentralized, institutional, multi-institutional, and mixed mode variants for organizing distance education.

James W. Hall (1990), President of Empire College, commented on open universities. His statements are equally relevant to other levels of open learning and training.

> Indeed, these new institutions have moved well beyond their tentative and experimental antecedents and are becoming a major force for change in higher education. Contemporary solutions to such central issues as access, curriculum, quality, and cost are being addressed most creatively and forcefully by these universities. Even as the flowering of the liberal arts colleges, the rise of the land grant and research universities and spread of community colleges were the most dramatic events of their respective generations in the United States, so today the distance universities are

emerging as the institutions most profoundly affecting higher education around the world. (p. 48)

Many agree that distance learning is the fastest growing instructional pattern in the world. Technologies of delivery, particularly those related to telecommunications, have had a "greening" effect on the distance learning enterprise. The potential to solve access, cost, time, place, and interactivity considerations that have plagued education since the beginning of time has never been greater. A look at the world's distance education programs confirms our heritage from a hundred years of distance education history and the hope we experience for the success of new educational patterns and technologies.

Case Scan

Interest in distance education has gripped the world. Today scarcely a periodical fails to mention new ways of educating, learning, and communicating. Education at a distance is widely heralded to solve the ills of society in a broad expanse of areas from basic literacy to re-training the global work force. Even a cursory scan of what is happening in distance education would fill volumes. Organization of a representative scan of cases sufficient to give a broad flavor of programs, technologies, and organizations involved in distance education is itself problematic. The following scan is done by geographic area, with an attempt to provide a variety of different organizational structures, scales of operation, varieties of technology, and outcomes. In no case can this brief overview be construed as comprehensive or fully representative of the world view.

One comprehends immediately the immense scope of distance education activity when browsing the Distance Education Database developed for the Commonwealth of Learning by the International Centre for Distance Learning (ICDL), on the campus of the Open University in the United Kingdom. The ICDL Database was prepared (April 1989–March 1992) under a grant of £2 million (approximately $3.7 million U.S.) from the British Government's Overseas Development Administration as an information service to the Commonwealth of Learning (Distance Education Data Base, 1991). The first phase—to include information on all major Commonwealth institutions and their distance taught courses by March, 1992—has been achieved. The database is available on-line and on CD ROM, free of charge to defined users in developing countries. Other users may purchase on-line subscriptions or CD ROM (four updates) at £200 (approximately $370 U.S.) per year.

Integrated access is available for:
- the course area, with approximately 18,000 records from about 150 Commonwealth institutions;
- the institution area, with information on about 590 institutions offering distance education;
- the literature area, with some 4,000 bibliographic entries on aspects of distance education.

The ICDL Database is simple to use on-line or by CD ROM. Searches are classified by "field of study" and the user may search these classifications by "level" or "search word." Institution search is by "region" in the first instance and "search word" to narrow the field. ICDL selected eight regions: Africa, Asia, Australasia, Middle East, Europe, North America, Caribbean, and Latin America. The authors of this chapter selected these regions as a suitable classification arrangement for the case scan. The literature search is by "subject area," "author," "title," "publication year," or "search word." All screens can be directed to output for creation of hard copy records.

The ICDL Database is a major contribution to the field of distance education. Although it includes primarily Commonwealth institutions, it is an invaluable resource for practitioners seeking information regarding programs and courses. Researchers will find it an excellent up-to-date resource. The authors found the 1992 database helpful in checking references and providing details concerning programs described in the literature. The ICDL Database has spawned a plethora of documentation, including the hard copy of *Distance education: A selective bibliography* (Harry, 1991), which arrived with the CD ROM version of the database. Lundin (1988) points out that global initiatives abound in distance education. The ICDL Database initiative, much as Lundin's communications and information technologies link the world, is rapidly becoming part of the global fabric.

This fabric, in the world view, is very much a patchwork, a mosaic. The patchwork is rapidly knitting together as educational communications technology becomes more pervasive and less expensive. Organizational patterns of technology, funding, and administration are becoming discernible across the world distance education mosaic. Most prevalent is the overall trend of institutions to move from a single-mode delivery strategy to multi-mode with a major interactive component. Two-way interaction between learner and teacher is gaining popularity both as a live component of the instructional process and as a mediated component made possible by emerging multimedia/computer technology. A comprehensive scan of world distance education shows distinct patterns developing along lines related to the geographical, technical, and funding imperatives of the region. A second pattern is the trend toward "open architecture" education that moves distance education from an institution-centered add-on to a process embodying a degree of collaboration and cooperation with the learner that transcends the insularity of traditional modes. The selection of cases for this scan emphasizes the differences and similarities of distance education programming throughout the world.

Africa

Africa is a continent of contrasts. Approximately 70–80 institutions provide distance education service. The University of South Africa became the world's first open university in 1951, as a dedicated correspondence university (Jenkins, 1989). The Zambian National Correspondence College was established in 1964 and the Malawi Correspondence College in 1965. Zambia and Malawi initiated a supervised study group system to provide alternative schooling for thousands of adolescents who could not enroll in secondary schools. The University of Zambia uses a mixed-mode organizational model (Rumble, 1986). The Department of Correspondence Studies academic staff are responsible for teaching both internal and external students, while the Department provides administrative services (Nyirenda, 1989). Tanzania trained 35,000 teachers by distance education over a five year period to staff a universal primary education program.

African distance education institutions have used mostly print and face-to-face media, although national broadcast radio has been used in a number of innovative programs. In 1965 Ethiopia established a small educational broadcasting program directed at 12,000 viewers. This undertaking has expanded to include television so that educational radio and television became available nation-wide (Gupta, 1991). Distance education strategies have been proposed to assist Africans with the educational crisis facing many countries, but as Jenkins (1989) points out:

> In order for all these programmes to be effective, more resources must be forthcoming and integration of distance education with the formal system is desirable. Otherwise distance education may remain at the periphery, its potential under-used. (p. 41)

Asia-Pacific

More than 100 major institutions and countless smaller ones in Asia have distance education courses and programs. The ICDL database differentiates between Asia, Australasia, and the South Pacific, although more recently these areas are referred to as the "Asia-Pacific Region." Diversity of population, geography, economics, culture, and distance characterize the Asia-Pacific Region, as compared with the greater homogeneity found in Europe and North America. Development of education and related services was sporadic until recently, when a surge in telecommunications created commonalities that tie the region together and portend enormous economic growth. The telecommunications revolution, fiber, wireless, and satellite, have potential to leap-frog the older copper infrastructure that has supported the rapid development in industrialized areas like Canada, United States, Japan, and some European countries. Without the liability of a highly capitalized older technology infrastructure, many of the less developed areas of the world have an opportunity to take advantage of new wireless developments that can be supported without intense terrestrial penetration. Distance education is poised to make use of the new pathways under development in the Asia-Pacific Region.

Distance education in Asia is increasingly spotlighted as an avenue for sharing resources among educational institutions and promoting participation of existing traditional institutions in open learning/multi-mode formats to increase cost-effective access. "Focus on Asia," a symposium arranged by the Commonwealth of Learning (COL) in Delhi, India in August 1992, brought together heads of university funding agencies to:

> Explore how the techniques usually associated with high quality distance education can be more closely integrated into the conventional approach

thereby increasing access, improving quality and accelerating the development of human resources so vital for all countries in their efforts to advance social and economic progress. (Commonwealth of Learning, 1992, p. 2)

The symposium analyzed ten case studies and agreed on the following conclusions:

1. The use of distance education offers significant potential in higher education, especially in addressing concerns for increasing access and improving quality.
2. While there are resource constraints, the implementation of distance education methods can be cost-effective and productive over time, providing that initial investments are well conceived and employed and resources are shared among institutions.
3. A "systems approach" should be adopted, in that all aspects of higher-education and higher-education institutions need to be considered in furthering of the application of distance education.
4. There is a strong case for integration of distance education methods throughout higher education, providing the flexibility and adaptability that will enable institutions to address many of the problems that they currently face.
5. There is a need for better informed politicians, bureaucrats, academicians, and members of the public as to the potential for distance education. The management and administration of distance education systems need more training and improvement. International cooperation is the key.
6. Continuing professional education, women's programs, and other specific areas also need support.
7. There is a need for further research in all aspects of distance education, including that of application of technology.
8. Participants also agreed on a general framework for the development and management of distance education programmes within the context of a dual-mode higher-education institution. (Commonwealth of Learning, 1992, pp. 2–3)

Emphasis has been placed on distance education for higher education in Asia, with primary and secondary education receiving less attention, perhaps because this segment of education has traditionally been better served by conventional methods. Indications are that alternative methods for primary and secondary education are now receiving more attention. Bangladesh, a populous country with a literacy rate of about 30 percent, established its first open learning institution of higher education in October, 1992. Concurrently, Bangladesh created an Institute of Distance Education charged with catering to the needs of primary and secondary schools and incorporating radio, television, and state-of-the-art communications technology. Bangladesh Open

University is unique in addressing the needs of the entire spectrum of education (Commonwealth of Learning, 1992, pp. 3–4).

Only a small number of institutions have been chosen for a brief review arranged according to the categories of Asia, Australasia, and the South Pacific as set out by the ICDL database. Type, format, scale, and geographic location guided the selection to provide an overview of the Asia-Pacific region.

Asia

Allama Iqbal Open University, Pakistan, was established in 1974 with jurisdiction over the entire country. Its mission is to provide educational "uplift for the masses" by "carrying education to their door-step" (ICDL, CD ROM, 1992). Four areas of academic programming feature functional education, general education, teacher education, and research and development. Allama Iqbal employs multi-media strategies such as correspondence kits, radio and television broadcasts, tutorial instruction by correspondence, at study centers, and workshops.

Andhra Pradesh Open University, India, was established in 1981 to provide equality of educational opportunity to a large segment of the population. It offers Bachelor's degrees in Arts, Science, Commerce, and Library/Information Science and has a budget of about $3.5 million U.S. Instructional strategies include print, audio cassettes, radio broadcasts, residential schools, face-to-face tutoring, and counselling. The university has 57 district study centers including one in the Central Prison at Hyderabad.

The Open Learning Institute of Hong Kong, opened in 1989, is the newest higher education institution established by the Hong Kong government. Some 17,500 students are enrolled, many without university entrance requirements. Courses are based on print materials, with some courses supported by supplementary materials, broadcasts, group tutorials, and day schools.

In China, a national network of Radio and Television Universities was established in the early 1960s to meet the demand for adult education. In 1978 the State Council approved establishment of the Central Radio and Television University (CRTVU), 43 Provincial Autonomous Regional and Municipal Universities (PRTVU), 279 Branch Schools, 625 Work Stations, and Television classes. The TVU system is operated administratively and academically by balancing centralization and decentralization. The system uses radio, television, and satellite to deliver programming, supplemented by printed teaching materials. TVU offers more than 200 degree level courses, while PRTVUs and their Branch Schools offer courses to suit the local needs, bringing the total to over 500 courses per year.

The TVU's target students are in-service adults, secondary school graduates, and school leavers waiting for job assignment. Students are admitted by national entrance examinations, and students who do not take the entrance examinations and who study on a self-instructional basis are called "free-viewers and listeners." They are issued diplomas or single course certificates if they take and pass the required examinations. CRTVU is the largest institution of higher education in China and the largest open learning institution in the world (China Radio and TV University, undated; Edgington, 1992).

The Open University of Sri Lanka (OUSL) was created in 1981 by amalgamation of the External Services Agency and the Institute of Distance Education. It offers certificates, diplomas, bachelor's degrees, M.Phil., and Ph.D. by distance education. No formal qualifications are required to study at the OUSL. Print is the main medium of instruction and is supplemented by audio and video cassettes, face-to-face teaching, seminars, workshops, laboratory, field work, radio, and television. A network of study centers provides administration of programs, registration, distribution of course materials, and face-to-face instructional and tutorial sessions.

In Singapore a distance education initiative called Fast Forward was instituted in 1990. Fast Forward offers companies and workers training programs that can be pursued any time, any place, at the pace suitable to the individual worker, and at relatively low cost. Workers' interest is stimulated and sustained by developing learning strategies adapted to their learning styles and offering progressive and continuous job-related skills upgrading. Courses are video based with supplementary television broadcasts. Participants receive course materials that reinforce video programs. Face-to-face tutorials are conducted at Fast Forward centers, and students can access their course leader for tele-tutoring over regular telephone lines (ICDL CD ROM, 1992).

Sukhothai Thammathirat Open University (STOU) was established by Royal Charter in 1978 as the eleventh state university in Thailand and the first in Southeast Asia to use a distance learning system. STOU subscribes to the principle of lifelong education, aims to improve the population's quality of life, seeks to upgrade the educational and professional qualifications of working people, and strives to expand educational opportunities at the tertiary level for the general public and those who have completed secondary education. STOU has devised a distance learning system that employs printed materials, radio and television programs, computer assisted instruction and other methods that enable students to study independently without having to enter a conventional classroom.

STOU offers bachelor's degree programs, certificate and continuing education programs in Liberal Arts, Educational Studies, Management Science, Law, Health Sciences, Economics, Home Economics, Political Science, Agricultural Extension, Cooperatives, and Communication Arts. By November 1992, 450,000 students were enrolled in distance education programs. An integrated approach to course development organizes material into course blocks of 15 units of approximately 12 hours, constituting a six credit course. Additional media, educational service centers, local and regional study centers, specialized practical centers, and area resources centers are available (Sukhothai, Undated; UNESCO, 1992).

Indonesia is the world's fifth most populous nation. Only a small portion of qualified applicants can be accepted into the government and private universities. To accommodate the need for tertiary education, Indonesia began experiments in distance education in 1955, and in 1984 Universitas Terbuka (UT) was created. It was modelled on the United Kingdom's Open University (Dunbar, 1991; Hiola & Moss, 1990). Enrollments exceeded 130,000 and constituted only a small fraction of those seeking admission.

United Nations Educational, Scientific, and Cultural Organization (UNESCO) and the International Council for Distance Education (ICDE) have identified operational problems at UT, including: over-centralization; difficulty producing required learning material; lack of interaction, supervision, and monitoring; and general unresponsiveness of the open learning system. Most investigators believe the cause of UT's problems lies in the juxtaposition of a Western model on an Asian culture. Many lessons may be learned by carefully reviewing the literature in respect to Universitas Terbuka (UNESCO, 1992/ICDE, 1990).

Australasia and the South Pacific

The Open Polytechnic of New Zealand, established in 1946, offers vocational and technical education by a home-study system in which students can be educated at every level, often without entering a classroom. The school provides over 900 programs serviced by teaching faculties from Applied Technology, Engineering Technology, Commerce, and General Studies. Students from Australia, the Pacific Islands, and Papua New Guinea are enrolled. Interaction with students is by mail, telephone, or an answerphone service that records queries for reply by mail the next day. Teleconferencing and workshops are options in some courses.

In Papua New Guinea, External Studies was established in 1974 as a department in the Education Faculty at the main University campus in Waigani. University Extension centers support the distance education programs and provide continuing education programs for local communities. A diploma in teaching and the first part of the Bachelor of Education degree are available externally. Students receive courses by correspondence and have face-to-face study groups in some centers.

Deakin University, Geelong, Australia was established in 1974. Having now merged with Warrnambool Institute of Advanced Education and Victoria College, it has five campuses, 26,000 students, and 7,000 faculty and staff. On campus, off campus, and international courses are available. Deakin is one of Australia's main providers of distance education courses and produces print, audio, and video cassettes to support external students. Teleconferencing, teletutorials, video, and computer conferencing are highly developed components of Deakin's off campus programs. The University is one of Australia's eight national Distance Education Centres.

The Queensland Open Learning Project (QOLP), Australia, is a state government project aimed at improving access and participation in tertiary education. Improvement in educational opportunity was to be achieved through the cooperative efforts of the universities and Technical and Further Education (TAFE) colleges via the design and delivery of courses using communication and information technologies. The pilot phase (1989–1991) was to establish an Open Learning Centre Network (OLCN) in 40 Queensland communities and carry out seven other pilot teaching projects designed to test effective ways of using OLCN technology. Thirty-three Open Learning Centres (OLC) have been set up to support programs offered by higher education institutions, TAFE Colleges, and the community. Each OLC provides a place to study, a microcomputer and software, electronic mail, facsimile machine, teleconferencing, career information material, 24 hour access to computing, and a personnel management structure. The final report on the pilot phase of QOLP identified varying levels of success in course design projects, the OLCN, government policies, future strategies, budget, and management. The Remote Area Teacher Education Program (RATEP) was singled out as having a high probability of providing a successful solution to the problem of Aboriginal and Torres Strait Island teacher preparation. The QOLP is worthy of close study by agencies looking at distance education networks with associated study centers, and requiring highly developed course design and production support (Lundin, 1990; Willett, 1991).

University of the South Pacific (USP), Fiji, was established in 1968 in Suva and serves ten other territories within a radius of 1500 miles and a sister campus in Apia, Western Samoa (Wallace & Maitava, 1990). USP has established centers in nine other regional countries. Each center has satellite terminal equipment that forms the USPNET connecting with the main campus and other centers. Students not able to attend campus programs enroll through a center and complete their courses through USP's Extension Services by print, audio tape, and satellite communication. Distance and the infrequency of boat traffic slows the transmission of conventional course materials, and careful planning is required to bridge the distance between student and campus. Satellite tutorials, electronic mail, and teleconferencing assist instruction and course administration.

Hawaii, consisting of some 121 islands, has a unique educational situation not experienced by mainland United States. The Hawaii Interactive Television System (HITS) educational network was created in 1988 to transform the way the Hawaiian education system could accomplish its mission. HITS is a state-wide, inter-campus, inter-island, closed circuit television network structured as an electronic communication service for the University of Hawaii (UH) and other state agencies. HITS serves Oahu, Kauai, Molokai, Lanai, Maui, and Hawaii using a combination of point to point microwave, Instructional Television Fixed Service (ITFS), satellite, fiber optic, and copper cable. Four outgoing channels of full motion analog video is transmitted from the main origination site at KHET/UH on the Manoa Campus of the University of Hawaii to all other sites. A single full motion return channel is transmitted from each island campus to provide two-way interaction. The Hawaii Public Broadcast Authority provides technical support, ensures reliable service, and allocates channels.

The University of Hawaii is the principal user of HITS. The state has identified a shortage of trained workers in certain disciplines and professions, and UH has committed itself to providing academic course work for those areas (Nursing, Education, Social Work, Library and Information Science, Medical Technology). UH has established a faculty development program to address the training of instructors to teach via the HITS network. In addition to credit programs, HITS is used for national conferences, workshops, teleconferences, and continuing education activities (Lassner, 1992).

Middle East

King Saud University (KSU), Saudi Arabia, was established in 1957. In 1959 King Saud established the General Presidency of Girls' Education and inaugurated formal education for girls. In 1961 four female students were enrolled in an external studies program established to educate women not able to participate in campus study due to cultural and religious considerations. Women are not allowed to be taught by men directly and therefore receive much of their instruction by closed circuit television and telephone link (Rawaf & Simmons, 1992). A conference on distance teaching was organized by the Arab Gulf region in the mid-80s and resulted in a recommendation to establish an open university for the Gulf region. The Al Quds Open University (QOU) was scheduled to begin operations in 1988. Rawaf and Simmons (1992) noted that at the time of writing, neither the QOU nor any of the other proposals described had come to fruition and that the Arab world was still without a working model of an open university.

In Turkey, civil unrest during the 1970s interfered with early development efforts to reduce inequalities in educational opportunity. Anadolu University (AU), formerly an academy, was formalized in 1981. Its main mission has been to increase availability of higher education to those for whom further education was previously not available (McIsaac, Murphy, & Demiray, 1988). Prior to establishing an open education program, there were 56,000 university places for the 515,000 students who applied. Open education doubled this number of spaces by 1985. Printed materials were supplemented by television and radio broadcasts. External students are served by Academic Service Centers, with university lecturers available to help them. AU operates a primary school teacher training project with 130,000 teachers taking courses via print and television. A second project undertaken by AU is "Training Turks in Germany" designed to serve more than two million Turks working in Germany. Turkey is constantly seeking ways to increase educational opportunities by use of new technologies within the financial constraints that face all developing nations.

Europe
Distance education initiatives in Europe are multi-faceted and multi-national. Europe has led in cross-border delivery of distance learning materials and development of collaborative software and networks. It is clear that all nations, like Europe as a whole, must establish an outward looking stance and participate as partners in global initiatives or be relegated to a passive flow of education across their boundaries. Rapid development of a new generation of powerful direct broadcast satellites, such as Olympus, will make political and physical borders transparent. In such an atmosphere of cooperation countries will be able to make great strides toward provision of basic education to vast numbers in a most efficient and cost effective manner (Brown, 1991).

Acronyms such as DELTA, EDEN, JANUS, EUROSTEP, EUROPACE occur in the line-up of European distance education programs. DELTA (Developing European Learning Through Technological Advance), was conceived by the Commission of European Communities as an exploratory action encompassing research and development in learning system design, collaborative development of advanced learning technology, testing and validation of communications, inter-operability, and creation of favorable conditions. A public call for proposals was generated, resulting in 30 pilot projects that looked at the market and users' requirements, relevance of emerging technologies such as expert systems, artificial intelligence, hypermedia, satellites, and smart cards, and different types of education and training delivery systems. Projects were awarded to numerous countries across Europe. The final technological report concluded that technology integration and validation led to a better understanding of user needs and priorities, standardization of activities, and improved inter-operability of services and portability of products, and pointed to further research on promising technologies (Rebel, 1990; Rodriguez-Rosello, 1991).

JANUS (Joint Academic Network Using Satellites) is a project within the framework of DELTA designed to link up voice and data/text communications among European institutions wishing to work together to produce distance learning materials for delivery on a Europe-wide basis and to transfer credits among institutions. The initial plan was to install low-cost, narrow-band, two-way earth stations at 12 European Association of Distance Teaching Universities (EADTU) to permit audio teleconferencing and computer conferencing among institutions. The JANUS concept is based on a shared two-way communications link with one voice channel and several data links enabling one-to-one, one-to-many, electronic mail, document transfer, cooperative working, and access to remote data bases (Bacsich, 1991).

In May, 1991, members of the Budapest Platform met in Prague, Czechoslovakia and agreed to establish EDEN, the European Distance Education Network, for promotion and development of distance education. The mandate was to involve not only educational institutions at all levels of teaching, but also broadcasting, publishing organizations, and employers with a commitment to professional development and training (Tait, 1991).

Other initiatives in Europe include SATURN, a 60 member, Europe-wide association of enterprises and universities concerned with using multimedia teaching techniques to meet training demands of 1990s. EUROSTEP (European Association of Users of Satellites in Training and Educational Programs) is an association of 65 institutions/consortia (350 educational institutions) that are using Olympus' European DBS satellite on an open access basis. EUROPACE, a consortium of universities and multi-national companies, uses commercial low-powered satellite for advanced training programs. The satellite beam covers 18 countries in which there are 329,000 educational institutions and a learning population of 44 million (Murray, 1989). EUROPACE is a 'federal' structure for supporting Europe-wide distance education, to enable economies of scale and maximize benefits of modern communications systems.

In Great Britain, Prime Minister Harold Wilson was responsible for initiating the Open University of the United Kingdom (OUUK) in 1969. He later stated, when commenting in the foreword to a book by Sir Walter Perry, the OU's first Vice-Chancellor, that the Open University "is now recognized in Britain, and in the wider world, as one of the most important educational and social developments of this century" (Perry, 1977, p.vii). Scope of recognition of the OUUK and emulation as a model for open learning throughout the world substantiates this view. The decision to create the "University of the Air" was a 1963 political commitment of the Labour Government. Despite massive opposition, the renamed Open University was created by Royal Charter and, as a university in its own right, was given the power to grant degrees and to act in all student, curriculum, and research matters as would any other university.

The OUUK is located in Milton Keynes, Buckinghamshire, and has offices in 13 regions throughout Britain. It offers undergraduate, postgraduate, and continuing education degrees. Print material forms the backbone of the courses and is supplemented with a mix of audio cassettes, radio broadcasts, video cassettes, television broadcasts, slides, home equipment kits, computer conferencing facilities, database access, field trips, summer school, weekend or day schools, tutorials, and counselling. Students form self-help and study groups, participate in a range of social activities, and publish a student newspaper. One hundred fifty undergraduate courses are available, as well as specialized short courses and free standing packs (ICDL CD ROM, 1992).

The Universidade Aberta (UA), Portugal, was created as a full degree granting, national distance teaching institution in 1988. UA evolved from an institute for distance education established by the Ministry of Education in 1981. It offers in-service teacher training, languages, and literature, parallel to the regular universities. Print-based materials are supplemented by radio and television programs and telephone tutoring. Counselling is available in support centers, located primarily in institutions of higher learning, with secondary centers in local areas such as libraries. Each center has a full complement of UA course materials, facsimile, telephone, audio, and video equipment.

North America

During the past several years distance education in North America has enjoyed unprecedented growth. Since the 1850s Canada and the United States have experimented with distance education, as the first correspondence schools attempted to bridge the huge, sparsely populated geographical expanse of North America. Both countries have led in advances in communications technology and have been quick to adopt these innovations for use in pilot distance education programs. Until the recent explosion of distance education in North America, adoption had occurred in an insular manner at institutional, state, province, and national levels. Early distance education programs, such as the Knowledge Network of British Columbia and the Midwest Program on Airborne Television Instruction (MPATI) in the United States, have caught and held the imagination of educators. Distance education in North America evolved slowly, however, because traditional institutions were plentiful, strong, and entrenched. It was the need for training in business and industry that prompted development of early educational networks and promoted use of modern media in instructional programming. Emerging technology and societal need have spurred the recent meteoric development of distance education systems at all educational levels.

In Canada responsibility for education rests at the provincial level, whereas in the United States the federal government has major responsibility for education. In Canada distance education has developed with eleven major signatures over the ten provinces, Yukon, and the Northwest Territories, whereas in the United States, not discounting state-wide development of distance education, the federal government has been able to mount major programs. In the U.S.A. the publication of *Linking for learning: A new course for education*, by the Congress of the United States (Office of Technology Assessment, 1989) provided the catalyst to drive development of distance education policy to the forefront of thinking. In Canada, development of British Columbia's Knowledge Network, initiated in 1979–80 with seven courses and 2,955 students, caught the imagination of Canadians and the world as a working model for distance education. In 1988 the Knowledge Network merged with the Open Learning Institute to form the Open Learning Agency, reaching 90 percent of B.C. households with 130 courses and a weekly viewing audience of 650,000.

Hundreds of distance education programs are in use or in the planning stage. Distance education in Canada and the United States has followed the emergence of satellite, fiber optic, compressed video, and broadband digital developments in carrier technology. Canada and the United States are testing the technology of education in a myriad of unrelated, independent initiatives. In contrast to the uniformity that grips the traditional schooling processes of classrooms, lectures, courses, credits, busing, curricula, and standardized tests, schools and higher education agencies have chosen a path of little or no uniformity in technology and distance education. Rapid developments in distance education technology have created a challenge in assessing the degree and extent to which distance education learning alternatives are being used by North American educational institutions (Levinson, 1990; Lowery, 1991; Mecklenburger, 1990; Weinstein & Roschwalb, 1990). Programs are so numerous that only highlights can be scanned.

United States

Prior to 1987 fewer than ten states were actively engaged in distance education in the United States. Today, spurred by federal and state grant programs, most states are involved in distance education programs at institution, system, and state levels. About 45 states share distance education programming across state borders, and a number of higher education institutions share programming across national borders (Doan, 1991; Lowery, 1991). Current educational philosophy in North America leans toward the use of distance education delivery technology to link all levels of education and to share costs with other sectors such as health, business, industry, and government. Integrated, shared-use, broadband (ISDN) distance education networks are rapidly forming cost-effective links among users. These networks, which combine copper cable technology with newer satellite and fiber-based delivery technologies, make it possible for North Americans to use older hybrid distance education systems employing teleconferencing, broadcast television, Instructional Television Fixed Service (ITFS), computer conferencing, cable, and fiber optic with new digital based, multimedia networks (Brown, 1992b). The term "digital fusion" or the convergence of existing and emerging technologies into one "delivery fabric" is placing the learner in the "digital drivers seat" (Brown, 1992a).

In the United States advances have occurred in distance learning because schools have partnered with telephone companies and telecommunications equipment suppliers (Gibson, 1990; Northern Telecom, 1991). Over the last two decades U.S. business and industry have used communication innovations to service widespread operations involving training and information dissemination throughout the country. Nation-wide teleconference, video conference, fiber, and satellite networks are commonplace in business and industry, where, e.g., automobile and fast food workers, firefighters, and accounting employees are trained. This broad base of installed capacity linked to a number of federal programs has resulted in astounding growth of distance education during the past five years. The STAR Schools Program and the President's Education 2000 Program accelerated the growth of distance education in the elementary and secondary sector (Krebs, 1991).

Congress created the STAR Schools Program to develop multi-state, multi-institution, elementary to secondary school distance education. Legislation enacted in 1988 authorized an expenditure of $100 million over a five-year period. Four programs were selected: Satellite Educational Resources Consortium (SERC), TI-IN United Star Network (TI-IN USN), Midlands Consortium, and Technical Education Research Centers (TERC). SERC, TI-IN, and Midlands are satellite-based while TERC uses computers on a telecommunications network. SERC encompasses 19 states and the cities of New York, Detroit, Kansas, and Cleveland. TI-IN USN includes three states, four universities, and one educational service center. The Midlands Consortium consists of five state universities and the Missouri School Boards Association. TERC members include museums, laboratories, universities, and curriculum developers. The Star Schools funding has established relationships among schools, universities, business, and telecommunications entities across the U.S., stimulating widespread interest in distance delivered education (OTA, 1989). An outgrowth of this and other distance education developments was the First National Policy Forum on Distance Learning held in Vermont in July, 1991, sponsored by the United States Distance Learning Association (USDLA). Representatives of 33 states and numerous private and public institutions met to discuss national educational and telecommunications policy issues (United States Distance Learning Association, 1991).

In the area known as the Oklahoma Panhandle, the economic downturn of the 80s severely limited educational resources. Realizing that distance education provided potential for resource sharing, school districts, business, industry, and government teamed up to revitalize education and the communities by creating the Share-Ed Video Network. A digital, fiber-based, two-way, full motion interactive video network was chosen to meet the objective of duplicating live classroom interaction. The network connects some rural Oklahoma schools and Panhandle State University, enabling schools to share resources, communities to conduct evening adult education activities, and the University to transmit undergraduate credit courses. The network consists of video classrooms connected to the telephone company central office, with interconnection to other offices and schools. The teacher controls programming from a video panel; students and teacher view programming on banks of monitors that allow remote locations to be seen, as well as the outgoing signal. A broad selection of programming including English, Spanish, mathematics, and undergraduate and graduate courses has been carried since the project originated in 1989 (Lane, 1991; Northern Telecom, 1991). In 1970 Oklahoma established the Oklahoma Televised Instruction System (TIS) as a state-wide television system providing high quality post-secondary educational opportunities by linking together public and private colleges, universities, junior colleges, and technical institutions. The system is microwave and Instructional Television Fixed Service (ITFS) based with multiplexed audio and leased telephone lines for student interaction. The efficiency and effectiveness of multiple independent networks within a state system is currently under careful scrutiny, as are single system models (Dillon & Gunawardena, 1990).

Share-Ed and other similar two-way television projects such as Project Blue Bonnet (Texas), Mississippi 2000, and Minnesota, Illinois, Iowa, and North and South Dakota rural education initiatives seem to be a formula for success in resource sharing. As many as 100 distance education state programs are now in use or in the development stage; they employ interactive strategies such as video conferencing, audio and audiographic teleconferencing, Instructional Television Fixed Service, and satellite programming. Information concerning specific technologies, strategies, and costs is readily available in the publications originating from industry partners.

Alaska is a state characterized by vast roadless expanses and diverse, multi-cultural educational needs for elementary, secondary, and post-secondary areas. Alaska has addressed these needs by application of a succession of distance learning modes beginning with correspondence courses in 1936. Past initiatives in Alaska were focused on single-technology approaches to distance education, while today's focus is on integration of voice, video, data, and print tools.

The terrain of Alaska warranted early consideration of satellite as a means of delivering learning. In the early 70s Alaska used the Applied Technology Satellite (ATS) system to deliver audio and data to 26 communities. In 1975 a demonstration project was established to reach rural areas with video programming. This service remains today, providing network and public television via low power transmitters, as the Rural Alaska Television Network (RATNET). The Learn Alaska Network (L/AN) was established in 1980 with state funding of an audioconferencing network for use by every school and university unit. At the same time a satellite transponder was leased and a 100 site network established. The Department of Education (DOE) and the university used the system during the day and evening, respectively. The audio conferencing component was used as stand-alone and with television programming. This system enjoyed varying levels of success, but came under attack with the drop in oil prices and a major downturn in the economy. Learn Alaska ceased to exist in 1987. Television programming was eliminated and the audio conferencing system was re-structured as the university-managed Alaska Teleconferencing Network (ATN).

"LiveNet" was established at the university level using transponder time obtained from a local carrier. LiveNet relies heavily on cooperative programming and technical support. This network and ATN use an integrated delivery approach incorporating audio, video, print, fax, and electronic mail. Electronic mail ensures student participation and interaction. Lap-top computers with external modems are issued to students in some programs. Alaska is experimenting with different multipoint-to-multipoint interactive digital graphics technologies, HyperCard, and videodisc. The Department of Education delivers programming by satellite to 113 elementary and secondary schools with receive capability. DOE is an active member of the Pacific Northwest Star Schools Partnership and is working with 35 school districts in Alaska in the installation and use of satellite delivered educational programs and services.

Perhaps the greatest strength of the Alaska system is that both the DOE and the university system have found that faculty development and inservice training are critical to long term effectiveness of distance education and have established a rigorous program of workshops, mentoring programs, and support services (Willis, 1991, 1992).

The Oregon Ed-Net is a technological infrastructure established through a 1990 appropriation to fund a state-wide telecommunications system. Motivation for the Ed-Net grew out of the need to provide equitable educational service to all residents of the state. Oregon's population resides primarily on the Western sea coast with a small population over the central and eastern areas. Ed-Net was created as a state agency to plan and operate the three network technical system. Network 1 is a color, full-motion, one-way video, two-way audio network delivering programming to 130 down-link sites throughout the state. Network 2 is a satellite based compressed video network providing 30 channels of two-way audio and video to 43 sites. Network 3, called Oregon Compass, is a data network that includes e-mail, computer conferencing, library access, and virtual classroom platform. A needs analysis preceded and supported development of a technical infrastructure for which funds were appropriated. No funds were provided for program development, and it was generally understood that Oregon Ed-Net would be self-sustaining within four years. Agencies using Ed-Net were dependent on re-direction of existing funding or through external grants. Perhaps of greatest interest in the Oregon model is the concept of a shared use, state-wide distance education infrastructure managed by an independent governance system. The effectiveness and efficiency of such a system remains a point of conjecture, but several states have selected an independently governed, shared use model to plan, coordinate, and implement wide-scale distance education programs (Hezel, 1991; Root, 1992).

North and South Dakota have established state-wide structures to plan, implement, and govern distance education. Both states initiated comprehensive needs assessment programs upon which to base their technological infrastructure and governance mechanisms.

In 1969, the North Dakota Legislature created the Educational Broadcasting Council to encourage the creation of educational broadcast facilities. In response to a severe economic downturn and massive demographic changes, educational technology was incorporated on a local, technologically autonomous basis with little prospect of state-wide compatibility or interconnection. To forestall the possibility of a conglomeration of incompatible systems throughout the state, the legislature created the Educational Telecommunications Council (ETC) in 1989, with power to: direct the implementation of telecommunications systems that were compatible; develop a comprehensive plan for development of state-wide telecommunications; coordinate the development of educational communications programs and systems; cooperate with state educational agencies and private organizations to develop state-wide projects; and study the needs, resources, and facilities available or required for establishing educational telecommunication programs and systems.

An initial recommendation was made to establish a training and teleconferencing network to serve 20 agencies. The state network supports voice, data, and video and provides interconnection of users, access to host library/database resources, and courseware. Interconnection of personal computers and peripherals at the local level is within the jurisdiction of that level and not part of the state network. Users are designated as "clusters" and remain autonomous in choice of technology to suit local needs, while the state network maintains interface standards that accommodate interconnection between clusters and state regions. Implementation of the North Dakota Telecommunications model involves a comprehensive system of grants to promote network and program development. This bold state-wide approach is receiving wide interest as a design for the 21st century (North Dakota, 1990).

The Rural Development Telecommunications Network for the State of South Dakota was established by the creation of the Governor's Telecommunications Task Force in late 1990. A needs assessment of elementary, secondary, post-secondary, and state government found that neither a terrestrial digital network nor a satellite transmission network could address all needs in a cost-effective manner. A network proposal called for two-way interactive video conferencing, one-way broadcast television, unlimited expansion capability without geographic restriction, and establishment of hardware network connection to allow existing local initiatives to proceed without interruption. The governance model selected was a modification of Oregon's shared-use integrated network scheme. After initial funding and a three-year start-up period, the network is to be self-supporting. South Dakota recognizes that technical obstacles are no longer the problem, but that the greatest challenge is programming and use of the network (Rural Development, 1991).

Canada

Responsibility for education in Canada is vested with the ten provinces, Yukon, and the Northwest Territories. Distance education developed with a distinct regional orientation. No other country in the world has such a wide range and diversity of distance education programming, and, while Canada has been an innovator in the use of technology in traditional and distance education, the great regional contrasts led to a charge that distance education in Canada is patchy, arbitrary, and incoherent (Bates, 1989). Sparsity of population and a vast geographic area promoted early interest in extending information and education to rural areas. Distance education was first introduced in Canada in 1889, with correspondence courses. Correspondence schools continue to form an important component of primary, secondary, and post-secondary education. New technologies were eagerly adopted by individual provinces and resulted in a leap-frogging of innovations province to province. The advent of satellite broadcasting and its early adoption by the majority of Canadian educational authorities solved many access problems not addressed by conventional distance education strategies (Brown & Fortosky, 1986). Although satellite footprints fall across provincial boundaries, the signals are not used by other than the provinces generating them. A number of provincial distance education models have received world attention. The Open Learning Agency (OLA) of British Columbia, an early adopter of satellite delivery for province-wide programming, has become a model emulated by other jurisdictions. Other early distance education systems have employed a broad spectrum of technologies to deliver education and have seldom relied on a single mode approach for dissemination of programs and interaction with learners.

The Open Learning Agency came into existence in 1988 when legislation combined the Open Learning Institute and the Knowledge Network (Mugridge, 1989; Open Learning Agency, 1991a). The mission of OLA is "to provide leadership in developing and maintaining a province-wide open learning system in order to make lifelong training and educational opportunities available to all people of British Columbia" (Open Learning Agency, 1991b, p.1). The mandate of OLA is carried out by three internal agencies: the Open College, the Open University, and the Knowledge Network, which deal respectively with workplace training and adult basic education, university degrees in collaboration with other institutions, and broadcast programming of a general nature to support school, college, and university instruction. Program components are articulated by a planning council created to identify program need, foster inter-institutional collaboration, set priorities, and make recommendations to the OLA board. A milestone in OLA's development has been the introduction in 1989 of the Education Credit Bank. The Credit Bank makes it possible to consolidate transferable credits, obtain credit for non-formal training, and establish foreign educational document equity to Canadian standards for employment purposes (Open Learning Agency pamphlet, undated).

British Columbia's Simon Fraser University typifies the commitment many Canadian institutions exhibit in providing an alternative to traditional classroom learning for students who wish to engage in formal training but cannot attend on-site or off-campus courses. In 1975 five distance education courses were offered to 55 students. In 1992 Simon Fraser offered 215 courses to over 10,000 students. Each student receives a full learning package containing notes, supplementary materials, audio cassettes, video cassettes, slides, and required course books. The OLA Knowledge Network is used to broadcast support materials for some courses. Each course is assigned a tutor/marker who holds scheduled office hours for toll free interaction with the learner. Courses carry full university credit. Campus and distance mode courses are treated equally in all aspects of quality, credit, and standards.

The Commonwealth of Learning (COL) was established in 1989, with headquarters in Vancouver, British Columbia, as an autonomous international organization to create and extend access to education using distance techniques and communications technologies to meet the particular requirements of member countries. COL is governed by a Board representative of all parts of the Commonwealth. Programs are carried out in collaboration with governments, relevant agencies, universities, colleges, and other educational establishments. The agency provides staff training and assists with acquisition, delivery, adaptation, and development of teaching materials. COL facilitates the channelling of resources to projects and programs in distance education and provides consultation on the choice of appropriate technology. Exchange of credit and the improvement of study-support systems have been a priority for student services. Initial COL efforts have focused on Africa, Asia, the Caribbean, and the Pacific. The Commonwealth of Learning is supported by its member countries, initially nine in number, with 27 at the time of writing (COL, Undated; Rubin, 1989; Wilson, 1992).

In Alberta three agencies stand out in providing learning at a distance: ACCESS Network, Athabasca University, and the Alberta Distance Education College. ACCESS provides broad spectrum production, acquisition, and satellite delivery of education resources to the entire province. Athabasca University, an open and distance institution, relies on print-based course packages supplemented by telephone tutor interaction, teleconference, audio, and video broadcasts over ACCESS Network. The Alberta Distance Education College, with roots in the correspondence system, has developed a modular approach to correspondence education that matches media to the needs and circumstances of the learner. Students may select print manual, videotape cassette, computer disk, audio cassette, or CD-ROM as their guide to instruction. Video and audio interaction provide learner support.

The Saskatchewan Communications Network (SCN) was created as a provincial entity in 1989 with a specific mandate "to provide equal access to information to all Saskatchewan residents" (Brown, 1990, p. 553). Creation of SCN was preceded by an eight year period of planning, public hearings, and a progenitor organization called the Saskatchewan Tele-Learning Association (STELLA). In 1981 the University of Saskatchewan began field trials (Uplink '81, '84, and '86) to deliver satellite programming to the post-secondary sector. These trials provided a framework for a major telecommunications initiative under the auspices of STELLA (Brown, 1989).

Traditions of cooperation and collaboration run deep in Saskatchewan people, and these traditions influenced the Saskatchewan telecommunications model. Funded in 1989 by an $18 million federal grant over a period of five years, SCN integrated the provincial fiber optic system with satellite to form a hybrid network reaching 92 regional learning centers with a Training Network and over 200 communities with a Cable Network. The Training Network uses point-to-multipoint one-way video, two-way audio and shares a multiplexed transponder with the Cable Network. Each SCN Center is equipped with a Ku-band satellite dish, receiver, decoder, video cassette, telephone, and facsimile machine. Most centers have computer access to library catalogues. The Training Network coordinates the delivery of programs from educational institutions, business and professional organizations. Credit courses are mounted by the two provincial universities, University of Saskatchewan and University of Regina. The Saskatchewan Institute of Applied Science and Technology (SIAST) and three provincial secondary schools offer programs. Nine regional colleges coordinate credit programming, initiate local programming, provide learner support, and student counselling.

SCN's Cable Network, moved by the theme "Bringing a world of learning to you," delivers a broad range of learning resources via satellite to local cable headends. SCN facilitates the development and acquisition of educational, cultural, and informational programs that reflect the needs of a diverse audience. Development of new resources is carried out by a "seed-money" program in collaboration with independent provincial production companies. The Saskatchewan education sector is kept in touch with the rest of Canada and the world by an aggressive policy of acquiring programming from outside the province and, in turn, distributing local programming beyond provincial boundaries.

In Manitoba, distance education has undergone a two year review resulting in a major reorganization of the Distance Education and Technology Branch to create two new areas—the Distance Education Program Unit (DEP) and the Technology Application and Training Unit (TATU). These changes created an integrated approach to independent study including: development, assessment, and acquisition of course materials; delivery and distribution of programming; professional development and training of educators and administrators; and development of pilot projects that incorporate emerging technologies. In addition to traditional delivery and interaction strategies, Manitoba operates the Manitoba Satellite Network (MSN) to 92 sites and the Manitoba Information Network (MINET) to over 550 sites. MSN distributes one-way video and two-way audio, while MINET provides electronic mail, bulletin boards, computer conferencing, direct facsimile links, storage, and transfer facilities. The unique aspect of MINET is the MILink software platform, which transcends most computer interfaces to make MINET accessible to virtually everyone with a computer. The Manitoba distance learning model has forged productive alliances with key private and public partners (Education Manitoba, 1991; Forster, 1992; Manitoba Education and Training, 1991).

In Ontario, Contact North (CN) is a provincial government initiative designed to increase educational opportunities to residents of Northern Ontario by the operation of a network of electronic classrooms. Introduced as a pilot project in 1986, Contact North achieved full program status in 1990. The key objective of CN was to improve access to formal educational opportunities at the secondary and post-secondary level and to establish long-term capacity to improve access to other training and informal educational opportunities. Referred to as a "neutral communications highway," the CN Network serves distance education program requirements of colleges, universities, and secondary schools in 92 Northern Ontario communities. CN was to ensure full access to network resources for special needs populations, such as Native people and Francophones. Each of CN's "access points" is equipped with Optel audiographic teleconference system, computer, facsimile, answering machine, convenor, videotape recorder, and monitor. Teleconferencing is supported by two 68-port Confertech bridges. In 1991–92 the CN Networks supported more than 65 secondary, 200 college, and 100 university courses. Contact North services include: assistance in audio conference design, instructional design expertise, bilingual expertise, participant and instructor training, technical support, on-site support, promotion, scheduling, liaison, and test-bedding effectiveness technology. Conceptually, CN was designed to supplement the resources of existing institutions and distribute their programming upon request (Arblaster, 1988; Contact North, 1990; Shaw, 1992).

Ontario's University of Waterloo (UW) provides one of Canada's largest correspondence education programs. Programs are offered in Applied Health Sciences, Arts, Engineering, Environmental Studies, Mathematics, and Science. The bulk of UW's correspondence courses consists of printed notes and audio tapes, with enhancement by video, slides, and textbooks. UW is noted for programs directed at students who drop courses prior to completion and has developed empirical evidence that confirms correspondence students maintain the same high standards that prevail throughout the institution. UW makes no distinction between different modes of study used for completion of degrees (University of Waterloo, 1992).

Newfoundland's Memorial University, which serves a half million people scattered over 350,000 square kilometers, provides access to remote locations and a widely dispersed student body. One of the original users of teleconference technology, Memorial has a 165 site audiographic teleconference network and a satellite network to deliver education and health services (Forster, 1992).

Television Northern Canada (TVNC), owned and operated by aboriginal people and northern residents, began broadcasting in January 1992 across an area covering 4.3 million square kilometers and spanning five time zones. TVNC broadcasts from the Yukon, through the Northwest Territories, across Arctic Quebec, and into Labrador, providing culturally relevant and educational television to native people who reside in Canada's north. TVNC has up-links in Iqaluit, Yellowknife, and Whitehorse, with down-links and re-broadcast facilities in 94 northern communities. This comprehensive network is a significant initiative from the stand-point of aboriginal input, sharing of resources, and cost-effectiveness (Forster, 1992).

Caribbean

Distance education in the Caribbean region is focused at the University of the West Indies (UWI). UWI is supported by 14 English speaking Caribbean countries encompassing the geographic area circumscribed by Belize, Jamaica, the Bahamas, British Virgin Islands, and Trinidad and Tobago. Population in this region is about 5.5 million. There are three campuses located in Jamaica, Trinidad, and Barbados, and Extra Mural Centers in non-campus countries. The challenge facing UWI has been to serve the needs of widely scattered, economically depressed countries throughout an enormous expanse of ocean. Early satellite experiments were successful and pointed to development of a telecommunications network supported by other forms of traditional media. The system is a combination of satellite, microwave, microwave radio, UHF, and leased four-wire telephone lines. An international collaborative project with Memorial University of Newfoundland, funded by the Canadian International Development Agency (CIDA), uses audiographic teleconferencing that employs slow-scan television, data, and voice communication between sites. These efforts have been carried out under the umbrella of the University of West Indies Distance Teaching Experiment (UWIDITE), which has established distance teaching programs for community aides, technicians, teachers, nurses, university undergraduates, and a variety of other professionals (Marrett, 1989).

Mexico

The Monterrey Institute of Technology and Higher Education (MITHE) began satellite transmissions in 1989. Three undergraduate programs (Ethics, Humanities I, and Humanities II) and five Masters degree programs (Education, Information Systems Administration, Industrial Engineering, Computer Sciences, and Business Administration) are transmitted on the network. The Morelos II satellite transmits to 26 receiver campuses from uplinks located in Mexico City and Monterrey. All transmitting and receiving classrooms have a computer terminal and telephone connected to the private satellite network. Using the telephone or specially prepared computer software, remote students can interact with the transmitting classroom where an expert moderates the interaction with the lecturer. The satellite channel is used 24 hours a day with pre-recorded courses in the Masters programs transmitted late at night. Limited ability to interact during class time has been solved by assigning an electronic mailbox to all undergraduate and graduate students in order for them to consult the instructor out of class time. The Monterrey network will form part of Going Global University to establish dialogue between Mexican and North American universities. Monterrey participates as a member of the National Technological University (NTU) and the National University Teleconference Network (NUTN) (Lane, 1992; Reyes, 1992).

Global Technologies of Distance Education

Across the world an unprecedented number of strategies are available for delivery of learning to the distant student. The scope, diversity, and rate of change make selection of appropriate delivery mechanisms difficult and risky. Yet these decisions must be made and a stake driven if education and training are to remain abreast of the need in both developed and developing countries. Lessons learned by early adopters of delivery mechanisms are beginning to percolate through the educational sphere, providing guidance for action.

Global investment in delivery technology is enormous, providing a richness of information transmission capacity and pathways almost beyond imagination a few years ago. Excess carriage capacity is commonplace among the developed world's telecommunications carriers. Yet articulation of this capacity to support education and training has been slow to develop, and initiatives using new and emerging technologies have not developed uniformly in developed or developing countries.

The underlying reasons for lag in adopting delivery technologies rest primarily with educators, administrators, and politicians. Review of world distance education reveals that a major holdback is the grip that traditional practice exercises over all aspects of education and training, preventing enthusiastic embrace of technologies that appear to be in constant change and always on the verge of a final breakthrough. A second holdback is financial; educational systems are operating to capacity in conventional modes of instruction and do not have the funds, personnel, or motivation to react to new needs, types of learners, and the development processes that accompany transition to distance education and open learning. Many agencies and countries face the choice between finding new funds to establish alternative formats for education and training or disrupting conventional formats, already operating to capacity, in order to divert funds to establish new formats.

Governments in every part of the world have been prompted to take steps to promote increased openness of learning opportunities because of changing patterns of work and the need for continuous learning, skilling, and re-skilling. Excess telecommunications capacity on satellite and fiber technologies has prompted carriers to establish "partner of choice" arrangements with educational systems to develop and resource local distance education networks.

Massive education need has promoted collaborative efforts to distribute instruction across state and country borders in an effort to achieve economies of scale for development and delivery of programming. The Maastricht Treaty is a notable example of crossing Europe's international borders to increase access to educational resources by means of new telecommunication advances (Oberst, 1992). In North America, as a consequence of the Star Schools Legislation, the Congress of the United States spurred cross-border programming from fewer than 10 states in 1989 to over 40 states in 1992.

A significant segment of change is occurring in video/computer technology. The "video/computer revolution" now of landslide proportions and gaining momentum, is due largely to advances in delivery technology. Television has been the mass medium of choice for over four decades, providing powerful life-shaping messages in areas of entertainment, news, and lifestyle. Video coupled with the organizing capability of the computer and delivered via new digital technologies is putting the learner and the instructional developer in the "digital driver's seat." The union of computer and television with the new technologies of digital storage, compression, and delivery produces a technology called "multimedia." Multimedia has created a global "buzz" among educators looking for a medium to support independent study. It provides an efficient connection to provider and data base for interaction and content. Telecommunications strategies for reaching and interacting with the learner demonstrate potential for establishing the 90s as a "decade of the independent learner."

Delivery methods such as print, postal service, audio cassette, videotape, radio, and television have enjoyed varying levels of success in addressing the needs of the distance learner. As evidenced in the case scan, conventional delivery methods are the norm in most parts of the world, with print holding a prime position as the medium of communication. Increased interaction between teacher and student and a desire to access information have been driving forces underlying development of new technologies to support the goal of learning at a distance. In the industrialized areas of Europe and North America, as a direct result of highly developed entertainment and business communications systems, educational telecommunications has advanced rapidly during the past five years. Major advances have also occurred in Pacific and Asian countries over the past three years. Globally the literature is emphatic in pointing out that emerging technologies, particularly those involving a telecommunications component, have the potential to catapult distance learning to the forefront of the educational scene. The client pool for non-traditional delivery of learning far exceeds the number of students now enrolled in traditional institution-based programs. Consensus is that the new and emerging technologies hold much promise as a means to attack the enormous task of education, training, and retraining facing the world as we hurtle through the few years remaining before being thrust into the twenty-first century.

The see-saw of the information and technology explosions during the 19th and 20th centuries has alternately created the need for and solution to the scope and level of education and training required to support the society of the time. The case scan establishes a global perspective on the breadth of strategies being used to deliver distance learning. Analysis reveals an evolution of distance learning delivery modes from the earliest person-to-person, local educational extension programming, to present day telecommunications developments with global capability. On the world front the trend is to rely on telecommunications as the backbone for distance education programming.

A lesson to be learned from a review of the many different distance education agencies around the world is that strategies for delivery of distance learning by telecommunications cannot be considered in isolation from the preceding older modes of delivery. Present day distance learning practice is a continuum from print to multimedia and from mail service to satellite service (Figure 1). New strategies for delivery and interaction have not instantly replaced serviceable existing modes. The old and the new must form an amalgam providing the best possible situation for the distance learner. Therefore, in the zeal to adopt the new, one must not lose sight of past and present methods. The increment results when the new is integrated with the old to take full advantage of the added dimension.

Cost-effectiveness is a factor in distance learning that is best served by evolution rather than by revolution. Numerous agencies have prematurely decommissioned low-tech practices in favor of high-tech methods that are allegedly less costly. Cost-effective paper-based print formed the backbone of instruction at a distance for the past century and will remain a major information carrier well into the next century. Although telecommunications may be the medium of choice, many agencies are returning to less exotic and expensive means of content delivery such as audio and video cassette. Where

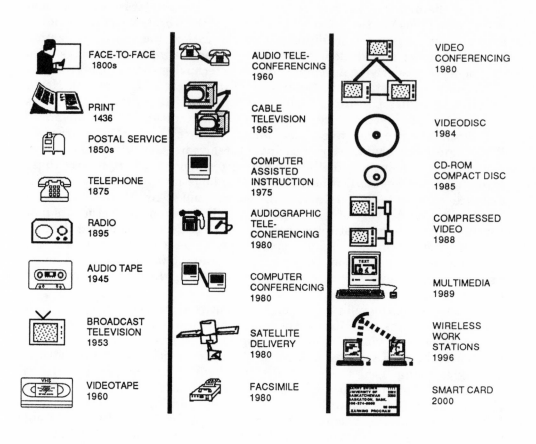

Figure 1. *A chronological continuum of devices and modes used to deliver learning to students distant from traditional sources of instruction (Brown, 1992b).*

cost is a limiting factor, the global trend has been to reserve real-time telecommunication linkages for interaction with the learner.

There is world-wide support for the idea that, as bandwidth availability increases and costs drop, a multimedia, computer/video approach using high density CD-ROM and laserdisc storage devices interconnected by fiber, satellite, and cellular networks will revolutionize the manner in which distance education is accomplished. Wireless work stations are now a test-bed reality. "Smart card" technology capable of tracking and organizing individual learning programs, with the same degree of efficiency and pervasiveness as credit cards track individual finances, are receiving good reports. Seamless world-covering communications using low earth orbiting (LEO) satellites such as Motorola's 77 satellite "Iridium" project promise wireless transparency of borders, time zones, and distances. New digital video compression and spectrum division technology herald 100 plus channel cable and satellite television reception to the home. Delivery technology is definitely on a roll and its eager adoption is tempered by a common, recurring theme expressing doubt as to the educator's ability to restructure, process and develop resources to accommodate its voracious appetite. Strategic planning processes abound in a world-wide effort to focus technological change on solutions to education and training in a changing society.

Pacey (1992) of the British Columbia Open Learning Agency, delivering the final keynote address to the 16th International Distance Education Conference, expressed the need for a strategic planning process to address the interface of distance and open learning with technology in order to breathe life into our organizational purposes and visions. She stated:

> If we are to create a powerful vision for distance education and open learning in the future, we have to view the system as a subtle whole with dynamic and complex interrelationships. We can no longer assume that what we do in our institutions, states or countries will not have an impact on the contiguous regions. As our organizations evolve we have to ensure that our connectedness to the whole is understood by the heads of state, political powers, as well as our respective colleagues and staff. It is no longer enough to use descriptors like single mode and dual mode institutions and to argue the merits and challenges faced by each. Instead, we need to understand our roles and relationships within the systems of learning and education, our connectedness to economic development and wealth generation, as well as our influence on the learner and the culture of learning. (Pacey, 1992, p. 7)

Summary

Foremost among major trends in the world view of distance education is the rapid increase of multi-mode and open learning educational institutions. Driven by problems of access and economics, governments are seeking alternative forms of delivery to fulfil the demand for basic education, continuing education, and training. Initially, learner access provided the main incentive for development of institutional distance education programming, but now, due to flagging economies, governments perceive distance education as a cost-effective means of serving the learner. Technological advances have permitted governments to link education and training quickly and effectively to state economy. Reaching learners and workers where they work or reside has many advantages over increasing the capacity of traditional institutions to accommodate the influx of learners. Determining the appropriate mix of traditional, multi-mode, and open educational institutions is central to the provision of equitable learner access and ultimately the economic success and cultural well being of the country.

The following generalizations are indicative of world trends gleaned from the case scan reflecting local, state, country, and international jurisdictions:

• World governments are "down-sizing or right-sizing" traditional educational institutions.

• The local, national, and world policy framework necessary to guide cost-effective introduction of alternative formats of instruction and training is under development in most countries.

• Micro and macro economic analysis is increasingly used to justify allocation and re-allocation of the education dollar in order to maximize educational benefit during times of fiscal constraint.

• As more jurisdictions introduce an "open architecture" model for education and training, education planners are adopting a strategic planning process to ensure effective articulation of existing personnel, development, and research services of the traditional institution with the specialized personnel skills and processes required for open learning modes.

• Evidence suggests that delivery/storage technology is receiving greater acceptance as an essential and integral component of the educational mix that affects learning structures and formats in the classroom, building, institution, system, country, and world continuum.

• There is a trend developing toward identification of student support systems as crucial to learner success. Successful systems hinge directly on determining an acceptable "attrition" rate and then targeting course materials, interaction, and personal student services to maintain or exceed this rate.

• Educational practitioners are moving toward an understanding that type and level of student support involves a complex interrelationship among student numbers, direct and indirect course production costs, distant and site interaction costs, open or multi-mode institutional strategies, and scale of institutional involvement with distance or open learning (Sewart, 1992).

• Effectiveness and efficiency are observable and expected outcomes of planned and managed distance learning and training programs, in contrast to programming in traditional institutions that remains largely within the purview of untrained content experts.

• Development of credit transfer mechanisms, credit banks, identification and accreditation for prior learning, greater reliance on the client as a "reflective practitioner," and client ability for self-assessment (Raggatt, 1992) are at various stages of development.

• Evidence is mounting that the high visibility of courses developed for distance education assures that principles of learning will be rigorously applied by course development experts in concert with content specialists, and the development of quality course material for distance education has had a beneficial spin-off effect on teaching practice in conventional courses.

• The challenge to individualize learning materials, extend mediation, and establish interaction between learner and provider is a priority in student support initiatives now under way.

• Educators and education provider systems are moving in the direction of broad-based, learner-centered, cooperative/collaborative relationships across educational sectors.

• Production-line, industrialized distance education modes are being replaced by open learning modes that respond to the students' needs for access, flexibility, learning strategies, and support systems.

• Digital telecommunications advances have fused video, audio, voice, and data into a single conduit, simplifying the hybrid delivery systems that support educational needs of distance and conventional programming. Distribution advances will soon have the capacity to provide seamless communications to every point on earth and make it technically possible to deliver learning experiences and information on an equitable basis world-wide.

The scan of distance education around the world reveals education to be at a crossroad, poised to follow the complex path of technological evolution, but holding back and viewing with nostalgia the former, simpler path. Technological evolution has been rapid and diverse, creating educational practice as an end in itself rather than as a means to establish new priorities to address changing global society. Globalization has become a world reality rendering borders and distance transparent to political, economic, and social reform. Telecommunication advances have contributed to globalization by forging partnerships, providing access to enormous databases, and reducing geographic isolation that had previously regionalized societal institutions such as education, health, and culture. Disappearance of the boundaries that once constrained these institutions has resulted in a form of social paralysis as new interrelationships are analyzed, evaluated, and adopted. A networked electronic environment has stripped the walls from our institutions and removed the constraints of time and place. Reaction, particularly by educators, has been cautious and measured as bearings are sought to provide the direction and stability that was lost as the walls crumbled. A sense of optimism is establishing a foothold as educators in all countries move to address the massive social and economic change with enlightened policy that adapts education to a changed world.

References

Arblaster, J. R. (1988, May). *Contact North: The concept, policy, development, and status of the Northern Ontario distance education access network.* Paper presented to the Canadian Association for Distance Education (CADE), Quebec City, Canada.

Bååth, J. A. (1978). Research in development work in correspondence education. *International Council for Correspondence Education Newsletter, 8* (4), 9–15.

Bacsich, P. (1991). Introduction to JANUS. In M. Moller & H. Shaughnessy (Eds.), *Telematic infrastructures for flexible and distance learning 'electronic universities'* (pp. 29–37). Commission of the European Communities.

Bates, T. (1982). Trends in the use of audio-visual media in distance education systems. In J. Daniel, M. Stroud & J. R. Thompson (Eds.), *Learning at a distance: A world perspective* (pp. 8–15). Edmonton, Alberta: Athabasca University/ International Council for Correspondence Education.

Bates, T. (1989). Diversity or chaos in Canadian distance education? A view from overseas. In R. Sweet (Ed.). *Post-secondary distance education in Canada: Policies, practices and priorities* (pp. 133–144). Edmonton, Alberta: Athabasca University/ Canadian Society for Studies in Education.

Brown, F. B. (1989). Bridging the distance: The Saskatchewan educational telecommunications experience. In L. S. Harms & D. J. Wedemeyer (Eds.),

Proceedings of Pacific Telecommunications Connectivity: Users, Networks, and Information Services (pp. 453–462). Honolulu: Pacific Telecommunications Council.

Brown. F. B. (1990). Saskatchewan Communications Advanced Network: Distance Education Saskatchewan Style. In D. J. Wedemeyer & M. D. Lofstrom (Eds.), *Proceedings of Pacific Telecommunications: Weaving the Technological and Social Fabric* (pp. 548–556). Honolulu: Pacific Telecommunications Council.

Brown, F. B. (1991). Mirror on distance education: Perspective on the 90s. *Australian Teleconferencing Directory*. Brisbane: Queensland University of Technology, Kelvin Grove.

Brown, F. B. (1992a, May). *In the digital driver's seat: Distance learning delivery, perspectives for new practitioners of distance education*. Paper presented at the meeting of the Canadian Association for Distance Education (CADE), Ottawa, Canada.

Brown, F. B. (1992b, June). *Distance learning: A perspective on delivery strategies*. Paper presented at the meeting of the Association for Media and Technology in Education in Canada (AMTEC), Vancouver, Canada.

Brown, F. D. & Fortosky, D. M. (1986). Use of television. In I. Mugridge & D. Kaufman (Eds.), *Distance Education in Canada*. London: Croom Helm.

Childs, G. D. (1971). Recent research developments in correspondence instruction. In O. MacKenzie & E. L. Christensen (Eds.), *The changing world of correspondence study: International readings*. State College, PA: Pennsylvania State University Press.

China Radio and Television University (undated). China: Author.

Coldeway, D. O. (1982). Recent research in distance learning. In J. Daniel, M. Stroud & J. R. Thompson (Eds.), *Learning at a distance: A world perspective* (pp. 29–37). Edmonton, Alberta: Athabasca University/International Council for Correspondence Education.

Commonwealth of Learning (undated). *Prospectus*. Vancouver, British Columbia: Author.

Commonwealth of Learning (1992). *Comlearn, 3*(2). Vancouver, British Columbia: Author.

Contact North (1990). *Annual Report, 1989–90*. Government of Ontario: Author.

Daniel, J., Stroud, M. A. & Thompson, J. R. (1982). (Eds.) *Learning at a distance: A world perspective*. Edmonton, Alberta: Athabasca University/International Council for Correspondence Education.

Dillon, C. L. & Gunawardena, C. (1990). *Learner support as the critical link in distance education: A study of the Oklahoma Televised Instruction System*. University of Oklahoma: Oklahoma Research Centre for Continuing Professional and Higher Education.

Distance education database prepared for Commonwealth of Learning (1991). Milton Keynes, U.K.: The Open University International Centre for Distance Learning.

Doan, M. (1991). Distance learning by satellite. *Satellite Education*, 8–11.

Dunbar, R. (1991). Adapting distance education for Indonesians: Problems with learner heteronomy and a strong oral tradition. *Distance Education, 12*(2), 163–174.

Edgington, C. (1992). *An integrated approach to teaching English as communication in China: A multi-media distance learning course*. Paper presented at the International Council for Distance Education Council's 16th World Conference, Sukhothai Thammathirat Open University, Thailand.

Education Manitoba (1991, May/June). *Distance Education*. Winnipeg, Manitoba: Distance Education and Technology Branch, Education Manitoba.

Forster, A. (1992). *Satellite technology: A versatile ingredient in distance education programs*. Ottawa, Canada: Telesat Canada.

Gibson, S. B. (1990). Distance education is a growth industry in the 90s. *Satellite Communications, 14*(12), 15.

Granger, D. (1990). Open universities: Closing the distances to learning. *Change: The Magazine of Higher Learning, 22*(4), 42–50.

Gupta, S. (1991). Distance education in Ethiopia. *Distance Education, 12*(2), 279–285.

Hall, J. W. (1990, July/August). Distance education: Reaching out to millions. *Change: The Magazine of Higher Learning, 22*(4), 48–50.

Harry, K. (1991). *Distance education: A selective bibliography*. Milton Keynes: The Open University International Centre for Distance Learning.

Hezel, R. T., (1991). Statewide planning for telecommunications in education: Some trends and issues. *Tech Trends, 36*(5), 17–20.

Hiola, Y. & Moss, D. (1990). Characteristics of distance learners at the University of Terbuka (Open University) Indonesia. *Distance Education, 11*(1), 116–124.

Holmberg, B. (1977). *Distance education: Survey and bibliography*. London: Kogan Page.

Holmberg, B. (1981). *Status and trends of distance education*. London: Kogan Page.

International Centre for Distance Learning (1992). *Distance education database*. (CD-ROM). Milton Keynes, UK: The Open University International Centre.

Jenkins, J. (1989). Some trends in distance education in Africa: An examination of the past and future role of distance education as a tool for national development. *Distance Education, 10*(1), 41–63.

Keegan, D. (1986). *The foundations of distance education*. London: Croom Helm.

Krebs, A. (1991). Distance educators forum. *Via Satellite, 6* (2), 18.

Lane, C. (1991) (Ed.). The Oklahoma Panhandle—ShareEd Video Network. *Ed., 5*(6), 7–8.

Lane, C. (1992) (Ed.). ITESM inaugurates digital satellite delivery system for education. *Ed., 6*(3), 4–8.

Lassner, D. (1992). HITS: Distance education and the use of interactive television. *Ed., 6*(12), 7–12.

Levinson, E. (1990). Will technology transform educators or will the schools co-opt technology? *Kappan, 72*(2), 121–126.

Lowery, L. (1991). Distance learning across state lines: The transborder study. *Ed., 5*(7), 3–10.

Lundin, R. (1988). "...and tomorrow the world?" Global initiatives in distance education. *Distance Education, 9*(2), 273–279.

Lundin, R. (1990). *The Queensland Open Learning Project: Annual report July 1989–June 1990*. Brisbane, Australia: Queensland University of Technology.

Manitoba Education and Training (1991). *MINET: The Manitoba Information Network*. Winnipeg, Manitoba: Author.

Marrett, C. (1989). Interactive distance teaching in the Caribbean. *Journal of Distance Education, 4*(2), 89–92.

Mathieson, D. E. (1971). *Correspondence study: A summary review of the research and development literature*. New York: ERIC Clearinghouse on Adult Education.

McIsaac, M. S., Murphy, K. L., & Demiray, U. (1988). Examining distance education in Turkey. *Distance Education, 9* (1), 106–114.

Mecklenburger, J. A. (1990). Educational technology is not enough. *Kappan, 72*(2), 105–108.

Mugridge, I. (1989). Distance education in Canada. *ACS Newsletter, 11*(3), 5–7.

Murray, J. F. (1989, Fall). The Olympus satellite project. *Technological Applications Committee Bulletin*. Edmonton, Canada: Grant MacEwan Community College.

Niemi, J. A. & Gooler, D. D. (1987). *Technologies for learning outside the classroom*. London: Jossey-Bass.

North Dakota Educational Telecommunications Study: Executive Summary (1990, April). Bismarck, North Dakota: Educational Telecommunication Council, Department of Public Instruction.

Northern Telecom (1991). *Distance learning using digital fiber optics: Applications, technologies, and benefits*. Richardson, Texas: Educational Systems.

Nyirenda, J. E. (1989). Organization of distance education at the University of Zambia: An analysis of practice. *Distance Education, 10*(1), 148–156.

Oberst, G. E., Jr. (1992). Distance learning via satellite in Europe. *Via Satellite, 7*(11) 22.

Office of Technology Assessment 1989. *Linking for learning: A new course for education*. Washington, DC: Congress of the United States.

Open Learning Agency (Pamphlet, no date). *British Columbia Educational Credit Bank: Giving credit where credit is due*. Richmond, British Columbia: Author.

Open Learning Agency (Pamphlet, no date). *Open learning and distance education: International partnerships*. Richmond, British Columbia: Author.

Open Learning Agency (1991a). *Only the beginning: 1988–1990*. Richmond, British Columbia: Author.

Open Learning Agency (1991b). *Strategic plan: 1991–1994*. Richmond, British Columbia: Author.

Pacey, L. (1992, November). *Strategic planning and open learning: Turkey tails and frogs*. Paper presented at the International Council for Distance Education Council's 16th World Conference, Sukhothai Thammathirat Open University, Thailand.

Perraton, H. (1982). Distance teaching north and south. In J. Daniel, M. Stroud & J. R. Thompson (Eds.), *Learning at a distance: A world perspective* (pp. 16–19). Edmonton, Alberta: Athabasca University/ International Council for Correspondence Education.

Perry, W. (1977). *The Open University*. San Francisco: Jossey-Bass.

Raggatt, P. (1992, November). *Serving individual needs: The new challenge for distance education*. Paper presented at the International Council for Distance Education Council's 16th World Conference, Sukhothai Thammathirat Open University, Thailand.

Rawaf, H. A. & Simmons, C. (1992). Distance higher education for women in Saudi Arabia: Present and proposed. *Distance Education, 13*(1), 65, 80.

Rebel, K. (1990). Modern teaching technologies and their importance for a "European open learning"—The DELTA example. *Research in Distance Education, 2*(2), 2–7.

Reyes, M. (1992). Monterrey Institute of Technology: Three years of experience in satellite technology, 1989–1992. Personal communication.

Rodriguez-Rosello, L. (1991). *Developing European learning through technological advance-DELTA-exploratory action—final technical report*. Commission of the European Communities (ref: DE2205).

Root, J. (1992, June). *Teaching from a distance: Television instruction via Oregon Ed-Net*. Paper presented at the meeting of the Association for Media and Technology in Education in Canada (AMTEC), Vancouver, Canada.

Rubin, E. (1989) (Ed.). The Commonwealth of Learning. *Research in Distance Education, 1*(1), 20.

Rumble, G. (1986). *The planning and management of distance education*. London: Croom Helm.

Rumble, G. & Keegan, D. (1982). General characteristics of distance teaching universities. In G. Rumble & K. Harry (Eds.), *The distance teaching universities* (pp. 9–14). London: Croom Helm.

Rural Development Telecommunications Network for the State of South Dakota: Governor Mickelson's telecommunications task force (1991, October). Pierre, South Dakota: The Bureau of Administration.

Sewart, D. (1992, November). *Student support systems in distance education.* Paper presented at the International Council for Distance Education Council's 16th World Conference, Sukhothai Thammathirat Open University, Thailand.

Shaw, W. A. (1992, January). *Contact North: A snapshot.* Paper presented at the meeting of Pacific Telecommunications Council Conference, Honolulu, Hawaii.

Sukhothai Thammathirat Open University (Pamphlet, no date). Thailand: Public Relations Unit, Sukhothai Thammathirat Open University.

Tait, A. (1991). Conference report. EDEN: The European Distance Education Network, 28–30 May 1991, Prague, Czechoslovakia. *Open Learning, 6*(3), 55–56.

Thorvaldsen, P. (1980). (Ed.) *From books to bytes: The impact of technology on education.* Toronto, Canada: TV Ontario.

United Nations Educational, Scientific, and Cultural Organization/International Council for Distance Education (1990). *Developments in distance education in Asia: An analysis of five case studies.* Bangkok: UNESCO

United Nations Educational, Scientific, and Cultural Organization/National Institute of Multimedia Education (1992). Survey of distance education in Thailand. In *A survey of distance education in Asia and the Pacific* (pp. 688–873). Paris: Author.

United States Distance Learning Association (1991). *National policy recommendations.* Unpublished USDLA document circulated to membership. San Ramon, CA: Author.

University of Hawaii (1991). *HITS: Hawaii Interactive Television System.* Honolulu, Hawaii: Author.

University of Waterloo (1992). *Reaching out: Correspondence courses 1992–93—A Canadian distance education program.* Waterloo, Ontario, Canada: Author.

Wallace, J. & Maitava, K. (1990). Improving management information at USP's Extension Services: The implementation of an electronic mail system by satellite. *Distance Education, 11*(2), 334–342.

Weinstein, S. & Roschwalb, S. A. (1990). Is there a role for educators in telecommunications policy? *Kappan, 72*(2), 115–117.

Willett, F. J. (1991). *Report to the Minister for Education, the Honourable Mr. Paul Braddy, on the Queensland Open Learning Project.* Brisbane, Australia: Queensland Government Publications.

Willis, B. (1991, October). Alaska. In *Reports from Western States: Educational telecommunications plans, policies, programs.* Unpublished report prepared for the third annual meeting of the Western Cooperative for Educational Telecommunications, San Diego, California.

Willis, B. (1992). *Effective distance education: A primer for faculty and administrators.* (Monograph Series in Distance Education, No. 2). Fairbanks, AK: University of Alaska Center for Cross-Cultural Studies.

Wilson, D. (1992) (Ed.) The Commonwealth of Learning: An historical synopsis. *COMLEARN, 3*(1), 11–12.

Chapter Two

Research in Distance Education

Robert Threlkeld and Karen Brzoska

Distance education, particularly with its current emphasis on the use of electronic technology, is being examined carefully by the educational community. As with any educational innovation, a standard set of questions is constantly asked: Is it as good as traditional education? What does it cost? What kinds of students benefit? What factors influence instructional effectiveness? Do instructors have to teach differently?

Fortunately, we now have a significant amount of information that provides tentative answers to these and other questions. This chapter will present some of that information. It will provide the reader with a sense of what we currently know (and don't yet know) about distance education, what some fruitful lines of inquiry may be, and how to use research information in a practical sense. We will use the term "research" in a rather loose sense, meaning any logical and systematic inquiry toward answering a question about distance learning and distance education. We will include evaluation data in the chapter. Evaluation data provides practitioners with ideas about what works and what doesn't in actual distance education programs.

The chapter will benefit the distance learning professional three ways. It will demonstrate that a good deal is already known about distance learning. It will also provide readers with concrete findings to keep the frequent critiques of distance education at bay. And perhaps most useful of all, it will provide suggestions on what to consider when designing a distance education program.

Information for this chapter comes from two sources: published formal studies and reports in journals, and unpublished evaluation summaries of distance learning at the secondary level. The latter are in-depth studies of distance learning that have yet to make their way into the research mainstream. Often these reports were done at the end of a demonstration project, to provide funding agencies with information on program outcomes and effectiveness.

Because novice distance learning practitioners often look first to the hardware, we will examine media variables at the beginning of the chapter. Researchers have looked at a variety of media over the past fifty years, and findings have been fairly consistent. Then we will look at instructional variables—interaction, instructor styles, learner satisfaction, and learner characteristics. At the end of the chapter we will examine research related to costs of both the distance education media and the instruction. While we will discuss distance learning findings for the general population, we will also draw from current experiences of secondary school students. Because of federal funding for high school distance learning over the past few years, substantial new data are now available.

Why are research and evaluation results important to the practitioner? Moore (1989) enumerates three reasons why research should be conducted and questions of effectiveness asked concerning distance education.

- Distance education uses technologies that are unfamiliar as the primary media of communication for teaching to most teachers and administrators.
- Distance education requires teachers to specialize in the various functions of teaching, especially those of content expert, facilitator of interaction, course designer, and learning counsellor, and such distinctions are unfamiliar to most teachers and administrators.
- Distance education requires planning, development, production and distribution on a larger scale than is familiar to most teachers and administrators, and requires major intervention by policy makers at national and state levels.

In its broadest definition, distance education can trace its roots into misty antiquity, when early civilizations used drums, fire and smoke, petroglyphs, and ultimately the printed word to communicate. Modern technological distance education was preceded by correspondence instruction. Prior to the age of electronic communication, for 80 years correspondence study was the only form of education that permitted learners to overcome barriers of time and distance to obtain an education. Particularly in the developing world, correspondence education remains an important form of distance education to reach mass audiences.

Media Variables

General Media Comparison Studies

The most common theme in distance education research is that which compares two or more media in relation to their effectiveness: "does it teach better than ..." Typically these studies are comparisons of traditional instruction with instruction by media such as computers, television, and radio. Although they often show some slight advantage for one medium or another, the most common outcome is "no significant difference" between mediated and face-to-face instruction. Literally hundreds of media comparison studies have been performed over the past forty years, and the results have been uniform: the instructional medium doesn't appear to make any important difference in student achievement, attitudes, and retention.

There have been so many media comparison studies that researchers are now writing reports that are reviews of the entire field of media comparison. For example, in 1967, Reid and MacLennan performed a broad review of 350 instructional media comparisons. They found a trend of no significant difference in comparisons of mediated instruction vs. face-to-face, regardless of whether the instruction was live or videotaped. In another review of media comparison literature, Dubin and Tavaggia did a longitudinal study of various approaches used in college teaching. They found the following:

> In the foregoing paragraphs we have reported the results of a reanalysis of the data from 91 comparable studies of college teaching technologies between 1921 and 1965. These data demonstrate clearly and unequivocally that there is no measurable difference among truly distinctive methods of college instruction when evaluated by student performance on final exams. (Dubin and Tavaggia, 1968, p. 35)

Visual-Based Instruction

The above summaries look at results from studies of a wide array of media. What about studies which focus on distance education which uses some form of visual-based instruction, such as television or audiographics (i.e., televised computer graphics)?

Cohen, Ebeling, and Kulik (1981) performed a meta-analysis of 74 studies which compared visual-based instruction with conventional instruction. They found that students learned slightly more from visual-based instruction than from traditional teaching, but there was typically no difference between the two groups in regard to course completion, student attitudes, or the correlation between attitudes and achievement.

Whittington (1987) performed the most widely quoted review of research on instructional television. Under contract to assess the instructional effectiveness of television for the Coordinating Board of the Texas College and University System, he reviewed studies done during the 1970s and 1980s and concluded the following:

1. Comparative studies indicate that students taking courses via television achieve, in most cases, as well as students taking courses via traditional methods.
2. Findings of equivalent student achievement hold even when rigorous methodological standards are applied.
3. Television is a technological device for transmitting communication and has no intrinsic effect, for good or ill, on student achievement.
4. Effective instructional design and techniques are the crucial elements in student achievement whether instruction is delivered by television or by traditional means.

Looking at one specific audience, high school students, we find similar results. Recent evaluation reports suggest that students who enroll in distance learning classes seem to do as well as students in traditional classroom settings. One group of high school students (SERC, 1990) taking a Japanese course learned slightly more than their traditional counterparts. Speth, Poggio, and Glasnapp (1991) found that satellite students received lower grades than students in conventional classes, although the researcher attributed this to differing student characteristics among the two groups. Satellite students tended to be better students, who had heretofore competed only with peers in a single (often small) school setting.

One audiographics report (Murray & Heil, 1987) stated that "... the pattern of scores across seven courses justifies the conclusion that receiving (distant) students do at least as well and perhaps better than their sending site counterparts and nonteleteaching control students" (p. 14).

As noted above, these findings which indicate that the medium doesn't have much effect are extremely common. Russell (1992b) reviewed media studies and abstracted sentences from studies which include terms such as "no significant difference." In nine single-spaced pages of research results snippets ("... students can learn about as well from television as from classroom instruction ... media comparison studies, regardless of media employed, tend to result in no significant differences ... over 24 years there was no significant difference in academic performance of the two groups ..."), he documents the dulling consistency of the findings.

Radio-Based Instruction

The use of radio for distance education began in the United States in the 1920s, and today is common throughout the developing world. It is a cost-effective way to reach a mass audience, and is used to provide literacy training and information about health, agriculture, and basic education. Gibbins (1989) gathered information on radio as an educational medium. She noted that most of the research on the effectiveness of instructional radio in the U.S. was conducted in the 1930s and 1940s. She listed half dozen studies from that period which demonstrated no difference in student performance between those who listened to radio lectures and those who attended live classes. She cites a report (Forsythe, 1970) for the Commission on Instruction Technology:

> Research clearly indicates that radio is effective in instruction. Experimental studies comparing radio teaching with other means or media have found radio as effective as the so-called 'conventional methods.' Even though radio has been criticized for being only an audio medium, studies have shown that visual elements in learning are not uniformly important. (p. 255)

Telephone-Based Instruction

Until recently, the telephone was the most widely used technology for interactive media-based distance education. The ubiquity of telephone in the U.S. and the relatively low cost of the technology has made telephone-based distance learning a wise choice for many distance education programs.

The telephone has been used widely for distance learning in rural areas of the United States, and evaluation results confirm its effectiveness in instruction. Kuramoto (1984) assessed the performance of nurses receiving continuing education via three delivery mechanisms: live, direct instruction; telephone-based courses; and print-based independent study. Nurses had comparable achievement regardless of the medium. Chute, Hulick, Messmer, and Hancock (1986) reported on the results of educational use of telephones by AT&T. The authors report:

> ... research conducted by Sales and Marketing Education Division has shown teletraining was as effective and in some cases more effective than face-to-face instruction. In general there were no significant differences between the amount of information students learned in classes that were teletrained and the amount they learned in face-to-face instruction. (p. 363)

Studies of media preference are common in comparing face-to-face instruction to telephone-based instruction. In general, there are no differences in preferred media. When faced with the option of traveling to a live class, students prefer learning by telephone. A representative study was reported by Kirkhorn (1985). She studied student media preferences for delivery of technical training. Kirkhorn found no significant difference in student satisfaction between a telephone-based course and a face-to-face course.

The popularity of media comparison studies among researchers may be due to its compatibility with classical research designs. The variable in question, the medium, can be manipulated while other variables can be held constant. However, Soloman and Gardner (1986, p. 14) suggest that such "stripping the medium down to its bare bones" accomplishes nothing. It simply demonstrates that "transporting" education via media does not alter its effectiveness for the learner. This highly controlled research environment does not allow for any modification of instruction to take advantage of a medium's particular strengths. Cambre (1987), in her review of instructional television, states:

> The classic example of this type of controlled comparison study is the comparison of the live teacher to the video-transmitted image of the teacher, with all other things being held constant. This, of course, is an appropriately controlled experiment but is not a test of the (potential) effectiveness of instructional television. Happily this point no longer needs to be labored and the media comparison studies that continue to find their way into the literature can, for the most part, be disregarded. (p. 30)

The most recent report on comparative media studies is Russell's (1992a) article. He draws the same conclusion as earlier studies. He believes that:

> ... no matter how it is produced, how it is delivered, whether or not it is interactive, low-tech or high-tech, students learn equally well with each technology and learn as well as their on-campus, face-to-face counterparts even though students would rather be on campus with the instructor if that were a real choice. (p. 2)

Clark (1983) summarizes current thinking succinctly when he states:

> The best current evidence is that media are mere vehicles that deliver instruction but do not influence student achievement any more than the truck that delivers our groceries causes changes in our nutrition ... only the content of the vehicle can influence achievement. (p. 445)

For the practitioner the choice of a medium in a particular distance education application need not be based on pedagogical advantages. If one believes, as decades of research results intimate, that one can teach almost anything over almost any medium, then implementation factors such as costs and maintenance may be the most salient dimensions. How many students need what content at which locations? What technologies are already in place? What do they cost to operate?

In a real sense the media comparison studies liberate decision-makers to concentrate their efforts more on the concrete elements in distance education systems. Once these media decisions are made, instructional strategies and program design can follow.

Distance education research has now moved to other areas of study, other variables which have an impact on the success or failure of a program. Olcott (1992) recently stated "... the research on student achievement is giving way to greater emphasis on student attitudes toward technology, economic analysis of ITV (instructional television), instructor effectiveness, course design features, and learning theory applied to media-based learning" (p. 3).

Instructional Variables

Live and Interactive Instruction

The ability of a student to interact with the instructor and other students is what distinguishes modern distance education from broadcast media and textbooks. Interaction can be categorized into that which is *individual*, between the student and course information in books, computer programs and lab experiments; and a student's *social* interaction with a teacher or other students. In common parlance, interaction in distance education refers to that which is social.

Social interaction may be *synchronous* (real-time, live and conversation-like during the instructional session) as in the case of two-way audio and two-way video. It may also be *asynchronous* (delayed, before or after the instruction session) as with correspondence, computer-mediated, and mailed communication. Most of the purely distance teaching institutions, such as the British Open University, utilize the latter. However, with the advent of some of the new communication media, traditional in-person colleges and universities have created distance education systems with fully interactive technologies designed to replicate the traditional classroom experience for distant learners. The replication model appears more expedient because it permits use of existing courses, and it is more acceptable to faculty because teaching models remain largely intact. The replication model assumes that synchronous interaction is critically important and that without it distance education would be vastly diminished in its effectiveness. But how important are live and fully interactive broadcasts to student learning and acceptance?

For the adult learner, it is not at all clear that live and interactive distance education is essential. One report on adult distance learners (Delbecq & Scates, 1989) views interactivity in the following light:

> In the beginning, most televised course programs operated according to a bias wherein they have tried to replicate the residential classroom situation. This bias favored an instructor in the presence of students with the opportunity for immediate feedback from students in the studio classroom and telephone communication with students at remote sites. Part of this attempt to duplicate as close as possible the existing residential classroom situation was an attempt to legitimize a new technology. However, evaluation of student performance across delivery designs do not show a clear pattern of increased performance associated with live interactions vs. later viewing ... Thus, one should not be prejudiced in favor of live broadcasts. There are significant disadvantages of utilizing only real-time broadcasts (without access to tapes) as the sole instructional technology. (p. 3)

Stone (1990), in his assessment of interactivity in distance learning for graduate engineers, believes that the need for live, interactive instruction is not supported by research and evaluation literature. He believes that off-campus graduate engineers do not suffer from the inability to "talk back" to faculty in real time. He argues that adult students may perform better in situations where they control not only *where* but *when* learning occurs. He believes that as long as students have some form of interactive access to faculty, high quality learning can occur.

These opinions are mirrored by other distance educators who work with adults. Swain (1990) stated "There is little apparent benefit from using the class time required for real-time interaction and there is reduced efficiency in transmitting course material" (p. 1). He believes that more important forms of interaction for adult engineers include: instructor's telephone hours, prompt feedback of homework and exam results, and peer interactions at the receiving locations.

If liveness and interactivity are of lesser importance to adult learners, what about for secondary school students? Most current distance education programs for secondary school students utilize live instruction, and all have some form of interactivity between instructor and student. The state of Utah operated a high school Spanish program by satellite in 1985–86. The series was live during its first year, then taped during the second year. Barker (1986), who evaluated the project, was very critical of this shift away from live and interactive instruction: "no matter how well produced the videotaped lessons may be, lack of a teacher (to interact with) greatly reduces the effectiveness of the teaching approach" (p. 11).

The above quotation presumes a lively, give-and-take classroom atmosphere in the distance learning environment, with distant students freely and spontaneously commenting and asking questions. The reality of distance learning, particularly satellite-based distance learning, is that students interact infrequently with instructors both on and off the air. Speth, Poggio, and Glasnapp (1991) reported that 42% of facilitators stated that students interacted only once per month, and 29% said their students *never* interacted. Another study (SERC, 1989) found that only 25% of students said they spoke with the teacher during or after class more than twice during the semester. With large numbers of students, and with many students watching tape delayed broadcasts, these are not unrealistically low levels of interaction.

Speth, Poggio, and Glasnapp (1991) intensely studied the interactions in a single, large foreign language class. They summarized their findings: "How important is the live, interactive feature in influencing cognitive and affective outcomes? This particular study did not indicate that interaction made much of a contribution to achievement ..." (p. 14).

However, throughout many of the secondary school evaluation studies the mystique of interaction is evident. For example, Speth, Poggio, and Glasnapp (1991) suggest that the linking process of live instruction was important. They state that "This course by satellite is a prime example of that process of unifying widely scattered learners; it brought together students and teachers from as far apart as eastern Montana and the gulf coast of Mississippi" (p. 10).

Although live on-air interaction may not be important for student outcomes, it may be important as a consumer variable, a requisite condition sought by some learners—even if not used. Synchronous interaction makes us feel more connected, a part of a "class." Live, interactive learning is what we are familiar with, it's "school." The early automobile was designed, perhaps unconsciously, to look like the horse-drawn carriage. It was decades before the automobile became an entity unto itself, developing according to its own potential. Distance education may require a similar aging period to evolve out of preconceived notions of what education should be.

We may already be seeing movement away from the "horseless carriage" model of distance education. One interesting development is that which Nipper (1989) calls "third generation" distance learning systems. These systems utilize electronic technologies for all forms of interaction. Bates (1991) reports that the technologies aren't used "... just in the 'one-to-many' form of print and broadcasting. These third generation technologies, using telecommunications and computers, provide far greater facility for two-way communications, resulting in a much more even access to communication between student and teacher (and also other students)" (p. 11).

The third generation models often use a combination of print, video tape, audio tape, fax, audio conferencing, and voice mail. However, the major tool for student-student and student-teacher interaction is computer conferencing (Waggoner, 1992). The interaction is almost exclusively asynchronous. Recent evaluation studies have indicated that this is highly acceptable both to students and faculty. Witherspoon (1992) taught an upper division university course using video taped lectures, print, and computer conferencing to 40 students. He found that, although students preferred live in-person interaction, by a margin of 2 to 1 they felt they learned more from other students' input than is usually the case in traditional classes, and by a margin of 3 to 1, students found the instructor to be more accessible than in usual classes. The author himself was very positive about the interactive nature of the course, and felt he got to know students better than in traditional classes.

The Western Cooperative for Educational Telecommunication (Markwood & Johnstone, 1992) recently published an interim evaluation report of an Annenberg/CPB-funded distance education project in higher education. Projects at two of the institutions (Rochester Institute of Technology and Northern Virginia Community College) utilized third-generation teaching structures. Interview results from both projects indicate that faculty and students feel that the asynchronous interaction from computer conferencing and voice mail was very useful and effective.

For the practitioner:

- The research literature doesn't confirm the need for live or synchronous interactivity in distance education. Its impact on learner outcome is elusive, at best.
- Live distance education with synchronous interaction, even if not used, is desired by some students and administrators. Distance learners may not participate in a distance learning system which doesn't provide it.
- As we gain experience with educational technologies, we may find ourselves interacting with teachers and other students in new and surprisingly satisfying ways.

Learner Elements

As noted, substantial research has been conducted to demonstrate "no significant difference" in achievement levels between distant and traditional learners. Much of this same research, however, reveals a considerable variance in student attitudes and satisfaction levels (Johnstone, 1991). This finding deserves attention since distance educators, like their counterparts in the traditional classroom, are concerned with the students' overall learning experience, not simply learning outcomes.

In an attempt to discern why such variance exists, research has been conducted to profile successful, satisfied distance learners. As a result of this profiling process, limitations have been imposed which ignore important variables such as individual learner characteristics. Speth (1991) makes a valid point when she says that "the literature in distance learning has paid an inordinate amount of attention trying to construct a profile of the typical learner" (p. 22). She believes that gathering large samples of distance learners and amalgamating them into averages produces an illusory "typical learner," which masks the tremendous variability which exists in the consumer population.

Rather than a focus on the typical learner, research which concentrates on individual differences and their impact on the learning process may prove more fruitful. As noted in the Midland evaluation report (Speth, Poggio, & Glasnapp, 1991), authors have discussed the possibility that individual differences among learners might affect their response to instruction, and regretted the lack of much research along those lines. Morgan (1984) criticized experimental studies in education for using an "agricultural-botany paradigm—assuming that students react to different educational treatments as consistently as plants react to fertilizers" (p. 8).

Understanding the varying backgrounds and needs of distant learners is important when planning a distance education program (Willis, 1992). Background and descriptive data will help in curriculum decisions, program design, and perhaps most importantly what to expect in terms of learning from distant students. We will consider research findings related to motivation and learning characteristics and how these elements might influence student attitudes and satisfaction.

Enrollment Motivation

Students choose to participate in distance education rather than traditional instruction for a myriad of reasons (Niemi, 1987). Studies have been conducted to see if a correlation exists between the reasons for participation and the subsequent educational experience of the distant learner. Due to their generic nature, three reasons for participation have been selected for review here: convenience and flexibility; lack of instructional alternatives; and educational mainstream alternative.

Convenience and Flexibility. Adult learners involved often cite convenience and flexibility as the primary reasons for enrolling in a distance education course. Family obligations, limited free time, and career/civic responsibilities can hinder enrollment in traditional, on-campus classes. Because the technology offers flexibility in the learning process (location of learning, time of learning), these learners are afforded the benefit of education they may not otherwise be able to receive (Holmberg & Bakshi, 1992; Shapiro & Hughes, 1992).

In a study which measured student perceptions of the effectiveness of correspondence instructions, Pierre and Olsen (1992) found that the majority of students (57%) in the study were employed forty or more hours per week. "The flexibility of correspondence study was cited by most students as the primary reason for choosing a correspondence course rather than a traditional course" (p. 67).

In a report on televised instruction, Delbecq and Scates (1989) note that students who participate in television courses are already busy people. They are attracted to what seems like an efficient means of study and said they would not have taken the course through any other medium.

For these adults, distance education has created an educational choice better suited than traditional instruction to their lifestyles. Because many of these learners are highly motivated, "they may be willing to endure almost any education environment or process to achieve a passing grade ..." (Wilkes & Burnham, 1991, p. 43).

Lack of instructional alternatives. Learners, particularly in rural areas, may choose distance education because of a lack of instructional alternatives. There are many areas in both developed and developing countries which are sparsely populated and/or separated from larger towns by geography. For the people who live in these areas, travel time and expense limit access to higher education. Realizing that technology may be their only bridge to education, these students are likely to persevere in their endeavors and receive some level of satisfaction with the process. Speth (1991) summarizes: "Simply stated, students are going to rate a televised program favorably if it saves them a large amount of travel time and earns them credit toward a professional qualification even if the content and presentation is poor" (p. 25).

For secondary students, a distance education class may provide the only means of receiving a particular class or specialized course of study. According to Bradshaw and Brown (1989), "an estimated one third of the country's school children get an inadequate education because of limited staff and resources related to small school size and geographic isolation" (p. 1). Today, limited resources are a reality for urban and inner-city schools as a result of personnel cutbacks and financial difficulties. These shortages, coupled with demands for increased student performance and access to a broader curriculum, have put administrators in a precarious position. To provide students with the classes they need and desire, many administrators have turned to distance education. But, are students satisfied with their learning experiences?

Research has suggested that learner response at the secondary level is varied. In a 1987 survey of students taking classes delivered over a satellite network, 70 percent indicated they would choose a traditionally taught course over the satellite course. Some of the reasons these students gave were too much work, some difficulty in hearing, difficulty in contacting the teacher, and inadequate teacher preparation and training. They also said, however, that they appreciated the increased number of course offerings and the interesting instruction (Johnstone, 1991, pp. 51–52).

In a recent study of the Midlands Consortium Star Schools Project, it was found that participating students were very satisfied with their satellite courses. Although the students occasionally felt frustrated because of the distance between them and their instructor, they felt that the overall experience was positive. " A majority of students indicated they believed the class had been a positive opportunity, not a better-than-nothing substitute" (Speth, Poggio, and Glasnapp, 1991, p. 33).

Educational Mainstream Alternative. Distance education is sometimes viewed as a substitute for traditional education; a route to be taken when traditional means are not available. For some learners, however, a chance to operate outside of the educational mainstream is what attracts them to the distance environment. Many of these students have participated in face-to-face instruction and have found it to be an unsatisfactory experience. As noted by Ohler:

> A footnote about who is a "distant" student: there are many reasons to cause people to turn to distance education, only some of which involve geographic separation of student and resources or a need for more flexible scheduling. Students can feel culturally or psychologically distant, or excluded from the education system as well, and turn to distance education in search of a system more sensitive to less mainstream audiences. (Ohler, 1989, p. 63)

Live interaction, an element that receives much attention in distance education literature, is not desired by all students. The idea of being in a traditional classroom, face to face with the instructor and other students may be disconcerting to some. For these students, the distance between them and the other participants is viewed as being positive.

For the practitioner:

- When designing a distance education program, consideration should be given to who the potential students are and their reasons for participation.

Learner Characteristics

Much research has been conducted to discern how learner characteristics affect learning in the traditional classroom. The models of these studies have been used to lay the groundwork for research concerning the distant student. Elements such as age, maturity, and learning styles have been identified as characteristics which can impact the learning process of the distant student (Campbell, 1992). To facilitate discussion of these learner characteristics, three audiences will be addressed—secondary, at-risk, and adult distant learners.

Secondary students. Many students participating at the secondary level have earned above average achievement levels in the traditional classroom. They are taking advanced placement courses via distance education to fulfill college acceptance requirements. These students are motivated to learn because, for many of them, distance education is the only way to access the courses they need.

When examining these students in terms of their approaches to learning, as outlined by Entwistle and Ramsden (1983), most would possess a Meaning-Oriented or Strategic approach to learning. Meaning-Oriented students are intrinsically motivated, enjoy learning for its own sake, and are actively involved with what they are learning. They use evidence, relate new information to previous knowledge, and try to see relationships among concepts. Strategics are often just as capable as the Meaning-Oriented students, but less interested in learning for its own sake and more interested in playing the system to get good grades. Students who use these approaches to learning are usually successful and satisfied with their distance education experience.

In the Midlands Consortium Star School Project (Speth, Poggio, & Glasnapp, 1991) it was reported that 85% of students taking the courses offered by satellite were planning to attend college. The author noted that although students in the Meaning-Oriented and Strategic groups can perform well in courses by satellite, students characterized by a Reproducing Orientation may warrant additional concern.

Students who approach learning with a Reproducing Orientation try to memorize or rote-learn disconnected pieces of information, are motived by fear of failure, and are not especially good at picking up cues as to what is expected of them. Although they are motivated to work hard, they are very easily discouraged. When planning a distance education course for students in this group, additional design elements should be taken into consideration.

These elements can include the use of detailed learning objectives, advanced organizers, learning reinforcers, and step-by-step instructions for student assignments.

These same design elements can also be used to assist students who are in the Non-Academic subgroups. These are students who are uninterested in their studies and disorganized in their study habits. Some lack both skills and motivation, others lack one or the other.

The potential for dissatisfaction and low achievement levels for distant students in this non-academic group is higher than in the other groups. It is very important to note, however, that this holds true for the traditional classroom, not just the distance learning classroom (Speth, 1991).

At-risk students. Rather than being viewed as an additional stumbling block for the at-risk or remedial student, distance education technology can be used to assist these students (Brey, 1988). Bates (1988) believes that televised instruction is especially useful to students who are struggling, because the visual medium allows them to understand concepts through the use of concrete examples.

One of the secondary school audiographic projects (Murray & Heil, 1987) offered several remedial courses through distance education and found the resulting achievement to be satisfactory. The Midlands satellite project (Speth, Poggio, & Glasnapp, 1991) found that young students and students who were low in academic skills were able to learn as well in satellite courses as in conventional Basic English and Reading courses. The report concluded that "there seems little basis for claiming that the satellite instruction puts the unmotivated, lower skilled student at a particular disadvantage compared to conventional instruction—the patterns of achievement are parallel" (p. 21).

Clearly, this is one area which deserves more study, particularly given the magnitude of remedial problems now endemic in rural areas.

Adult learners. The majority of adult learners involved in distance education do not routinely receive the same level of structure and support provided to secondary students. This is especially true of those adults who are involved in telecourses and correspondence instruction. In such cases, maturity, high motivation levels, and self-discipline have been shown to be necessary characteristics of successful, satisfied students (Delbecq & Scates, 1989).

In a study conducted to identify predictors of high risk among community college telecourse students, it was found that the average age of the forty-three non-successful students was 25.14, compared to an average age of 28.46 for the 108 successful students (Dille & Mezack, 1991). The authors contend that older students can be expected to perform better in telecourses for several reasons:

> First, age often brings greater maturity and self-discipline which would be needed in the telecourse format, which requires self-discipline and independent learning. Second, older students are more likely to have completed more college credit hours than younger students. In the study the number of college hours completed was shown to be significant to success. And, finally, older students are more likely to have full-time

careers, have a family, and be paying for their own education. For these students, dropping out of a telecourse would be considered a waste of time, money, and effort. (p. 32)

Adults who are most likely to complete courses using distance technology have a cluster of important characteristics, such as tolerance for ambiguity, a need for autonomy, and an ability to be flexible. In contrast, those who are more likely to drop out tend to prefer a great deal of structure, face-to-face lectures, and the opportunity to interact with the instructor. These research findings may be easily explained in terms of the classical dichotomy of Field-Dependence versus Field-Independence (Speth, 1991).

Field-Independent persons tend to be detached from others and enjoy autonomy. These learners can flourish in a distance education course which requires minimal interaction with the instructor and other students. Field-Dependent learners require goals to be defined for them and also need a good deal of reinforcement (Levano-Kerr, 1982). They may have more difficulty in distance education classes where continual reinforcement through constant interaction is limited.

Campbell-Coggins (1989) described Moore's (1976) study of the interaction between field independence and attitude to independent study among adult learners. His findings show:

> the distribution of personality characteristics of field independence among correspondence learners is higher than chance, and a likely explanation is that by a self-selection process, only those who can tolerate non-social learning conditions survive in a program where dialogue is so low. (p. 152)

Learner characteristics play an important role in achievement and satisfaction levels of the distant student. Because these characteristics are so varied, it is important to conduct a learner analysis prior to developing a distance education course (Moller, 1991). Information concerning the potential student's preferred learning style will influence design considerations and instructional strategies.

For the Practitioner:

- A learner analysis of the potential audience should be conducted prior to course development. This learner analysis should include information about demographics, learner styles, motivation, and cultural background.
- Learners with all types of learning styles can be successfully taught using distance learning technologies, if the proper design elements are incorporated into the course.
- Student expectations about the technology need to be considered when developing a program. A point of consideration is a pre-class training program which reorients students to the proper use of the medium in relation to the distance education class.

Learner Support

Many distance learners require support and guidance to make the most of their distance learning experience. Be they adults studying engineering via satellite or secondary students learning through computer conferencing, they need support structures which augment the instructional process. This support can be academic in nature (e.g., feedback on class assignments, academic counseling) or can be related to non-content areas, such as student enrollment and orientation.

The same technologies that are used to disseminate distance education classes are now being used to provide learner support services. Wright (1992) notes that there appears to be an increase in the use of more advanced technologies, such as computer networking and fax machines, for providing support services to the distance learner. This method of offering assistance is especially beneficial to those students who cannot travel to the origination site due to time or travel constraints.

A broad range of support services have been identified, the presence of which seem to have a positive affect on learner satisfaction. Three services appear repeatedly throughout the research literature and are now discussed in brief.

Timely student feedback. Cited again and again as being a critical component of learner support, students who receive timely feedback on their assignments respond more positively to the class than those who must wait for feedback (Delbecq & Scates, 1989). Distance educators who realize the importance of "turn-around time" on assignments are making use of the technology to expedite the process. "Again, using microcomputers, modems, fax and telephone communication, rapid turn-around of corrections and comments is presently feasible" (Delbecq and Scates, 1989, p. 5). If such technology is not available to both the instructor and students, a reliable courier or mail system needs to be in place.

On-site support. Most secondary school distance education programs have the requirement that a local person be in the receiving classroom with the students. These assistants, called facilitators, coordinators, or teaching partners, proctor exams, monitor activities, coach or mentor students, and conduct local off-air exercises. This position may be filled by a fully qualified teacher, a librarian, or an aide.

Many assistants assume more of a coordinator role by ensuring that materials are distributed when needed, that tests are proctored, and that deadlines are met. Others may take on more of a facilitator role and act as "a bridge between the students and instructor, keeping informed of student interests and progress, and providing guidance and answering questions as needed" (Willis, 1992, p. 28).

The support provided by the receive-site facilitator has been consistently cited as critical to the effectiveness of a distance education program (McCleary & Egan, 1989; Chute, Balthazar, & Poston, 1988). In studying student responses to an electronic classroom (EC) project, Moore, Burton, and Dodl (1991) found that "the role and performance of the facilitator was a major factor in determining the success of the electronic classroom class." Principals and students alike noted that the facilitator's attitude and interest in the projects was vital in allowing students to get the most value from the programming.

Focusing attention on secondary students, Moore (1989) suggested that "teachers, highly qualified and experienced in the understanding of learners and learning, but not necessarily in the academic subject, support students by:

- providing skilled diagnostic counseling and orientation programs;
- assisting students to organize their time and develop study skills;
- providing active tutorial assistance during the course, face-to-face if needed and feasible;
- monitoring written work not only for cognitive achievement but for affective responses;
- ensuring that the instructors involve the students in the instruction of the course; and
- giving assistance when illness, financial, family or work difficulties threaten to overcome the motivation to study" (p. 6).

Threlkeld (1992a, b), in his case studies of rural distance education, reinforces the position that the learner support person is critical to the success of distance education programs. He describes one particularly effective support person in rural California who provided many of the above supports for secondary school distant learners:

> One gets the strong feeling that this facilitator views her role as something much more than the person who opens the door and turns on the equipment for the distance learning student. These are *her* kids in *her* classes. She is the central person in the student's distance learning class, and the television is the information source.... (p. 27)

Because the on-site facilitators play such a vital role, their importance or contributions should not be diminished in any way. A successful distance education program must be sensitive to the needs of the facilitators and offer support on a continual basis.

Access to library materials. A key component in distance education is the student's ability to obtain library materials. Imagine the following situation: Dr. Smith has just assigned a research project for her students participating in "Economics by Satellite." As the project requirements are being discussed, Patty in urban New York makes a mental note to go to the city library after class to begin her research. At the same time, Alvin in rural Alaska begins to panic. For him, the closest library is an hour away by plane ...

Situations such as this are not uncommon. For the adult learner who may be taking a course at home, access to library resources may be limited. And, although many secondary-level distance students have access to their high school library, often the holdings are limited or dated. This can create problems for the distance learner. As pointed out by Dillon, Gunawardena, and Parker (1992), who conducted an evaluation of learner support:

> Library resources are very important to distance students as the majority of them (57.3 percent) indicated that success in the course required access to library materials. The effectiveness of the library services provided seemed to be a significant barrier to distance students who are required to use the library. (p. 2)

One alternative for students with limited access is to put all relevant library materials on-line for access by personal computer. If this is not practical, specific articles and papers could be put on computer or mailed to the distance students. Another alternative is to structure assignments which can utilize newspapers or other resources that are common to most learners.

Instructor Elements

When analyzing existing distance education programs, a wide array of teaching styles can be noted. Upon closer examination, one can identify instructors who have successfully adapted their traditional strategies to suit their new teaching environment. Unfortunately, close inspection is not needed to spot those instructors who have not redesigned their course. These instructors seem to have packed their traditional course into a suitcase, travelled across campus to the distance learning studio, and unpacked this same course to use with the technology—wrinkles and all. To compound the situation, these wrinkles become even more apparent through the accentuating effects of the technology.

As noted in *Linking for Learning* (U. S. Congress, 1989), "The critical role of the teacher in the distance learning setting makes it imperative that teachers get adequate training not only in the technical aspects of the system, but also in the educational applications of the technology" (p. 95). This report contends that training is a critical component of any distance education program and should not be overlooked. Asking an instructor to bring to the distance education environment a class that has been developed for the traditional setting, without providing suggestions for redesign, would be unfair to both the instructor and the students (Gehlauf, Shatz, & Frye, 1991).

Redesign of the course should be based on the type of technology to be used, the nature of the content to be presented and the needs of the distant learners (Willis, 1989). For example, technologies which utilize synchronous interaction but provide no visual feedback for the instructor (e.g., one-way video, two-way audio) should incorporate strategies for increasing interaction and gauging comprehension levels. Without the benefit of non-verbal student response, instructors must structure into their class specific activities which will help determine student receptivity and comprehension of the material (Holden & Vivian, 1988).

What the learner needs (or desires) in terms of effective instruction will vary based on learning styles and learner characteristics. Research studies have revealed, however, a number of instructor characteristics that have been identified as effective by a large number of distant learners. Haaland and Newby (1984) conducted studies to investigate student perceptions of teaching behaviors necessary for effective delivery of courses both conventionally and via distance education. This study revealed five statistically significant differences in the frequency of effective teaching behavior of those teaching by teleconference. Effective teleconference teachers: (1) used students' names, (2) set out clear statements of purpose, (3) made use of printed material, (4) encouraged discussion, and (5) did not speak in a monotone. Furthermore, these authors found that the delivery mode (e.g., video) has no effect on students' overall ratings of the courses or on ratings of instructors' ability.

When measuring the impact of system design on instruction, Hackman and Walker (1990) found that distant students viewed favorably instructors who employed strategies for enhancing social presence. These strategies incorporated elements such as encouraging involvement, offering individual feedback, and promoting interpersonal relationships with distant learners. Baird (1976) in addressing findings of the extensive Wisconsin Educational Telephone Network, noted that the instructor's ability to listen is a requirement for effective distance instruction.

Bradshaw and Brown (1989) reinforce the idea that teleteachers should possess a willingness to become comfortable with the technology. Teleteachers should plan their teaching with a view to the strengths and weaknesses of the technology. These authors cite effective instructor characteristics which include voice quality, self-confidence, stage presence, a flair for the dramatic, and spontaneous creativity. "While these are characteristics most teachers need, they are especially critical for teaching 'in absentia' " (p. 4).

For the practitioner:

- Specific teaching strategies have been developed to complement different distance education technologies and varying student needs. To be effective distance educators, instructors should take part in a training program designed specifically to meet their needs (see Chapter 13, Enhancing Faculty Effectiveness in Distance Education, for additional information).

Cost Variables

Both in the developed and developing worlds, the driving energy behind the establishment of distance education systems is often the desire to provide education to a population in the least costly fashion. Although there are instances where the social or political needs (i.e., to serve an isolated population) are the major forces, distance education is more often touted as a way to either reduce costs or serve greater numbers with the same funds. Indeed, as Dively (1989) points out, legislatures are very concerned about costs when examining new, alternative technologies. At first glance, one assumes that it is more economical to use some form of media to move information to the learner rather than the other way around. However, cost comparisons between distance education and traditional education are often neither as simple as one might hope, nor, as with media comparison studies, as useful.

Bates (1991) lists three main cost components in distance education:

- **delivery:** the costs of getting teaching materials to students; these can be transmission costs, telephone costs, mailing costs, etc.;

- **production:** the costs of creating teaching materials; these would include the costs of teachers developing materials, television or computer-assisted learning or other media production costs, etc.;
- **support:** the additional costs needed to ensure that the system works successfully; these can be administrative costs, such as registration and examinations, local support costs, such as local tutors or coordinators, and institutional overheads, such as building costs, etc.

Although limited in number, some costs studies have appeared in the distance education literature. Rumble (1988), in discussing traditional preproduced distance education courses, believes that there are consistent findings in cost studies of distance education. He believes that the cost structures of distance education and traditional education are different. Distance education is characterized by high fixed costs (course development, technology) and lower variable costs (materials, logistics, correspondence with individual students). He notes that conventional British universities have a fixed to variable cost ratio of 8:1, whereas the British Open University has a ratio of 2000:1.

Rule, Dewulf, and Stowitschek (1988) summarized a three-year comparative study of distance education in Utah. They found that per student costs declined markedly over the three-year period, particularly costs related to travel and personnel. The system proved its cost-competitiveness to conventional instruction *when given sufficient time.* Chute, Balthazar, and Poston (1988) reported similar results in corporate training at AT&T. They found that major savings were realized through distance education in internal courses, one-hour updates, and specialized internal seminars. Once initial start-up costs were amortized, significant savings were found in travel and lost productivity from workers who otherwise would have had to travel to a training site.

Ellertson, Wydra, and Jolley (1987) studied costs of distance learning in public secondary schools. From a mailed questionnaire to projects providing service to 812 students in 47 schools, the authors concluded that fewer than half of the courses were less expensive than a live teacher, but because of the lack of a qualified local teacher, most of the courses would not have been offered without some form of mediated instruction.

Studies which examine computer-mediated communication (CMC) costs are rare in the distance education literature. However, the number of courses which use the computer as a primary communication medium are increasing rapidly. A report by Phelps, Wells, Ashworth, and Hahn (1991) provides some insight into costs and effectiveness of CMC compared to classroom instruction. The authors studied two U.S. Army Reserve courses which were taught to groups of students in residence and students who received the course modified for computerized instruction. They found that the courses were both equally effective in terms of student achievement and comparable in costs, if the expenses related to course redesign were amortized over several cycles of instruction.

Often an educational organization's decision to utilize distance education or not is based on a number of factors in addition to economics. Price (1990) suggests that organizational politics are an important element, as are the social missions of an organization. He notes that higher education is often governed by the tradition of small, intimate classes, and distance education may violate that tradition. Simply showing that some form of distance education would be less costly might be irrelevant in some organizations.

Educational values also must be considered when approaching costs. Dillon, Gibson, and Confessore (1992) suggest that two factors—distribution and interactivity—need to be considered when analyzing distance learning costs. The distributive element in distance education offers access to greater numbers of students at steadily decreasing per-student costs and represents efficiency. A delivery system which permits wide distribution of a course or regular re-use of preproduced materials can be shown to significantly reduce costs. As Rumble (1988) says, "Because variable costs per-student can be low, distance education systems can be cheaper per student and/or graduate than conventional systems, but only if the high costs can be spread across sufficient students to bring the average cost per student down below the level attained in traditional instruction" (p. 4).

However, as numbers of students increase through increased distribution, either the amount of interaction with learners decreases or the total cost for student-faculty interaction increases. Dillon, Gibson, and Confessore (1992) suggest that the nature of learner interactions is one indicator of educational quality, particularly in higher-order learning. A cost model which is acceptable to an organization will mirror the organization's values and the relative importance of efficiency and effectiveness. An institution which has a high need to teach large numbers of students will support expansive course delivery and limited interaction. One which prizes small group experiences will spend funds supporting interaction. One needs to understand the pedagogical needs and values of an organization before making judgments related to costs.

Because distance education impacts on the spending decisions within host organizations, Cowen and Nemiec (1983) believe that it is essential to involve the chief financial officer in any cost study, to be certain that the data collected are viewed as pertinent and credible by an organization's decision-makers. Their study of a two-way interactive video network in central Maine showed substantial travel and productivity savings over time and led to the continued funding of what appeared at first to be an overly expensive program.

Adding to the complexity of cost analyzing distance education is the lack of experience by universities and colleges in quantifying educational outputs and the absence of uniform ways of calculating such major expenses as overhead. Because of the high initial hardware and course productions costs of many distance education systems, depreciation and replacement expenses need to be included in any rigorous cost analysis.

Apart from simple economic value, distance education may provide many unmeasured benefits, such as increased parental involvement (U. S. Congress, 1989) and exposing students to new technologies. Clark (1989) points out that in many cases, older technologies (e.g., books, audio cassettes, television, the mail system) are cheaper in monetary terms but very "expensive in delivery time and reliability. Evaluation of costs should always consider trade-offs with cheaper and more traditional delivery options" (p. 21).

For the practitioner:

- Distance education systems which deliver instruction to large numbers of students employing limited interaction tend to show cost-effectiveness over an extended period.

- Distance education systems which transport traditional instruction using electronic technology may or may not be cost-effective, depending on the on-going costs of delivery and support, and in particular the costs of synchronous interaction.

- Distance education may provide benefits which are difficult to measure in dollars, such as reaching unserved students or providing isolated rural students with connections with the world around them.

- Marketing distance learning as a way to cut educational costs is risky, at best. In the short run, there is little evidence in the United States that distance education reduces costs over traditional instruction.

Conclusion

Hopefully the reader will now have learned a good deal about findings from the research in distance education. In the minds of the distance learning professional, at least, sufficient evidence exists to affirm that teaching via media does not do violence to teaching. The media is a mere vehicle and successful learning comes from other factors related to learners, support, course design, motivation, and need. We have gone beyond the initial phase of using media to teach students at a distance, during which we had to demonstrate over and over again that teachers could teach and that students could learn.

Perhaps we have entered a second phase, one which Miller (1992) calls " a period of integration and convergence." We may be moving away from single medium distance education systems typically operated by quasi-external units attached to institutions. We may be moving toward the internalization of distance education, in which traditional institutions use multi-media technology to provide mainstream education to their regular students. Indeed, some educators who use technology dislike the term "distance education," because it implies that students must be off-campus to learn from it. Today, some of the most intriguing work in distance education does not focus on any specific barrier such as time or space. Designers are asking the question, "given the technologies of today and tomorrow, how can we best design instructional systems which meet learners needs, wherever and whenever."

At the present time, distance education is very visible, and is being debated on campuses around the world. As this chapter has shown, teachers, students, administrators, and the interested public are examining this assumed new way of learning. As Brand (1987, p. 15) says, "There is a natural instinct to see either revolution or conspiracy in every new technology that comes down the pike."

As practitioners struggle to get distance education technologies imple-mented and accepted, another technology—the fax—has quietly slipped into general public use. With little fanfare, we see that legal information, financial information, letters home, and deli orders are skimming along the wires. We can hope the work of the researchers described in this chapter will help move the public to a point where distance education is not just accepted, it is *assumed.*

We are reminded of a statement made recently by a school superintendent in rural California. He has been using distance education, and using it well, for eight years. He said:

> When distance learning is ultimately successful, it will cease to be viewed by students, teachers, administrators, and parents as an add-on. It will no longer be a big deal. We will have arrived where we want to be when the kid no longer bursts through the door and says, "guess what, we got to use the computers today!"

Summary

Distance education has been the subject of study for at least 60 years. Results from research and evaluation studies can guide a distance education professional in making good decisions. This chapter examined general media comparison research as well as research related to specific media. Results from a multitude of studies suggest that the media itself is not as important to instruction as other variables, such as learner characteristics, motivation, and instructional alternatives. There is little empirical evidence to support the current drive for live and interactive instruction, although this type of distance learning seems to be preferred by many students.

What does seem to be very important is support for the distant learner. Students want and need rapid feedback from instructors as well as access to library resources and other supporting materials. Distant learners also value help from a local person (often called a facilitator or coordinator) who can offer advice and encouragement. Distant teaching faculty also need assistance in designing courses to maximize the potential of various media for meeting the needs of distant learners.

Finally, to date, findings are mixed regarding the cost-effectiveness of distance education. Proving that distance education is less expensive than traditional instruction is difficult, when one factors in the cost of media, program development, and long-term student support. There is some evidence that cost-effectiveness can be demonstrated, if one examines cost over an extended period of time.

References

Baird, M. (1976). Designing teleconference programs: Some clues from the Wisconsin experience. *The status of the telephone in education.* Madison, WI: University of Wisconsin–Extension.

Barker, B. (1986). *Interactive satellite instruction: How rural schools benefit.* Paper presented at the Annual Conference of the Rural Education Association, Little Rock, AR.

Barker, B. & Platten, R. (1988). Student perceptions of the effectiveness of college credit courses taught via satellite. *The American Journal of Distance Education, 2*(2), 44–50.

Bates, A. (1988). Television, learning, and distance education. *Journal of Education Television, 14*(3), 213–225.

Bates, A. (1991). Third generation distance education: The challenge of new technology. *Research in Distance Education, 3*(2), 10–15.

Bradshaw, D. & Brown, P. (1989). The promise of distance learning. Far West Laboratory, Policy Briefs, Number Eight.

Brand, S. (1987). *The Media Lab: Inventing the future at MIT.* New York: Penguin Books.

Brey, R. (1988). Expanding the classroom through technology. Meeting the mission of the community colleges. *American Association of Community and Junior Colleges*, Feb./March, 29–31.

Cambre, M. (1987). *A reappraisal of instructional television.* Syracuse, NY: Syracuse University, ERIC Clearinghouse on Information Resources.

Campbell, G. C. (1992). Changing perceptions of learners and learning at a distance: a review of selected recent research. *DEOSNEWS, 2*(4).

Campbell-Coggins, C. (1989). Preferred learning styles and their impact on completion of external degree programs. *The American Journal of Distance Education, 2*(1), 25–347.

Chute, A., Balthazar, L. & Poston, C. (1988). Learning from teletraining. *American Journal of Distance Education, 2*(3), 55–64.

Chute, A., Hulick, M., Messmer, C. & Hancock, P. (1986). Teletraining in the corporate environment. In L. Parker & C. Ohlgren (Eds.), *Teleconferencing and electronic communications V* (pp. 362–365). Madison, WI: University of Wisconsin, Center for Interactive Programs.

Chute, A. & Shatzer, L. (1989). Designing for international teletraining. Paper published in International Teleconference Association 1989 Yearbook.

Clark, R. (1983). Reconsidering research on learning from media. *Review of Educational Research, 53*(4), 445–459.

Clark, R. (1989). *Evaluating distance learning technology.* Washington, DC: U.S. Congress, Office of Technology Assessment. (ERIC Document Reproduction Service ED 325 097).

Cohen, P., Ebeling, B. & Kulik, J. (1981). A meta-analysis of outcome studies of visual-based instruction. *Educational Communications and Technology Journal, 29*, 26-36.

Cowen, R. & Nemiec, A. (1983). Evaluation considerations when documenting teleconferencing cost-benefits. In L. Parker & C. Ohlgren (Eds.), *Teleconferencing and electronic communications II* (pp. 290–292). Madison, WI: University of Wisconsin, Center for Interactive Programs.

Delbecq, A. & Scates, D. (1989). *Distance education through telecommunications: A review of lessons learned.* A special report of the American Assembly of Collegiate Schools of Business, August 1989.

Dille, B. & Mezack, M. (1991). Identifying predictors of high risk among community college telecourse students. *The American Journal of Distance Education, 5*(1), 24–35.

Dillon, C., Gibson, C. & Confessore, S. (1992). The economics of interaction in technology-based distance education. *Proceedings of the Seventh Annual Conference on Distance Teaching and Learning* (August, 1991). Madison, WI: University of Wisconsin.

Dillon, C., Gunawardena, C. & Parker, R. (1992). An evaluation of learner support services in a distance education system. *Distance Education, 13*(1), 29–45.

Dively, D. (1989). *Educational telecommunications in the west: 1989 state legislative actions.* Publication No. 2A195 of the Western Interstate Commission for Higher Education, Boulder, CO.

Dubin, R. & Tavaggia, T. (1968). *The teaching-learning paradox: A comparative analysis of college teaching methods.* Eugene, OR: Oregon University, Center for Advanced Study of Educational Administration. (ERIC Document Reproduction Service ED 026 988).

Ellertson, E., Wydra, D. & Jolley, H. (1987). *Report on distance learning: A national effectiveness study.* Mansfield, PA: Mansfield University and the Pennsylvania Teleteaching Project.

Entwistle, N. & Ramsden, P. (1983). *Understanding student learning.* London: Croom Helm.

Forsythe, R. (1970). Instructional radio. In S. Tickton (Ed.), *An evaluation of instructional technology* (pp. 12–34). New York: Bowker & Co.

Gehlauf, A., Shatz, M. & Frye, T. (1991). Faculty perceptions of interactive instructional strategies: Implications for training. *The American Journal of Distance Education, 5*(3), 20–28.

Gibbins, M. (1989). *The effectiveness of technology applied to instruction: A summary of the research literature.* San Diego: San Diego State University, Center for Communications.

Haaland, B. & Newby, W. (1984). Student perceptions of effective teaching behaviors: An examination of conventional and teleconference based instruction. In L. Parker & C. Ohlgren (Eds.), *Teleconferencing and electronic communications III* (pp. 211–217). Madison, WI: University of Wisconsin, Center for Interactive Programs.

Hackman, M. & Walker, K. (1990). The impact of systems design and instructional style on student reactions to distance education. *Research in Distance Education, 2*(2), 7–8.

Haughey, M. (1983). Teaching and learning via interactive satellite: A Janus view. (ERIC Document Reproduction Service No. ED 325 791).

Holden, D. & Vivian, R. (1988). Sure, satellite teaching is neat, now let's learn to use it well. *The Executive Educator, 10*(7), 23–24.

Holmberg, R. & Bakshi, T. (1992). Postmortem on a distance education course. Successes and failures. *The American Journal of Distance Education, 6*(1), 27–39.

Johnson, G., O'Connor, M. & Rossing, R. (1983–84). Interactive two-way television vs. in-person teaching. *Journal of Educational Technology Systems, 12*(3), 265–272.

Johnstone, S. (1991). Research on telecommunicated learning: Past, present, and future. *The Annals of the American Academy of Political Science, 514,* 49–57.

Julian, A. (1982). Utilizing telecommunications for non-traditional instruction in the North Carolina Community College System. (ERIC Document Reproduction Service No. ED 224 957).

Kirkhorn, J. (1985). A teletraining study: Student learning preferences. In L. Parker & C. Ohlgren (Eds.), *Teleconferencing and electronic communications IV* (pp. 223–231). Madison, WI: University of Wisconsin, Center for interactive Programs.

Kuramoto, A. (1984). Teleconferencing for nurses: Evaluating its effectiveness. In L. Parker & C. Ohlgren (Eds.), *Teleconferencing and electronic communications III* (pp. 262–268). Madison, WI: University of Wisconsin, Center for Interactive Programs.

Levano-Kerr, J. (1982). Cognitive style revisited. Implication for research. Paper presented at the Annual Meeting of the American Educational Research Association, New York, March 19–23, 1982.

Markwood, R. & Johnstone, S. (1992). *New pathways to a degree.* (Project evaluation: first year report), Western Cooperative for Educational Communications, Boulder, CO.

McCleary, E. & Egan, M. W. (1989). Program design and evaluation: Two-way interactive television. *The American Journal of Distance Education, 3*(1), 55–60.

Miller, G. (1992). Long-term trends in distance education. *DEOSNEWS, 2*(23).

Moller, L. (1991). Planning programs for distant learners. Using the Assure model. *TechTrends, 36*(1), 55–57.

Moore, M. (1976). Investigation of the interaction between cognitive style of field independence and attitude to independent study among adult learners who use correspondence independent study and self-directed independent study. Ph.D. diss., University of Wisconsin–Madison.

Moore, D. M., Burton, J. K. & Dodl, N. (1991). The role of facilitators in Virginia's electronic classroom project. *The American Journal of Distance Education, 5*(3), 29–38.

Moore, M. (1989). *Effects of distance learning: A summary of the literature.* Washington, DC: U. S. Congress, Office of Technology Assessment.

Morgan, A. (1984). A report on qualitative methodologies in research in distance education. *Distance Education, 5,* 252–265.

Murray, J. & Heil, M. (1987). *Project Evaluation: 1986–87 Pennsylvania Teleteaching Project.* Mansfield, PA: Mansfield University, Rural Services Institute.

Niemi, J. (1987). Contexts of using technologies for learning outside the classroom. In J. Niemi and D. Gooler (Eds.), *New directions for continuing education. Technologies for learning outside the classroom.* San Francisco: Jossey-Bass.

Nipper, S. (1989). Third generation distance learning and computer conferencing. In R. Mason & A. Kaye (Eds.), *Mindweave: Communication, computers, and distance education* (pp. 63–73). Oxford: Pergamon.

Ohler, J. (1989). TechTrends interview. *TechTrends, 34*(5), 62–67.

Olcott, D. (1992). Instruction television: A review of selected research. *Using comprehensive evaluation for distance education.* Panel presentation, National University Continuing Education Annual Meeting, San Diego, CA.

Phelps, R., Wells, R., Ashworth, R. & Hahn, H. (1991). Effectiveness and costs of distance education using computer-mediated communication. *American Journal of Distance Education, 5*(3), 7–17.

Pierre, S. & Olsen, L. (1992). Student Perspectives on the effectiveness of correspondence instruction. *The American Journal of Distance Education, 5*(3), 65–71.

Price, M. (1990). Perspectives and procedures for cost analysis of distance education methods in higher education. Unpublished manuscript. Stillwater, OK: Oklahoma State University.

Reid, J. & MacLennan, D. (1967). *Research in instructional television and film: Summaries of studies.* Washington, DC: Office of Education, U. S. Department of Health, Education, and Welfare.

Rule, S., Dewulf, M. & Stowitschek, J. (1988). An economic analysis of inservice teacher training. *The American Journal of Distance Education, 2*(2), 12–22.

Rumble, G. (1988). Economics in distance education: Time for a change of direction? In D. Steward & J. Daniel (Eds.), *Developing distance education: Papers submitted to the World Conference of the International Council for Distance Education* (pp. 63–70). Oslo, Norway.

Russell, T. (1992a). Television's indelible impact on distance education: What we should have learned from comparative research. *Research in Distance Education, 3*(4), 2–4.

Russell, T. (1992b). The "no significant difference" phenomenon as reported in research reports, summaries, and papers. Unpublished manuscript, North Carolina State University, Raleigh, NC.

SERC demonstration year evaluation studies. (1990). Bethesda, MD: Levine Communications, Inc.

SERC pilot semester evaluation project. (1989). Volume I, executive summary. Bethesda, MD: Levine Communications.

Shapiro, J. & Hughes, S. (1992). Networked information resources in distance graduate education for adults. *T.H.E. Journal, 19*(11), 66–69.

Soloman, G. & Gardner, H. (1986). The computer as educator: Lessons from television research. *Educational Researcher, 15*(1), 13–19.

Speth, C. (1991). *Important themes and concepts in technology based distance education: A review of the research literature.* Monograph Reviewing Research Literature. Manhattan, KS: University of Kansas.

Speth, C., Poggio, J. & Glasnapp, D. (1991). *Midlands final evaluation report.* Final draft, Manhattan, KS: University of Kansas.

Stone, H. (1990). Does interactivity matter in video-based off-campus graduate engineering education? Unpublished manuscript.

Strain, J. (1987). The role of the faculty member in distance education. *The American Journal of Distance Education, 1*(2), 61–65.

Swain, P. (1990). Interaction: An "engineering" perspective. Unpublished paper.

Threlkeld, R. (1992a). Recent Research and Evaluation Studies for High School Distance Learning. Panel presentation, National University Continuing Education Annual Meeting, San Diego, CA.

Threlkeld, R. (1992b). Rural Voices: Conversations about distance learning with four rural California schools. Submitted for Publication.

U. S. Congress, Office of Technology Assessment. (1989). *Linking for learning: A new course for education*, OTA-SET-430. Washington, DC: U. S. Government Printing Office.

Waggoner, M. D. (Ed.) (1992). *Empowering networks: Computer conferencing in education.* Englewood Cliffs, NJ: Educational Technology Publications.

Whittington, N. (1987). Is instructional television educationally effective? A research review. *American Journal of Distance Education, 1*(1), 47–57.

Wilkes, C. & Burnham, B. (1991). Adult learner motivations and electronic distance education. *The American Journal of Distance Education, 5*(1), 43–50.

Willis, B. (1989). Teaching at a distance: Planning for success. *International Journal of Instructional Media, 16*(2), 137–141.

Willis, B. (1992). *Effective distance education, A primer for faculty and administrators.* (Monograph Series in Distance Education, No. 2). Fairbanks, AK: University of Alaska Center for Cross-Cultural Studies.

Witherspoon, J. (1992). Teaching with computer communication, video, and print. Unpublished manuscript, San Diego State University.

Wright, S. (1992). Research on selected aspects of learner support in distance education programming: A review. *DEOSNEWS, 2*(4).

Chapter Three

Strategic Planning and Academic Planning for Distance Education

Robert Albrecht and Gary Bardsley

Introduction

Strategic planning for distance learning represents a significant challenge to an educational institution, as it requires the expansion of thinking and operational planning beyond that of the core business of resident teaching, yet also requires the integration of new activities with those of the operational units and functions. Even as it may require educators to address contentious institutional issues, it can promote the expansion of educational alternatives by providing a greater variety and quality to prospective students. Educators are no longer limited to the physical classroom, and students are no longer restricted to courses offered on a campus. While such programs can produce revenue, extend the institution's presence to the corners of a state, and satisfy consumer demands for more delivery sites, they can also raise costs beyond benefits, create new patterns of competition, divide a faculty, and violate state regulations. In order to minimize the social, political, and financial costs, a comprehensive and coordinated planning process must be developed. Strategic planning offers five primary benefits: (1) the communication of a strategic vision, (2) the increase in external support that normally follows a clear articulation of vision, (3) the increased certainty it brings to the lives of organizational members, (4) a context for resource allocation and reallocation on campus, and (5) improvement of the institution's image (see Keller, 1983).

This chapter will explore the basic tenets of strategic planning for distance education as they apply to both Kindergarten–12th grade (K–12) and higher education environments. Fundamental principles of strategic planning and case study examples are provided to illustrate the application of these principles to conditions typically encountered in distance education situations. This process of planning must be regarded as a primary activity.

The process must be carefully thought out and shared through both written and verbal communications. This is essential so that the leadership and all other participants have involvement with and confidence in the process. Without full participation, the process will be incomplete and likely to fail, no matter how well it is diagrammed from beginning to end.

Even though distance education may appear to represent an economic solution to the problems of resource availability and access to educational opportunities, attention must be paid to underlying academic needs and processes. In some cases, such as in the laboratory or interactive skills development aspects of a curriculum, all learning goals may not be adequately or easily met through distance learning methods. Some disciplines are easily adapted to distance education applications, while others will require more care and thoughtful application in order to fully meet educational and academic requirements. Only through the enthusiastic participation of planners, providers, and students can satisfactory and successful solutions be found.

Throughout this chapter the authors have used models of video delivery. The two forms of distance learning methods most often implemented are those of curriculum sharing and broadcast instruction. In the case of curriculum sharing, teachers in geographically distributed schools share the instructional responsibilities through the use of bi-directional telecommunications facilities arranged to provide a video network. These networks are increasingly popular in rural areas, as they substantially reduce the costs of development and instruction, as well as providing for an exchange mechanism for each school to contribute to the educational community formed by this network. Minnesota has demonstrated a very strong commitment to curriculum sharing in that one-third of the state's school districts have some form of interactive distance learning capability (see Parker, 1991).

The second form, more common at the university level, is that of broadcast instruction. The most widespread examples are those of the National Technological University (NTU) and Mind Extension University (MEU) in that satellite and terrestrial networks are used to broadcast one-way video signals to students in remote locations. The educational services of PBS and the Learning Channel portion of the Discovery Channel also represent good examples of broadcast instruction. In instructional broadcast situations, additional coordinative and supportive considerations must be taken into account. Specifically, how will student-teacher interactions be facilitated; tests, homework, and other learning tools distributed; and management of the financial, administration, and other key student interfaces be handled?

The Strategic Planning Process for Distance Education

The process of strategic planning for distance education should not be perceived as essentially different from other forms of academic planning. To seize opportunity while avoiding pitfalls, strategic planning permits an institution to gather data, analyze information, and rationally move toward the implementation of a plan that has a high probability of achieving expectations. Any strategic plan seeks to avoid common mistakes: in distance education those include the premature selection of a technology, the emphasis on technical planning, and the neglect of market factors and program resources. The traditional framework of a strategic academic plan still applies; however, the planning elements differ somewhat, and the range and impact of elements to be considered often exceed that of other strategic academic planning processes. As shown in Figure 1, the planning process is not linear. Each module has an impact on the others, and this influence is continual throughout the planning process. The assessment of these interrelated impacts must be continual throughout the planning and implementation processes.

For example, if an initial mission statement is to "provide targeted educational outreach to an industrial base within a region," the availability of facilities, the current academic curriculum available, and the cost/benefit implications of this outreach would impact the final definition of the mission and determine the scope of actions to be taken. It may well be that the mission would be refined from providing full degree programs to a continuing education curriculum of certain engineering or specialized business courses of most interest to this industrial base. The coverage area might consist of sites only within reach of an existing or proposed Instructional Television Fixed Service (ITFS) educational channel or even a fiber optic network. Conversely, there may be such a large and distributed curriculum demand that nationwide satellite distribution facilities are warranted. In a K–12 environment, it might be necessary to include district or state perspectives in the analysis to ensure both conformance with broader areas of policy and an appropriate academic and geographic range of the outreach program.

Outreach program planning must involve both the providers and receivers of the intended distance education program as well as include an analysis of competitors or other positive or impacted alliances. Without this complete analysis and the involvement and cooperation of administrators, students, and instructors at each site, success is unlikely.

The Mission Statement

A clearly defined and articulate mission statement is essential to the development of a successful distance learning strategic plan. It is also an often overlooked or inadequately prepared part of the academic distance learning project. Everyone assumes that her vision of the program is the same as that of all other participants. In reality, the view by individual participants and even whole departments will vary widely without the unifying effect of a clearly stated and shared mission statement. This mission statement is not just the generation of a carefully worded statement of purpose; it must also have accompanying supportive goals and objectives (see Marrus, 1989). These goals and objectives clearly define the scope of the impact of the distance learning process and provide unambiguous measures that can be compared with current levels of achievement. It is important that these goals and objectives be available for use in the entire planning process. Their development will facilitate the planning team's understanding of interrelationships and the needs of other units.

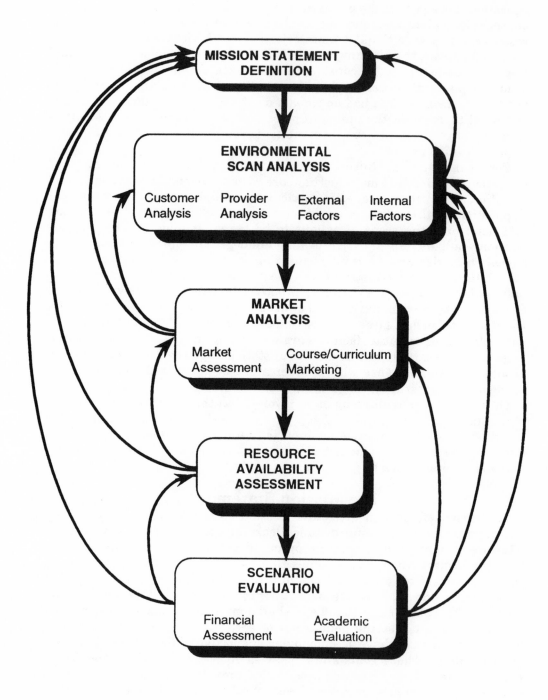

Figure 1. *The strategic planning process.*

For example, the views taken by personnel from the budget office, academic affairs, student counseling, public relations, and the teaching faculty itself probably differ from those of the administration. Comprehensive understanding and participation in the definition process is essential to achieving consistent efforts toward the desired end result. The mission statement itself should be drafted by a team of knowledgeable representatives for key units and edited as necessary by work performed during the remaining steps of the planning process.

For K–12, for example, this would typically include the use of a focus group composed of district personnel from curriculum planning, instructional design, and budgeting, together with experienced administrators and teachers. If the plan in question involves activities outside a single district, then involvement by appropriate representatives from the other areas must be present. This initial group would concentrate on the development of a concise definition of the mission statement and the identification of key "stakeholders" that would be crucial to the development of the final plan and implementation. This process may typically require, at the appropriate points, the involvement of "external" but vital components such as the school board, representatives of the state government, and the state office of education. One must not forget the role of the customer, the student or parents as their representatives, but their involvement should typically be delayed until at least a prototype mission statement is available. A careful assessment of their goals within the mission statement will demonstrate that their concerns have been considered. As an example, a parental goal of a K–12 plan could be quantified through anticipated impacts on college preparatory test scores or college admissions.

In a university environment, a similar mission definition process is appropriate, although there are different cohort members to be included. These include the offices of admissions and registration, student counseling, continuing education, personnel from the schools or colleges involved with the actual educational delivery, and of course representatives from potential student populations. Often, employers must be included, even when they are not primary sources of financial support. The planning process can thus be used as an opportunity to bring together personnel from the university with representatives of customer or client groups.

These initial planning stages for either higher education or K–12 must be handled in a careful and sensitive manner. The process must balance the necessity for a concise, clear mission statement with the potentially negative impacts of a strictly top-down process or the exclusion of key factions or individuals. For that reason, the mission must first be stated with the understanding that it be modified during the process with the participation of all involved in academic planning. As mentioned earlier, this process will also identify the key groups to be involved in the remainder of the planning. By producing both of these products, criticism can properly be channeled through participation in the remainder of the planning process.

As in all other parts of the planning process, definition of the mission must be seen as cyclical and repetitive. Once the initial mission statement and participants are identified, the structure and tasks for the remainder of the planning process can be assigned. The first and most comprehensive of these steps is that of the environmental scan.

The Environmental Scan

The task of accomplishing this vital component of the planning process should be given to a team of representatives who are able to contact others inside and outside the organization to determine the appropriate characteristics of the current and proposed environments (see Shirley, Peters, & El-Ansary, 1981). The environment changes constantly and provides a wide variety of constraints and opportunities. The major topics of consideration for the environmental scan are: a customer analysis, a provider analysis, an evaluation of external factors, and an assessment of internal factors. These topics actually provide a number of dimensions which must be considered in the planning process.

Figure 2 is a model that can be useful in the environmental scan process as a means to assess the various scenarios which will be developed to meet the overall goal.

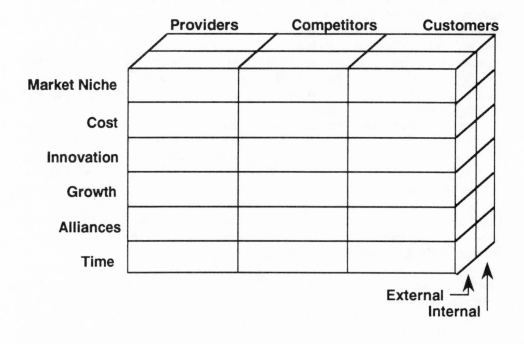

Figure 2. *An adaptation of the Porter/Wiseman/Frenzel model (see Frenzel, 1992).*

This model highlights the integration of strategic influences into the planning process, encouraging the consideration of key factors from a number of perspectives. It is helpful to describe the implications on each three-dimensional cell for a typical case. For example, one plan may produce a scenario with a large, new potential market niche, few competitors, many new customers and providers, but with some negative impact on current internal customers and traditional providers. This plan could require substantial up-front costs; promote the development of innovative teaching methods; cause growth in various areas of the academic organization; and foster the need for new internal and external alliances over a very short time frame. While this model cannot generate solutions, it is helpful for ensuring that impacted elements are considered.

Educational system planners at all levels must consider each of these influences shown in the model as they explore potential ways to accomplish the mission. Technology is providing new methods of delivery to traditional audiences and also allows new competitive opportunities for reaching a changing educational market. New paradigms of format, scope, and standards are being defined on an almost continual basis. An educational institution, at the K–12 level or at the college or university level, that does not recognize the changing dynamics for provider and receiver relations in distance learning will miss the opportunities associated with the new technology and may be ineffective as measured against new competitors. A popular form of analysis of the many aspects associated with a final product is *value chain* analysis (see Porter, 1985).

A key group that must be considered in K–12 is one which has a dual role, the parents. Parents represent both a surrogate for the educational customer, the student, and a provider of revenues and managerial input. This managerial role may take place directly through discussions with the school board, administrators, principals, and teachers, or indirectly via letters to the editor, In any case, it is both their right and responsibility to provide input to the process. As administrators well know, this input is both vital and potentially volatile in the sense that there will undoubtedly be both pro and con positions represented. It is usually best to solicit their involvement early enough to be able to recognize their input and needs, but not so early as to provide a less than well thought out proposal.

Following is a brief summary of typical discussions for four major areas of an environmental scan.

Customer Analysis. The analysis of the market for distance education must include needs, resources, size, and demographics. (See Chapter 4 for a more comprehensive discussion on needs analysis.) Here we merely emphasize the need for a very practical and precise analysis of the market. Many of us have gone through the experience of identifying a large market for a particular program only to discover that this market existed only as a potential market. Potential customers may lack the financial resources, means of access, or some other key element that would allow them to take advantage of the proposed program. Successful efforts in distance education are based on tapping a real market that is not only interested but behaviorally able to take advantage of the programs. This distinction is one that must be made and should be included with the task assignment to the interdisciplinary team charged with this effort.

Provider Analysis. The ability to deliver programs can be under-estimated by planners. For example, having a faculty academically qualified to teach a particular program by no means ensures that this faculty is willing and able to deliver this program in a different way or time. The faculty must be actually contracted before one can assume that delivery is possible. The resources must be identified; the salary or other compensation levels must be agreed upon. The means of meeting the faculty needs of the target population must be clearly identified before a final plan can be formed. The task of identifying such faculty considerations often rests on the selection of the participants in the planning process. The identification of participants in the process must be clear. How does one go about ascertaining the availability of faculty to teach at a particular time and within a particular program?

The nature of the institution may dictate whether the appropriate participants should be the faculty themselves, the principal of a particular school, the department chairs, deans of schools, or the office of academic affairs. The group that is ultimately identified for this project in one institution may not be appropriate for another situation. For example, if one were working on a project in continuing legal education, the office of academic affairs is not a sufficient contact; one would go early to the dean of the law school. Similarly, if an institution were setting up a program in continuing education for nurses, it would be appropriate to begin with the dean or faculty representative for the medical discipline to be delivered. Given the typical independence of university faculty members, it will also be necessary to seek out individual faculty members willing and able to "champion" the effort. In K–12, the organizational structure typically dictates that more than just random teacher or district contacts be made. More likely, it will be necessary to look at individual schools and their faculties as well as providing a more comprehensive, district-wide analysis of impacts and resources.

The provider analysis at any level must extend to the technology and the development of instructor expertise suitable to the technology. Essentially, it must be recognized that the classroom cannot be transformed by technology alone. The involvement of trainers and others, such as instructional design professionals, must occur to enable the instructors to accomplish their roles. The provider analysis should reveal what technology and expertise are available and what must be acquired.

External Factors. In any environmental scan, factors such as regulation and competition come early to attention. These factors change and should always be reviewed, particularly with a view towards recent changes in competitor presence or in interpretation of laws or regulatory practices. For example, Mind Extension University (MEU) has altered the pattern of distance education in several states. (Note: MEU, created and offered by Jones Intercable, offers coursework and degree programs; faculty from a number of institutions deliver the courses over Jones Intercable companies; credit is awarded by their institutions and aggregated by Colorado State University and others as degrees are earned.) In at least one state, MEU has not been subject to many of the rules and regulations that have been imposed on public institutions within that state. An enterprise such as MEU can change the regulations in a state; and certainly the presence of a new, highly visible enterprise will impact the way others operate in distance education. At the present time some states leave telecommunicated instruction unregulated, while others are imposing extended regulations that require specific licensing.

In a similar fashion, the commencement of satellite delivery has raised policy issues in state after state concerning the regulation of distance education, since the regulations are typically founded on practices associated with correspondence study or the off-campus delivery of courses by traveling faculty. Regulations that function satisfactorily for one delivery system can be outdated by a new technology. The planning group that considers such factors as part of the environmental scan can avoid significant problems or move politically to change the legal environment. Schools may no longer have to hire their own language teachers on site, but they must still address issues associated with the accreditation of instruction.

Internal Factors. Planners and decision-makers must be very conscious of the culture of their own institution. Distance education opportunities do vary: College North may be able to offer an off-campus MBA, while College South may have a better market opportunity but lack the "cultural permission" to accomplish it. Similarly, the college of education within a university may be free to move into distance education, while the college of arts and sciences faculty within the same university will reject the opportunity regardless of the advantages. Distance education presents differences in delivery methods, faculty development, funding, competition, and students. Academic administrators, as well as faculty, differ in their willingness to encounter these factors.

The example of a university that is considering course delivery to corporate sites dictates a close examination of a number of internal factors. Does the institution have the experience of delivering courses off campus to a particular site? Considerations of an internal attitude towards such a move can be particularly complex if the institution has no such history. Documented institutional policies cannot accurately reveal the current climate or situation. Furthermore, the choice of participants in the planning process to identify these factors can be crucial and often represents a very difficult task. Should the institution hire new people or train existing staff? Should it hire outside consultants or rely on internal planners?

It often may be the case that the very fact of distance education delivery will upset traditional service areas and the agreed upon balance of curriculum coverage specialties between multiple campuses, state supported institutions, or K–12 districts. The other campus sites, institutions, or districts may well strongly object to this new competition within their geographical or academic territories. Such objections could have unforeseen financial or geopolitical consequences if their realities are not included within the planning process.

The implications of the model and the broad areas of the environmental scan can perhaps be best illustrated through a specific case.

Case Study

The College of Engineering in a public university has decided to investigate distance learning in order to better serve the population of the state. The College must work within the restrictive role and mission of the whole institution, which is limited in its permitted outreach. It is allowed to utilize distance education technology but cannot interfere with the residential offerings of other institutions and cannot receive state funds to support its outreach activities.

A customer analysis has discovered several possible customer bases, one of which is the work force in the state's high technology industry. This industry is concentrated in and around a major metropolitan area that is within the area served by the university's campuses and covered by its individual ITFS (Instructional Television Fixed Service) licenses.

As a part of the environmental scan it was discovered that the existing individual ITFS systems were not interconnected and thus coverage of the entire region would require the duplication of courses on at least two campus sites. The costs and academic implications of such duplication were examined and it was determined that interconnecting all the campus sites with fiber optic cable links would be the best solution and would also offer additional benefits to the institution.

The fiber and ITFS microwave networks are shown in Figure 3. The scope of the customer analysis can be simplified in that only markets within reach of this network are candidates for the initial outreach program. The needs of this potential audience are assessed through a provider analysis and matched with the capabilities of the university most appropriate to meeting those needs. Should initial matches appear to be positive, a more detailed analysis and plan would be developed (as discussed within the "marketing" section of this chapter). In this example, specific matches were found between the graduate programs of the engineering and business schools of the university and workers and management employees of the high technology industry. The particular implications for these two schools then become the focus for additional planning efforts.

Next, external factors must be analyzed. These should include an assessment of the offerings of other colleges, universities, and specialized training programs. Some of the offerings may come from institutions such as National Technological University which provide programs over many states. The analysis must ask whether such providers currently serve the potential customer base and whether the intended program is more cost effective, more timely, or otherwise more attractive. Will it attract a sufficient number of students to warrant pursuit of the market?

The next layer of analysis addresses questions such as, "will the state system governing board(s) permit an overlap of programs into non-traditional territories on a selective or more general basis?" It will also be necessary to ascertain whether adequate library resources are available and appropriately accessible to students. The scope of this survey must include on-campus as well as remote students if it is to correctly forecast the additional demands on existing library resources. This would take into account the impact of additional students as well as a longer period for the circulation of materials

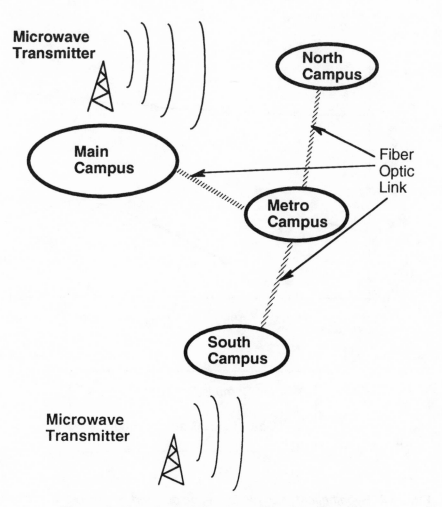

Figure 3. *Hypothetical distance education network.*

due to reciprocal lending agreements and the associated time for processing. All of these and many more areas must be considered and addressed.

Finally, the internal factors mentioned earlier must be considered. The graduate enrollments of a college may be significantly altered; a 20–25% jump cannot always be easily accommodated. (See Figure 4 for an example of the size of off-campus enrollments.) In this instance, the graduate entrance requirements for the engineering disciplines must be accommodated and degree requirements for the curriculum carefully examined. In many states, a Master of Science degree in engineering or other subjects may require a certain number of hours or semesters of on-campus residency in order to meet graduation requirements. This may not be the case, however, for a Master of Engineering or other alternatives. Specific curriculums to be made available would also be considered. Is there a requirement for laboratory sessions which cannot be adequately met through distance education modes of

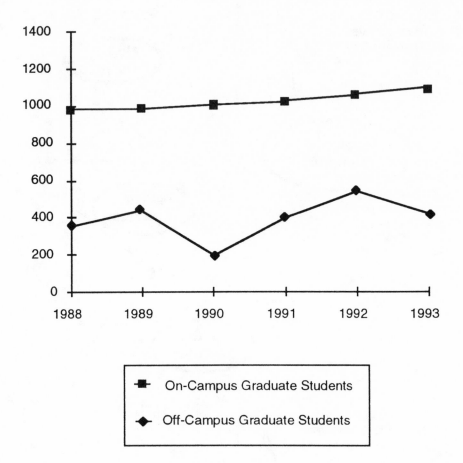

Figure 4. *Hypothetical example of on-campus and off-campus enrollments.*

instruction? Are faculty members from all necessary areas of specialization able and willing to adapt to distance education methods of teaching? Will this require additional time and expense to modify instructional materials and support systems, such as pre-printed illustrations, that have traditionally been done on the blackboard? Will special mail, FAX, or courier services be required to provide timely collection and distribution of student and instructional materials, such as hand-outs, homework, and tests?

None of these concerns or potential problems should represent a fatal flaw or halt to the planning process. In fact, an in-depth assessment of ways to meet these concerns by a motivated and interested faculty can provide a healthy improvement to the educational process for on-campus students as well.

There may be serious problems found as a part of the analysis that will force the abandonment or modification of the plan. The market may be small, the costs may be high, or the faculty resources may be inadequate. Finally, operational and administrative difficulties, such as high costs of attracting students or the alienation of existing alliances, could force the abandonment of the plan.

Market Analysis

Many of the factors associated with a market analysis have been discussed in general terms in the customer analysis section of the environmental scan. However, a comprehensive demographic approach should be included in the planning process so that details of the potential customer base are well understood and accommodated within the design of the intended program. As a minimum, student demographics should be collected and segmented by age, geographic distributions, degrees sought, occupations, financial support/ status, and educational demand trends. For K–12 populations, careful consideration of topic coverage in previous grades and curriculums is necessary to avoid redundancy or inadvertent gaps in knowledge; alternative sources may also need to be considered. Localized needs and requirements should be carefully addressed so as to minimize the potential for overlooking important considerations that could result in a disenfranchisement of the distance learning student. This can be through various social factors, or even by neglecting to recognize local holidays which are assumed at one location but slighted at another.

Specific items which can well have an impact on the distance education process can be the same as those that affect on-campus or K–12 local school environments. It is likely, however, that distance education students may have very different characteristics which must be addressed. In the K–12 environment, distant communities may have different racial, ethnic, or cultural backgrounds which might impact the educational processes. For example, if a specific course is offered from an urban school to a rural environment, the assumed values for the urban developed product need to be screened to ensure compatibility with the needs of the rural student. In a post-secondary environment, the distance education student may be older or offer significant practical experience. In both instances, the mix of backgrounds and perspectives can enrich the educational experiences for both distant and on-site students if handled appropriately.

The eventual product must be marketed to both potential students and faculty members. While these two constituent groups are quite different, both must be approached with an intent to meet their needs. The approaches will be as dissimilar as the groups and must be tailored to their expectations if the program is to succeed. The competition for both must be evaluated. The questions for the student market may be obvious, while the questions for the provider less so. Are there adequate numbers of trained faculty willing to participate at a given salary? In either case, their motivating factors and potential sources of dissatisfaction must be understood if a satisfactory attempt is to be accomplished.

The means of marketing the product or program to dissimilar groups will also need to be quite different in order to be successful. For example, for the situation in the case study, it may well be that the best marketing approach would include close coordination with employers in the high technology industry. This would include an understanding of their tuition and educational support policies, the use of their in-house distribution and newsletter media, and cooperation with the human resources departments. For the K–12 audience, the teachers, administrators, and parents of students in the recipient area must be included in the planning and information dissemination process. Their knowledge and participation is essential to the development of a successful approach.

Resource Availability Assessment

The technologies now available present a daunting opportunity to those responsible for distance education. Until recently, most institutions were limited to two processes of distance education; offering correspondence courses or sending faculty members to off-campus sites. The introduction of video through satellite, ITFS, tapes, and cable have greatly expanded the list of alternatives. This development of alternatives has also raised the cost and complexities of distance education. Understandably, some planners have been reluctant to adopt new technologies, while others have tended to look to the technologies to solve old problems. The distance education planner must maintain perspective and not expect the technology to solve problems. To the contrary, the new technologies often contribute complexity and cost, which can be offset by wider distribution and sources of revenue.

The following case exemplifies such problems: the School of Nursing at Zeta University has been pressured by many constituents and encouraged by state legislators to develop a comprehensive, state-wide offering of continuing education. Although several institutions offer nursing programs, all are campus based and much of the geographic area of the state is not served by any program. Citizens of the rural areas of the state must move to attend nursing programs. While the specific needs have changed from time to time, the basic need for providing continuing and core education to the nurses at various sites has existed for a long time. In the past, typical alternatives were correspondence courses, audio tapes, and circuit-riding faculty. With the introduction of various forms of video, the university has decided to look again at the possibility of delivering the nursing program to schools and hospitals throughout the state. As planners consider the alternatives of cable, compressed video over phone lines, satellite, and video tape, as well as the many variations and combinations within these systems, they quickly come to issues of cost. The costs include not only those of delivering the instruction but also of registering and counseling students, training the faculty, etc. The planners in their early meetings came to realize that the technological alternatives present a new set of problems at least as much as they present solutions. The technology offers new delivery systems, but it does not provide new, trained faculty. It does not necessarily represent significantly lower incremental costs for the additional students; it does not in itself permit the simple establishment of sites and locations for students to gather, and so forth. Rather, it will take innovative planning and design to provide an adequate product at an acceptable cost.

Fiscal resources must be carefully considered within all aspects of the planning process. This will include an analysis of capital and expense requirements, marketing expenses, and the potential for additional sources of revenues. It may also be that there can be implications for traditional funding formulas in the form of cross-elastic student registrations. Planners must measure revenue and cost streams to determine the net over-all effect. Table 1 summarizes costs for the delivery of typical video courses in the United States in 1993.

Conversion of Tele-education Classroom (includes 2 cameras, video monitors, microphones, video recorders, control equipment, audio bridge, etc. Does not include cost of the classroom, desks, chairs and heating/cooling support)	**$75,000**
Amortized maintenance (covers cost of maintenance, and prorated repairs)	**$18/hour**
Personnel Costs (single operator plus prorated manager, Does not include Faculty costs)	**$23/hour**
ITFS Broadcast Expenses (includes studio and facilities costs)	**$25/hour**

Table 1. *Typical costs for distance education infrastructure & operation.*

Distance education is currently enjoying a wide basis of support, both intellectually and financially. Numerous telecommunications vendors and providers are funding or otherwise sponsoring joint ventures with schools at all levels. The federal government has also provided leadership in the form of the Star Schools Program and the Public Telecommunications Program, which provides funds for hardware such as microwave and satellite equipment, and for project planning assistance. The Star Schools Act supports the formation of multistate organizationally diverse partnerships to prepare and deliver curriculum, and to create opportunities for disadvantaged students to receive remote instruction. The Rural Electrification Administration announced a Distance Learning and Medical Link Grant Program (May 26, 1992 *Federal Register*) to promote advanced telecommunications and computer networks in rural areas. In addition, numerous foundations, state and federal agencies are providing funds and other support to assist in the expansion of distance education projects and initiatives.

New sources of funding may have to be explored if schools and colleges are to be successful in extending their boundaries. Two recent examples of innovative educational funding are the establishment of a tax on video cassette rentals to benefit distance education and the allocation of excess profits from telecommunications common carrier operations to fund innovative educational programs. Other states are applying the profits from lotteries and other operations to provide the needed additional sources of revenue for distance education.

The curriculum of the institution amounts to a significant but limited resource. For the most part, institutions are not able to extend through distance education programs which are not present on the campus. The issues of trained faculty and the application of standards represent limitations to the curricular resources of the institution. In some situations at both K–12 and university levels the brokering of programs from third party providers enables the development of distance education programs beyond the traditional patterns that once seemed restricted but firm.

Evaluation

Even the most careful planning process does not result in one right answer. The process typically results in a series of scenarios that can meet the requirements and objectives. The evaluation of the scenarios must go beyond a traditional cost/benefit analysis. How does the anticipated accomplishment of each scenario compare with the expectations of the planners? How are potentially dissimilar requirements satisfied? A system of evaluation that anticipates such situations must be built into the planning process. Outcomes including student learning, revenue streams, and impact on educational resources must be included. The evaluation of these factors should drive the planning group back through the process to achieve those outcomes most valued.

If a continuing education unit or K–12 school system embarks upon the planning process for distance education, it may be that financial indicators will tend to determine if the process has been successful. The authors would suggest that this is an insufficient indicator of the planning process. While financial success may be an indication of the success of the program, it should not be the single metric used to judge the success of the process. The planning process is more appropriately judged by the outcome of the process; namely the accomplishment of important goals and objectives by putting in place new programs and dropping old programs as a result of the plan. The success of the individual program depends on the validity of the needs analysis, the application of resources, appropriate marketing, and the delivery of courses. The planning process is not responsible for those factors.

A negative example illustrates this point: Delta University, an urban university with a School of Education that enrolls many students in a graduate program in counseling, offers an off-campus program in counseling, designed particularly for high school counselors. The courses are offered at a number of sites around the state. These sites are staffed by faculty members who drive to the sites, deliver the courses, and return home. The program is not a large one and rests on the shoulders of four regular faculty and a number of adjuncts. One of the key faculty members has little interest in the program, habitually misses classes, and conducts himself in such a way that students drop from the program and seek alternatives elsewhere. A carefully managed planning process might well have led to the development and implementation of this program. The planning process might have been sound in every way, but the program which eventually was delivered rests upon the shoulders of the faculty, not upon the planners who perhaps rightly identified this as a program which in every respect could carry out the purposes of the institution and meet the needs of a viable constituency.

Such an example points out the need for on-going review and analysis of educational processes in general. By their very nature these processes tend to be dependent on the efforts and dedication of the teacher, not on the best intentions of the many planners and administrators involved in the process. A positive implication of a distance learning environment is that it often requires a more dedicated and capable individual, while also providing a means to quickly expose less than excellent performance. The increasing availability of electronic forms of distance education provides even more opportunities to monitor and assess the effectiveness of the educational process.

It should also be obvious that the evaluation process actually consists of two major components. The first, the evaluation of alternatives, has already been described. The second is often neglected. This important action is the evaluation of the actual processes and results achieved once the planning alternative is put into place. Not even the finest collection of planners, operating under perfect conditions can correctly determine all the facets of an operation as complex as a new educational process. The realities will be different than the expectations, and appropriate fine-tuning of personnel, facilities, and procedures must be made early. Otherwise, a commendable effort may easily go astray due to relatively minor details cascading into major problems.

The Final Step: Making the Right Decision

Although the planning diagram shown in Figure 1 with its many feedback loops has now been completed, the process is actually not finished with the evaluation of the scenarios or alternatives that were developed. In fact, the whole process can be seen as a wasted effort if decisions are not made, using the facts and expert analyses that have been gathered and incorporated into the plan.

How is the right decision made? It is likely that any decision that is made will be subject to second guessing and even attacks by those who support a different decision than the path selected. How do you minimize the risk of making a choice which later turns out to be incorrect given the actual situation encountered? Although it can never be "proven" that the plan selected was the "best" course of action, it can almost certainly be demonstrated that the "status quo" alternative does not meet the mission statement, its goals or objectives. If it did, then this would have been the winning alternative. It is not a failure to find that the current form of education is still most suited to accomplishment of the educational mission.

If, however, a departure from the norm appears to be appropriate, the minimum course of action to be considered is that of a limited trial of the plan. Such an approach could include controls on the number of students, geographic or curricular scope, or phased implementation. This technique allows for the previously discussed operational evaluation to take place and to instill confidence that the process truly works.

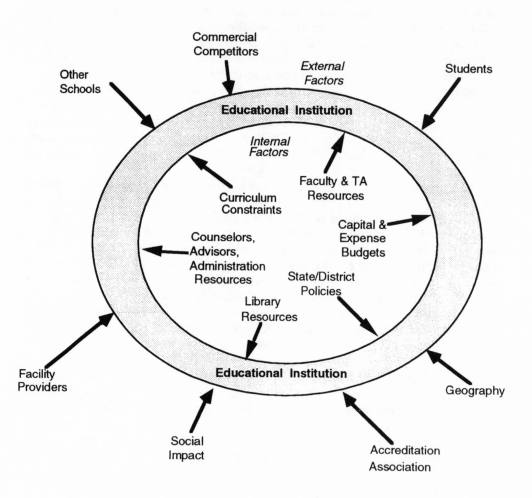

Figure 5. *Explosion/implosion model.*

Summary

The strategic planning process presented in Figure 1 defines the steps in strategic academic planning from the mission statement to evaluation, taking into account the environmental scan, both internally and externally, as well as the analysis of the market and the resources. These steps direct the attention of the planning team to the common factors that determine the success or failure of many efforts. Throughout the chapter the process of planning is emphasized as the key to success: merely following the steps without adequate participation from relevant constituencies will not guarantee that expectations are met. The faculty, to a greater or lesser extent in the various segments of education, control the content of the curriculum; to impose new curricular elements on them rather than incorporating them in the planning endangers any academic planning process.

This chapter is anchored in case studies from different disciplines to illustrate realistic situations. The tools offered in the chapter are helpful in those situations. But the lack of internal direction, a "soft" market, the "wrong" technology, or the lack of human resources often present simply the opportunity to choose an alternative. A program that may not have the resources for satellite technology may be able to use video tape. However, if an institution's primary purpose is to establish a satellite delivery program, the planning process should be so structured.

Figure 5 illustrates typical factors that might be encountered, internally and externally. A structured planning process such as the one described in this chapter enables a planning group to resolve these diverse elements into an outcome that accomplishes their original mission.

References

Annenberg/CPB Project (1992). *Going the distance: A handbook for developing distance degree programs using television courses and telecommunication technologies.* Washington, DC: Annenberg/CPB Project.

Frenzel, C. (1992). *Management of information technology.* Boston, MA: Boyd and Fraser Publishing.

Keller, G. (1983). *Academic strategy.* Baltimore, MD: The Johns Hopkins Press.

Marrus, S. K. (1989). *Building the strategic plan: Find, analyze, and present the right information.* New York: John Wiley & Sons.

National Telecommunications and Information Administration (1991). *The NTIA infrastructure report: telecommunications in the age of information.* U.S. Department of Commerce: NTIA Special Publication 91–26.

Norris, D. M. & Poulton, N. L. (1991). *A guide for new planners.* Ann Arbor, MI: The Society for College and University Planning.

Parker, E. B. & Hudson, H. E. (1991). *Electronic byways: State policies for rural development through telecommunications.* Boulder, CO: Westview Publishing.

Porter, M. E. (1985). *Competitive advantage.* New York: The Free Press.

Rossman, P. (1992). *The emerging worldwide electronic university: Information age global higher education.* Westport, CN: Greenwood Press.

Shirley, R. C., Peters, M. H. & El-Ansary, A. I. (1981). *Strategy and policy formation: A multifunctional orientation.* New York: John Wiley & Sons.

U. S. Congress, Office of Technology Assessment (1991). *Rural America at the crossroads: Networking for the future.* Washington, DC: Government Printing Office, OTA-TCT-471.

Warner, L. & Wilkinson, J. (1992, July). Evaluation of on-campus activities in disciplines necessitating compulsory attendance. *Research in Distance Education, 4*(3).

Chapter Four

Assessing Needs, Developing Instruction, and Evaluating Results in Distance Education

Nick Eastmond

How feasible is the new distance education technology you saw at the latest national convention, for your particular locale? Who are the learners to be served, and what are their learning needs? How can relevant instruction be delivered to a diverse audience at myriad sites? And how can we be sure that instruction was effective, i.e., that messages sent were received, that relevant learning took place, and that the learner's needs have been met?

These are the central questions for distance education to answer, and this chapter takes them on. In doing so, current practice and the suboptimal "conventional wisdom" (Galbraith, 1958) will be contrasted with the optimal solutions, the very best in practice, in the opinion of this author. Actual cases of the best practical solutions will be noted. This chapter should raise the sights of people conducting the current generation of distance education, at both the faculty and the administrator level.

Assumptions and Definitions

The assumption made in this chapter is that principles of conventional instruction—as varied as that enterprise is—can be adopted in the distance setting, but only with both caution and ingenuity. The ingenuity might be exercised, for example, by adapting an in-class exercise using a contest-type format for chapter review to an audioconference or videoconference class, by making some changes in the rules to allow students to signal they have a right answer (e.g., pushing the "press to talk" switch on the audio microphone). The necessary caution might be to ensure that all students are given an opportunity to respond and participate, and if the cultural norms of certain students (e.g., Native Americans) made competition a taboo, the competition might have to be adapted from the level of the individual, for example, to teams at each receiving site. The essential element for success in the distance education enterprise will be wisdom in the broadest sense, ideas that transcend conventional wisdom and strike out boldly into new directions. Good ideas make fine programs, since they energize all involved.

This chapter assumes that the reader will have had some prior exposure to distance education, either as participant or as observer. The chapter will use the definitions given previously in the book, defining distance education as "the organizational framework and process of providing instruction at a distance," and distance learning as "the desired outcome of distance education programs, i.e., learning at a distance." Two other important terms are defined below:

Needs assessment: A need has been defined as "a gap between 'what is' and 'what should be' in terms of results" (Kaufman, 1972). A needs assessment is a systematic inquiry into the most important needs to be met.

Evaluation: The process of determining the merit or worth or value of something; or the product of that process. The special features of evaluation, as a special form of investigation (distinguished, e.g., from traditional empirical research in the social sciences) include a characteristic concern with cost, comparisons, needs, ethics, and its own political, ethical, presentational, and cost dimensions; and with the supporting and making of sound value judgments, rather than hypothesis testing (Scriven, 1980, p. 47).

Introduction

Of the settings where systematic instructional design has been implemented most successfully in recent years, distance education has been the most receptive, with the other competitor being corporate training. Both of these are growth areas, where many problems remain to be solved and where the challenges of teaching are daunting at best. Hence, the successful innovator remains "teachable" and searches for the best solution possible.

Distance education is having major impact in a variety of countries on a global scale (see Chapter 1). The success of the British Open University has been noted worldwide, and has been emulated in adaptations from Turkey to China, from Finland to British Columbia. The potential cost savings in reaching the distant learner with a university education, judged at roughly one-sixth of the cost of providing a conventional university education, in the case of the Turkish Open Education Facility (Murphy, 1989), cannot fail to capture the attention of policy-makers worldwide.

Delivering instruction in a distance education environment requires skills in assessing needs, designing instruction, and evaluating the results that go far beyond the demands of more traditional educational modes. The following quotation refers to the science education-based Jason Project, but it is applicable to most distance education settings:

> To date, most distance learning projects have attempted to replicate as closely as possible the existing classroom model of face-to-face instruction. In this traditional view, transmitting the image and voice of the teacher from a remote location into the classroom is seen as a necessary evil, a

second choice. This view assumes that it is always better to interact with students face-to-face, rather than through a limited medium like television. Body language, the dynamism of a great teacher, puzzled faces, boredom—all of these elements of classroom management are perceived as compromised in distance learning.

In (effective distance education) projects ..., however, the traditional classroom setting is reversed: instead of the teacher coming to the students, the students are electronically transported to a new site where teaching can occur. And rather than the media being a compromise, it now makes possible experiences previously out of the reach of students, and, for that matter, out of the reach of most adults as well ... Such experiences, built into a valid pedagogical framework, have the potential to broaden and invigorate the educational experience for children.

   (U. S. Congress, Office of Technology Assessment, 1989, pp. 16–17).

The point of this quotation is not to suggest that non-technology-assisted, face-to-face instruction is not important, but rather that a "more of the same" mentality in designing distance education may doom the enterprise to failure. Instead, by following a systematic development process, more innovative instruction becomes possible.

And how is this systematic development work done? By first assessing needs systematically, a range of solution strategies will become possible that far exceeds the initial vision. By evaluating at strategic intervals, a project's progress can be monitored and its performance improved in substantial ways. The kinds of innovative approaches suggested above become possible and can succeed in the distance education setting if stages of systematic planning of instruction are clearly followed.

This chapter attempts to demonstrate that needs assessment, program development, and evaluation are inseparable and that examining them holistically, as a series of cycles, has its advantages. It further assumes that a working model for evaluation and for needs assessment can draw upon similar techniques for data collection, analysis, and reporting, once the study's ends are established. Figure 1 models how these three cycles interconnect. Note that the place for beginning the needs assessment is remarkably close to the ending point for the evaluation effort. That proximity is by design, to show symbolically that the ending of one cycle of needs assessment, program development, and evaluation will necessarily be followed by another, at least if the program is to continue in viable fashion. For each of the cycles illustrated, this chapter will attempt to show how the concepts can be applied in practical ways by the teacher of distance education classes as well as the administrator of a system-wide effort, i.e., the microcosm and the macrocosm.

Needs Assessment

The logic of needs assessment is fairly straightforward: before beginning to solve a problem or making any improvement, it is worth being sure that the right problem is being solved, that the effort is directed toward real needs. Determining what those needs are is what needs assessment is all about.

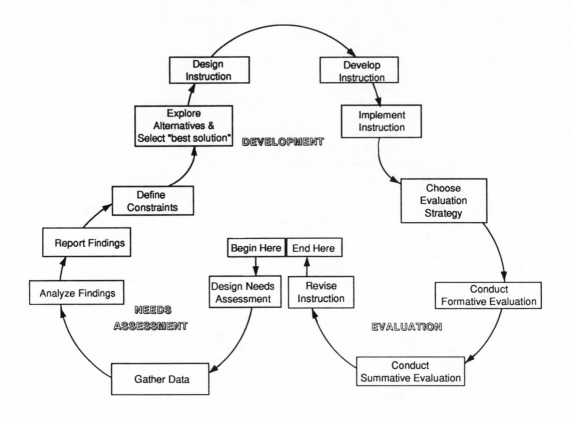

Figure 1. *Formulating instruction step-by-step.*

A useful distinction made by Kaufman (1972) and others involved in the founding of the needs assessment movement has been the distinction between "needs" and "solutions." Needs are viewed as a gap between "what is" and "what should be," defined at the level of the learner. In the case of distance education, the learner level would be the student participant in a distance education class. For example, a need might be determined to be that a majority of 10th grade students in a rural Alaska school are currently reading at a 5th grade reading level, often because of linguistic and cultural differences between Native American culture and the culture of the predominant Anglo schools. Assuming that representatives from their respective communities would want students to be reading in English at their particular grade level, the gap between current reality and community expectations is a need. A vehicle for resolving that need—for example, a culturally appropriate set of reading materials—would rightly be labeled a "solution."

Until the need has been adequately identified, an appropriate solution is unlikely to be found. Once the need has been specified, an amazing number of potential solutions become possible. In our example of the Alaska reading problem, the solution chosen for implementation might be a peer tutoring program or cooperative learning arrangement for students. It is important to note that distance education is itself a kind of solution, involving certain technologies. Some learners (for example, those with auditory impairments), might not succeed with audioconferencing, in spite of a high level of need or considerable motivation, but might do well using correspondence study or computer conferencing. Some learners, lacking certain basic learning skills or incapable of performing with the level of independence required, may simply not be prepared to have their particular needs met via distance education. Appropriate needs assessment helps make such determinations clear.

System-wide Needs Assessment

If you are an administrator of a distance education system, you may feel that a system-wide needs assessment could provide you and others with important information to affect decisions made. You may want to see a profile of present or potential students, to discern current unmet needs, and to assess the potential for expansion of a current or proposed distance education system. Needs assessment addresses these types of questions; and, as was evident in the section above, the answers are seldom definitive, but rather are snapshots of a process in motion.

Decisions, Decisions ... As you enter the design phase of a needs assessment (see Figure 1), you necessarily encounter important decisions to be made. Consider the following:

—Inside or outside? Do you want the study done internally, or by someone from the outside, a consultant or researcher? Each option has its advantages and disadvantages. In either case, steps should be taken for quality assurance, as described below.

—What information is of most worth? Obtaining information entails costs, either in money or in time and energy. Are you facing equipment decisions or ones affecting curriculum offerings or marketing questions? Or all of the above? It will help keep the needs assessment within reasonable limits if the scope of inquiry can be narrowed appropriately (Witkin & Eastmond, 1988).

—Who are the important stakeholders? Frequently, assessing needs forces political questions into the open, where the vital interests of one group may conflict with those of another. An important "hidden agenda" of many committed to needs assessment is faith in the "democratic process," that the needs of many can be met openly and in rational fashion. The best policy is to get these issues out on the table early, in the planning stages.

Responding to these questions early and reviewing them as the needs assessment progresses can avoid a variety of problems from arising.

Institutional Commitment and Quality Assurance. Before embarking upon any formal needs assessment study, some guarantees of institutional commitment are crucial. Without these, political roadblocks may derail the study, or needed resources may run short, causing the study to fail. The project should be "scoped out" from beginning to end, and appropriate administrative approval obtained.

A "quality assurance committee" can provide a valuable anchor in the organization for a needs assessment. This committee will consist of 3–5 people who can meet periodically with the person conducting the study to oversee the work. Use of this committee has two important results: (1) its members serve as a sounding board for the needs assessor in the course of the work, helping identify important questions to be asked and constituencies to be sampled; and (2) when the report is final, these committee members can serve as advocates for its adoption and use, since they were closely involved in the decisions made. Selecting the 3–5 people who oversee the needs assessment effort can usually be done best by the administrator who commissions the work; they should be representative of various interests, but more than that they should be professionally responsible and available for consultation.

Data collection. Given the commitment to assess needs and a certain degree of focus provided in the design stage, there are many options for data collection (see Eastmond, 1980–81). Needs assessments commonly draw upon opinion data through interviews, questionnaires, or various group procedures. Institutional data available through census files, accreditation reports, and the like should be used to supplement and help explain findings. The whole field of needs assessment is characterized by a unity of ends and a diversity of means. Some examples of data-collection methods employed by practitioners follows:

—Sponder (1989) used participant observation of several distance education classes to unobtrusively gather data at Kuskokwim College in rural Alaska.

—Williams, Van Monfrans, Eastmond, and Hart (1987) used a series of vignettes of various receive sites to help understand the needs of rural learners.

—Hébert (1986) used an anthropological approach to determine needs, through living with and interacting with students in a rural village.

Other group-centered approaches to data collection are promising, such as those described by Witkin (1987) in her resource on needs assessment. These approaches include fault-tree analysis (examining a system for potential sources of failure, then working to insure that these potential problems are solved), focus groups (convening groups for discussion of a particular topic, recording results), "nominal group technique" (where members list concerns individually and then discuss collectively), and "community speak ups" (where a public meeting is announced, opened with a keynote speaker, and then broken into smaller groups for discussion purposes). These techniques have the advantage of involving many people to generate data about concerns and values; and, in addition, to refine the expressions through discussion with others, with each opinion expressed having been informed by the opinions expressed previously.

Data Analysis. The resulting information is seldom structured for easy entry into quantitative computer analysis, although at least part of the information (e.g., through a questionnaire) may be handled in this way. More frequently, multiple sources of data and multiple types of information will require careful study and synthesis by a skilled researcher. One technique used successfully in rural China (Eastmond, Sr., 1991), is a group technique called "Concerns Analysis," in which a representative group of 25–35 people convene to sort out community facts and values, and then to prioritize these for program intervention.

Analyzing needs assessment data requires considerable expertise with quantitative, but especially qualitative data analysis techniques (see Lincoln & Guba, 1985; McKillip, 1986). In addition to prioritizing of identified needs, this stage also include expressions of minority opinion, areas requiring compromise, and descriptions of areas of remaining ambiguity. In some cases, as in the prescriptions for the individual teacher given below, promising solutions will appear. These should be stored for later use, as valuable ideas emerge at this stage.

Concluding the needs assessment. Usually, researchers report findings both orally and in writing, to make them as widely known as possible. A common problem in assessing needs is to overcommit resources to the needs assessment, to the detriment of the actual program (Witkin & Eastmond, 1988). It is simply not possible to answer every question. Important concerns should be addressed, and then planning of instruction should occur. The process should avoid becoming bogged down in detail.

What should happen as a result of the needs assessment process is a certain enlightenment on the part of course designers. Given information generated in the needs assessment, the designer of instruction should be able to move ahead with development, confident that important needs have been addressed and that others, apparently less important, may emerge during formative evaluation; or, in any case, these will be re-examined as the needs assessment effort is encountered in a subsequent program cycle.

Needs Assessment for Teachers of Distance Education

Coming to know the needs of your students in a distance education setting can be a daunting task for the teacher first introduced to a system. Your situation will likely be the assignment to teach a certain course in distance education fashion, and if you are fortunate, you will have the opportunity and time to help design the course materials. In the all too typical scenario, you will be asked to teach a course that you have taught traditionally, and then given little lead time or few instructional resources to make any adaptations. While sounding cost-effective to some administrators, the latter approach is perilous for all concerned, since the way you will learn will be entirely by trial and error, with the emphasis upon error.

Assuming that you do have some lead time (say 4–6 months) and some limited resources (technical assistance for materials development) available for redesign of the course, how can you assess the needs of your students? Particularly if you have never met this set of students, you have a challenge ahead.

Prior to course beginning. For starters, become acquainted with some of the students involved in taking courses such as yours. Your needs assessment, from design to analysis, will likely be done informally for your own use or for members of a design team you will be working with. You would be wise to ask and pursue questions like the following:

—*Who are the students involved? How many of them can be expected to enroll in my class? What are their strengths and weaknesses evident to others who have had contact with them?*

If there is a "receive site" nearby and classes are now going on, you might sit in on one or more classes to observe current students in action. In audioconferencing, since any telephone may serve as a "receive site," you may coordinate with the teacher(s) to be a non-participant observer and simply listen in. Interviewing one or several of these students might reveal a lot about their motivation for taking the course, their previous experience, and their frustrations.

Other faculty, in elementary, secondary, or college teaching situations, particularly those with a reputation for good teaching or those with responsibility to travel to distant sites, can provide insights into the nature of the learners. Such teachers can also suggest solutions to commonly encountered problems—solutions that should be recorded and held in reserve until the design phase described next is completed.

Examine published materials that might help you better understand your students. The central office or university office of institutional research may provide a statistical profile of students in your program that may help you anticipate their needs. What is the ratio of males and females? How many students are taking courses for a specific degree as opposed to taking courses for enrichment? What are their ages, cultural backgrounds, previous experience in the subject matter, or prior exposure to the distance learning environment? Answers to these questions can be most helpful, and frequently can be gleaned from published sources.

—*What is the technical system, and what limitations does it present? How does "the entire system" work, to include the personnel and operating modes: e.g., how are assignments collected, exams given, and individual counseling handled? What opportunities does the system provide?*

While the information gained in answering these questions rightfully belongs in the "specify constraints" step of the design phase, this information is too valuable not to pick up while conducting the needs assessment. You need to know what the main channel for information delivery is. Will audioconferencing be the main vehicle for sustaining a class, or will video be involved (full motion or slow scan)? If the vehicle is essentially "electronic mail," as in a computer conferencing mode, you will have a different set of concerns than if your contact is with the spoken word. For example, you will rightfully be more concerned with students' writing abilities over computer conferencing than over an audio system.

As the course unfolds. You have made your best assessment of needs prior to course beginning, but frequently these needs will become clearer as you begin to learn about your students through their participation in class. Some suggestions follow:

—Design class exercises that require some self-disclosure on the part of students, not because you want to pry into their lives but because they will be more engaged in the class if real sharing takes place. For example, you may decide to begin each class period with a writing exercise applying course topics with your students' everyday lives. As you read their papers, be alert to personal factors underlying the content.

—Stay alert to the student skill levels and deficiencies on written assignments or oral presentations. Depending upon the objectives of the class and your capabilities, you may help students in developing skills or may refer them to other sources of help.

—If possible, teach from or at least visit some other sites. Some distance education systems allow the teacher to originate at any site; in others, there is a central teaching station only. In any case, try to arrange to visit your students in their own setting. Alternatively, try to participate in a face-to-face meeting early in the term to establish a personal relationship with students. If that is impossible, try to arrange the next best thing, probably person-to-person conversation over the telephone during advising time.

Obviously, there is an infinite amount of information possible in your coming to know your students, and you have finite time and energy resources. But you should tune your ear to listen for the real human needs that your instruction must help to meet. *Assessing needs is not something done once and for all and then forgotten about; it extends over the time of your teaching involvement and will have an observable difference in your effectiveness in instructing.* Students will let you know when you are succeeding in this endeavor by confiding their own concerns, often sensitive information, to you. And of course, there will be some students more willing to share such information than others. In any case, staying alert to student needs requires genuine concern over a long-term and is part of the essence of teaching.

Having examined needs assessment at both the formal, institutional level and at the more informal level of the individual teacher, we next use these findings for developing need-based instruction.

Developing Instruction

While all portions of the instructional development process require expertise and finesse (as shown in Figure 1), it is in the design and development of instruction that the most creative work is needed. The designer of instruction, working alone as a distance education teacher or as a member of a team, must be resourceful and capable of trying out new ideas. With the results of the needs assessment in hand, the designer is ready to go to work. The steps outlined in this chapter parallel prominent models in the field (e.g., Dick & Reiser, 1989), but place emphasis upon areas of particular concern for distance education: e.g., specifying constraints (i.e., limitations), exploring alternative solutions, selecting and implementing the "best" solution, and designing, developing, and implementing this instruction.

The so-called "best" solution always requires an optimization of factors, and is consequently subject to change and revision, never the last word. A danger in examining many options can be the "paralysis of analysis," i.e., an inability or unwillingness to make a decision, holding out for the ultimate best one. By staying tentative with the chosen solution, that malady can be more easily avoided.

For distance education, the developing of instruction is of major importance. In its absence, instruction relies upon traditions, often archaic, of what should be taught, or even worse becomes a sort of "stream-of-consciousness" teaching where no structure or organization in the presentation is apparent to the student. On the other hand, when instruction is systematically developed, the course has organization, logical consistency, and wholeness that can engage students and supply the conditions for efficient learning.

Developing System Level Instruction for Distance Education

Two decisions lead to the type of instructional decisions shown in Figure 1. The first decision is a choice between adapting existing instruction or creation of entirely new material. The second decision follows from the first and entails a team or an individual faculty approach, either for developing the course materials or for teaching the course. Each course of action has its advantages and disadvantages.

The development of large-scale instruction for distance education can be handled with a "team approach." Team members typically include instructional designers—specialists in the systematic design process; content experts—persons most knowledgeable about the subject matter being taught (frequently the former or present teacher of the course), and media producers—specialists in the particular form of media to be used (e.g., video, microcomputer, audio production). Such an approach has been exemplified for the past three decades by the British Open University or more recently by the producers of large scale telecourses, such as the Coast Community Colleges consortium or the Annenberg/CPB Project offerings in the United States. Rather than rely upon individual faculty to make all instructional decisions, these courses are developed on a large scale, for distribution to a regional or national audience, for adoption and use by local teachers. Just as in the past a teacher would adopt a textbook, the decision now is to adopt an entire course to include media and print materials. For one of the Annenberg CPB courses like *Destinos*, an introductory course in Spanish released in 1992, the purchaser can acquire a full set of 52 videotapes or videodiscs, each one-half hour in length; a student text, workbook, instructor's manual, and set of audiotapes for practice.

Another approach, frequently more popular with local teachers, requires that they individually develop course materials. In many cases, although not always, they have the option to team with other specialists—to design the course, or to produce graphics, video, or other special class resources.

With either a large-scale or a small-scale approach, the steps outlined in Figure 1 under "Development" are applicable. While they may not always be followed in a fixed, linear order, they must each be addressed. The first step of defining the constraints of budgets, time until delivery, and technical specifications of the delivery system must be taken into account. Given the possible framework provided by these constraints, alternative teaching strategies should be explored: i.e., what approaches can be used to teach this material most effectively? Once a "best solution" or optimal mix of potential solutions has been chosen, a formal design process for the instruction should be undertaken: writing objectives, developing criterion test items, structuring content into hierarchies, and selecting appropriate media forms (see Dick & Reiser, 1989). The resulting tasks for developing instruction can be parceled out to team members or contracted outside. Given adequate time to carry out this process, the result should be coordinated instruction.

Developing Instruction at the Teacher Level

The biggest temptation for the new instructor over distance education is to duplicate the tried-and-true formulas for instruction in a traditional classroom, either those experienced as a student or as a teacher. While skills such as being an entertaining storyteller or clearly explaining basic concepts will transfer, others (like reading the expressions on students' faces for feedback) will not, except possibly with two-way interactive television (Lochte, 1993).

As has been pointed out repeatedly (Eastmond, 1987; Willis, 1992), the major difference between successful and unsuccessful distance instruction is *prior planning*. The practice of "just in time" delivery—deciding the hour prior to class to show a film or engage in a group activity—will likely not work out if attempted under the conditions of distance education.

The major difference in thinking that this author has experienced personally has led to a different way of viewing all college level instruction. That difference puts the responsibility for learning the course's basic concepts squarely on the shoulders of the learner and expects that, given appropriate resources, most of this basic learning will occur outside of class time. Class time (and here my own experience is with an enhanced form of audioconferencing) can then be spent in integration or enrichment activities, where connections between basic concepts are established and activities can be more lively than a lecture-type presentation. This approach requires advance planning and a "systematic design of instruction" to succeed.

Designing Instruction Involving
Student Work Outside of Class

The vehicle to ensure that such learning takes place outside of class is an adequate text and a well designed course syllabus, hereafter referred to as an "extended syllabus." This extended syllabus, usually many chapters long, provides the continuity for the student studying away from the professor. If well designed, the syllabus will be explicit about learning objectives for each module of instruction, will include a variety of sources of information such as articles to be read or activities to be completed, and will suggest a path for the learner to follow in completing the work. The extended syllabus will include assignments and deadlines, criteria for grading, and even some motivational humor to keep the material in perspective. Given that sort of guidebook, the following types of activities are possible.

—Assign pre-reading and contact the author. Have students read an article or text and formulate questions. Telephone the author during class time (prearranged beforehand) to allow students to ask their questions directly. Certain kinds of classes—e.g., current issues seminars or electronic-mail courses—lend themselves well to this kind of work.

—Incorporate a local activity. Suggest a learning activity that can be completed at the local site, a kind of mini-field trip that students can carry out locally, write up, and discuss later in class. Activities such as agency visits, interviews or field trips could be used. For example, students might be required to visit and observe another kind of distance education occurring locally, if only another class using their class' particular system. Frequently the number of the options uncovered by students in rural communities will be surprising, and the resulting discussion better informed than most.

—Have students view videos outside of class. For a class dealing with the topic of distance education, students might be offered "extra credit points" for locating and watching the video "Educating Rita" (about a young woman's intellectual growth at the British Open University, and the repercussions in her personal life). The author's past experience would show that many class members will find a way to rent and watch the video, and they will be ready to provide examples of similar disruptions in their own lives. Another course might provide a video with clips illustrating specific principles being studied. In order to complete particular unit worksheets, students need to watch and respond to the video segments before coming to class.

—Have students work in teams to prepare presentations. Students studying at the same site can work together to plan and present enriching material for class. If the students are working solo, with no one else at the same site, they can contact each other by telephone and plan their group presentation. If extensive telephoning is required, the instructor should be certain that the long distance charges are billed to the class and not to the individuals completing the assignment, possibly through the use of an "800 number." These student presentations should be short and lively, seldom exceeding six to eight minutes in length. Students have to be coached beforehand to listen to their peers, and skillful teachers will test on the material covered in the student presentations to make certain that its importance is communicated to all class members.

The point of this type of teaching is to engineer learning experiences for students outside of class that can then be synthesized while in class. These kinds of experiences require prior planning and preparation; the best courses have a set of requirements and experiences evident to the student from the first day. A learning contract or similar device may be a way of orchestrating these activities with class time. Given guidelines and options, such an approach can be empowering for students, in a way too often found lacking in present distance education and traditional courses (Sponder, 1989).

Delivering instruction at a distance. If the development of the instruction took a coordinated effort, its actual delivery to learners at local sites requires even more. All materials must be presented for copyright clearance, duplication, and distribution well in advance of the beginning of class. And even that is not enough, since it is possible to have materials present on site but locked in a cabinet at the time learners actually need to use them. Elaborate coordination is required, with all persons in the network doing their jobs.

In some distance education settings, where groups convene at several locations, the on-site coordinator or technical person is critical to the system's success. In the author's experience, these people are frequently a neglected resource in the distance delivery system. Frequently, with minimal prior instruction, these people can do more than move a camera from place to place; they can become involved as "group discussion leaders" in some forms of instruction. In any case, their conscientious fulfillment of such essential tasks as sending in assignments, proctoring exams, and fielding student suggestions can make a world of difference for the teacher at a distance. Where these people are available, they are extremely valuable: recruit selectively, keep them accountable, and put them to work!

Evaluation

Evaluation is an area of concern in everyday life. We constantly consider the positive and negative aspects of every experience, placing a value on each. Evaluation of programs or classes is not much different: we simply try to make these judgments more systematic and based upon extensive evidence.

Educational program evaluation has undergone a number of refinements since it was proposed as a discipline in the 1950s, from an emphasis upon tests and measurements, to behavioral objectives, to supplying information to decision-makers, to an emphasis upon judgment and values. It seems that each succeeding refinement in the concept of evaluation builds upon ideas previously expressed and tested.

Evaluation, as defined earlier in this chapter, was seen to be the step of determining the effectiveness and worth of instruction. Clearly, the success of a program in distance education must be judged based upon the learner needs determined in the needs assessment. If the program does not meet these needs, it must be judged as ineffective.

As is seen in the root of the word, the assignment of "value" is central to the concept of evaluation. That this assignment is done fairly, accurately, and systematically is the concern of both evaluators and clients.

One important way of distinguishing evaluations is by classifying them according to the object being evaluated, often called the "evaluand" (Scriven, 1980). Common distinctions are made between personnel (the people), programs (long-term or ongoing organized efforts), projects (short-term organized efforts), and instructional products (materials). This chapter deals with all but personnel evaluation, deliberately keeping the focus upon instruction rather than the skills or traits of the people involved. This distinction is made for strategic reasons, to minimize the perceived threat of evaluation; recognizing, however, that the success or failure of a program or project will certainly reflect upon the performance of those involved.

Program evaluations—evaluations that assess educational activities which provide services on a continuing basis and often involve curricular offerings. Some examples are evaluations of a school district's reading program, a state's special education program, or a university's continuing education program (Joint Committee on Standards for Educational Evaluation, 1981, p. 12).

Project evaluations—evaluations that assess activities funded for a defined period of time to perform a specific task. Some examples are a three-day workshop on behavioral objectives or a three-year career educational demonstration project. A key distinction between a program and a project is that the former is expected to continue for an indefinite period of time, whereas the latter is usually expected to be short-lived. Projects that become institutionalized in effect become programs (Joint Committee, 1981, pp. 12–13).

Materials evaluation (instructional products)—evaluations that assess the merit or worth of content-related physical items, including books, curricular guides, films, tapes, and other tangible instructional products (Joint Committee, 1981, p. 13).

For the past decade and more, a division in the field of evaluation has emphasized the differences between qualitative and quantitative forms of inquiry. In the past, the "hard data" provided by quantitative analysis has often been the more highly valued.

Early practitioners of program evaluation such as Ralph Tyler (Tyler, 1942; Stufflebeam *et al.*, 1971) were highly influenced by the quantitative bias of the then prevalent behaviorism and operationalism in social science research. These theorists emphasized experimental designs, control groups, objective postures toward data collection, and analysis. Qualitative considerations were present, but frequently neglected, or included only as an afterthought.

In a more recent position taken by proponents of qualitative inquiry (Fetterman, 1988; Guba & Lincoln, 1989) investigation relies upon the human observer to record significant events. Earmarks of this kind of research include participant observation over lengthy periods of time, unstructured interviewing, and analysis to uncover meaningful patterns in the phenomena observed. Specific methodologies for doing qualitative evaluation include ethnography (Fetterman, 1989), an anthropological approach to the study of a particular culture; naturalistic inquiry (Lincoln & Guba, 1985), an approach drawn from sociology, emphasizing observation in the natural setting; and educational criticism (Eisner, 1991), drawn from connoisseurship in the arts and art criticism.

Recognizing that reality is not exclusively numerical or categorical, current consensus thinking (Fetterman, 1988; Worthen & Sanders, 1987) stresses a more balanced approach, emphasizing that both are important and that both should be incorporated in some way to provide an adequate description of reality. For the purposes of this chapter, it will be assumed that both qualitative and quantitative techniques can be incorporated into a single model for use in evaluating distance education (see also Eastmond, 1991).

An important additional consideration is the distinction between two main purposes of evaluation: evaluation done primarily to improve and evaluation as a final judge of worth. These two types of evaluation were distinguished by Scriven (1980), who has provided definitions for these two activities as follows:

Formative evaluation is conducted *during* the development or improvement of a program or product (or person). It is an evaluation which is conducted *for* the in-house staff of the program and normally remains in-house; but it may be *done by* an internal *or* an external evaluator or (preferably) a combination. The distinction between formative and summative has been well summed up in a sentence of Robert Stake's "When the cook tastes the soup, that's formative; when the guests taste the soup, that's summative" (Scriven, 1980, p. 56).

Summative evaluation of a program (etc.) is conducted *after* completion and *for* the benefit of some *external* audience or decision-maker (e.g., funding agency, or future possible users) though it may be done by either internal or external evaluators or a mixture. For reasons of credibility, it is much more likely to involve external evaluators than is a formative evaluation. It should not be confused with **outcome evaluation**, which is simply an evaluation focused on outcomes rather than on process—it could be either formative or summative (Scriven, 1980, p. 130, italics in original).

At both the level of the administrator and the teacher, these distinctions will prove to be important.

Evaluation of Distance Education for Administrators

Recognizing that good programs are made that way through constant vigilance and by learning from feedback received along the way, the administrator of distance education will be faced with several preliminary decisions:

—What are the decisions to be made as a result of evaluation? Are you primarily interested in program improvement or in justifying the existence (or expansion) of your program to funding agencies? (Another way of asking this question, commonly posed by evaluators, is: "If you had the results of the proposed study in front of you, what is the range of decisions you would be prepared to make?")

—Inside or outside evaluator? Do you want the program scrutinized by a person from within the organization or by an external observer. The answers to the previous questions (in the paragraph above) may give the basis for this decision.

A Basic Model for Distance Education Program Evaluation

Referring to the diagram in Figure 1, the four steps of the evaluation cycle are as follows:

Choose an evaluation strategy. This step is best accomplished in cooperation with a practicing evaluator. What kind of information do you seek? A quantitative approach might examine numbers of enrollees, their ratings of program quality, the percentage of graduates, and the perceptions of persons dropping out or graduating. Because of the technology involved in distance education, for example, with use of electronic mail as a mainstay of a course, it may be possible to set up automatic indicators of query response time, for example, or weekly utilization rates (Tucker, 1991). On the other hand, a qualitative approach might examine an inside view of the process of distance education. It might show profiles of the social climate at three contrasting receive sites—how studying takes place, how leadership is exerted, how good grades are obtained, etc. The one perspective would possibly be more useful in taking program action, say, for instance, to expand course offerings or add a new track to a degree. The second is more useful in understanding the process, what is going on, and how it might be influenced from within or from the outside to provide a more satisfying educational experience.

Conduct formative evaluation. This process of providing feedback to monitor day-to-day progress of the distance education program can be set up on an ongoing basis, allowing a kind of "management by exception." When some element of the process seems to be out of line from normal expectation, then administrative attention can be turned to providing needed remediation. For example, an ongoing formative evaluation process might tap into several sources of routine data: student course evaluation results, response time lags on the electronic mail system, and a series of exit interviews with persons completing various courses. As an evaluator, one would look for aberrations from the norm—e.g., a marked drop in course evaluations or a different pattern of electronic mail responses—before taking any steps toward intervention.

Conduct summative evaluation. Any funding source will rightfully expect to receive information showing the degree of accomplishment of program objectives. Sometimes the source of such information will be external, e.g., from an external visit team set up to review various aspects of a program. Many programs in higher education will require accreditation team visits, and these become, in one sense, a source of summative evaluation. Where important indicators can be determined and then measures put into place, a program can insure that needed information will be forthcoming at the time it is needed.

Report findings. A frequent problem with evaluation information is that it does not receive the attention it deserves from people within or outside the distance education system. A system of reporting, both formal and informal, can make sure that results receive a wide hearing. In order for needed revisions to take place, these results must find their way into the design process at both the system level and the level of the individual teacher.

Evaluation at the Level of the Teacher

Conduct formative evaluation. For the individual teacher conducting class over a distance education system, the indicators of how the class is going are in many ways similar to on-campus instruction. Some sources of information to help shape up and maintain quality in a course you are teaching are listed as follows:

—Messages from students, feedback about the class, and expressions of sentiment, favorable or unfavorable, are common in any sort of class.

—Student course evaluations provide a more formal mechanism for such feedback. Skillful teachers often find additional ways of obtaining such feedback (e.g., midway through the course, rather than at the end, with a form designed specifically for a particular class).

—Consider the various sources of miscommunication that can occur in teacher-student communication. Sponder (1989), in his monograph about teaching and learning practices in audioconference courses in rural Alaska, has done a skillful analysis of communication difficulties. Such common occurrences as "bypassing" when sender and receiver miss each other with their meanings, and a variety of other pitfalls are examined. It seems that the distance education context opens up a range of possibilities for miscommunication that requires sensitive listening and response on the part of the teacher. A style of open and receptive communication is a good place to begin.

Sorting out such feedback to understand exactly what is meant is complex. Good advice for a new faculty member is to sit down with a more seasoned colleague and get additional help from that person in interpretation.

Conduct summative evaluation. At the present time, in most distance education courses, the sole source of summative evaluation remains the end-of-course student evaluation. For university faculty, these serve for promotion and tenure purposes. As pointed out in earlier articles (Eastmond, 1986, 1987), these may not have much weight in important decisions affecting the career of most university faculty. Alternative means of conducting evaluations should be developed, to include self-evaluation and peer evaluation (Licata, 1986). One simple procedure for a teacher is to institute the practice of filling out an evaluation form for the course at the same time as the students do, and then later comparing one's own ratings with those provided by the students. Where discrepancies exist in perceptions, more thorough investigation (e.g., by personal interviews with students) may be needed. The important point to be made is that end of course or program evaluation procedures can both significantly improve instruction and serve as justification for continued effort or support.

Dealing with Misconceptions

It seems that the skeptics about distance education are never far away. Being a new field, there are areas where practice in distance education falls short of the theory, and the detractors are quick to fault the entire enterprise.

Some commonly encountered views contain misconceptions and half-truths. Figure 2 summarizes some of the commonly encountered ones and provides an alternate view, generally more optimistic toward distance education's possibilities. The alternate view could be summarized as follows:

—Needs assessments can be sufficiently focused and efficiently conducted to provide timely information for developing instruction.

—Distance education need not be the "poor stepchild" but can have results at least as positive as face-to-face instruction.

—Evaluation involves attention to the political context, but can be conducted impartially and fairly.

—Creative teachers can succeed under both individual and team approaches to instructional design. There is no substitute for imagination and diligent effort, however.

The argument in this chapter has been for the alternative view, avoiding where possible the prevalent "conventional wisdom" of the status quo and the

Heard in passing. . .   An alternate view

Needs assessments are amorphous, like "pinning jelly to the wall", not worth the time and resources expended.	Needs assessments can be adequately defined for a system's specific purposes. Resources spent on needs assessment are vital, since the results drive the entire development process.

Distance education is a poor sub-stitute for "face-to-face" instruction. It is impersonal and lacks the impact of direct contact with the teacher.	Distance education, skillfully conducted, can have results at least as positive as face-to-face instruction. In some subject areas, distance education may be better suited than in others.

Evaluation is political and must remain so. Attempts to be objective are smokescreen favoring the status quo. Evaluators work for project directors and look out for the project directors' interests.	Evaluation has multiple purposes and serves multiple audiences. Formative evaluation is vital to provide feedback and encourage improvement. Summative evaluation can be conducted fairly and credibly, with particular attention given to keeping it fair.

As a team approach is applied to developing distance education, the room for creative teaching will be reduced. The days of autonomy of the teacher, and consequent freedom, are numbered.	A team approach allows each person to perform in the area of his or her expertise. Creative teachers will always be needed, and the appetite of people for relevant, lifelong education seems nearly insatiable.

Figure 2. *Some misconceptions about distance education, needs assessment, and evaluation.*

pessimism of the skeptic. If we can learn to follow the sound principles that we know about assessing needs, developing instruction, and evaluating results in distance education, the future of the enterprise is bright.

Summary

This chapter has examined the process of developing instruction, from needs assessment through development of instruction to evaluation and revision. For a graphic summary of this process, Figure 1 should be helpful.

This chapter has examined **needs assessment** at the level of the system and, alternatively, at the level of the distance education instructor. In either case, the focus of attention was prescribed at the level of the learner, suggesting gaps between the existing and desired conditions. Steps required for quality assurance were outlined. While it is important to do a thorough job of assessing needs, it is also important to keep the task focused and to manage it efficiently; if not, the entire enterprise is at risk of bogging down in excessive detail. Once needs of the learners have been identified, the way is open for a variety of methods and means to meet those needs.

In **developing distance education instruction**, this chapter suggested defining constraints in resources and equipment first, and then generating alternative solution strategies to determine the "best" solution. (A "best" solution is always tentative and subject to revision further along.) At this point, instruction can be developed, to include objectives, activities, and assessment techniques. Having planned and developed the instruction adequately, the results should be implemented in the distance education setting.

Evaluation should provide feedback to improve the implementation process (**formative evaluation**) and should give a final assessment of the instruction's effectiveness (**summative evaluation**). Based upon these findings, instruction should be revised.

It is worth remembering that in practice these activities are rarely conducted in a strict linear fashion. More frequently, the flow of activities is in the general direction suggested, but with the sequence of activities varying somewhat. For example, a distance education system might have tried out a couple of courses before conducting a full needs assessment or, alternatively, the design process may include elements of formative evaluation before the final shape of the instructional system is apparent. As in most human processes, the actual practice will seldom follow the theoretical steps exactly, and often will be varied for good reason. Keeping this feature in mind, the reader should avoid compulsiveness about strict adherence to a linear flow of activities.

Similarly, needs assessment, and formative and summative evaluation represent ways of more closely examining the educational needs and the performance of the resulting program. As strategies for research, they frequently overlap in their use of particular techniques. For example, surveys or focus groups could be appropriate techniques for both.

Conducted properly, these steps for formulating instruction liberate the designer to be able to use a variety of means, rather than locking onto a single solution or failing to respond to feedback that could improve the program's functioning. If conducted properly, the steps outlined in this chapter can make major differences in the responsiveness of distance education to its remote but all-important clientele.

References

Dick, W. & Reiser, R. (1989). *Planning effective instruction.* Englewood Cliffs, NJ: Prentice-Hall.

Eastmond, J. N. (1980–81). Assessing instructional needs at the departmental level: Why and how. *International Journal of Instructional Media, 8*(4), 317–327.

Eastmond, J. N. (1986). Extension teaching: New technologies and old insights. *Innovation Abstracts, 7,* p. 23.

Eastmond, J. N. (1987). Proving the critics wrong. *Innovation Abstracts, 9*(27).

Eastmond, J. N. (1991). Educational evaluation: The future. *Theory into Practice, 30*(1), 74–79

Eastmond, J. N., Sr. (1991). An assessment of training needs of educational leaders in the minority nationalities in the south central region of China. *Educational Technology Research & Development, 39*(2), 98–105.

Eisner, E. W. (1991). *The enlightened eye: Qualitative inquiry and the enhancement of educational practice.* New York: Macmillan.

Fetterman, D. M. (1988). *Qualitative approaches to evaluation in education: The silent scientific revolution.* New York: Praeger.

Fetterman, D. M. (1989). *Ethnography step by step.* Newbury Park, CA: Sage.

Galbraith, J. K. (1958, revised 1969). *The affluent society.* New York: Mentor.

Guba, E. G. & Lincoln, Y. S. (1989). *Fourth generation evaluation.* Newbury Park, CA: Sage.

Hébert, Y. M. (1986). Naturalistic Evaluation in Practice: A Case Study. In D. D. Williams (Ed.), *Naturalistic evaluation.* (New Directions for Program Evaluation, No. 30). San Francisco: Jossey-Bass.

Joint Committee on Standards for Educational Evaluation. (1981). *Standards for evaluations of educational programs, projects, and materials.* New York: McGraw-Hill.

Kaufman, R. (1972). *Educational system planning.* Englewood Cliffs, NJ: Prentice-Hall.

Licata, C. M. (1986). *Post-tenure faculty evaluation: Threat or opportunity?* (ASHE-ERIC Higher Education Report No. 1, 1986) Washington, DC: Association for the Study of Higher Education.

Lincoln, Y. S. & Guba, E. G. (1985). *Naturalistic inquiry.* Beverly Hills, CA: Sage.

Lochte, R. H. (1993). *Interactive television and instruction.* Englewood Cliffs, NJ: Educational Technology Publications.

Murphy, K. L. (1989). Turkey's Open Education Policy. *Educational Technology Research & Development, 37*(2), 122–125.

McKillip, J. (1986). *Need analysis: Tools for the human services and education.* Newbury Park, CA: Sage.

Scriven, M. (1980). *Evaluation thesaurus* (2nd ed.). Inverness, CA: Edgepress.

Sponder, B. (1989). *Distance education in rural Alaska: An overview of teaching and learning practices in audioconference courses* (2nd ed.). Fairbanks, AK: University of Alaska Center for Cross-Cultural Studies.

Stufflebeam, D. L., Foley, W. J., Gephart, W. J., Guba, E. G., Hammond, R. L., Merriman, H. O. & Provus, M. M. (1971). *Educational evaluation and decision-making.* Itasca, IL: Peacock.

Tucker, R. W. (1991). Electronic Process and Outcomes Assessment in the Electronic University. Paper presented at the annual meeting of the American Evaluation Association, Chicago, Il.

Tyler, R. W. (1942). General statement on evaluation. *Journal of Educational Research, 35,* 492–501.

U. S. Congress, Office of Technology Assessment. (1989). *Linking for learning: A new course for education.* Washington, DC: U. S. Government Printing Office.

Williams, D., Van Monfrans, A., Eastmond, J. N. & Hart, A. (1987). Statewide Evaluation report on productivity project studies related to improved use of technology to extend educational programs: Sub-Report One: Six case studies and participant survey. Provo, UT: Wasatch Institute of Research and Evaluation.

Willis, B. (1992). *Effective distance education: A primer for faculty and administrators.* (Monograph Series in Distance Education, No. 2). Fairbanks, AK: University of Alaska Center for Cross-Cultural Studies.

Witkin, B. R. (1987). *Assessing needs in educational and social programs.* San Francisco, CA: Jossey-Bass.

Witkin, B. R. & Eastmond, J. N. (1987). Bringing focus to the needs assessment study: The pre-assessment phase. *Educational Planning, 6*(4), 12–23.

Worthen, B. R. & Sanders, J. R. (1987). *Educational evaluation: Alternative approaches and practical guidelines.* New York: Longman.

Chapter Five

Print Tools for Distance Education

Earl R. Misanchuk

Without going into great historical detail, it must be acknowledged at the outset that distance education is deeply rooted in the medium of print, having evolved primarily from what were earlier called *correspondence courses*. Sherow and Wedemeyer (1990) succinctly trace the evolution of modern North American distance education delivery systems from correspondence courses developed at Oxford University about 1870. Print still plays a significant role in the delivery of distance education, both in North America and around the world, despite the emergence of powerful and attractive "high-tech" alternatives. Why? Because, as Willis (1993) and others point out, print has a number of significant advantages.

Advantages of Print

- It is familiar to, reasonably well understood by, and accepted by learners—no learning curve is involved.
- It is completely learner-paced.
- It can be navigated easily; random access of specific portions is convenient and fast.
- The technology is familiar to and reasonably well understood by instructional designers and subject-matter experts (SMEs) alike.
- No distribution/reception timetable is required (i.e., the learner does not have to be at a specific time and place to use it).
- No special facilities or equipment are needed to use it; it is generally highly portable.
- The medium is "transparent," allowing the message to come through without distraction or dazzle from the delivery technology.
- It has a low unit cost (relative to the alternatives) for both the preparation of the master copy and for duplication.
- It is a very efficient format for delivering large quantities of content.
- It is easy to revise, given word processing and desktop publishing.

- It is cost-effective to produce small print runs ("just-in-time" printing) via xerography, thereby facilitating revisions and minimizing storage costs.

Surveying the numerous and powerful advantages, it is easy to see why print has endured as a delivery medium for distance education. If the goal is simply communicating content cheaply and effectively, as opposed to employing the latest and most sophisticated technology available, then print must be a strong contender. However, print does have some limitations.

Limitations of Print

- Interactivity is more difficult to achieve with print than with some other media (e.g., computers).
- Motion cannot be shown.
- Color, if needed, is more expensive than monochrome.
- A significant proportion of learners do not know how to make optimal use of print materials (members of the "Sesame Street" or "sound-bite" generations—those who were raised primarily on television rather than on print—appear to be less adept at using print than they could be).

With the exception of the first and last, careful examination shows that the limitations identified are not really limitations at all—they are simply characteristics which, for many instructional and educational situations, may not be relevant. That is, when the depiction of motion and color are not salient considerations (as is often the case), print is not disadvantaged.

Formats of Print Materials

Print materials come in a number of formats (Willis, 1993), including:

- textbooks,
- study guides,
- workbooks,
- course syllabi, and
- case studies.

While an increasing number of textbooks are showing evidence of the application of instructional design principles, a disheartening number still are produced on the apparent premise that all a textbook has to do is organize and present content. To make such textbooks function as effective distance education tools almost always requires the creation of supplementary materials, such as study guides, workbooks, or syllabi. A study guide offers supplementary material and advice on how to proceed with learning; a workbook provides interactive "read-and-do" activities; and a syllabus outlines the goals and objectives of a course, the expectations the instructor has for student performance, a list of readings and assignments/activities (often described on a day-by-day or week-by-week basis), and descriptions of evaluation and grading methods and procedures. Whatever the particular format employed, certain considerations must be undertaken in the preparation of instructional text; these are the substance of this chapter. To help put into perspective the discussion below, it may be useful to know that most of the distance education courses at our university employ standard textbooks supplemented by a locally-developed *Course Guide* (a combination of study guide, workbook, and syllabus) containing many of the elements described herein. These are frequently accompanied by reprints of journal articles and/or other source materials. The print materials may be augmented with videocassettes, audiocassettes, slides, etc. In a few courses, print is combined with television.

Utilization Strategies

A good deal of experience has been built up regarding the effective use of text. However, teachers' and instructional designers' knowledge of how to use text is usually acquired through "the school of hard knocks" rather than through formal education. This is even more true for how instructional text is created, designed, and laid out than it is for the ways in which we make use of text prepared by others. This section is intended to address that shortcoming in our educations.

Access Structure and Orienting Devices

Whatever the length of a document, it will contain certain common features, many of which we take so much for granted as to devote little thought to them. Obviously, however, part of the instructional designer's role is to examine some of those "givens" closely.

Waller (1979) focused attention on the *access structure* of documents, which he defined as the "... coordinated use of typographically signalled structural cues that help students to read texts using selective sampling strategies" (p. 175). Waller's contention was that learners don't simply begin at the beginning of a document and work through to the end, reading most things only once. They browse through some portions, read others intensively, and skim still others. They skip forward and back as necessary. They come back to the document after an absence in order to locate specific information. The access structure of the document, composed of features such as the following, facilitate that kind of behavior:

- content broken into chapters or modules;
- titles and headings, paragraphs, and "point form" (itemized lists preceded by bullets, like this one);
- pagination;
- headers and footers;
- table and figure numbers;
- tables of content and indexes; and
- glossaries.

Modularization

Breaking the course content into modules helps learners by establishing the "borders" of certain topics, and by making small "chunks" out of what could otherwise be an overwhelming amount of content.

A frequently-asked question is "How many modules should comprise a course?" The standard answer is "Just as many as it takes to do the job; no more, no fewer." Instructional designers and (especially) administrators in distance education programs sometimes feel that all courses must have exactly the same structure, including the number of modules and assignments. To my mind, that's simplistic and constraining. Mathematics, history, chemistry, and philosophy are different disciplines. They use different approaches and techniques for both the generation and transmission of knowledge. Why should anyone expect them to be organized in exactly the same way?

Headings and Titles

Headings and titles are short descriptions used to identify and demarcate the contents of sections of text. Properly used, they make plain the structure of the content, showing how every bit of it relates to every other bit. Headings should be used liberally in instructional materials. Research has shown that the use of headings is beneficial to learning for learners older than about 12 or 13, especially for long-term retention (Brooks, Danserau, Spurlin, & Holley, 1983; Hartley & Jonassen, 1985; Hartley & Trueman, 1983, 1985). The exact form of the heading doesn't seem to matter: headings that are embedded in the text (as they are in this book) are just as effective as headings printed in the margins, and headings stated as questions are as effective as headings in the form of statements. Generally speaking, you should use no more than three levels of headings (e.g., major headings, minor headings, sub-headings) unless the work is very long, as readers appear to have difficulty making effective use of more levels.

Headers and Footers

Headers and footers are information printed in the top and bottom margins, respectively. In addition to page numbers, headers and footers can be used to indicate chapter or module names, and even section titles. Obviously, the page numbers are of greatest importance. Headers and footers should be set apart from the body text by a sufficient distance to eliminate confusion with body text. It helps to use a font and/or font size for headers and footers that is different from that used in the body.

Tables of Content and Lists of Figures or Tables

Any document longer than a few pages and a few headings should have a table of contents to facilitate accessing information. Similarly, if there are figures or tables in the document, they should have their own listing. Figure captions and table titles (in shortened form, if they are lengthy) should form the entries.

Tables of content are most useful when they reflect the heading structure of the document. That is, subordinate headings are indented under superordinate headings. The more subordinate they are, the more they should be indented. All levels of headings should be represented in the table of contents.

Whether the page numbers should immediately follow the entry (Figure 1a) or align at the right margin (with or without leader lines) (Figure 1b) is a matter of taste rather than functionality. A form they should *not* follow is the run-in one (Figure 1c), as accessibility is severely hampered.

Background 1
    Advantages of Print 1
    Limitations of Print 2
Utilization Strategies 2
    Access Structure and Orienting Devices 2
    Layout and Design 7
    Software Requirements 12
    A Few Practical Tips 12
    Integrating Text with Other Technologies 14
Interaction 14
    Instructional Design Elements 14
    Writing for Instructional Materials 18
Summary Case Study 18

Figure 1a. *Nested style of table of contents.*

Background	1
Advantages of Print	1
Limitations of Print	2
Utilization Strategies	2
Access Structure and Orienting Devices	2
Layout and Design	7
Software Requirements	12
A Few Practical Tips	12
Integrating Text with Other Technologies	14
Interaction	14
Instructional Design Elements	14
Writing for Instructional Materials	18
Summary Case Study	18

Figure 1b. *Nested style of table of contents, with leader lines.*

Background 1; Advantages of Print 1; Limitations of Print 2; **Utilization Strategies** 2; Access Structure and Orienting Devices 2; Layout and Design 7; Software Requirements 12; A Few Practical Tips 12; Integrating Text with Other Technologies 14; **Interaction** 14; Instructional Design Elements 14; Writing for Instructional Materials 18; **Summary Case Study** 18;

Figure 1c. *Run-in style of table of contents. This style is a poor choice.*

Figure and Table Numbers

Figures and tables should be numbered for ease of reference to them from within the body text. It is common in academic circles to have separate lists of figures and of tables. Frequently, the numbers are preceded by the chapter number, as in *Figure 4-7* or *Table 8-3*, indicating the seventh figure in the fourth chapter, and the third table in the eighth chapter, respectively. There is no necessity for having two series, however. As long as you make it clear to the learner (through explanation early in the document), all non-body-text items could be numbered sequentially. If it seems untoward to use a sequence like *Figure 4-1*, *Figure 4-2*, *Table 4-3*, *Figure 4-4*, etc., to indicate the first three figures and the first table in Chapter 4, then perhaps the designation can be changed to *Display 4-1*, *Display 4-2*, etc. There is a certain logic to numbering all non-text items sequentially, in that it makes it easier to locate a specific item. One knows that 6-3 comes between 6-2 and 6-4, no matter whether it is a table or a figure. Since this is a little unconventional, however, it should be explained to the learner.

Indention and Lists (Point Form)

Instructional materials make much more use of point form presentation that do most other kinds of written material. This is an effective and efficient format for presenting a series of more than two or three points.

When using point form, second and subsequent lines of text in a paragraph should be aligned with the text in the first line (Figure 2a), not with the bullet (•) (Figure 2b). In the typewriter days, asterisks or hyphens had to be used to delineate points. Now, most word processors have bullets, so why not use them instead?

- Course content changes (new theories emerge; new research evidence is incorporated; new SMEs bring new ideas on how the material should be presented).
- Other course materials (e.g., textbooks) undergo revision, and new editions differ from the old.
- Instructional designers determine through formative evaluation that learners are having difficulty with portions of the course, and want changes.

Figure 2a. *Properly wrapped outdention.*

• Course content changes (new theories emerge; new research
evidence is incorporated; new SMEs bring new ideas on how the
material should be presented).
• Other course materials (e.g., textbooks) undergo revision, and new
editions differ from the old.
• Instructional designers determine through formative evaluation
that learners are having difficulty with portions of the course, and
want changes.

Figure 2b. *Improperly wrapped outdention.*

Indexes

An index is an invaluable access tool for locating specific information on a topic. Many high-end word processors have built-in indexing routines, which greatly facilitate creating an index. By issuing a certain command in appropriate places, words or phrases are "marked" electronically so that, upon a different command, an index can be generated automatically. Although the indexing feature may take a little study to master, it is well worth the investment. Creating an effective index appears to require a knack for such work, and formative evaluation is a good way for determining who has the knack: Have several people create an index for a document, then have several typical students use the index to locate information, using the various versions of the index. Select the index that seems to be most useful.

Glossaries

A glossary summarizes in one place all the new, often technical, terminology encountered in a document. Typically, glossaries are placed at the end of a document. In modularized instruction, glossaries are usually placed at the end of all modules, or sometimes even in a separate document. To facilitate the use of a glossary, it is helpful to delineate glossary entries in a specific way (e.g., with **boldface type**). Learners then know (because we told them so in the introduction to the document) that they can find the term in the glossary. One way of facilitating the introduction of new terms even more is to provide a definition of the term the first time it is used (perhaps as a footnote on the page where it is first encountered), as well as placing it in the glossary for easy access during subsequent encounters.

Formative evaluation of the distance education materials is essential to determine what words to include in a glossary: Representative students can be asked to identify words that they feel should be included in the glossary during their trial use of the materials.

Pagination by Modules

Paginating by modules (e.g., *page 4–3* designates the third page in the fourth module) is a common means of accommodating frequent revision of materials. If a few pages have to be added or deleted in the middle of a document, the worst-case scenario is that one module (rather than the entire document) must be reprinted to make the pagination adjustment. Indeed, if cost is a major concern, it is possible to simply identify a page as *14a* if it must be added between pages *14* and *15* (assuming loose-leaf binding or something similar is used). Pagination by modules therefore can be very useful from the designers' point of view, and learners seem to have no trouble using such pagination, provided they are instructed in advance as to how the pagination system works.

Color Coding

Color coding of pages can be an effective means of distinguishing activities within a distance education course (provided a loose-leaf binding is employed). For instance, assignments that are to be sent in for evaluation can be printed on, for example, blue paper; self-assessment questions might be on yellow; answers to self-assessment questions on gray, etc. While color-coding activities in this way facilitates the learners' locating them, it has the disadvantage of (probably) requiring more pages in the overall instructional package (unless each color-coded activity is exactly some multiple of a page long).

Icons

Icons are small, simple graphics which can be used to direct learners' attention to specific learning activities. Learners can lapse into "reading mode," and skim right over questions designed to promote reflection, or exercises designed to consolidate the knowledge gained through previous reading. An icon can help break the reading pattern, as illustrated in Figure 3, extracted from a course on the sociology of religion.

Background to Weber's Analysis

Before beginning *The Protestant Ethic*, it is necessary to place Weber's approach in the context of his times. A scholar who lived from 1864 to 1920, Weber studied and wrote a good deal of his work during a period dominated intellectually by Marx's legacy. In the following two selections, McGuire provides some comparisons between Marx (along with Engels) and Weber. The first reading concerns each author's respective views about religion's conservative role or, in other words, how religion protects the status quo. The second reading notes how Weber saw the relationship between religion and social change, as compared to the positions held by Marx and some of his intellectual descendants.

 Religion often acts to support a society's existing stratification system (the "status quo"). How is Weber's position on this subject similar to that held by Marx? In what ways is Weber's position different?

 McGuire, "Religion Supports the Status Quo," pp. 190-197.
McGuire, "Religion Promotes Social Change," pp. 197-204.

Exercise 4.1

Theme: In a sentence or two, summarize the author's main purposes in writing each of these two sections.

Figure 3. *Example of icons used in instructional materials.*

The first kind of icon, we explained to learners early in the course, identifies a Guiding Question—one which is intended to help them determine what questions they should be able to answer after doing a particular reading. The second kind of icon signifies the need to consult a particular textbook. The third one signals the learner to write out an answer to a question posed. Some icons that we have found useful are shown in Figure 4, along with their suggested meanings.

Assignment or exercise that involves writing or recording answers.

Send in this assignment for grading.

Read the following page(s)/section(s)/chapter(s) in one of the textbooks.

Make notes on something (e.g., a reading).

Telephone someone (instructor, another student, etc.).

Talk to someone (instructor, another student, etc.) about this; discuss this; consult with other team members.

Do this activity on a Macintosh computer.

View broadcast or narrowcast television program.

View a videotape.

Listen to a cassette recording.

Figure 4. *Some icons and their suggested meanings.*

When icons are employed, care must be taken to define their meanings to learners in the introduction to the course and/or the very first time they are used. Furthermore, it is important to use icons in a consistent way in different documents (i.e., across all courses), otherwise you risk confusing learners.

Layout and Design

Layout and design are concerned with such factors as:
- whether pages will be printed on one side or two,
- the type of binding to be used,
- the size and shape of the page,
- the size and shape of margins on the page,
- the number of columns of print employed,
- the length of the printed line,
- whether or not text is right-justified,

- the font and font size to be used,
- the consistent use of variants of the font chosen (e.g., *italics*, **boldface**, CAPITALS, etc.),
- leading (vertical spacing between lines),
- the amount and distribution of white space employed,
- the location, size, and style of headings, and
- the positioning of figures and tables.

Timing of Layout/Design Decisions

Some seemingly simple decisions should be made early in the process of producing an instructional document, because they can have profound effects on how the document is constructed; others can, through the graces of desktop publishing, be delayed and even experimented with. The list of factors above is roughly in order of increasing freedom to defer decisions. Items near the top of the list must be decided more firmly and earlier in the design/layout process than items lower in the list. Failure to make early decisions at the beginning can increase risk in terms of the amount of effort necessary to accommodate a change later on. At the same time, many of the decisions involved are interrelated. For example, the decision to print on one or both sides of a page not only affects the quality and opacity of the paper you must use, but also may determine whether you choose a mirror-image layout or a single-page layout. The layout may also affect, and be affected by, the type of binding used (e.g., loose-leaf or ring-binding, comb-type plastic binding, edge-stapled, etc.). The page size and shape may influence the margins used, which in turn (along with the number of columns deemed necessary) influences the line length. Research has shown that the optimum font size and leading are integrally related to the line length.

Given that virtually all design/layout decisions are exquisitely "intertwingled," where does one begin? Due to the limited amount of space available in this volume, and the fact that more complete descriptions of and rationales for the process exist elsewhere (e.g., Misanchuk, 1992), the design/layout process will be reduced here to recommendations and rules of thumb, with little justification for their existence. These rules represent *good* ways of laying out instructional text, albeit not necessarily the best possible for all circumstances. While they may not represent the *only* good ways of doing the job, they are safe. Violating the rules is something that can be done by skilled practitioners, sometimes with salient effect; in the hands of a novice, however, it can wreak instructional and/or aesthetic havoc.

Likelihood of Revision: Implications

One of the fundamental considerations that should guide your decision-making about design and layout is the likelihood of revision of the materials. The overwhelming majority of distance education materials are likely to be revised fairly frequently, for a variety of reasons:

- Course content changes (new theories emerge; new research evidence is incorporated; new content experts bring new ideas on how the material should be presented).

- Other course materials (e.g., textbooks) undergo revision, and new editions differ from the old.
- Instructional designers determine through formative evaluation that learners are having difficulty with portions of the course, and want changes.

Printing on one side of a page makes revisions easier. If only a few changes are necessary, a single replacement page may be printed. Intermediate pages can be inserted between two existing pages, if necessary, to accommodate lengthier revisions. If there is little likelihood of revision, printing on both sides of a page may be necessary or desirable. For the reasons identified above, a loose-leaf binding, where individual pages can be inserted or deleted, is desirable if revisions are likely.

Page Size and Related Factors

The *de facto* standard for page size is 8 ½ × 11" for most educational units in North America. Given those dimensions, the range of possibilities for margin size and line length (and therefore number of columns of text) are fairly limited. Although research has shown that margins *per se* are not necessary for legibility (Tinker, 1963), readers seem to expect them, and they should probably be included for that reason. There are several rules of thumb in the publishing industry for determining the size of margins. However, there is probably no "right" set of margins for instructional materials. In general, the bottom margin should be slightly larger than the others, purportedly to give a feeling of stability and solidity to the page. If pages are printed on one side only, there do not appear to be empirically-based reasons to make the left margin larger than the right, or vice versa. However, simply centering the column on the page may, some feel, makes for a very staid and conservative layout. Too, some argue that making one margin larger than the other provides space for learners to make notes.

White Space

White space is space in which nothing is printed. It should be used liberally in instructional materials to "lighten" the page, thereby making it more inviting. Short line length relative to page width (i.e., wide side margins) help achieve this "lightening," as does the use of point form. White space should not be distributed randomly, however; it should be used to separate disparate elements, thereby uniting the elements themselves through contiguity (e.g., see the recommendation below about white space and headings). As suggested in "Positioning Figures and Tables," bottom margins needn't be strictly adhered to (Hartley, 1978, 1982; Hartley & Burnhill, 1977). Indeed, there may be valid reasons for not making bottom margins uniform. Gropper (1991) asserts that a legitimate concern for designers is facilitating the order in which items are processed mentally by the learner. Since adjacency of items affects the order in which processing occurs, and since page breaks don't always occur at instructionally logical places, larger-than-normal amounts of white space may have to be left at page bottoms.

Positioning Figures and Tables

Figures and tables should be placed as close as possible to the text that refers to them, even if this means that bottom margins are larger or smaller than normal. Presumably the reason a figure or table is included is because the designer wants the learner to refer to it and glean some information. Making it difficult for the learner to avoid confronting the figure or table (by placing it right where it is first referenced) should facilitate that process. Introducing new ideas after referring the learner to a figure or table (perhaps in order to fill the remainder of the page, to the bottom margin, with text) may interrupt the desired interaction.

Fonts

A font, in common terminology, is the complete set of all characters available in a given size and style of typeface (although more stringent definitions are used in the publishing industry). Figure 5 illustrates some fonts commonly used in desktop publishing, with variants—plain (or roman) text, italic text, and bold text.

This font is Avant Garde: roman, *italic*, **bold**.
This font is Bookman: roman, *italic*, **bold**.
This font is Helvetica: roman, *italic*, **bold**.
This font is New Century Schoolbook: roman, *italic*, **bold**.
This font is Palatino: roman, *italic*, **bold**.
This font is Times: roman, *italic*, **bold**.

Figure 5. *Some fonts commonly used in desktop publishing.*

Print size, leading, and line length are all interrelated (Tinker, 1963, 1965). Although more complete and explicit guidelines exist for selecting appropriate parameters for these variables (see Misanchuk, 1992, pp. 156–159), approximate guidelines are:

- Font size should be between 9- and 12-point for general body text. (A point is approximately $1/72''$.) Smaller text may be used in limited quantities for table entries or reference material, but text smaller than 6- or 7-point is likely too small for most learners to read comfortably. Larger sizes may be used for headings and titles.
- Although a small range of leading will produce satisfactory results for 9- to 12-point text, 2 additional points of leading is a safe choice across the range.
- Given an $8 \ 1/2 \times 11''$ page size, using two columns of text produces line lengths that are just barely long enough to be efficient. Short line lengths lead to very jagged right margins, due to long words falling at the end of the line. The alternative of hyphenating those words causes unnecessary interruption of the flow of reading (Lichty, 1989; White, 1983), leading to decreased reading efficiency. Two-column layouts generally involve extra work, especially when headings and/or

graphics are included that span more than one column, and given the
potential for frequent revision of instructional materials, it seems
prudent to stick with single-column layouts. In that event, the line
should be as long as possible without causing reading problems—
about 4 1/2–4 3/4" (certainly no longer than 5").

Although equivalent legibility is about equal across a fairly wide range of
common fonts, learners have strong preferences about what fonts they like to
read. Sans-serif fonts (e.g., Helvetica) are generally disliked by readers, as are
relatively compact ones (e.g., Times) (Tinker, 1963, 1965; Misanchuk, 1989).
(Ironically, Helvetica and Times are perhaps the most widely-used fonts in
the world!) Choose a font that has:

- a serif,
- a heavy stroke (bordering on boldface),
- clearly distinguishing characteristics between letters,
- considerable white space within letters, and
- substantial width to the letters.

Bookman and New Century Schoolbook (used in this volume) are both good
choices.

No more than two fonts should be used on a given page. Instead, use
variations (**bold**, *italic*, different size) of the same font. Avoid "fancy" variations,
such as outline or shadow, as they are difficult to read. If you use them for
effect, use them sparingly. The use of all capital letters is not recommended,
since all-caps text is more difficult to read than that using capitals and lower-
case (Tinker, 1965; Tinker & Patterson, 1928).

Justified Margins

Right-justified margins are those in which the right margin forms a
straight vertical line, with all the lines exactly the same length, as in this
paragraph. Instructional text should not be right-justified, since that process
inhibits legibility (Davis, Barry, & Wiesenberg, 1986; Kleper, 1987; Muncer,
Gorman, Gorman, & Bibel, 1986; Spiegelman, 1987; Trollip & Sales, 1986;
White, 1983), presumably due to the variable inter-letter and inter-word
spacing necessitated by right-justification. Inter-letter spacing can be kept
fairly constant through the use of hyphens at the right margin, of course;
however, hyphenation appears to cause legibility problems of its own (Lichty,
1989; Misanchuk, 1992; White, 1983). In addition, right-justification
frequently introduces "rivers of white" into a body of text (sinuous vertical
"trails" of white space), which require extra effort to eliminate.

Headings

As noted earlier, headings should be used liberally. Even the most minor
heading should be larger than the body text, and the more major the heading,
the larger should be the font used for it. The so-called *Rule of X's* suggests
appropriate sizes for different headings: The capital X of the body text should
be the same physical size as the lower-case x of the lowest order of heading
(i.e., the heading pertaining to that body text). The capital X of the text used
for the lowest-order heading should be the same physical size as the lower-
case x of the next-higher order of heading, etc. White space should be used

around headings to help establish the structure of the subject-matter: the more major the heading, the more white space should surround it. In all cases, the amount of white space separating the heading from body text that follows it should be less than the amount of white space separating the heading from body text that precedes it.

Software Requirements

The production of print-based instructional materials benefits greatly from the use of computer-based technologies like word processing and desktop publishing (DTP). A few years ago, the distinction between word processing and DTP was fairly clear: Software packages performed functions that either fell into one category or the other. Word processors were used to prepare text, and page-layout or DTP programs were used to place and arrange text on the page. Today, the categories have blended together; most software that is touted as being in either category performs many or all of the functions typically found in the other category. Many of the fancy "extras" provided in some DTP programs today are either necessary only for specialized uses (e.g., color separations) or for processes that are often counter-productive from an instructional point of view (e.g., runarounds). Instructional designers of distance education materials will likely find that page-layout (DTP) software is not really necessary, since most "high-end" word processing programs provide virtually all the page-layout functionality they need.

A Few Practical Tips

Whatever software you use, there are some practices that will make your work easier and more efficient. Here are a few:

The Advantage of Working With WYSIWYG

It is a great advantage to be able to do your work in a computing environment that is WYSIWYG (pronounced *wissy-wig,* and derived from What You See Is What You Get). Fortunately, the computer industry is moving in the direction of becoming more WYSIWYG. Even if you have to use a small screen which allows you to see only a portion of an entire page at one time, the advantage of seeing exactly what you will be getting, in more-or-less actual size, is very facilitative of design and layout work.

Screen Size

Of course, having a screen that permits the display of a whole page (or even two pages, especially when laying out material that will be printed on both sides of the page) is best.

Keep it Electronic

Digitize as much as is reasonably possible. One of the greatest benefits to instructional designers of the DTP revolution is the ability to revise material quickly and inexpensively. Of course, this is facilitated greatly by having illustrations, as well as text, in electronic form. Currently, scanners and video digitizers are sufficiently affordable that even small instructional design units can own them. On the other hand, reason must prevail: If the materials are expected to have longevity, or if the software just isn't working as it is supposed to (and that *does* happen!), you may find it more expeditious to revert to scissors and glue-pot to accomplish your objective. Designers have been known to struggle with truculent software for a half day or more, trying to make it work the way it is supposed to (i.e., trying to keep everything in the document electronic), when a simple manual cut and paste could have done the job in two minutes.

Keep a Single Master

You can get yourself into a pack of trouble when there is more than one copy of a document floating around a work group. Of course, you should (no, you **must**!) keep backup copies, but establish a procedure that everyone involved can follow to ensure that there is only one master copy in existence. Ongoing work should be done on a copy of that master, and the master should be replaced with the updated copy only when all work is completed. This implies that some individual act as a controller, doling out "permission" to work on a given document to only one person at a time.

The Word Processor Is Not a Typewriter

Most teachers and instructional designers come to word processing and desktop publishing bringing along familiarity and experience with typewriters. This "baggage" can be both functional and dysfunctional when designing instructional print materials with DTP. There are a number of practices that are common to typewriter use that are dysfunctional to word processor use. They are too numerous to describe and defend in detail here, but are well covered by Williams (1990) and Misanchuk (1992). Among these are:

- Learn how to use the word processor's "ruler" (i.e., margin and word-wrap settings); they are different from those on a typewriter.
- If you touch the space bar twice or more in succession (even between sentences!), you are doing something wrong.
- If you touch the return key twice or more in succession (even between paragraphs!), there is probably a better way to do the job.
- Use the tab key rather than the space bar to accomplish horizontal spacing, but don't use tabs to emulate outdented word-wrapping.
- Use features such as "hard" and "soft" carriage returns, and non-breaking spaces, judiciously.
- Use the proper keys for numerals, ellipses (...), dashes (—), and bullets (•).
- Make use of style sheets, template documents, and glossaries or macros.

Breaking well-established typewriter-use habits and substituting proper word-processor-use habits may take a little work on your part, but you will save immeasurable time in the long run when you revise materials.

Integrating Text with Other Technologies

Although this chapter isolates text as a distance education medium, this is an opportune time to recall that text can be invaluable in a supporting role to other media, as well as in its frequent role as a primary medium of distance instruction. The low cost, permanence, and ease of traversal of text makes it an ideal accompaniment to instruction offered by televised, audio-conferencing, and computer-based methods. When such integration is contemplated, it is essential that the designer consider the text component from the outset of the project, rather than "tacking it on" near the end. Only through involvement in the entire project will the designer responsible for the text component be able to integrate the text component fully with other media used.

Interaction

As noted in the list of limitations of text, interaction is difficult to achieve. Print is largely a one-way communication medium. However, there are some devices that an instructional designer can employ to maximize the amount of interaction in distance education print materials. By and large, these consist of formalizing and codifying many pieces of information that are communicated via other means—sometimes non-verbal—to a typical learner in a classroom situation. Too, the kind of language used for distance education print materials is terribly important; properly used, language can entice learners into experiencing interactivity even within the confines of a largely one-way communication medium.

Some of the instructional design elements readily worked into print materials are described in this section, as are some tips for writing more effectively. Generic approaches to fostering interaction (e.g., using telephony, computer networking and electronic mail, developing "learning buddy" and proctor support systems), which can be effective in conjunction with print but are not unique to it, are discussed elsewhere in this book.

Instructional Design Elements

There are certain things—which are called here, for lack of a better term, instructional design elements—that can foster a feeling of interactivity. Some of these have to do with the way the course materials are introduced to the learner, others have to do with the way in which expectations are communicated. The use of examples and analogies, and the required application of newly-learned material are others. More elaborate and formal exercises and assignments, both self-corrected and instructor-evaluated, round out the possibilities.

Introduction to the Course

The very first thing a learner should see when he opens the package of materials is an introduction to the course. This may be a separate document, or the first number of pages of a larger document, and should contain a number of elements:

- *Welcome and overview.* Almost no instructor would think of walking into a classroom and begin teaching without first introducing herself, and probably doing the same for the subject-matter. No less should be done for distance education materials. Having the instructor provide a little background information about herself, both as a scholar or professional, and as an individual—a human being concerned with not only the subject-matter at hand, but also with mortgage payments, raising children, hot-rodding or gardening or some other hobby—sets the tone for establishing a dialogue between her and the learner.

By the same token, the content of the course should be put into perspective. After reading the welcome, learners should know how what they are about to learn in the course fits into the "big picture." Writing a welcome is just a matter of putting onto paper what you might say to a group of learners the first time you meet them in a classroom.

- *Goals and aims.* In a face-to-face course, the goals and aims of the course (in fairly general terms) are communicated to learners in a number of ways over a considerable period of time (i.e., over numerous class meetings). The instructor may make comments and asides that help clarify to learners what she considers important outcomes of the course. In print-based distance education, of course, these opportunities are absent, so it is important that the goals or aims of the course be set out clearly and completely at the beginning. Learners have a right to know early on what they are getting into.

- *Course map or table of contents.* A convenient device for communicating the structure and scope of a course is a course map or concept map (Waller, 1982), which displays the content to be covered in graphical or semi-graphical form. An alternative to a course map is a simple table of contents, which should be a minimum requirement.

- *Text(s) and/or additional materials needed.* Part of the introduction to the course should be a listing of any textbooks or ancillary learning materials that will be needed, whether included in the package of course materials or available separately. Instructions and sources for acquiring them should also be provided. Any conventions used (e.g., bibliographic format used in the course materials or required in assignments; abbreviations or acronyms used) should be explained.

- *Typographic/icon conventions used.* Other conventions, such as typographic cues (e.g., boldface terms can be found in the glossary) or icons used (e.g., the book icon refers you to a reading you are expected to do) should also be explained as part of the introduction to the course materials.

- *Assignments, examinations, and grading.* Learners should know exactly what will be expected from them in terms of assignments that must be submitted for grading by the instructor; how many examinations there will be, where they will be held and when, and what their nature will be (e.g., essay-type, short-answer, multiple choice); what the weight of each assignment and/or exam will be in terms of contribution to the final grade; and any other stipulations having to do with evaluation.

- *Pagination.* The pagination system, if other than the most common incremental system, should be explained, with an example. The

pagination scheme advocated earlier, which consists of the module or chapter number, followed by the page number, can be confusing to anyone who has not encountered it previously. (This doesn't mean you shouldn't use it, however. Just explain it first.)
- *Headings.* You should make a point of elaborating the heading system used, and pointing out how it can be used to contribute to the learner's understanding of the structure of the subject-matter.

Instructional Objectives and Other Means of Communicating Expectations

Instructional objectives (Mager, 1962; Gronlund, 1990) are a staple of instructional design—so much so that designers sometimes forget that there are other ways they can use to communicate expectations of learning to learners (e.g., self-assessment checklists, pre-tests, orienting questions, or a list of questions to be addressed by the module). Distance education students probably don't use instructional objectives in the manner in which they were intended to be used, according to some research (Macdonald-Ross, 1978). While the value of instructional objectives for helping SMEs and instructional designers clarify their own intentions is undeniable, their value for communicating those intentions to learners is less certain (Macdonald-Ross, 1978; Davies, 1976; Hartley & Davies, 1976). The important thing is that *some* means of communicating expectations of learning be used; the exact form is probably less critical.

Advance Organizers and Other "Contextualizers"

Since their introduction, advance organizers (Ausubel, 1963; Ausubel & Robinson, 1969) have been the subject of considerable research and debate. The research suggests that they don't always work, but neither should we expect them to in all cases (Jonassen, 1982). As with instructional objectives, there may be other ways of equally effectively capitalizing on learners' schemata (e.g., overviews, orienting questions, epitomes [Reigeluth, 1979], rationales [Canfield, 1968]). As with communicating expectations, it probably matters less exactly *how* it is done, than that it *is* done.

Examples

One extremely common flaw in print materials is not providing enough examples. One would think that this is so basic that it shouldn't require mention; unfortunately, perusal of any sample of print-based instructional materials—whether for distance education or otherwise—quickly shows that most teachers and writers don't use examples nearly often enough. This may not be such a big concern for classroom teachers, because they can, on the spur of the moment, concoct an example or two to illustrate a point which they perceive their students to be having difficulty with. In distance education, it becomes doubly important that the frequency and quality of examples is attended to in the first instance.

Analogies

Analogies have been shown through both experience and research to be powerful tools for assisting learners to incorporate new ideas into their existing schemata (Newby & Stepich, 1987). Like examples, analogies are easy to generate on the spot, when difficulty in understanding is detected. Since the detection is much more difficult in distance education (it may be delayed a great deal), it is best to make a conscious effort to provide analogies right from the beginning.

Processing and Application

Important contributions to the effectiveness of instruction are mental processing and the application of new ideas (i.e., practice). Many years ago, behavioral psychologists showed quite conclusively that activity and practice were important to learning. In subsequent years, however, in part due to the *malpractice* of practice and the ensuing trivialization of learner activity in programmed instruction, this notion has been forgotten. That mental processing and the application of learning is facilitative of learning, however, is beyond dispute (Salisbury, Richards, & Klein, 1985). Most writers of self-instructional materials could do a better job of providing for mental processing and application of new knowledge. Part of the reason may be that teachers are often accustomed to thinking about evaluation (which is closely related to practice) only well after instruction occurs. It takes conscious effort to ensure that knowledge presented, in appropriately-sized chunks, is followed immediately by some device that promotes thought about (processing) and application (practice) of the knowledge.

Writing for Instructional Materials

Writing for instructional materials is qualitatively different than writing for other purposes. By virtue of a post-secondary education, most of us write in a fairly scholarly manner—quite differently than we would speak to a class. Yet instruction frequently benefits from the use of language more like that used for speaking than for writing journal articles and books. Following are some tips for writing more appropriately for instructional materials; more elaborate justifications and explanations can be found in Felker, Pickering, Charrow, Holland, & Redish (1981), Jonassen (1982; 1985), Noble (1989), and Race (1989):

- Use short sentences.
- Avoid compound sentences.
- Avoid excess information in a sentence.
- Use the active voice.
- Use personal pronouns.
- Avoid nouns created from verbs; use action verbs.
- Keep equivalent items parallel.
- List conditions separately.
- Avoid multiple negatives.
- Use point form.
- Use familiar examples.
- Write as you would speak.

- Avoid unnecessary and difficult words.
- Avoid jargon; use technical terms only when necessary.
- Put sentences and paragraphs into a logical sequence: first things that affect many, then things that affect few; first the general, then the specific; first permanent provisions, then temporary ones.
- Avoid cultural and gender stereotyping.

Applying the suggestions above will probably not come naturally to you as you write. Furthermore, you may find colleagues and reviewers of your materials reacting negatively to the "different" language used. Remember, however, that you are doing this for the learner, not for those detractors, and continue to apply those rules of thumb as diligently as you can.

Case Study

The Problem

In Canada, the University of Saskatchewan Independent Studies Program serves a population of less than a million scattered over an area of a quarter-million square miles; about 40% is rural. Students are generally so dispersed that finding cohorts of even a half-dozen taking the same course in the same locale is quite rare.

Distance education evolved from a correspondence course program established in 1929. About 65 undergraduate degree and diploma courses make up the current calendar. Print-based courses outnumber televised and multi-mode courses by a ratio of 8:1. As the program evolved over the last decade, it became obvious that some degree of uniformity and quality control had to be built in. Consequently, instructional designers were given the responsibility of working with subject-matter experts to prepare course materials. For the last dozen years (and for the foreseeable future) university budgets were extremely tight: low-cost solutions were imperative. The use of print—but print with a difference, employing instructional design principles and capitalizing on emergent word-processing, desktop publishing, and xerographic reproduction technology—appeared virtually the only viable delivery option.

As the number of instructional designers involved in the enterprise grew, and began to include part-time and contract (i.e., non-resident) designers, it became increasingly difficult to communicate the evolving format specifications for courses. Full-time designers were settling on a format for course materials that included locally-prepared *Course Guides*, textbooks, and, frequently, ancillary readings (journal articles or portions of other texts). *Course Guides* generally favored a step-by-step approach to the course, providing an integration of the information typically found in a syllabus, suggestions on how to study the material, reading assignments, interactive exercises and self-check evaluations, and assignments to be sent in for grading. (Figure 3 shows a typical page from a *Course Guide*.) Supplementary text prepared by the subject-matter expert might also be part of the *Guide* if the textbooks and/or readings were deemed inadequate. *Course Guides* also began to incorporate some of the instructional design elements, access structure and orienting devices, and layout and design principles described throughout this chapter. However, their use was not uniform across courses or designers. As designers experimented with new elements (using formative evaluation information from students to aid their decision-making), they would apply them to newly-designed courses, but rarely have the opportunity to go back and incorporate them into existing courses. The result was that courses showed a distinct lack of uniformity in format and in quality.

A Solution

In an attempt to ensure that distance education print materials were done in a consistent way, a set of course design standards was developed for the program. The standards include reference to the following, often in considerable detail:

- why standards are necessary or desirable;
- how rigidly the standards should be interpreted;
- a description of the standard design environment (hardware/ software);
- the responsibilities of instructional designers in the course development process;
- a description of the standard components of the *Course Guide* and *Article Reprints* (instructor information, annual schedule, cover and title pages, table of contents, list of figures and tables, course introduction, standard module contents, optional module components);
- standard layout parameters (page size and orientation, margins, fonts, leading, banners, pagination, headings, figures and tables, indention, font variations, printing procedures);
- module design elements (module introductions, icons, mental processing adjuncts, white space, graphics, tables, color coding, reference lists, glossaries);
- copyright clearance procedures;
- using template documents.

The kind of information that might be included in the section on standard layout parameters, for example, is that all major headings are to be in 24-point bold Helvetica type, with 20 points of white space preceding them and 9 points of space following them, centered on the page; that minor headings be done flush left in 18-point Bookman type, with 9 points of white space preceding and 6 points following; etc. The standards might also describe what kinds of margins should be used, how pagination is to be done, and a host of similar details.

Standards must reflect local realities. The number of students involved, the type and level of subject-matter, institutional requirements, the number of sites (if group meetings form part of the educational experience), support personnel (proctors, tutors, etc.) involved, the delivery technologies used, the specific characteristics of equipment used for course material production—all these and more influence what the standards must address. Standards therefore should be devised locally, rather than adopted from elsewhere.

However, certain aspects of others' standards may be useful as starting points for helping formulate your own.

We found it easiest to have the standards developed first by an individual (although a *very* small group might be effective, too). All the instructional designers were then asked whether or not the standards were acceptable, and/or what needed to be added, deleted, or changed. The fundamental question was "Can you live with these standards?" If the question had been "How do you like these standards?," we probably would have generated a great deal of discussion and disagreement: Despite the advice in this chapter and elsewhere, many of the layout and design decisions are necessarily arbitrary (albeit within limits), and individual preferences come into play. The primary requirements for establishing useful standards, aside from advice and research findings such as elaborated in this chapter and in Misanchuk (1990), were common sense and the ability to identify the details that need to be considered.

Experience has shown that it is important that standards not be too restrictive, because the moment a rule is constructed, an exception to it will be identified. Rather, the standards should be detailed enough to ensure consistency, but flexible enough that a designer can exercise discretion to accomplish what is necessary in a given instance. Perhaps the greatest value of a set of document standards is that formulating them requires designers to confront document design and layout issues such as those raised throughout this chapter, make decisions about them, then apply them consistently to the documents they produce, rather than making them *ad hoc*.

Of course, design and layout standards do little good unless they are communicated to all people involved in course design. This usually means writing them out, although it is frequently useful to encode some layout standards in a template document, as well. We have found such written standards to be very useful when there are several designers working on courses in a given program, and especially when part-time or contract people are involved. While it is necessary to revise standards every couple of years, their very existence creates stability and consistency in the "look and feel" of the course materials.

Summary

Although decidedly not a "high-tech" medium, print has a number of very powerful advantages that make it a staple alternative for distance education materials. Print materials can be used in a variety of ways in distance education. Whatever form they take, however, distance education documents should have certain features (identified here as access structure and orienting devices) to make them more useful. These can include some combination of modularization, headings and titles, headers and footers, tables of content and lists of figures or tables, figure and table numbers, indented lists, indexes, glossaries, page numbers, color coding, and icons. A number of layout and design decisions need to be made during the creation of any print-based distance education materials; while some can be deferred, some are best made early in the process. A prime consideration is the likelihood that the materials will have to be revised in the near future. Other considerations include page size and format, the use of white space, positioning of figures and tables, and the typography to be used. Some tips and short-cuts are listed in this chapter that can facilitate the preparation of print-based distance education materials regardless of the sophistication of the software used to do it. Interaction with print-based distance education materials is relatively difficult to accomplish; however, a number of instructional design elements are identified which can ameliorate the problem. Writing distance education materials is different from writing journal articles, conference papers, and other kinds of documents that academics have had more experience with. For that reason, a number of specific suggestions are provided to facilitate the process. A case study, describing how and why a set of document-preparation standards was devised for the preparation of distance education print materials, rounds out the chapter.

References

Ausubel, D. P. (1963). *The psychology of meaningful verbal learning*. New York: Grune & Stratton.

Ausubel, D. P. & Robinson, F. G. (1969). *School learning: An introduction to educational psychology*. New York: Holt, Rinehart & Winston. Cited in Marland, P. W. & Store, R. E. (1982). Some instructional strategies for improved learning from distance teaching materials. *Distance Education, 3*(1), 72–106.

Brooks, L. W., Danserau, D. F., Spurlin, J. E. & Holley, C. D. (1983). Effects of headings on text processing. *Journal of Educational Psychology, 75*, 292–302.

Canfield, A. A. (1968). A rationale for performance objectives. *Audiovisual Instruction, 8*(2), 127–129.

Davies, I. K. (1976). *Objectives in curriculum design*. London: McGraw-Hill.

Davis, F. E., Barry, J. & Wiesenberg, M. (1986). *Desktop publishing*. Homewood, IL: Dow Jones-Irwin.

Felker, D. B., Pickering, F., Charrow, V. R., Holland, V. M. & Redish, J. C. (1981). *Guidelines for document designers*. Washington, DC: American Institutes for Research.

Gronlund, N. E. (1990). *How to write instructional objectives*. New York: Macmillan.

Gropper, G. L. (1991). *Text displays: Analysis and systematic design*. Englewood Cliffs, NJ: Educational Technology Publications, Inc.

Hartley, J. (1978). *Designing instructional text*. London: Kogan Page.

Hartley, J. (1982). Designing instructional text. In D. H. Jonassen (Ed.), *The technology of text: Principles for structuring, designing, and displaying text* (pp. 193–214). Englewood Cliffs, NJ: Educational Technology Publications.

Hartley, J. & Burnhill, P. (1977). Fifty guidelines for improving instructional text. *Programmed Learning and Educational Technology, 14*, 65–73.

Hartley, J. & Davies, I. K. (1976). Pre-instructional strategies. The role of pretests, behavioral objectives, overviews, and advance organizers. *Review of Educational Research, 46*, 239–265.

Hartley, J. & Jonassen, D. H. (1985). The role of headings in printed and electronic text. In D. H. Jonassen (Ed.), *The technology of text (volume two): Principles for structuring, designing, and displaying text* (pp. 237–263). Englewood Cliffs, NJ: Educational Technology Publications.

Hartley, J. & Trueman, M. (1983). The effects of headings in text on recall, search and retrieval. *British Journal of Educational Psychology, 53,* 205–214.

Hartley, J. & Trueman, M. (1985). A research strategy for text designers: The role of headings. *Instructional Science, 14,* 95–155.

Jonassen, D. H. (Ed.) (1982). *The technology of text: Principles for structuring, designing, and displaying text.* Englewood Cliffs, NJ: Educational Technology Publications.

Jonassen, D. H. (Ed.) (1985). *The technology of text (volume two): Principles for structuring, designing, and displaying text.* Englewood Cliffs, NJ: Educational Technology Publications.

Kleper, M. L. (1987). *The illustrated handbook of desktop publishing and typesetting.* Blue Ridge Summit, PA: Tab Books.

Lichty, T. (1989). *Design principles for desktop publishers.* Glenview, IL: Scott, Foresman and Co.

Macdonald-Ross, M. (1978). Language in text. In L. S. Shulman (Ed.), *Review of research in education, vol. 6.* Itasca, IL: F. E. Peacock.

Mager, R. F. (1962). *Preparing instructional objectives.* Palo Alto, CA: Fearon.

Misanchuk, E. R. (1989). *Learner preferences for typeface (font) and leading in print materials.* Saskatoon, SK: Division of Extension and Community Relations, The University of Saskatchewan. (ERIC Document Reproduction Service No. ED 307 854)

Misanchuk, E. R. (1990). *Standards and procedures for designing independent studies course materials at the University of Saskatchewan.* Saskatoon, SK: Extension Division, University of Saskatchewan.

Misanchuk, E. R. (1992). *Preparing instructional text: Document design using desktop publishing.* Englewood Cliffs, NJ: Educational Technology Publications.

Muncer, S. J., Gorman, B. S., Gorman, S. & Bibel, D. (1986). Right is wrong: An examination of the effect of right justification on reading. *British Journal of Educational Technology, 17,* 5–10.

Newby, T. J. & Stepich, D. A. (1987). Learning abstract concepts: The use of analogies as a mediational strategy. *Journal of Instructional Development, 10*(2), 20–26.

Noble, K. A. (1989). Good writing: What role for the educator? *British Journal of Educational Technology, 20,* 142–144.

Race, P. (1989). Writing to promote learning. *British Journal of Educational Technology, 20,* 215.

Reigeluth, C. M. (1979). In search of a better way to organize instruction: The elaboration theory. *Journal of Instructional Development, 2*(3), 8–15.

Salisbury, D. F., Richards, B. F. & Klein, J. D. (1985). Designing practice: A review of prescriptions and recommendations from instructional design theories. *Journal of Instructional Development, 8*(4), 9–19.

Sherow, S. & Wedemeyer, C. A. (1990). Origins of distance education in the United States. In D. R. Garrison & D. Shale (Eds.), *Education at a distance: From issues to practice* (pp. 7–22). Malabar, FL: Robert E. Krieger Publishing Co.

Spiegelman, M. (1987). Interior design for documents. *PC World,* March, 178–185.

Tinker, M. A. (1963). *Legibility of print.* Ames, IA: Iowa State University Press.

Tinker, M. A. (1965). *Bases for effective reading.* Minneapolis: University of Minnesota Press.

Tinker, M. A. & Patterson, D. G. (1928). Influence of type form on speed of reading. *Journal of Applied Psychology, 12,* 359–368.

Trollip, S. R. & Sales, G. (1986, January). *Readability of computer-generated fill-justified text.* Paper presented at the Annual Convention of the Association for Educational Communications and Technology, Las Vegas, NV.

Waller, R. H. W. (1979). Typographic access structures for educational texts. In P. A. Kolers, M. E. Wrolstad, & H. Bouma (Eds.), *Processing of visible language* (Vol. 1, pp. 175–187). New York: Plenum Press.

Waller, R. (1982). Text as diagram: Using typography to improve access and understanding. In D. H. Jonassen (Ed.), *The technology of text: Principles for structuring, designing, and displaying text* (pp. 137–166). Englewood Cliffs, NJ: Educational Technology Publications.

White, J. V. (1983). *Mastering graphics*. New York: Bowker.

Williams, R. (1990). *The Mac is not a typewriter*. Berkeley, CA: Peachpit Press.

Willis, B. (1993). *Distance education: A practical guide*. Englewood Cliffs, NJ: Educational Technology Publications.

Chapter 6

Audio Tools for Distance Education

Linda Lachance Wolcott

with assistance from Vicki S. Napper and Robert E. Lindsay

Distance education delivered through audio technology relies principally and often exclusively on voice communications for instruction. Labeled "the true interaction" by Garrison (1990, p. 16), audio interaction serves as the basis for much of distance delivery today. While some distance education systems use interactive television and satellite transmissions to provide greater options for visual interaction, audio communication is the mainstay of these telecommunications systems. Few systems of electronic delivery operate without a strong oral component.

This chapter focuses on distance instruction that is delivered live and interactively by audio technologies. The goal is to provide the reader with a foundation on which to build effective practice. To that end, the author takes an approach that is both reflective and practical. The chapter begins with a description of those features that make audio delivery unique and challenging, and follows with recommendations for reflecting on practice. The third section offers strategies drawn from research and practice to meet the challenges. The chapter concludes with an extended example that illustrates some of the strategies in action.

An Overview of Audio Applications in Distance Education

Distance education in the form of correspondence study has a formal history of approximately 150 years. While correspondence was and continues to be an important and flexible form of education (Van Kekerix & Andrews, 1991), advances in communication technologies have come to provide alternative delivery options that supplement and often replace it (Moore & Thompson, 1990). Audio enhancements and alternatives include: radio, pre-recorded media, and telephone.

Radio provided the earliest means of delivering education apart from the classroom setting. The University of Iowa and the University of Wisconsin were among the colleges and universities to broadcast courses by radio in the early part of the century. The University of Iowa, which began offering radio courses in 1911, discontinued the service in 1928. The University of Wisconsin, however, met with greater success, initiating radio courses in 1919. This service led to the creation of WHA, the first federally licensed educational broadcasting station, which continues today to provide radio courses through its "University of the Air." Early attempts at educational radio broadcasting were often plagued by interference from and competition with commercial radio stations. Eventually, radio as a medium for delivering distance education in the United States declined despite FCC allocation of educational AM and FM channels in the 1940s and 1950s. Today, though widespread in developing countries, the use of radio is limited in the United States (Office of Technology Assessment, 1989) due in part to its lack of interactivity and the proliferation of video technologies. Both Alaska and Australia use two-way interactive radio for distance education.

Pre-recorded instruction on phonograph records, audio tapes, and audio cassettes provides other audio delivery options. These technologies are used much like correspondence courses and in combination with them. For example, records, tapes, and cassettes have been used extensively to teach foreign languages. Though assessments of their current use in the United States are contradictory (see Takemoto, 1987; Lewis, 1985), pre-recorded audio components have been an integral part of distance instruction provided through the British Open University (Verduin & Clark, 1991). In the future, compact discs may offer greater options when used independently as sources of audio instruction or interactively with other media to store and retrieve large amounts of data.

Since the 1970s, telephone technology has been the preeminent mode of audio delivery. Today, audio instruction in the United States extensively utilizes the public telephone network. The divestiture of American Telephone & Telegraph (AT&T) and federal mandates for equal access to education have provided the motivation for state educational institutions to use teleconferencing technologies to deliver elementary and secondary school instruction as well as certification programming for educators at a distance (Office of Technology Assessment, 1989). Telephone technologies to provide education and training range from the common telephone conference calls to more sophisticated transmissions of visual and data enhancements to supplement voice communications. For example, a pioneer in audio-based delivery, the University of Wisconsin–Extension, continues its commitment to distance education with the Education Telephone Network (ETN) and the Statewide Extension Network (SEEN). Currently, computer technologies can augment telephone systems with simultaneous voice and data transmissions to provide even greater opportunities for delivering audio-based distance education.

Audioconferencing Technologies for Distance Education

Using public telephone lines to hold electronic meetings and to provide access to education and training opportunities is a form of teleconferencing. Teleconferencing links people at two or more locations in an electronic conversation that takes place in real time; hence, it is both synchronous and interactive. While a number of technologies such as television, satellite, cable, microwave, and computer systems can facilitate audio communications, telephone technology remains a common means of providing instruction at a distance in business and education communities. Two types of telephone formats are currently used: analog and digital. Analog telephone service has been the primary source of communication since the development of the public telephone network. An analog signal is a continuous electrical signal transmitted electronically in a form resembling a spoken word. Analog telephone systems are used primarily to send voice messages. Digital transmission of electrical signals through telephone circuits is an emerging technology. Digital signals differ from analog in that they are sent as discrete binary signals, while analog signals have continuously varying or wave-like signals. Digital networks enable faster switching and have the capacity to simultaneously transmit voice, data, and compressed video signals over the same line.

Audio-based teleconferencing called audioconferencing or audio teleconferencing consists of two types: (1) communication that is audio-only, and (2) communication in which the audio communication is supported or enhanced by image or data transmissions—audiographic conferencing. Teleconferencing by audio differs from other audio technologies in that communication is interactive, that is, interaction flows back and forth between participants who act alternately as sender and receiver. Audio communication such as radio broadcasts (with the exception of short wave radio) and pre-recorded tapes is limited to the transmission of a message in one direction—from a sender to a receiver. In addition to facilitating two-way communication, audio-based teleconferencing occurs in a synchronous rather than asynchronous manner. Asynchronous communication is delayed by hours, days, or perhaps weeks. For example, in an asynchronous system, a student may listen to a radio broadcast or an audio recording and respond by making a recording of her own or by exchanging messages with the teacher using voice or electronic mail. Synchronous communication is live, permitting participants to communicate without delay.

Audio-Only Conferencing

According to Ostendorf (1989), the audio-only system is the simplest and most prevalent means of delivering distance education. Audio-only conferencing can be classified as simplex, quasi- or half-duplex, and full-duplex. All three systems allow two-way communication, but not necessarily simultaneously. Communication in a simplex system flows in one direction at a time. Half-duplex systems are similar, yet faster switching makes it easier for parties to interrupt and to change the directional flow of the communication. Full-duplex systems permit simultaneous two-way communication as in a telephone conversation. Because participants interact without delay, audioconferencing "offers the interaction format most like the traditional classroom" (Ostendorf, 1989, p. 9).

The transmission of audio signals is typically accomplished by the use of analog transmission technologies utilizing the public telephone network. Standard home or office telephone sets and speaker phones are adequate for conversations involving two parties; but when three or more parties participate, additional devices are required to facilitate a larger group and to reduce noise and interference such as echo. Components of a typical audio-only conferencing arrangement include: (1) telephone hand sets, speaker phones, or microphones; (2) an audio bridge that interconnects multiple phone lines and controls noise; and (3) a speaker device to facilitate multiple interactions. Institutions either purchase an on-site bridge system or use commercial audio bridging services. Through its bridging system, the site hosting the conference may call participants individually, connecting them to the conference, or participants may directly call into the bridge in what is known as a "meet-me" teleconference. A bridging service provides the same function where there is no bridge on site. Some settings where audioconferencing use is heavy among specific sites have dedicated teleconferencing or "hot" lines for which no dialing is required.

Audio-only conferencing offers the advantage of live interactivity at a relatively low cost in a medium based on a familiar and available technology. Widely dispersed participants can communicate directly, engaging in discussion and providing one another with verbal feedback. Systems are cost-effective and can be combined with peripherals to supplement voice communication with print, video and data communication. Among the disadvantages of teleconferencing by audio, Willis (1992) lists: initial resistance from users unfamiliar with the technology, the potential for communication to be impersonal sans nonverbal cues, and a restriction on the type of content that can be delivered.

Audiographic Conferencing

Audiographic conferencing combines technologies for voice communication with those that allow image or data transmissions. While voice remains the primary communication medium, audiographic technologies transmit pictorial or electronic data using regular telephone lines to both supplement and enhance the audio message. Various audiographic peripherals provide the visual component; they include the facsimile machine (fax), electronic blackboard, still video technology, and the personal computer.

Audiographic devices such as these reduce the amount of time required to send printed materials by mail or courier and facilitate the simultaneous transmission of voice and data on a single telephone line. Because they add another dimension of interaction, audiographic components can introduce more immediate feedback into audioconferencing. The relative disadvantage (a point open to controversy) remains that audiographic systems, lacking full-motion, are not fully interactive.

Facsimile (fax) machines. Widely used in applications such as business and law enforcement, fax machines transmit documents or printed images. In distance education, the use of fax machines facilitates the sending and receiving of instructional materials and assignments, as well as the exchange of personal communication. Fax machines are photocopiers that scan an image at one copier and use a telephone connection to transmit the information necessary to reproduce the image on paper at another copier. Fax machines are favored because of their availability, low cost and ability to deliver information more quickly than by mail. The disadvantage of facsimile machines occurs in terms of interaction: there is a slight delay in the transmission of printed materials, hence they are not the best choice for real-time interaction. Additionally, the quality of copies varies among machines.

Electronic blackboards. Electronic blackboards are one of the earliest enhancements to audio-only conferencing. As with the customary blackboard, the instructor writes or draws on the pressure-sensitive board. The image is translated into a series of coordinates that is transmitted to the receiving sites on a telephone line separate from the voice line. The incoming signal is displayed in black and white on a television monitor. With appropriate equipment at the receiving sites, students can also respond using the electronic blackboard. The electronic blackboard is an attractive option in education because it closely resembles a medium to which teachers are accustomed. The primary advantage of electronic blackboards is real-time writing; there are disadvantages in terms of legibility, however. The quality of the image is subject to both the quality of the monitor on which the image is displayed and on the quality of the instructor's handwriting. Images must conform to TV ratio (3:4) and to the limited viewing area displayed on monitors at the receiving sites. The electronic blackboard requires writing larger and perhaps more clearly than normal. As a result, less information can be displayed on the screen than on a traditional blackboard.

Video images. Still video images can enhance audioconferences (for information on full-motion video conferencing, see Chapter 7). Known variously as still-frame, slow-scan, or freeze-frame, these video-based systems capture a single image and transmit that still or "frozen" message to the receiving sites. The image, which can be that of an illustration, a three-dimensional object, or a person (typically the instructor), is "shot" with a video camera. The image, akin to a snapshot or slide, is generally sent over a separate telephone line and regenerated on a video monitor at the receive sites in a scanning motion that recreates the image in approximately 15–30 seconds. Both black and white and color systems are available.

Still video systems have numerous advantages: they are convenient, easy to use, and affordable. Since they are relatively portable and built to be compatible with and utilize existing telephone technology, slow-scan systems can be used virtually anywhere there is a telephone and electrical power. The obvious instructional advantage offered by still video systems is the ability to transmit visual images that allow a wider range of options for illustrating an idea or showing examples. If the equipment is available at both the originating and the receiving sites, the instructor and students can exchange visual messages. Widner (1990) suggests that still-image systems may be superior to full-motion systems in terms of interactivity.

The obvious disadvantages are that still video systems transmit a delayed image without motion. Limited by a 3:4 TV ratio and by the quality of television monitors at the receive end, images generally have low resolution and may lose clarity during transmission. Transmission time may also be a factor; for example, color images take longer to transmit than black and white images. Communication among sites can be slowed considerably if one telephone line is used for both conversation and the transmission of visuals. The lack of full-motion video can be overcome by distributing copies of pre-recorded video tapes or disks to be played at each site independent of the delivery system or instructional time. In such cases, it is mandatory to secure permission from the copyright holder to copy and distribute tapes (see Chapter 11 concerning copyright issues). Systems such as the electronic blackboard and slow-scan can be used in combination to augment audioconferencing.

Widner (1990) notes that the use of slow-scan teleconferencing is not widespread and may, in fact, have declined since the early 1980s. While they will likely continue to be displaced by newer technologies that allow full-motion video, slow-scan technologies, as assessed by Bransford in 1984, had yet to reach their potential.

Computers. Computer technologies provide a means of enhancing audioconferencing by transmitting both images and data over telephone lines. Combined with voice capabilities, computer-based systems permit the use of a variety of visual images and allow writing without transmission delays. Computer-based systems offer advantages over slow-scan technologies in terms of additional visual stimuli, more immediate interaction, and improved visual quality. The computer keyboard and a graphics or writing tablet are the counterparts to the electronic blackboard; output from these devices typically share a common display on a monitor at the other sites. The instructor can prepare materials in advance, store and retrieve pre-recorded data and still video images, and transmit them in class much as teachers use overhead transparencies. With a computer at each site, users can exchange and annotate text and visual data live or by transferring information to and from disks. Data such as instructional materials and records of instructional transactions can be exchanged in printed form or conveyed through a modem.

On the downside, audiographic conferencing is more hardware intensive, requiring computer and video components and perhaps an additional phone line. For successful audiographic conferencing, participants need to be well-versed in the use of peripherals, especially the computer. In Johnstone and Gilcher's assessment (1989), computer-based audiographic systems constitute a "major development in low-cost, fully interactive communication technologies" (p. 59) whose use is increasing.

Audio-based systems are widely used to add real-time interaction to distance instruction. Their popularity can be attributed to their comparatively low cost to install, operate, and maintain. Because they use available telephone technology, audio-based systems can potentially go anywhere. There is the added advantage that this technology is generally familiar to teachers and students and is relatively easy to use. When full-motion is not required, audio-based systems are effective in allowing live interaction among participants. However, teaching through an audio-based system does require a considerable investment of time and energy in planning, preparation, and teaching. The following section outlines the major challenges and offers solutions to guide the design and teaching of courses delivered using an audioconferencing system.

The Challenges of Audioconference Teaching

In many ways, distance teaching is similar to teaching face-to-face. Yet the experiences of teaching and learning at a distance are different because participants are separated from one another and their communication is mediated, typically by electronic means. These conditions change the role of the teacher (Beaudoin, 1990) and the nature of the transactions between the teacher and the learners (Dewal, 1988; Rumble, 1989). In audioconferencing, the difference is readily apparent because the visual channel that typically carries much of the instructional and interpersonal messages is absent or significantly modified. This aspect of audioconferencing is its defining characteristic and sets it apart from face-to-face and other modes of distance education.

The lack of a visual component results in the loss of information ordinarily derived from sources such as seeing the gestures and facial expressions of the speaker and other participants, observing a demonstration of a process or the manipulation of objects, and viewing instructional materials. The abilities to both convey messages and to relate interpersonally is strained when the participants cannot see one another. Ironically, the delivery mode intended to actuate communication across distances can itself set up obstacles to communication. More in this environment than in a face-to-face setting, there is the potential for increased interpersonal distance, reduction in the amount and frequency of interaction, loss of feedback, and interference in the transfer of messages.

Increased Interpersonal Distance

Interpersonal distance refers to perceived closeness among participants. Feelings of psychological closeness decrease as one moves from an information rich environment (such as face-to-face conversation) to an information lean environment where sensory channels are reduced as in audioconferencing (Wellens, 1986). Lacking both physical proximity and a visual reference, participants find it difficult to establish a rapport. Greater interpersonal distance is a threat to identifying and communicating with one's peers. Learning alone or in a small group, students may feel isolated and lack a sense of belonging. This is particularly true when, in addition to students distributed among a number of remote sites, there are students present with the teacher at the origination site.

Reduction in the Amount and Frequency of Interaction

Patterns of communication in distance education differ from those of face-to-face instruction because of the separation of learners, mediated communication, and the lack of nonverbal cues (Zvacek, 1991). Specifically, increased interpersonal distance contributes to less spontaneous interaction

(Wellens, 1986), while the necessity of communicating through telecommunications technology can impede the free-flowing conversation.

It is common for teachers to notice less interaction when teaching distance courses than in face-to-face classes (Gilcher & Johnstone, 1988). Various devices such as push-to-talk microphones can make the act of communicating awkward or one-sided. Unaccustomed to using the communication technologies for instruction, participants often feel intimidated and self-conscious as did students in Burge and Howard's study (1990). Students' reticence also threatens spontaneity and lessens the amount and frequency of interaction between the teacher and among the students themselves. Indeed, Sponder (1990) cites student-to-student interaction as the least utilized pattern of communication in audioconferencing. With less spontaneous interaction, teachers have a tendency to fill air time with lecture, pausing infrequently to ask or allow questions. Students are inclined to react passively, reluctant to interrupt with questions.

Loss of Feedback

Coincident with the reduction in interaction is the loss of feedback resulting primarily from the absence of nonverbal communications. In teaching, faculty members traditionally rely on nonverbal means such as eye contact, facial expressions, and body language to gauge the reactions of the students: a puzzled look prompts them to rephrase, clarify or make connections more explicit, while a nod of the head lets them know the point has gotten across. By indicating the degree of success in the transmission of the message, these nonverbal cues help regulate the pace and contribute to both the success and spontaneity of the instructional transaction. Without feedback, communication is inhibited. Sponder (1990) observes that audioconferencing compounds miscommunication by impeding participants' ability to predict and gauge the success of their messages and by providing fewer opportunities to correct mistaken messages if, in fact, a mistake is recognized.

Interference in Message Transfer

Considering that over 80% of what people learn comes from what they see (Heinich, Molenda, & Russell, 1989), audioconference learners are at a disadvantage. Learning which emphasizes listening and excludes or greatly diminishes visual communication taxes the learner's capacity to attend to the instructional message. Students are, for the most part, without visual reference points. Their success in audioconferencing is often defined by the proficiency of their listening skills, as well as by their ability to learn independently.

With emphasis on the verbal message, greater demands are placed on the organization and presentation of content. Lacking nonverbal cues and with feedback diminished, there is a greater likelihood that messages may be misinterpreted (Neumann, 1986). Comprehension can be threatened when messages are limited in their form, frequency, and immediacy (Garrison, 1989). Moreover, it has been suggested that technology-based instruction might be unsuitable for fostering creative thinking (Heinzen & Alberico,

1990) and may, in fact, be a hindrance to cognitive growth (Wiesner, 1983) due to the demands placed on attention and to the loss of contact, respectively.

Distance teaching raises new issues and places new demands on teachers and learners. Indeed, the absence of a visual modality introduces obstacles that in teaching and learning face-to-face one does not necessarily encounter. To minimize the effects resulting from the loss of visual communication, teachers are challenged in audioconferencing to:

- reduce interpersonal distance,
- nurture interaction,
- increase feedback, and
- enhance learning and message transfer.

Distance teaching is a departure from the familiar (Massoumian, 1989) and, as such, represents what Schön (1983) describes as an unstable situation of practice. These situations present new problems for which one's routine approach is challenged. What has worked in the past, may not be adequate for dealing with the unique situation presented. As suggested by a number of distance educators (e.g., Ohler, 1989; Sparkes, 1983), customary classroom practices applied in the audioconference environment may fail to effectively bridge the distance. Teachers may find that the skills are not the same (Knapper, Lumsden, & Stubbs, 1985); solving problems posed by distance teaching requires more than experience with face-to-face teaching (Sparkes, 1983). There is no simple prescription. Meeting the challenges presented by audioconference teaching necessitates both thoughtful planning and skillful deployment of planned strategies. The following sections propose two approaches to addressing the challenges posed by audioconference teaching. The first suggests that teachers reflect on their practice, and the second offers specific strategies for meeting the major challenges of audioconference teaching.

Meeting the Challenges Through Reflection

One solution to adapting to a unique or unstable environment is to reflect on practice. Schön (1983) describes reflection as a process through which people think about what they are doing and "turn thought back on action" (p. 50). Reflecting on the practice of teaching requires scrutiny of one's underlying philosophies of education and teaching—examining assumptions and questioning preconceptions about learners; about one's role, approach, and methods; and about the teaching/learning process. Reflection is an integral part of planning and an essential component of effective teaching (Romberg, 1980). Planning has several dimensions: it is both a mental activity in which one thinks about the variables involved in teaching, and a practical activity in which one puts ideas and abstractions into a plan to guide action (Clark & Peterson, 1986).

Haughey (1983) cautions that distance education, in general, "causes one to re-examine one's dearly held views on teaching and learning" (p. 12). The significance of planning in audioconference teaching is underscored in interviews with distance teachers (Gilcher & Johnstone, 1988; Ohler, 1989; and Wolcott, 1991). Both novice and veteran distance teachers attest to the time and energy involved, as well as to the benefits derived from planning distance courses. Further, reflecting on audioconference teaching has been found to be beneficial beyond the distance setting. Faculty members teaching on Utah State University's audiographic COM-NET system were among those who reported improvements in their on-campus teaching as a result of rethinking the same course when taught at a distance (Gilcher & Johnstone, 1988; Wolcott, 1991). In preparing to teach via audio-based systems, teachers should reflect on the challenges with respect to the context, the learners, and the methods and procedures they employ.

Reflecting on Context

Altered by the separation of participants, mediated by the use of telecommunications technology, and lacking visual modality, the teaching environment takes on a new complexion. Within this environment of microphones, telephones, monitors, and electronic writing devices, there is both the facilitation of communication and the potential to inhibit it. While telecommunication technologies provide a means of linking a widely dispersed group of students, such technologies exert an influence on the teaching and learning process. After interviewing numerous distance teachers nationwide, Gilcher and Johnstone (1988) found that the technology of audioconference teaching impacted course content, the method of instruction, the degree of interactivity among participants, and the quality of both the instructor's and the students' performance.

To teach effectively, teachers have to acknowledge a changed environment and its contextual influences. Specifically, they have to work within the capabilities of the medium and adapt to the limitations it imposes on their approach to instruction. Faculty can acquire a feel for the context and experience of distance teaching and learning by:

- talking with distance teachers and reading about others' experiences;
- observing distance taught classes, particularly from the students' point of view;
- learning about the capabilities and limitations of the equipment and practicing with it;
- talking with administrative, technical personnel, and site facilitators to become familiar with the routines and procedures; and
- talking with distance students to identify their needs and concerns.

In reflecting on the context, distance teachers should ask themselves questions such as the following:

- What are my expectations of this delivery medium?
- What can I count on to be the same and what will be different about teaching and learning in this environment?
- Can the objectives I have for this course be adequately met in this context?
- What are the influences, both positive and negative, on learning in this setting?
- How do I make maximum use of this medium while minimizing its limitations?

Reflecting on Learners

Because distance teaching is different from conventional classroom teaching, learning at a distance is likewise different for students participating in the instructional experience by electronic means. Students in programs which are chiefly audio experience learning differently and thus have a different perspective from students who are not separated from the locus of instruction.

To begin to effectively bridge the gaps between classroom and distance teaching, faculty need to look at distance teaching and learning from the students' point of view. They need to be aware of and sensitive to the psychological, social, and technical obstacles that distant learners face. For example, separated by distance, students often suffer "the loneliness of the long-distance learner" (Thiagarajan, 1978, p. 22). They have fewer opportunities for contact with their instructor, both formally in class or more casually outside of class meetings. Geographically dispersed, distant students lack contact with students at other locations and often the support of a peer learning group. Students can feel isolated from or second class citizens to students present with the teacher at the origination site.

Under the weight of quasi-independent learning, students encounter cognitive challenges as well; they are challenged to be self-motivated and self-disciplined. They have to hone their listening skills to attend to audio-carried messages and to assert themselves as active participants in the learning process. A constant danger in audioconference teaching is that students—unseen—may become invisible to the instructor. Projecting oneself into the students' frame of reference can help to identify with students' needs and concerns. Experiencing distance learning from the other side of the microphone can provide suggestions for drawing students together as a learning community.

Since the distant learners in higher education are typically adults, teachers should give prominent consideration to the characteristics of adults as learners. As Knowles (1984) contends, adult learners differ from the more traditional college students in several unique ways. They are characterized as self-directed and intrinsically motivated, endowed with a wealth of experience, and inclined toward practical and immediate application of the information they have acquired. Distance education speaks to adults because of its convenience and economy; their needs, motivations and learning attributes become paramount in planning distance instruction. To guide reflecting on learners, ask yourself:

- What are students' needs and what do they expect from this course?
- What do I know (and how can I find out) about the students' entry skills, cognitive styles and background?
- What do students find motivating about instruction?
- How can I build on students' experiences and provide instruction that is relevant and applicable?
- How do I assure the students a quality learning experience?

Reflecting on Methods

A growing body of research identifies teacher behaviors and instructional strategies that make a difference in student achievement (see Brophy & Good, 1986). A major conclusion of the teacher-effects research holds that "what constitutes effective instruction varies with context" (p. 370). In audioconference teaching, then, it is not safe to assume that a teacher who is good at teaching in a face-to-face setting is equally as good at teaching in distance settings. Nor is it safe to automatically apply preferred face-to-face techniques considering repeated warnings that the transition from one context to the next is not necessarily a natural nor easy one (Haughey, 1983; Sparkes, 1983; Sponder, 1990). Audioconference teachers must adapt to an instructional environment for which customary instructional practice may be inadequate.

In planning instruction, faculty in higher education emphasize the selection of content (Stark *et al.*, 1988). But more than considering what to cover, teachers should also reflect on methods by analyzing the rationale for and the effectiveness of the instructional strategies they employ. They should think about the desired outcomes and the expectations they hold of their students and ask: What are the optimal means of fulfilling goals and expectations? Is there congruence between goals and the means through which they are achieved? If, for example, one expects to develop critical thinkers, it is inappropriate to test primarily for comprehension and recall.

Distance educators caution against simply replicating traditional methods used in a face-to-face setting (e.g., Haughey, 1983; Knapper, 1988). Considering Sparkes' (1983) admonition that "successful face-to-face teaching methods do not readily translate to the distance teaching mode" (p. 183), it becomes especially important for prospective distance teachers to explore alternative strategies for teaching within a distance framework. Ask:

- Am I considering methods because they are familiar and comfortable?
- Are the methods under consideration those which utilize the medium to its best advantage or are they attempts to reproduce face-to-face instruction?
- What strategies would optimally achieve expectations in light of the variables of students, content, and context?
- What adjustments are required to accommodate instructional activities and visuals to audioconferencing delivery?
- Are the methods and techniques likely to encourage participation and interaction?

Meeting the Challenges Through Design

Reflecting on the nature of and interaction among the context, the learners, and methods in a distance teaching situation is requisite to further planning. Answers to questions such as those posed above are the foundation for designing a course that anticipates and accommodates the challenges of audioconference teaching. From reflection, specific strategies can be devised for reducing interpersonal distance, nurturing interaction, increasing feedback, and enhancing learning and message transfer.

Reducing Interpersonal Distance

Physical separation and the absence of visual communication among participants can increase psychological distance, posing some unique challenges to learners. But as Garrison (1990) contends, "Physical distance of the student does not necessitate a cognitive and affective separation from the teacher.... Distance education should not, and does not, have to be viewed as a shearing away of a sense of belonging to a larger group" (p. 23). The key to group identity and cohesion is to establish and maintain a rapport between teacher and students and among the students themselves. Lacking nonverbal strategies such as eye contact and facial expressions, teachers in audio-based systems must find alternative means of establishing rapport. The following techniques have been utilized by distance teachers to build rewarding teaching/learning relationships unhindered by distance.

Establish a climate for learning. In outlining steps for planning programs for adult learners, Knowles and Associates (1984) advocate creating a climate conducive to learning which addresses both physical and psychological dimensions. These suggestions are especially pertinent to audioconferencing programs where visual stimulation and familiarity with the teaching/learning environment may be lacking. Baird and Monson (1988) refer to the concept of creating a conducive climate as humanizing, "the creation of an environment which emphasizes the importance of the individual and which overcomes any sense of distance by generating a feeling of group rapport" (p. 37). Humanizing involves conveying a personal interest in your students as well as creating an atmosphere which is non-threatening and in which students are treated equally and with respect. Students in Burge and Howard's (1990) study indicated that peer behavior along with technology performance were as important for a good instructional experience as were the instructor's attitudes and skills. The following are among the suggestions for creating a conducive learning environment.

Address "creature comforts." To the degree that you have control over such elements, see that the ventilation, temperature, lighting, noise level, and seating arrangement do not interfere with students' learning at the various sites. Work with technical staff to insure the quality of visual and voice transmissions. If a session runs longer than an hour, take a ten minute break each hour.

Set ground rules. On the first day of class, instruct students in the proper use of the communication equipment and establish a protocol for commenting and asking questions. For example, how do students signal that they have a question? Can students interrupt the teacher or other students? Set limits to the amount of time a student can "tie-up" the system.

Learn students' names. A particularly effective technique to build rapport is to learn and to use students' names. Create a list of students at each site and share it with the class. Use the list to address students by name and to direct questions and comments to them specifically. Getting to know students' names is both a sign of respect and an indication of interest and caring which reduces distance and heightens rapport. Perhaps no single behavior does more to tell students that you care about them as individuals than taking the time to learn and use their names.

Get acquainted. Most teachers want to know about their students. Whether the information is used to determine course objectives, to develop relevant examples and activities, or for purely humanistic reasons, learning about your students is an important part of teaching. In distance education, it is often difficult to get information about students before the course begins. Some techniques for becoming better acquainted with students include the following:

Send out introductory materials. Prior to the first class meeting, mail prospective students materials about the course or program. Materials might include a course syllabus, suggestions for making the most of distance learning, or a welcoming letter in which you introduce yourself and the goals you have set. One teacher sent a photo of herself along with a biographical statement to her students (Rezabek, Nordmann, & Shaeffer, 1989).

Hold introductions. At the first meeting of the class, have students introduce themselves to one another; ask them to share some background information including personal and professional interests as well as their goals and expectations for the course. Introductions break down barriers to communication as students discover characteristics they have in common. Additionally, introductions perform the important function of acquainting students with the teleconferencing equipment and getting them talking on the system under conditions of minimal risk. Don't forget to introduce yourself!

Collect student data. Some teachers request a data sheet, a brief student biography, and/or a photograph as other means of learning about their students and of increasing the human element in audioconferencing. Together with introductions, collecting information about students can build a profile of students' characteristics and learning styles. During the term, call on students to share their experiences and look for commonalities among their diverse backgrounds and goals. Capitalize on students' experiences by drawing background information into discussions and examples.

Break the ice. In addition to introductions, other ice-breaking activities can function as rapport-builders. Initial low-risk games, simulations, and small group activities can get students acquainted and interacting while reducing anxieties. Informal conversation and humor can help break down barriers, but humor should be used cautiously because it is so subjective.

Take daily attendance. You can do so formally through a roll call or informally by asking questions and engaging students in casual conversation before and after class or during breaks. Until you are familiar with individual voices, ask students to identify themselves and their site each time they ask a question or comment.

Meet face-to-face. Circumstances permitting, schedule a face-to-face session including as many participants as possible. Some programs conduct orientations or hold occasional seminars requiring participants to congregate at a central location. A widely-used and recommended alternative is for the instructor to visit participating sites and originate from them when possible.

Nurturing Interaction

Moore (1989) identifies three types of interaction: (1) learner-to-content, (2) learner-to-teacher, and (3) learner-to-learner. With experience, instruction achieves a certain flow in which the exchange among faculty and students is quite seamless and natural. This spontaneous dynamic of presentation, questioning, discussion, and responding develops as participants, familiar with the classroom environment and protocol, become engaged in learning. Because teachers are intimately familiar with classroom teaching, they can take a lot for granted about the dynamics of the instructional interchange in a distance setting. Teaching via a system that lacks real time, two-way visual communication can upset the spontaneous dynamic that teachers have come to expect. Achieving a similar quality of interaction in audioconferencing is more difficult; and though it sounds contradictory, interaction must be planned or (in the words of an experienced distance teacher) "orchestrated." There are many strategies that distance teachers have successfully utilized to nurture interaction among participants.

Encourage participation. One of the main concerns that novice distance teachers have is how to engage students in their learning. The answer is to challenge them to inquire, to think critically about what they are learning, and to interact with course materials and with other members of the class. The following strategies are designed to encourage participation.

Use a variety of active learning techniques. Engage students in discussing, debating, or role playing. These techniques require students to not only talk with you, but also to interact with instructional materials and one another. Activities that involve student-to-student communication and intra-group exchange can foster a sense of learning community and reduce the students' dependence on the instructor as the source of their learning. Practitioners recommend a number of student-centered techniques, many of which can be undertaken as individual or small group activities.

For example, assign the responsibility for a particular question, activity, or portion of discussion to a specific individual or group (Monson, 1978). A group can consist of students from the same site, or can be formed by combining several sites or mixing students from various sites. With groups, designate a discussion leader and/or a reporter. Depending on group configuration and logistical constraints, students can work on the assignment in several smaller conferences during class time, or off-air between one class meeting and another or throughout the term. Here's an opportunity to use interactive capabilities to advantage. Where interactive writing is available have students write their own questions and comments or annotate graphics that the instructor has displayed. Shale and Garrison (1989) found that "the 'best' interaction occurred when students were able to use the technology actively as a tool in their participation" (p. 7).

Segment instruction into shorter blocks that vary the type, pace, and focus of activity. For example, alternate blocks of time when you are lecturing with blocks in which students are meeting in small groups to discuss a question that you or other students have posed. Dividing instruction also reduces the strain of listening for extended periods of time; Monson (1978) suggests limiting concentrated listening to blocks of 10-15 minutes. Johnstone and

Gilcher (1989) note that the more successful instructors combine lecture and interaction.

Build activities into the course manual or syllabus that encourage independent study and bridge to class activities where knowledge and skills are applied and elaborated through interaction with peers. Study or discussion questions focus students' attention on the important concepts, and also serve as a framework for group interaction.

Ask questions. Skillful teachers know when to ask questions, what questions to ask, how to ask, and how to respond. Where visual cues are absent, questioning becomes the primary means of obtaining feedback from students and drawing them into an instructional dialogue. Here, the phrasing and type of question are important. For example, asking rhetorical, non-directed questions such as, "Does everyone understand?" or "Are there any questions?" is not likely to generate a lot of participation. Rather, questions should be specific and directed as in, "Susan, what parallels do you see between A's theory of B and X's theory of Y?" Likewise, questions that are open-ended (as in the previous example) encourage students to respond in greater detail than does a closed or forced-choice question. Additionally, ask questions for which there is no right or wrong answer—questions that allow students to engage in some original thinking as in, "If it were up to you, Jeff, how would you deal with the problem presented by this situation?" Monson (1978) suggests "planting" some questions among the students to generate interaction.

Manage silence. Silence in response to a query can be disconcerting to faculty accustomed to a more free-flowing dialogue. There may be any number of reasons for a lack of response. Initially, for example, students in audioconferencing may be intimidated by the medium and hesitant to use devices such as microphones. They may be reluctant to assert themselves into the electronic conversation for fear of interrupting or sounding "stupid." A student may simply not have heard the question or s/he may be taking a moment to think and formulate a response. Whatever the reason for a student's reticence, distance teachers need skill, not to mention patience, in dealing with silence. Simply put: don't take silence for an answer. Wait; give students time to respond. If no response appears forthcoming, tactfully confirm whether the student has heard the question. After a reasonable pause, rephrase the question or re-direct the question to another student. Willis (1992) advises teachers to be sensitive to students' different styles of communicating. Burge and Howard (1990) caution instructors to also consider the hour at which the course is being taught.

Maximize the medium. Designing an audio-based course is a balancing act of maximizing the capabilities of the medium while minimizing its limitations. The advantage that synchronous audio-based systems have over correspondence or asynchronous systems is that communication takes place in real time allowing for spontaneous dialogue and feedback. Hence, interactivity is not only a distinguishing attribute but a feature to be exploited. A majority of the contact time in audioconferencing should be devoted to permitting students to interact with the instructor and one another about the content. Consider using pre-recorded audio tapes instead of audioconferencing if it is your intent to present information with little or no interaction.

A delivery system that is predominantly audio challenges teachers to think visually. Though audio-based systems are often limited with respect to the transmission of visuals, teachers designing instruction for audioconference courses are not without opportunities for visual communication. Even so-called audio-only systems are rarely that, for print materials (including illustrations) can be distributed by mail or electronic means to supplement instruction. Despite the apparent absence of or delay in such transmissions, teachers should seize every opportunity to utilize available visual capabilities of the audioconferencing system. Consider some of the following examples:

- In slow-scan systems, position a camera to "shoot" real objects or printed materials that in a conventional setting might be presented on overhead transparencies. With cameras at remote sites, images of students or prepared materials may be exchanged.
- When using an audiographic system, prepare visual materials such as slides in advance; store them and use them on demand.
- With permission, duplicate and distribute video tapes for use concurrently at individual sites.
- Use the telephone. Eastmond (1987) frequently makes half-hour telephone interviews with resource persons from around the country an integral part of his audioconference classes.

Audioconferencing also permits an instructor to originate a class from their office or home, or while "on the road." Whatever the particulars, faculty should capitalize on the system capabilities available to them to complement conversation with visual images that illustrate key concepts, make abstractions concrete, and contribute to comprehension.

Increasing Feedback

In the communication process, feedback is information that is fed back to its source (DeVito, 1986). Feedback provides information to both parties; for example, a teacher can learn how well the students are "getting" concepts and students can clarify misunderstandings and receive information about their performance. Two aspects of feedback are important in instruction but can be problematic in audioconference teaching: giving and receiving feedback in the absence of nonverbal cues, and evaluating students' performance. The following strategies can increase opportunities for and the amount of feedback.

Solicit and provide feedback. A widely voiced concern of audio-teaching faculty is that of knowing whether students are "with you" if you can't see them. Unable to make direct eye contact with the students and to read their faces and body language, teachers lose a primary source of feedback. To compensate for the absence of nonverbal communication, faculty teaching by audio need to make it a point to give and receive feedback. The key is to routinely provide the opportunities; there are numerous tactics.

Use written feedback. A typical means of receiving feedback is through course evaluation forms distributed to all students during the course as well as at its conclusion. You can collect feedback by sampling; that is, ask some of the students representing different portions of your class to respond to a particular item of concern or to prepared questions. Monson (1978) suggests including "message mailers" in printed course materials. Provide feedback by making written comments on assignments, and returning assignments as promptly as possible (Willis, 1992).

Ask questions. Feedback does not necessarily need to be written, nor restricted to questions about content. Utilize informal moments such as before class and during breaks to poll students about their satisfaction with the course and its conduct, about problems they may be encountering, or about their understanding of the course material. Set aside some time during each class session for asking and answering questions. Pause frequently and long enough during presentations to allow students to ask their own questions. Be sure to acknowledge students' questions and comments, and to ask confirming questions such as, "Have I answered your question?" Praising and making reinforcing comments are forms of feedback that may also contribute to students' confidence and motivation. Eastmond (1986) suggests letting the technical assistants at the sites be your eyes and ears by reporting on what works well and what doesn't.

Maintain open channels of communication. Distance teachers have conveyed their desire for open communication by holding telephone office hours and providing students with their office, fax, and home phone numbers. Some distance education systems utilize toll-free telephone numbers, voice-mail or electronic mail (E-mail) services for easier communication especially at odd hours. Since feedback is a two-way street, get your students' numbers and initiate calls to them to check on their progress and to address any difficulties they may be having.

Evaluate student performance. With students dispersed among a number of distant sites, assessing student performance may pose some logistical problems for the distribution, collection, and administration of tests. At the very least, there is likely some delay in getting materials to and from the instructor when relying on mail or courier delivery. A number of communications technologies such as E-mail or fax can be used to speed the transmission of assignments between the distant and home sites. More important than delay, however, distance teaching challenges the use of some traditional methods of testing. For example, is it a good use of limited on-air time to schedule tests during a class meeting? Some faculty are concerned about cheating and the conditions under which students at remote sites take tests. Alternatives to in-class testing require a change in philosophy—one that suits both the setting and the typical distance student, the adult learner.

Assign "take-home" tests or applied projects as alternatives to in-class tests. Evaluations such as these typically address higher order objectives and eliminate some of the concerns associated with the practicality and equity of giving multiple choice tests.

Utilize the features of the electronic delivery system for evaluating student performance. In lieu of a paper and pencil test, for example, consider having students prepare their exams or make their project presentations on audio or video tape. Vandehaar (1986) suggests conducting individual appraisal interviews with each student. For privacy and optimal use of on-air time, conduct interviews by telephone at mutually convenient times.

Use non-graded (no risk) quizzes or exercises. While faculty need to provide students with formal assessments of their performance, these non-threatening measures can be useful in gauging comprehension.

Provide self-assessment materials. Students can measure their own progress through self-assessments items such as study questions, checklists, and self-tests provided with the course materials.

Enhancing Learning and Message Transfer

Holznagel (1988) observes that in distance education, some of the components of quality instruction are problematic to provide from the delivery end. Teachers face increased pressure to design and deliver instruction that facilitates student learning. In particular, teachers need (perhaps more than in face-to-face instruction) to motivate learners and provide them with the appropriate framework or supporting structure to facilitate memory and comprehension.

Take a student-centered approach. In higher education, faculty typically have an egocentric view of teaching and assume the dominant role in instruction—a role that is reinforced in an audioconferencing format (Sponder, 1990). Teachers plan instruction in terms of what they will do, asking themselves, for example: "What content will I cover?" "What assignments will I give?" "What questions will I ask?" They present the material, ask the questions, and set the pace. Conversely, the students' role is subordinate: they listen, respond, do assignments, and take tests.

The nature of distance teaching in an audio-based mode calls this teacher-centered focus into question for several reasons. First, predicated on the tenets of open and life-long learning and as an outgrowth of correspondence learning, electronically delivered distance education emphasizes a greater degree of independence in learning. Students are expected to do more learning on their own, often with a course manual serving as a study guide. Second, distance education is an attractive educational option for adult students because of its convenience and economy. Since adult learners are likely to be quite self-directed, motivated, and inclined to want more control of their learning, instruction that is perceived as irrelevant or not immediately applicable to their needs is not readily tolerated. Thirdly, adult instruction should foster students' intellectual as well as cognitive growth (Chickering, 1969).

In designing an audioconference course, then, teachers should adopt an approach that shifts the focus of instruction from the teacher to the students. Students are called upon to be less dependent on the teacher, to work collaboratively with other students, and to be actively involved in the processes of teaching and learning. A student-centered approach is characterized by teachers taking a more facilitative and less expository role in instruction, sharing responsibilities for teaching/learning, creating opportunities for active participation and interaction among students, and responding to needs of students as adults and as distant learners. Student-centered approaches enhance critical and higher order thinking (Brookfield, 1986).

Toward student-centered design:

- Write course objectives in terms of what students as opposed to the teacher will do.
- Provide students with choices in activities and assignments, e.g., allow students to set some of their own objectives and work toward their own goals.
- Be realistic in the amount of content covered and the assignments given. It may take longer in audioconference teaching to cover the same ground.
- Decrease the amount of lecture while increasing the use of active instructional techniques such as case studies, debates, and role playing that accommodate a variety of learning styles.
- Assist students in learning to learn.
- Provide for the practical application of skills and knowledge.
- Encourage collaborative learning through student-to-student interaction and by utilizing teams and small group activities.
- Aim objectives at the higher-order thinking skills, encouraging students to apply, analyze, synthesize, and solve problems.

A student-centered approach to audio course design facilitates active participation; students have more of a stake in learning if they have some say in the objectives they strive to achieve and in the activities they pursue. With student-centered instruction, the responsibility for teaching and learning is more equally shared between the instructor and the students.

Motivate students. According to the ARCS Model of motivational instructional design (Keller, 1983), four components contribute to students' effort and interest in a course: attention, relevance, confidence, and satisfaction. In a study of adult distance students learning through an audio-based system (Wolcott & Burnham, 1991), findings favored strategies that built students' confidence and enhanced course relevance. Specifically, in terms of effort expended it was most important to students that requirements for success were made clear, that they perceived a benefit from the knowledge they acquired and that the information was useful, and that they could set and achieve high standards. From the viewpoint of their interest in a course, it was most important that the students feel enthusiastic about the subject and that they received timely feedback. The following strategies address motivation.

Clearly spell out course requirements and expectations. From your initial meeting, let students know what they can expect from the course and what is expected of them. List course goals, objectives and major assignments in the syllabus. Share specific lesson objectives with them as well.

Emphasize the relevance of the information. Make connections to known skills and knowledge apparent, and point out the practical value of applying the material to common problems. Look for opportunities to make connections with students' background, experiences and interests, and provide examples to which they can relate. Studies by Haaland and Newby (1984) and Shaeffer and Roe (1985) found that students' satisfaction was positively correlated to the instructor's encouraging discussion of the practical application of content and relating subject matter to students' interests and background.

Build enthusiasm for the subject. Relevance can contribute to motivation as can the instructor's own enthusiasm for the subject (Keller, 1983). Lacking a full range of visual and nonverbal channels, teachers must rely on verbal means to convey enthusiasm. Share your excitement and personal interest in the subject. Like an actor, become proficient in using the vocal qualities of pitch, volume, and other dimensions of vocal expression to communicate enthusiasm in your speech.

Incorporate timely feedback. The value of feedback lies in providing it when it can do the most good. Build opportunities for feedback into your instructional plan; utilize strategies such as questioning and discussion for providing students with immediate correcting or confirming feedback (see section on Increasing Feedback for additional suggestions).

Build a framework for learning. In audioconferencing, faculty rely on the oral communication channel to carry the substance of instruction. What this means for teachers is that greater demand is placed on their ability to organize information and convey concepts, often without the benefit of visual illustration. Providing students with a framework or supporting structure is important for making connections and developing the associations on which to attach new learning.

Provide support materials. Prepare and distribute content outlines and copies of visual materials. Some faculty give students a complete outline; others find it useful to distribute a skeletal or partial outline of the material which leaves room for the students to fill-in and add to the structure provided. Supplying hard copies of visuals such as transparencies or other graphics used in instruction not only gives students an organizational framework and common visual reference point, but also saves note-taking time. Using materials such as textbooks, course outlines, handouts and illustrations, and a variety of audio-visual media are ways to support abstract ideas with graphics to aid memory and provide structure.

Develop a course manual. Provide structure by creating a manual or guide to accompany the audioconference course. In a successful approach used at Utah State University, faculty in the Liberal Arts and Sciences program developed an "enhanced" or "extended" syllabus. Borrowing from correspondence practice, these distance educators supplemented audio instruction with a print component that carried additional content while guiding independent learning and providing organization and structure (Wolcott, 1991). Along the same lines, faculty members at New Mexico State University create "interactive study guides" that provide word pictures and skeletal outlines to use in conjunction with their telelectures (Cyrs & Smith, 1991). In addition to the customary contents, syllabi might include: supplemental readings, hard copies of visuals and other illustrations, study questions and exercises, bibliographies, and original text materials.

Research suggests a danger in structuring too rigidly. In several studies (Gilcher & Johnstone, 1988; Wolcott, 1991), audioconference faculty reported feeling "tied" to their course syllabus or agenda. Having specified in detail the content and structure of the course and individual class sessions, faculty were reluctant to deviate from their plans and lamented the loss of spontaneity. Beaudoin (1990) warns of "syllabism," a similar tendency in which students "work in a 'syllabus bound' manner, i.e., to focus study only on what is prescribed in the syllabus rather than pursuing new ideas" (p. 26). To nurture interaction, faculty must be flexible enough to depart from plans to pursue equally beneficial activities or lines of inquiry and encourage students to do the same.

Use visuals. Think visually (Wileman, 1993). Identify those concepts which could and ought to be presented in a visual form, and find means within the delivery system to convey them. Veteran distance teachers suggest integrating visuals where appropriate and changing visuals frequently to hold students' attention. Work with instructional designers and technical personnel to assure optimal message design and legibility. Smeltzer and Vance (1989) contend that it is more important that visuals complement the message than follow good design principles because inappropriate use of graphics can distract or confuse students.

Incorporate structuring elements. Teacher effects research finds that student achievement is maximized when teachers incorporated elements such as the following into instruction: begin with overviews or advance organizers, review objectives, outline content, signal transitions between topics, point out main ideas, summarize important points, and review main ideas (Brophy & Good, 1986). When instruction is presented primarily in an audio mode, teachers need to make statements that help students see the structure of the content and connect new information with previously learned information. Audioconference teachers can use the following techniques to provide structure that is integral to the instruction.

Use previewing, presentation, and reviewing techniques. Introduce lessons by overviewing the topic and stating instructional goals and objectives. Review the main points of the preceding lesson and show relationships with previous instruction. At the end of the session, summarize important concepts, and provide a brief preview to material which will be the topic of the next session.

Call attention to the main points as well as to the organization and structure of material by using advance organizers in printed form such as a presentation outline or through statements such as, "There are three important factors that contribute to ...." Other techniques that assist the students in structuring their learning include:

- making the relationship among concepts explicit;
- indicating emphasis with simple but direct statements such as "This is an important point";
- developing ideas logically and incrementally;
- signaling transitions when moving from one topic to the next, and indicating connections between topics; and
- repeating important points, and spelling out unfamiliar names and terms.

Facilitate access to resources. In addition to instructional support materials used in class, students need access to a broad range of information resources. Students in Threlkeld's (1990) study rated available library resources a top priority in distance learning. Providing such support for learning is problematic, because distance education presupposes the lack of proximity to an institution of higher education. Living at some distance from campus, distance students lack academic support services available to campus students. Access to information resources, though ameliorated somewhat by interlibrary loan services and electronic document delivery, presents a significant obstacle to learning particularly in upper division and graduate level courses. Since it is rarely possible to anticipate the materials a student would need or practical to provide them in duplicate, the instructor is faced with the choice of modifying objectives and course requirements or finding creative alternatives.

Learn about library and information center facilities within the reach of the remote sites. Either directly or through the academic library staff, survey the depth and breadth of local collections to determine the availability of relevant materials. To what extent can local collections support students' information needs? What finding-tools such as indexes, abstracts, and bibliographies are on hand? What periodicals are held?

Explore options for connecting distant students with resources. Fortunately, the very technologies that make distance education possible are revolutionizing access to information. On-line and CD-ROM technologies give us access to library catalogs, databases and interlibrary loan services. Facsimile and computer technologies speed electronic document delivery. Some options to campus services include satellite collections at remote sites on a permanent or temporary basis, a library professional designated to coordinate and provide services to distant students, and networking to provide remote access to on-line public access catalogs and other electronic databases.

Conclusion

In audio-based teaching, many of the instructional components remain unchanged (e.g., the content to be taught, the needs of students, and the goals of instruction), but conveying the instructional message, meeting the needs of students, and accomplishing the goals may prove problematic. The techniques discussed in this section may not represent anything that is actually new; a "good" teacher might plan and implement similar strategies. Certainly, distance teachers are required to do no less than is required for good classroom teaching.

But while some teacher behaviors and skills drawn from previous practice may transfer, there is no guarantee that a teacher will be successful in audioconference teaching without a greater awareness of and sensitivity to the challenges that distance teaching presents. Much of one's success in distance teaching depends on approaching audioconference teaching with a predisposition to meeting the challenges. The following case study illustrates how a distance teacher, reflecting on context, learners, and methods, met some of the challenges of audioconference teaching.

A Case Study in Teaching by Audioconference

Dr. Doe has been assigned to teach a course about the role of library media programs in schools. LMA 515 serves as an introductory course for students entering a Master's program in Library Media Administration, but it is anticipated that students at both the undergraduate and graduate levels will enroll. The audience could include teachers, administrators, and library media personnel. The course is a new distance education offering. Dr. Doe has been fortunate in being given some release time this semester and six month's lead time to prepare her course.

The course will be delivered by an audiographic conferencing system which combines audio communication with telewriting via a writing pad and slow-scan transmission of live images and graphics. Both the originating and the receive sites are equipped with these capabilities. Instructors wear wireless microphones to permit movement around the classroom; students use push-to-talk mics. Students and teacher can use a fax machine and electronic mail to transmit assignments.

This will be Dr. Doe's first distance teaching or learning experience. She has considerable experience in teaching public school students, college students, and adult learners from whom she has received excellent evaluations. However, the thought of teaching students most of whom she can't see has unnerved her somewhat. She has heard other faculty relate distance teaching "horror stories," but she is convinced that distance teaching and learning can be positive and rewarding experiences. She assumes an optimistic outlook and pursues the challenge with enthusiasm. She finds the prospect of totally rethinking her approach to the content and instruction invigorating.

Dr. Doe approaches her new charge methodically. She begins by visiting with the instructional designer with whom she will be working; they discuss possible formats of the course, the capabilities and limitations of the delivery system, and the preparation of course materials, especially the course manual and visual materials. She inquires about exemplary distance teachers and makes plans to observe several classes. The instructional designer tells her about a mentoring program they are initiating; she eagerly volunteers to participate. She leaves the designer's office with some recommended background reading and spirits high.

During the next week, however, she is less optimistic. After observing a political science course that reaches 45 students enrolled at 12 sites, she is having serious doubts about her ability to manage on-air instruction for such a large group. Specifically, she's worried about how to create the rapport with the students that she considers a hallmark and the foundation of her teaching style. She calls her newly-assigned mentor and makes an appointment to discuss her mounting concerns with her over coffee.

Her mentor is both empathetic and reassuring. She shares some of the techniques she has used, such as creating student profiles, sharing "portraits," and tricks to learning students' names. She suggests that Dr. Doe chat with some students who are veteran distant learners and recommends several to her. With renewed confidence, the prospective distance teacher goes back to planning. She decides to watch her mentor "in action."

Over the past term, Dr. Doe has been immersing herself in the distance teaching and learning experience. She has observed numerous classes, talked with students as well as teachers, and read materials from which she has gleaned many ideas. The topic never far from her mind, she has been living and breathing distance education and reflecting on her approach. She turns her attention now to the more concrete aspects of planning.

Since her goals for the course include having the students define their philosophy of library media services and come to an understanding of current issues facing the field, Dr. Doe chooses a seminar approach to instruction. She believes that this method will both appeal to the adult learners who will constitute the majority of the class and facilitate participation. She has gathered a collection of appropriate readings which, together with objectives, study questions, assignments, and self-assessment items, will be bound as the course manual. If time permits, she'll add lesson outlines and hard copies of visuals she is developing with the instructional design staff; otherwise she'll send the materials separately during the term.

The availability of library resources is a particular concern. Since the course is issues-oriented, she wants students to access recent materials for writing the "status quo" and "reaction" essays she will assign. Hesitant to compromise her objectives, she meets with the university library staff to determine the feasibility of getting the necessary materials, especially relevant periodical articles, to students at the more remote locations. With the overall structure established, Dr. Doe details the major assignments, individual lesson plans and activities, and plans for evaluating students' performance. She selects activities such as debates and small group discussions that will get students actively involved in the class and interacting with both the content and one another. After six months of planning, Dr. Doe feels that she has organized the course content and structured materials and activities to achieve both her content and process goals.

At the first class meeting, there are twenty-five students enrolled. Five students are with her at the origination site; the remaining twenty are distributed among seven additional sites. The most students at any one site is four; there are several sites that only have one student. Following introductions, Dr. Doe is disappointed to discover that a number of students lack public school teaching or administrative experience. However, the diversity among the students is an advantage. There are more women than men and, judging from voices alone, there appears to be a wide range of ages, but as anticipated, most students appear to be adult learners. The majority of students are attending at rural centers, including two students at the state prison.

The initial session goes quite well. From her experience, Dr. Doe knows the importance of setting expectations and the tone of the course during the first meeting. She makes it a point to be enthusiastic and to clearly state what she expects of the students and to ask them to tell her something about themselves, their interests, and goals. She begins with an activity that has students meet in small groups to respond to a brief "in-basket" activity. She's pleased with the responses and the level of thinking that they represent.

Given that it's the first meeting, she's not disturbed that she has to probe for responses, but she's concerned about getting the class to "go with the flow" as her face-to-face classes do with the same content. Long pauses are disconcerting. She puzzles that even between students who have been in her on-campus classes, she feels a loss of rapport.

The class session goes quickly; she doesn't cover all that she had planned. Much time has been taken up with "housekeeping" activities, including orienting students to the equipment and protocol. She makes a mental note to limit chores of a housekeeping nature to the opening ten minutes of each class. She finds that she has to repeat directions several times, and even at the end of the session there is confusion about the activities and assigned readings for the next meeting. Despite some initial butterflies, she feels quite positive about her performance and much relieved that there were no technical problems.

She leaves the classroom generally pleased with the evening's outcome, but somewhat uneasy about the experience from the students' point of view. She asks herself many questions. Was I sensitive to students' needs and the possible difficulties of learning at a distance? Have I outlined reasonable expectations considering the distance that separates students from campus? What might I have done to make the experience better especially for the students learning alone? How can I create a sense of community? Did I favor the students who are in the classroom with me and neglect those I can't see? How can I draw out students who are reticent? How will I know what students are thinking if I can't see their faces? Will they let me know if there's something they don't understand? Walking to her car, Dr. Doe decides to keep a journal and to later discuss with her mentor these and other questions that will undoubtedly come up during the term.

Summary

With the rapid advances in telecommunications, distance education entered a new generation. Today, synchronous and interactive media can link a widely dispersed group of students in a common instructional dialogue. Instruction is no longer confined to voice communication. Technological developments such as fax, electronic writing devices, and computers make it possible to transmit visual images and data as well. Audio teleconferencing deliveries are extensively used and effective distance education options.

Teaching and learning via audio-based systems is different enough from face-to-face instruction that it poses some unique challenges to teachers and students. While many aspects of teaching are similar regardless of the environment, some considerations take on added salience because participants are separated by distance and their communication is mediated by technology. In audio-based teaching, the absence of a channel for the transmission of live visual and nonverbal information presents a potential barrier to rapport-building, interaction, feedback, and optimal learning. Teachers find that audioconference teaching requires adjustments in their approach, planning, and presentation of instruction.

To meet the challenges, this chapter has proposed two approaches. First, it was recommended that teachers reflect on the variables of context, learners, and methods in the essential planning phase of instruction. Second, the chapter offered teachers guidelines drawn from practice and research for designing and implementing effective audio-based distance instruction. A concluding example presents a look at how guidelines can be applied to reduce interpersonal distance, nurture interaction, increase feedback, and enhance learning and message transfer.

References

Baird, M. & Monson, M. (1988). Strategies for applying audio teleconferencing to distance education and training. In *Changing roles in education and training.* Proceedings of the Fourth Annual Conference on Teaching at a Distance (pp. 36–40). Madison, WI.

Beaudoin, M. (1990). The instructor's changing role in distance education. *American Journal of Distance Education, 4*(2), 21–29.

Bransford, L. (1984). *Slow-scan television utilization in education.* Washington, DC: The Annenberg/CPB Project.

Brookfield, S. D. (1986). *Understanding and facilitating adult learning.* San Francisco: Jossey-Bass.

Brophy, J. & Good, T. L. (1986). Teacher behavior and student achievement. In M. C. Wittrock (Ed.), *Handbook of research on teaching* (3rd ed.) (pp. 328–375). New York: Macmillan.

Burge, E. & Howard, J. L. (1990). Audio-conferencing in graduate education: A case study. *American Journal of Distance Education, 4*(2), 3–13.

Chickering, A. W. (1969). *Education and identity.* San Francisco: Jossey-Bass.

Clark, C. M. & Peterson, P. L. (1986). Teacher's thought processes. In M.C. Wittrock (Ed.), *Handbook of research on teaching* (3rd ed.) (pp. 255–296). New York: Macmillan.

Cyrs, T. E. & Smith, F. A. (1991). Designing interactive study guides with word pictures for teleclass teaching. *TechTrends, 36*(1), 37–39.

DeVito, J. A. (1986). *The communication handbook: A dictionary.* New York: Harper & Row.

Dewal, O. S. (1988). Pedagogical issues in distance education. *Prospects, 18* (1), 63–73.

Eastmond, N. (1986). Extension teaching: New technologies and old insights. *Innovation Abstracts, 8*(23).

Eastmond, N. (1987). Proving the critiques wrong. *Innovation Abstracts, 9*(27).

Garrison, D. R. (1989). Distance education. In S. B. Merriam & P. M. Cunningham (Eds.), *Handbook of adult and continuing education* (pp. 221–232). San Francisco: Jossey-Bass.

Garrison, D. R. (1990). An analysis and evaluation of audio teleconferencing to facilitate education at a distance. *American Journal of Distance Education, 4*(3),13–25.

Gilcher, K. W. & Johnstone, S. (1988). A critical review of the use of audiographic conferencing systems by selected educational institutions. College Park: University of Maryland and the Annenberg/CPB Project. (ERIC Document Reproduction Service No. ED 313 003).

Haaland, B. A. & Newby, W. G. (1984). Student perception of effective teaching behaviors: An examination of conventional and teleconference-based instruction. In L. A. Parker & O. H. Olgren (Eds.), *Teleconferencing and electronic communication III* (pp. 211–217). Madison, WI: University of Wisconsin–Extension.

Haughey, M. (1983). Teaching and learning via satellite. Victoria, British Columbia: University of Victoria. (ERIC Document Reproduction Service No. ED 235 791).

Heinich, R., Molenda, M. & Russell, J. D. (1989). *Instructional media and the new technologies of instruction* (3rd ed.). New York: Macmillan.

Heinzen, T. E. & Alberico, S. (1990). Using a creativity paradigm to evaluate teleconferencing. *American Journal of Distance Education, 4*(3),3–12.

Holznagel, D. C. (1988). *Distance education: Promise, practice and pedagogy.* Portland, OR: Northwest Regional Educational Lab. (ERIC Document Reproduction Service No. ED 308 052)

Johnstone, S. & Gilcher, K. W. (1989). Audiographic conferencing: A primer. In K. J. Hansell (Ed.), *Teleconferencing manager's guide.* White Plains, NY: Knowledge Industry Publications.

Keller, J. (1983). Motivational design of instruction. In C. M. Reigeluth (Ed.), *Instructional-design theories and models: An overview of their current status.* Hillsdale, NJ: Lawrence Erlbaum.

Knapper, C. (1988). Lifelong learning and distance education. *American Journal of Distance Education, 2*(1), 63–72.

Knapper, C., Lumsden, B. & Stubbs, J. (1985, August). Instructional development for distance education. Paper presented at the 13th World Conference of the International Council for Distance Education, Melbourne, Australia. (ERIC Document Reproduction Service No. ED 265 638)

Knowles, M. S. (1984). *The adult learner: A neglected species* (3rd ed.). Houston: Gulf.

Knowles, M. S. & Associates. (1984). *Andragogy in action.* San Francisco: Jossey-Bass.

Lewis, R. J. (1985). *Instructional applications of information technologies: A survey of higher education in the West.* Boulder, CO: Western Interstate Commission for Higher Education.

Massoumian, B. (1989). Successful teaching via two-way interactive video. *TechTrends, 34*(2), 16–19.

Monson, M. K. (1978). *Bridging the distance.* Madison, WI: University of Wisconsin–Extension.

Moore, M. G. (1989). Editorial: Three types of interaction. *American Journal of Distance Education, 3*(2), 1–6.

Moore, M. G. & Thompson, M. M. (1990). *The effects of distance learning: A summary of literature* (Research Monograph No. 2). University Park, PA: American Center for the Study of Distance Education.

Neumann, D. R. (1986). Teleconferencing as a public speaking platform. In L. A. Parker & O. H. Olgren (Eds.), *Teleconferencing and electronic communication V* (pp. 327–331). Madison, WI: University of Wisconsin–Extension.

Office of Technology Assessment. (1989). *Linking for learning: A new course for education* (OTA-SET-430). Washington DC: U. S. Government Printing Office.

Ohler, J. (1989). TechTrends interview: Jason Ohler. *TechTrends, 34*(5), 62–67.

Ostendorf, V. A. (1989). *What every principal, teacher, and school board member should know about distance education.* Little, CO: Virginia A. Ostendorf, Inc.

Rezabek, L. L., Nordmann, D. D. & Shaeffer, J. M. (1989, November). Using a computer-based audiographic telecommunication system for distance learning. Paper presented at the International Conference of the Association for the Development of Computer-based Instructional Systems, Washington, DC (ERIC Document Reproduction Service No. ED 332 662).

Romberg, T. A. (1980). Salient features of the BTES framework of teacher behaviors. In C. Denham & A. Lieberman, *Time to learn* (pp. 73–93). Sacramento, CA: State Commission for Teacher Preparation.

Rumble, G. (1989). On defining distance education. *American Journal of Distance Education, 3*(2), 8–12.

Schön, D. (1983). *The reflective practitioner: How professionals think in action.* New York: Basic Books.

Shaeffer, J. M. & Roe, R. G. (1985). Effective teacher behavior as perceived by students in a face-to-face and teleconference course. In L. A. Parker & O. H. Olgren (Eds.), *Teleconferencing and electronic communication IV* (pp. 216–222). Madison, WI: University of Wisconsin–Extension.

Shale, D. & Garrison, D. R. (1989, June). Instructional design considerations in telewriter applications to distance education. Paper presented at the annual conference on the Canadian Association for the Study of Adult Education, Ottawa, Ontario.

Smeltzer, L. R. & Vance, C. M. (1989). An analysis of graphics use in audio-graphic teleconferences. *Journal of Business Communication, 26,* 123–141.

Sparkes, J. J. (1983). The problem of creating a discipline of distance education. *Distance Education, 4,* 179–186.

Sponder, B. M. (1990). *Distance education in rural Alaska: An overview of teaching and learning practices in audioconference courses.* (Monograph Series in Distance Education No. 1). Fairbanks, AK: University of Alaska Center for Cross-Cultural Studies.

Stark, J. S., Lowther, M. A., Ryan, M., Bomotti, S. S., Genthon, M., Martens, G. & Haven, C. L. (1988). *Reflections on course planning: Faculty and students consider influences and goals.* Ann Arbor: National Center for Research to Improve Postsecondary Teaching and Learning, University of Michigan.

Takemoto, P. A. (1987). Exploring the educational potential of audio. In J. A. Niemi & D. D. Gooler (Eds.), *Technologies for learning outside the classroom* (New directions for Continuing Education, No. 34). San Francisco: Jossey-Bass.

Thiagarajan, S. (1978). The loneliness of the long-distance learner. *Audiovisual Instruction, 23*(1), 22+.

Threlkeld, R. M. (1990). *California distance learning survey: 1989–90.* Pomona, CA: California State Polytechnic University, California Technology Project.

Vandehaar, D (1986). Learning between here and there: Quality teleconference classrooms. In L. A. Parker & O. H. Olgren (Eds.), *Teleconferencing and electronic communication V* (pp. 338–346). Madison, WI: University of Wisconsin–Extension.

Van Kekerix, M. & Andrews, J. (1991). Electronic media and independent study. In B. L. Watkins & S. J. Wright (Eds.), *Foundations of American distance education: A century of collegiate correspondence study* (pp. 135–157). Dubuque, IA: Kendall/Hunt.

Verduin, J. R. & Clark, T. A. (1991). *Distance education: The foundations of effective practice.* San Francisco: Jossey-Bass.

Wellens, R. A. (1986). Use of a psychological distancing model to assess differences in telecommunications media. In L. A. Parker & O. H. Olgren (Eds.), *Teleconferencing and electronic communication V* (pp. 347–361). Madison, WI: University of Wisconsin–Extension.

Widner, D. (1990). Revisiting slow-scan in distance education. *American Journal of Distance Education, 4*(2), 57–63.

Wiesner, P. (1983). Some observations on telecourse research and practice. *Adult Education Quarterly, 33,* 215–221.

Wileman, R. (1993). *Visual communicating.* Englewood Cliffs, NJ: Educational Technology Publications.

Willis, B. (1992). *Effective distance education: A primer for faculty and administrators.* (Monograph Series in Distance Education No. 2). Fairbanks, AK: University of Alaska Center for Cross-Cultural Studies.

Wolcott, L. L. (1991). A qualitative study of teachers' planning of instruction in a telecommunications-based distance education environment. (Doctoral dissertation, The University of Georgia, 1990). *Dissertation Abstracts International, 52,* 03A.

Wolcott, L. L. & Burnham, B. R. (1991). Tapping into motivation: What adult learners find motivating about distance instruction. In *Designing for learner access: Challenges and practices for distance education.* Proceedings of the 7th Annual Conference on Distance Teaching and Learning (pp. 220–207). Madison, WI.

Zvacek, S. M. (1991). Effective affective design for distance education. *TechTrends, 36*(1), 40–43.

Chapter Seven

Video Tools for Distance Education

E. Lynn Oliver

"Visual experience is primary in learning to understand and respond to the environment; visual information is the oldest record of human history" (Donis, 1973, p. 2). From ancient cave paintings to contemporary video technology, visual symbols and codes provide the connection between thought and experience.

Video is a Latin word that means "I see" and is defined as "the display of pictures on a television-type screen" (Heinich, Molenda, & Russell, 1989, p. 218). The amalgam of both visual images and sound in one highly sensory medium makes video a versatile and appealing ingredient in the array of instructional technologies available to the distance educator. This chapter will describe the presentational characteristics of instructional television, survey the technologies that comprise the video tool kit, and discuss the effective utilization of video in distance education. The chapter will conclude with a case study of video-based applications.

Instructional Video: An Overview

Instructional applications of video in distance education fall into four general categories (Gunawardena, 1990). The technologies and characteristics of each application will be discussed in greater detail later in the chapter.

1. Pre-produced video. The video component of a single instructional unit or a series of lessons comprising a telecourse consists of programs that have been designed and produced according to specific instructional objectives. Programs may be distributed by video cassette or by video-based technologies such as broadcast, cable, or satellite.

2. Televised instruction. Televised instruction transmits a classroom lecture to off-campus locations. "In this delivery system, only the technology of television transmission is used, not the 'presentational' characteristics unique to the medium" (Gunawardena, 1990, p. 111).

Instruction may be enhanced by telephone interaction among remote students and the instructor.

3. Interactive video. Interactive video integrates video with a computer. This melding of technologies creates a medium that "capitalizes on the features of both instructional television and computer-assisted instruction" (Heinich, Molenda, & Russell, 1989, p. 200). Learners interact with the subject matter by computer-controlled instructions, activities, and feedback.

4. Videoconferencing. A videoconference emulates a face-to-face meeting or conference and may consist of a single workshop, seminar, or training unit or a full course of instruction delivered at a distance. While similar to televised instruction, it is usually designed to incorporate the presentational characteristics of television. A two-way communications link permits participants to interact with each other. Videoconferencing and televised instruction (if a two-way communication link is provided) are also described as interactive television (Lochte, 1993).

Advantages of Video

Instructional television draws on an eclectic assortment of visual devices ranging from simple artistic representations to complex computer generated and controlled images. Heinich, Molenda, and Russell (1989) and Brown and Fortosky (1986) describe its advantages:

- Video provides vicarious experiences and visual access to a world outside the classroom.
- Complex, abstract concepts can be simplified through visualization.
- The medium is familiar and "user friendly."
- Video is an evocative medium. Drama and documentary can stimulate thought and emotions.
- Simulations and role playing can demonstrate and model behavior.
- Video is a close-up medium capable of showing microscopic intricacies.
- Video can collapse time and space, capturing and relaying events as they happen.

Limitations of the Medium

While video is familiar and pervasive, its apparent simplicity is deceptive. The effective utilization of the medium's richness and potential as a distance delivery mechanism requires time, tenacity and creative visualization skills. As Willis (1992), Bates (1991), and Rowntree (1990) indicate, video has limitations:

- Professional video is expensive. Broadcast quality production requires access to sophisticated studio facilities.
- Video production is time consuming, requires specialized assistance, and places heavy demands on teachers.
- Professional video is expected to have a shelf life. Revisions and updates may be complicated and costly.
- Interactive television requires high-cost specialized equipment and communications systems.

- Viewers are conditioned by commercial television to be passive recipients of information. Motivating active participation and interaction requires highly skilled teachers, systematic planning, and creative design.

Instructional Television in Distance Education

The inauguration of the British Open University in 1971 heralded a new era in distance education. Its extensive use of broadcast media, especially television, expanded distance learning opportunities and enhanced traditional correspondence study with alternative channels of communication (Garrison, 1990). Since then, advances in telecommunications have ignited an "explosion of alternative instructional delivery systems" (Barker, Frisbie, & Patrick, 1989, p. 20). These systems facilitate varying levels of interactivity that bridge the distance between instructor and student. "It is this added component of live interaction that breaks the field of distance education into two major categories—correspondence-based distance education and telecommunications-based distance education" (p. 22).

The emergence of interactive technologies over broadcast media "can extend the influence of the educator and benefit the learner through immediate and sustained two-way communication" (Garrison, 1990, p. 42). Interactive technologies extend the educational transaction beyond the cognitive exchange of information to a learning environment that fosters group support and social affiliation.

Video and its numerous technological permutations have facilitated the development and rapid growth of interactive television networks across North America. Over half of the universities and colleges providing distance education in Canada employ some form of "tele-education," from terrestrial voice communications to satellite telecommunications (Telesat Canada, 1991). In the United States, video-based distance education is pervasive, including one-way broadcast and cable transmission and two-way interactive television with telephone feedback (Gunawardena, 1989). Despite the prevalence of technology utilization, Gunawardena concludes:

> There is a dearth of information on current practices in the use of new technologies for delivering instruction, the difficulties encountered in their use, and techniques employed by institutions to integrate the delivery medium with the distance education system. (p. 171)

This chapter will endeavor to address this gap. The balance of the chapter will examine video-based technologies and the effective deployment of video as an instructional medium and communications conduit in distance education.

Video-Based Technologies

From the learner's perspective, whether the program arrives in the mail, by courier, horseback, or satellite would not appear to be relevant. However,

> the speed of arrival, the time it takes to get feedback, the feeling of isolation,
> and the ability to interact with other learners are all affected by the
> distribution system. (Forster, 1992, p. 9)

Video-based technologies and distribution systems may be broadly
delineated by how messages are sent and received. "If the message simply
stimulates the receiver in isolation, then we must classify this as one-way
communication" (Garrison & Shale, 1990, p. 32). By contrast, two-way
communication occurs when participants in an educational transaction
are both senders *and* receivers and "messages go in both directions" (p. 32).
One-way communication is characterized by delayed or asynchronous
interaction between teacher and student, while two-way communication
facilitates immediate real-time or synchronous interaction.

One-way Asynchronous Communication

Broadcast television. Open-air broadcast television provides convenient
and ready access to instructional video, usually in the student's own home.
The method of delivery is of particular appeal to handicapped or
institutionalized individuals, to parents with small children, retirees, and
those intimidated by the thought of attending a regular class (Zigerell,
1986). Broadcast video is typically of high quality and is designed to employ
the attributes of the medium to best advantage.

The Achilles' heel of broadcast television is its mass media approach.
The economic viability of television broadcasters requires large viewing
audiences; therefore, instructional objectives may be sacrificed for greater
entertainment appeal. The mass media approach seldom accommodates the
individual needs of the learner. As Bates (1984) observes, "Broadcasts are
ephemeral, cannot be reviewed, are uninterruptable, and are presented at
the same pace for all students" (p. 31).

Broadcast delivery encourages passive viewing rather than active
participation. Students lack control over the medium and are unable to stop
the flow of information to ask questions and clarify understanding. With
little exposure to either an instructor or other learners, students may feel
isolated in the experience.

The integration of ancillary media alleviates some of the weaknesses of
broadcast television and increases the level of learner participation. A
well-designed "telecourse," for example, combines the benefits of
professionally produced video with the elements of self-paced, independent
study. Zigerell (1986) describes a telecourse as "a system of instruction
whose parts are interrelated and provide stimuli—print, sound, visual
images—that reinforce each other" (p. 1). The basic components of a
telecourse that accompany the broadcast of pre-produced programs are a
study guide, textbook, and a collection of readings, references, and
activities.

Video cassette. The video cassette as an instructional tool and a
distribution medium relies on the increasingly popular video cassette
recorder (VCR) for playback. Whether a non-broadcast version of a
telecourse or a custom designed video-enhanced independent study course,

the integration of video with other media will enhance learner control and interaction with the subject matter. As Brown (1984) notes, the video cassette offers flexibility and control by permitting utilization at a time convenient to the learner and by permitting the learner to adjust the pace of the instruction through the VCR's pause, replay, and fast forward capability.

Learner interaction and participation with the materials and subject matter may be increased with the addition of "participative exercises," a strategy which counters passive viewing (Gunawardena, 1990). The author suggests including instructions which direct students to stop the tape periodically and respond to questions, summarize conclusions, complete a checklist, or engage in an activity found in the study guide.

Asynchronous interaction, primarily through the exchange of written assignments and feedback, is the norm for broadcast and video cassette delivery. Interaction may be enhanced with the provision of supplementary communication, either by telephone tutoring or periodic face-to-face and audioconference sessions. Telephone tutors designate office hours during which students may call and ask for assistance. Group sessions, facilitating direct contact with the instructor and other students, help to alleviate the isolation of independent study.

Videodisc. The videodisc is a durable plastic disc that resembles a long-playing phonograph album. Its laser encoded surface is capable of storing up to 54,000 still images and 30 minutes of full-motion video per side or a combination of the two. Unlike the video cassette, random access to information located anywhere on a disc is instantaneous.

Interactive video. This is the term used to describe the integration of a microcomputer and a videodisc. The hybrid technology is a powerful, self-paced system that facilitates learner interaction with the subject matter through computer-controlled branching, multiple pathways, and instant feedback (Kemp & Smellie, 1989). "By requiring frequent responses, interactive video captures learners' attention and holds their interest to a greater extent than does videotape alone" (Heinich, Molenda, & Russell, 1989, p. 201). By virtue of its design, interactive video is a highly individualized medium conducive to independent study.

Multimedia. The term "multimedia" can be confusing. Traditionally, it has described an instructional approach that incorporated a variety of audio, visual, and print media. However, the term has been adopted by the computer industry and re-defined to mean "the integration of video, audio, graphics, and data within a single computer workstation" (Bates, Harrington, Gilmore, & van Soest, 1992, p. 6). This technological fusion holds tremendous promise for distance education. Multimedia software enables the instructor to custom design and individualize instruction and the learner to "plan, execute, and manage his or her learning experience at the rate, place, and time of the learner's choice" (Schwier, Brown, Misanchuk, & Proctor, 1992, p. 67).

Multimedia systems have the potential to combine the advantages of self-paced, learner-managed study with built-in opportunities for two-way communication. By linking workstations in multiple locations through telephone lines, computer teleconferencing facilitates both synchronous interaction with peers and the instructor and asynchronous interaction by forwarding and retrieving stored information.

Interactive video and multimedia technologies require specialized equipment and software and a high degree of computer competence in both teachers and students. Workstations must also be available in sufficient numbers to accommodate self-paced learners. These conditions have implications for computer literacy training and the administration and equipping of centers in which students may gain access to workstations. The high cost of original video production and custom designed computer software may also deter the implementation of these technologies on a wide scale in distance education programs. As the cost of hardware declines and the availability of appropriate and affordable application software increases, integrated workstations will undoubtedly become a valuable conduit for distance education.

Two-way Synchronous Communication

Cable television. Cable television systems capture video signals and retransmit them to subscribers primarily by coaxial and fiber optic cable. Subscribers receive several signals or channels that are individually selected by a tuner on the television receiver. While mass distribution of instructional video via cable television shares the same weaknesses as broadcast television transmission, cable networks have the capacity to transmit signals in both directions permitting two-way communication between subscribers.

In densely populated areas where cable distribution is prevalent, video transmission can be integrated with telephone and audioconferencing capability to accommodate immediate feedback and interaction. However, in rural areas where cable networks are sporadic or in terrain that resists the laying of cable, other transmission technologies are required.

Instructional television fixed service (ITFS). ITFS is a terrestrial microwave distribution system in which an omnidirectional transmission tower is positioned on high ground in direct line-of-sight of sending and receiving locations (Weinstein, 1986). Microwaves are low-powered electromagnetic waves that travel between transmission towers. Because microwave transmission is low-powered and travels by line of sight, ITFS is limited to locations in close geographic proximity.

Multi-channel ITFS service can deliver as many as eight channels reserved exclusively for educational use (Noll, 1988). The system is a low-cost distribution alternative because it does not require the complex and expensive installation of a cable network. ITFS incorporates two-way audio communication by telephone or microwave radio.

Satellite point-to-multipoint delivery. A satellite is a device which circles the earth in a fixed path or orbit. It is capable of receiving video and audio signals from a powerful antenna called an uplink. The satellite receives and re-transmits signals to a Television Receive Only (TVRO) earth station called a downlink. The downlink comprises the equipment needed to capture and reconstruct the video signal. The most visible part of the downlink is a large dish-shaped antenna aimed in the direction of the satellite. Other components include a receiver that selects designated video and audio signals, a television, a VCR, and in some cases, a decoding device. Two-way communication occurs with ancillary telephone or audioconferencing equipment.

While ITFS is sensitive to geographic impediments and distance, satellite telecommunications collapse distance and space anywhere within an electronic "footprint," the geographic area of the earth served by a satellite. Satellite transmission, with all terrain blanket coverage, is particularly suited to multipoint signal distribution. Any number of receive locations can be added to the network configuration without increasing satellite transmission costs.

Although satellite delivery is a versatile technology, capable of transmitting data, voice, and video, a satellite network configuration requires a complex technical infrastructure with considerable investment in specialized equipment. Highly trained technical personnel are required to operate and maintain the system.

Compressed video. To understand compressed video, it is helpful to understand "bandwidth." Bandwidth is a term used to describe the electronic pathway along which voice, video, and data travel. It is the width of a band of frequencies that constitutes a signal (Noll, 1988). Different signals require different bandwidths. Video transmission, for example, needs far greater bandwidth than voice transmission. One full-motion video signal requires the same bandwidth as 600 telephone calls. Typically, the greater the bandwidth required for delivery, the higher the cost of transmission. Compressed video provides a cost-effective alternative.

Compression technology converts an electromagnetic or analog video signal into a digital signal made up of bits of data. A digitized signal is transmitted more efficiently along a narrower bandwidth. Several digital signals can be sandwiched together and transmitted in place of one analog video signal. The amount of visual information transmitted in a compressed signal is reduced; therefore, the quality of the visual image is altered. The rate of compression determines the nature of the signal. Very high compression transmits still images in the form of freeze-frame video; low compression transmits the equivalent of full-motion video.

A highly compressed signal is characterized by motion that appears to be blurred and slowed. Quickly executed actions will seem stilted. Where crisp detail and full motion are not essential to the subject matter, signal degradation appears to be acceptable for many applications, especially in light of its reduced transmission cost. Compressed video is particularly amenable to two-way video communication and is gaining rapidly in acceptance and popularity.

Teleconference. A teleconference utilizes telecommunications technologies to facilitate meetings, workshops, courses, and conversations among groups or individuals at two or more locations (Willis, 1993). The teleconference may involve audio, data, or video communication or a combination of media. It is, as Garrison (1990) says, "the quintessential technology" (p. 43) distinguished by its capacity to facilitate synchronous, real-time communication among participants. This communicative capability when combined with the attributes of video results in a high impact mode of communication.

Videoconference. A teleconference that uses video technology as its primary communication link is called a videoconference. There are two types of videoconference configurations: (a) one-way video, two-way audio, and (b) two-way video, two-way audio. In a one-way video, two-way audio configuration, students at receive sites can see and hear the instructor on a television monitor, but the instructor cannot see the students. Two-way audio communication occurs via telephone lines.

In a two-way video configuration, the students and the instructor can both see and hear each other. This process is facilitated by television cameras and microphones at receive locations and technology that permits video to be transmitted in both directions.

Business TV. The videoconference method is often referred to as "Business TV" (BTV). "BTV provides business and industry with a cost-effective way to disseminate information and training to multiple, distant sites without incurring high personnel, travel and time costs associated with on-site meetings" (Schwier, Brown, Misanchuk, & Proctor, 1992, p. 64). The advantages of live interactive communication, timely dissemination of information, and greater accessibility to corporate training have made videoconferencing an important adjunct of information transfer in the corporate setting. Large scale BTV users often establish their own network configurations enabling instant communication among multisite locations.

Summary

Instructional video in distance education can be represented by four categories: pre-produced video, televised instruction, interactive television, and videoconferencing. The video medium has strengths and limitations which require careful consideration when selecting a video-based technology for distance delivery.

Instructional television in distance education can be delineated by one- and two-way communication capability. In general, one-way technologies include broadcast television, video cassettes, videodiscs, and multimedia configurations. Two-way video is inherent in cable television distribution, ITFS, satellite delivery, and compressed video. Teleconferencing, including videoconferencing and BTV delivery, is an effective vehicle for two-way communication.

While video is a powerful medium, Brown and Fortosky (1986) remind us of the following:

> Television's contribution to distance education, or any form of education, is proportional to the extent that its cold technology can be animated by human design and expression. (p. 267)

The type of video technology used in distance delivery is just one piece of the instructional puzzle. The following section will examine a mediated classroom model that amalgamates technology and an integrated support infrastructure.

Explanatory Model of a Mediated Classroom

Dick and Carey (1985) describe the instructional process as a system. They write:

> The purpose of the system is to bring about learning. The components of the system are the learners, the instructor, the instructional materials, and the learning environment. These components interact in order to achieve the goal. (p. 3)

The instructional process that is mediated by telecommunications technology is a complex and multifaceted system. The technology poses challenges to administrators, instructional designers, instructors, television production personnel, technicians, remote site attendants, and students. Yet the capacity to provide educational opportunities to geographically-bound individuals motivates thoughtful reflection about utilizing the technology to best advantage.

The mediated classroom model represented in Figure 1 identifies the interrelated components of an infrastructure that supports and facilitates interactive televised instruction (Oliver, 1993). While there is a tendency, particularly with video-based technologies, to focus attention on the technology, it is essential to consider the nature of "human-to-human" interactions in addition to "human-to-machine" interactions in the learning process (Wong, 1987). As Garrison and Shale (1990) state:

> While considerable attention has been given to the use of technological media, less attention has been paid to the nature of the communication process and the role of technologies in supporting it. (p. 31)

As indicated in the model, pre-instructional planning components and the contextual conditions of both the originating studio facility and the receive site are vital considerations in developing and implementing mediated instruction via interactive television.

Prior to actual instruction in a studio facility, interactive television involves an antecedent phase consisting of four components:
- instructional design
- system design
- administration
- media production and print support.

Instructional Design

Instructional design is the systematic process of analyzing learning goals and developing, implementing, and evaluating instruction (see Dick & Carey, 1985; Gagné, Briggs, & Wager, 1988). The instructional design and development process entails three stages (Wagner, 1991):

1. Analysis. Of jobs, tasks, objectives, content, and audience.

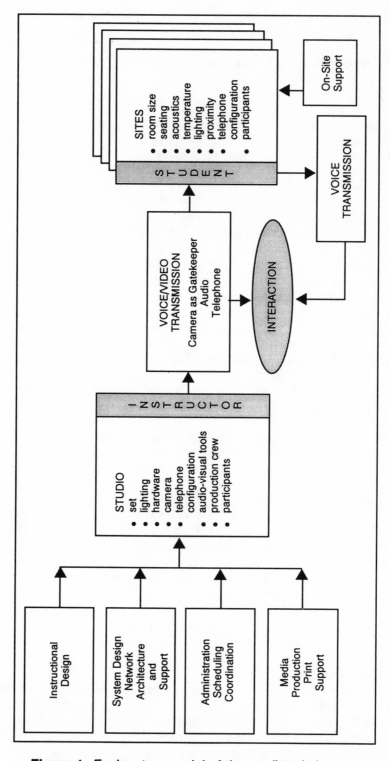

Figure 1. *Explanatory model of the mediated classroom.*

2. *Design and Development.* Of lessons, units, and curricula; of delivery systems, strategies, media, and materials.
3. *Evaluation.* Both formative and summative, from entire instructional systems to individual instructional exercises within lessons.

The instructional design of an interactive television class will differ substantially from one delivered face-to-face. A televised class requires a team approach and a well-constructed instructional plan that clearly establishes goals, objectives, media resources, support systems, instructional strategies, and a plan to evaluate the effectiveness of the delivery strategy.

System Design

Video-based technologies vary in network architecture, interactive capability, geographic reach, information capacity, cost, and administrative complexity. Each technology must be analyzed on multiple levels when constructing a mediated delivery mechanism. A well designed system will contribute to the technological transparency of the medium and accommodate the needs of both the instructor and the distant learner.

Administration

The administration and coordination of video-delivered instruction requires interaction among a number of players: technical support personnel, course administrators, subject matter experts, instructors, production personnel, network administrators, site coordinators, library services, instructional designers, tutors, and student counselors. Coordinating and scheduling courses, designating receive sites, and establishing a communications strategy among stakeholders is a complex, yet essential administrative task. Accommodating the needs of the learner through the distribution and collection of back-up videotapes, textbooks, print packages, exams, and assignments is critical in the administration of televised courses. The formation of an administrative unit or team with clearly defined roles and responsibilities will contribute greatly to an effective and efficiently operated system.

Media Production and Print Support

While characteristically diverse, video-based technologies share in common the visual medium. Video offers a plethora of visual devices, the building blocks of effective televised instruction, capable of enhancing communication and the subsequent cognitive benefits of visual stimulation and reinforcement. "Thinking visually" (Wileman, 1993) is an important first step in a series of steps devoted to planning and implementing instruction via interactive television.

The production and reformatting of visual materials requires preparation and adequate lead time. Some visual resources may require original art work or computer design. Identifying, screening, evaluating, and acquiring pre-produced materials is also a time-consuming process.

Permission to use still images may have to be obtained and some video programs may require the purchase of broadcast rights (permission to electronically transmit a program). If original video is used, sufficient time and resources must be allocated for pre-production planning, production, and post-production editing.

Still Images

Photographs. Photographs, enlarged and mounted, can be brought to life in front of the television camera. The content of the photograph can be manipulated by camera movement, from a display of the entire photograph to a close-up of a part of the image. This attention-focusing technique can cue the learner to analyze details of the image and relate them to the whole.

Slides. Color, clarity, and aesthetic appeal make 35mm slides a useful visual resource. Slides can illustrate close-up detail, establish a mood, and simulate movement, particularly when combined with music. When slides are projected from behind a translucent screen, the camera can take the viewer inside the scene by zooming into a close-up or panning across the image.

Graphics. Graphics are artistic representations of ideas, concepts, and information contained in the subject matter. Graphics include words, diagrams, bar graphs, charts, and illustrations. A graphic may be produced manually as an "art card" or generated electronically by a computer. Art cards, mounted on poster board, are placed on an easel in front of the camera. A series of art cards may be videotaped for later playback during the presentation.

A computer graphic is generated using specialized software and may combine the artistic elements of an art card with movement or animation. Animation is an effective attention-getting device and especially appropriate in illustrating concepts that require motion.

Whether a graphic is produced manually or by computer, the message depicted must be easily and quickly understood. Bold, simple designs free of busy detail will be most effective. Color, contrast, balance, and legibility of lettering are important considerations in effective graphics design (see Kemp & Smellie, 1989).

Aspect ratio. A graphic must conform to the size and shape of the television screen. The screen is a rectangle, four units wide by three units high. This four to three ratio is called an aspect ratio. To ensure complete visibility of the entire image, graphics must conform to these dimensions.

Character generator (CG). The CG is a computer that generates text and numeric information. It is an extremely useful tool in displaying titles, captions, and brief messages. The CG is also effective in providing a simple outline, visually reinforcing an instructional objective with words or numbers, displaying an unfamiliar term or phrase, highlighting instructional objectives, and providing simple written instructions. Text may be displayed on a colored or black video background or superimposed on another video image.

Still images and textual information must be carefully designed and adapted for the television screen. To the dismay of many instructors, visual materials such as overhead transparencies, wall maps and charts, and other reliable classroom devices are not suited to television and must be reformatted. The instructor is well advised to collect all visual material used in the classroom, and with the aid of television support personnel, test the materials on camera. Camera-checking each visual will sort out those that can be used as is from those that must be redesigned.

Moving Images

Roll-ins and video clips. A pre-produced television program used in a larger video presentation is called a "roll-in." It is played or "rolled in" at a pre-determined point in the lesson. A video "clip" is a short video segment that illustrates a specific point and adds visual punch to a message.

Roll-ins and clips enrich the presentation of information by importing people, events, and activities into the studio. Ostendorf (1989) lists four situations in which roll-ins are particularly effective:

1. to illustrate a step-by-step procedure
2. to demonstrate an activity that could not easily be done in the studio
3. to provide excerpts from professionally produced documentary or news footage
4. to provide access to a guest presenter unable to appear in person during the studio presentation.

Print Support

Print materials are an essential component of effective interactive television. Print is an "agent of interaction" just as video, audio, and data are (Wong, 1987). The printed word provides a structural and organizational mechanism that lessens the psychological distance among participants. A course syllabus, for example, can address administrative matters, provide general course information, and act as a road map for each televised session. "The syllabus will constitute the major communication link, aside from television" (Cyrs & Smith, 1990, p. 44). As with the preparation of visual materials, print materials require sufficient time to develop and produce. Because the print component sets the stage for effective video instruction, advance distribution of print materials will contribute to a successful televised session.

The Television Studio

In a face-to-face instructional setting, the eyes of the participant determine, for the most part, what is to be observed. A student is capable of selecting relevant visual information at any given moment. The television camera changes that personal selection process, choosing instead what is to be looked at. Selectivity is narrowed to the structured visual images contained within the frame.

The television camera's selection and interpretation of events mold the visual images and messages transmitted to the distant student. As the mediated classroom model suggests, the television camera becomes the "gatekeeper," determining what the viewer will see on the remote site's television monitor. It is, therefore, worthwhile to acquire a basic understanding of television production elements and the medium's codes and conventions to better understand the impact of the visual message on the instructional process.

Television's codes and conventions are formulated by the selective representation of the television camera: the camera's point of view or perspective and the camera's field of view.

Point of View

The television camera represents three perspectives or points of view: (a) reportorial, (b) objective, and (c) subjective (Burrows and Wood, 1986).

Reportorial. The reportorial or presentational point of view is that of direct address; the presenter ("reporter") speaks directly through the camera to the audience just as the journalist does when delivering the news.

Objective. The objective point of view places the viewer in the role of eavesdropper. "No one is addressing the camera directly; the camera is just an observer of the action" (Burrows & Wood, 1986, p. 139).

Subjective. The subjective point of view is achieved when the viewer assumes the television presenter's perspective and observes the environment through the presenter's eyes.

Field of View

The field of view is determined by the amount of information contained within the camera's shot. The three basic shots are: (a) long, (b) medium, and (c) close-up. According to Millerson (1990), long shots are used "to show where the action is taking place, to allow the audience to follow broad movements, to show the relative positions of subjects, and to establish mood" (p. 101). Closer shots are used "to show detail, to emphasize, to reveal reactions, and to dramatize" (p. 101). Shots are described by how the subject is framed on the television screen:

Long Shot (LS). The entire body, head to feet, and much of the surroundings are within the frame. In an Extreme Long Shot (ELS) the subject appears as a small figure embedded in the surroundings.

Medium Shot (MS). Most of the body is within the frame including the head and torso to just slightly above or below the waist.

Close-up (CU). The head and top of the shoulders are within the frame. An Extreme Close-up (ECU) shows only the eyes, nose, and mouth of the subject.

Camera Angle

"The angle from which you shoot can have a considerable influence on the audience's attitude towards it" (Millerson, 1990). There are three basic camera angles: (a) flat (normal) angle, (b) low angle, and (c) high angle.

The flat angle represents normal eye-level observation. A low angle shot occurs when the camera looks up at the subject; a high angle shot looks down on the subject. Subjects portrayed by a low angle shot may appear to be overpowering and authoritative while high angle shots tend to diminish the authority of the subject.

Camera Movement

Shots can be further defined by the camera movement involved. The four basic movements are:

Pan. Movement of the camera head horizontally on its axis, left or right.

Tilt. The camera head tilts up or down on its axis.

Dolly. Movement of the entire camera toward or away from the subject.

Truck. Movement of the entire camera from side to side.

Lens Movement

The camera's zoom lens permits adjustment of the content of a shot by zooming in or out. Zooming in fills the screen with close-up details of the image, while zooming out reveals the entire image.

Television Production

The eye of the camera has the potential to enhance or detract from the relationship between the televised instructor and the distant learner attending to the television monitor. Communication among the camera operator, the director who selects the camera's shots, and the instructor is vital. All must work together to project the appropriate image at the right time. A skillfully executed television production will ensure that information is conveyed effectively and that the quality of the instructor's presentation is maximized. To achieve these aims the following production techniques are suggested:

1. *Camera angle.* A normal, flat angle medium long to medium shot is the recommended camera angle and field of view. Avoid high or low angle shots and minimize long shots and close-ups of the instructor. Long shots increase the psychological distance between the instructor and viewer. Close-up shots are appropriate when showing detail of objects but are invasive when framing the instructor.

2. *Point of view.* The reportorial point of view is recommended as the dominant perspective. It has the potential to enhance a feeling of viewer participation, in contrast to the objective "eavesdropper" perspective. The reportorial point of view most closely emulates face-to-face conversation and enables the instructor to maintain eye contact, through the lens of the camera, with the distant learner.

3. *Movement.* Camera and lens movement should be minimal. Any movement should be executed smoothly and slowly to avoid distraction. Cutting between cameras should serve an instructional or practical purpose. Instructors should be cued to the on-air camera in order to preserve the reportorial point of view.

4. *Camera shots.* Shots should be pre-selected and composed off air. Conventional framing techniques are advised to avoid viewer distraction. The instructor and the message will be enhanced by stable, appropriately framed flat angle shots in the range of a medium long to a medium shot.

5. *Special techniques.* Special effects, reaction shots, and cut-aways should be used purposefully, judiciously, and sparingly. Overuse of these special techniques may be distracting. The transmission of instruction

should be as technologically transparent as possible to ensure the learner's concentration on function, not form.

6. *Board work.* Distant students often complain of not being able to write adequate notes from the board. A balance must be achieved in the length of time that textual information from the board, a graphic, or the character generator remains on screen. Inordinate amounts of textual information are more appropriately delivered in print.

7. *Legibility.* Visual aids such as charts, graphs, and tables must be appropriately designed and adapted to the television medium. Textual information must be clearly written and easy to read.

Excessive cutting from camera to camera, particularly when shifting from the reportorial to the objective point of view; frequent use of camera and lens movement (pans, tilts, and zooms); obscure framing techniques; and visual images at variance with the action are intrusive and will inordinately remind the viewer of the technological medium.

Instructor Orientation

Instructors must feel at ease in front of the camera and in the studio environment. This comfort level is vital to an effective presentation, the efficient operation of studio equipment, and the enhancement of the instructor's personal and presentational qualities. As Gehlauf, Shatz, and Frye (1991) state:

> Instructors do not want to be told how to teach; rather, they want to "get a feel" for the equipment and the specific techniques they need to use to be more effective in interactive television classrooms. To facilitate this type of training, the technical system must be as "user-friendly" as possible so that the technology is transparent to the educational process. (p. 26)

Hands-on orientation and practice sessions with mock telephone calls will help. The instructor, the camera operator, and the director should discuss ways in which they will communicate. The use of hand signals, cue cards, and other on-air communication strategies should be thought out and agreed upon well in advance of the first televised class. Illustration of the different points of view, camera shots and angles, and the effect of eye contact with the camera will assist the instructor in understanding the ways in which the medium influences the message.

The Receive Site

Situational Variables

Situational variables at remote sites include the number of students; the size and position of the television monitor; the angle of viewing and proximity to the screen; the location of the telephone; and the environmental conditions of the room such as acoustics, temperature, lighting, furniture, and seating arrangements (Meyrowitz, 1986). The situational variables ascribed to the classroom are as important a consideration as those of the studio. The best of televised instruction will suffer if remote students are under environmental duress while participating in a televised class.

Student Orientation and Support

Distance education is for many an unfamiliar method of learning. When sophisticated technology is involved, it can also be intimidating. Therefore, site support and student orientation to the system are important elements in the mediated classroom. It is essential to provide remote students with both technical support at the site and training in the use of the equipment. An introduction to the technology will reduce anxiety and pay dividends later, particularly when an instructor expects active participation from students during a class.

A site facilitator or coordinator can bridge the distance between the instructor in the studio and participants on site. The facilitator provides the "warm body" presence often missing in instruction at a distance.

Role of the Site Facilitator

While the site facilitator is not necessarily a content expert, an effective facilitator does need to be "a good planner, organizer, communicator, and decision-maker" (Stahmer & Green, 1992, p. 25). The facilitator's role may include the following tasks:

- arrives well in advance of "air time" and prepares the room, from adjusting the thermostat for comfort level to arranging the furniture for discussion groups;
- distributes materials and sets up ancillary audio-visual equipment;
- welcomes participants and orients newcomers to the facility;
- warms the climate by encouraging participants to introduce themselves;
- explains protocols and procedures;
- guides discussion and manages the group process;
- coordinates and facilitates telephone interaction; and
- troubleshoots in the event of technical failure.

A tutor may also act as a site facilitator and perform tasks more closely associated with the subject matter. The tutor serves as a "guide" to students, helping them find their way through a body of knowledge (Wong, 1987). The role of the tutor will be discussed further in the Case Study at the end of this chapter.

Utilization

The essence of television is visual imagery. In designing instruction for televised delivery, one is compelled to think in visual terms: How can each instructional session exploit the visual channel of communication? The fundamental principle that shapes the answer to that question is video's dynamic capacity to *show* instead of to *tell*. Creative analysis and planning for visual communication will counter the over-reliance on "talking heads," a term used to describe the often tedious practice of "telling" too much. However, as Massoumian (1989) cautions, "haphazard use of visuals

may lead to minimal or no instructional gain and gradual loss of effectiveness as an instructional tool" (p. 19). The author suggests the following as particularly amenable to visual representation:
- presenting outlines or lists;
- illustrating key points;
- presenting complex material in a step-by-step fashion;
- illustrating relationships; and
- summarizing information for retention and recall.

Leshin, Pollock, & Reigeluth (1992) note the "attention-focusing" capability of visual devices such as: zoom lens movement to emphasize important details, split screens, shading and contrast, voice-over narration, text, and graphics. The authors suggest that visual images can facilitate comprehension and retention of information through organizational, structural, and mnemonic (assisting memory) functions. Five forms of visual illustration noted are:
- representational pictures that show what things look like;
- diagrams illustrating conceptual relationships, organization, and structure of content material;
- maps showing spatial relationships;
- graphic organizers illustrating representations of conceptual relationships; and
- graphic presentations such as graphs, tables, and charts.

Rowntree (1990) identifies motion as a valuable characteristic of video. The author suggests the following video applications in which movement is an attribute:
- to demonstrate the operation of tools or equipment;
- to demonstrate skills that learners are expected to emulate;
- to conduct experiments in which the processes must be observed;
- to present a dramatic or musical performance in which it is necessary for learners to see as well as hear the performers;
- to analyze change over time using animation, slow motion, or time lapse photography;
- to reveal the spatial, three-dimensional qualities of an object or structure;
- to transport learners into situations that could not otherwise be experienced; and
- to present primary source material for analysis, such as archival film of historical events or videotapes of naturally occurring situations.

Distant Teaching via Interactive Television

The mediated classroom demands adaptation of instructional approaches and resources. This adaptive process requires instructional design decisions that ensure the effective utilization of media resources and the implementation of instructional strategies that maximize two-way communication. Whether conducting a two-hour videoconference or teaching a complete university course at a distance, utilizing interactive television requires a special set of skills and an understanding of how technology filters the instruction and influences interaction among participants (Carl, 1986).

Florini (1989) reminds us that "instructional effectiveness is rooted in how instructors use the technology, not in the technology itself" (p. 50). An intervening technology frequently requires the adjustment of an instructor's teaching style and the implementation of ways to compensate for lack of physical presence. Interactive television typically requires instructional techniques that differ from those used face-to-face. Time and effort must be expended to develop the "prerequisite skills and abilities to effectively present material in an interactive televised setting" (Gehlauf, Shatz, & Frye, 1991, p. 20).

Having planned and designed an instructional television session with visual communication in mind, the instructor is prepared to enter the television studio armed with an arsenal of video tools and an understanding of the basic elements of television production.

Presentational Tips

Teacher immediacy. "Teacher immediacy" involves a set of behaviors that reduces the psychological distance between instructor and student. Because distance imposes physical separation in a mediated classroom situation, immediacy behaviors assume added significance in attempts to reduce psychological distance. Immediacy can be enhanced by increased sensory stimulation through multiple channels of communication. "When a person communicates through words, facial expressions, tone of voice, body movements, and direct eye contact, there is greater immediacy than when a person communicates only through words and body movement" (Anderson, 1979, p. 544). Hackman and Walker (1990) found that teacher immediacy behaviors positively influenced perceived learning and student attitudes toward televised instruction. The authors conclude:

> ... satisfying televised courses were taught by instructors who used humor, asked questions, involved students, praised student contributions, and maintained a confident, expressive nonverbal demeanor. (p. 7)

Those instructors who exhibit a friendly and relaxed demeanor, who smile at and engage in eye contact with the camera, and who actively engage distant learners in telephone conversation exhibit a high degree of immediacy.

An effective presentation requires a level of energy and dynamism that will attract and hold the attention of the distant learner. Warmth, expressiveness, vocal variety, and sincerity will collectively influence the mediated rapport between the televised instructor and the learner.

Instructional strategies. "Enthusiasm is contagious. So is boredom" (Willis, 1992, p. 77). *Good teaching*, not technology or advanced television production, ensures an effective mediated presentation. The following is a collection of instructional strategies gleaned from Stahmer and Green (1992), Willis (1993), and Ostendorf (1989):

- Limit lectures to 20 minutes, or divide a lecture into 10-minute units and combine with alternative presentation strategies.
- Keep the structure simple and clear.
- Do not read material.
- Maintain a moderate speaking pace.
- Do not digress—keep participants on track.
- Vary instructors, maintaining viewer interest with a change of voice, image, and presentation style.
- Include different kinds of student involvement, from watching and reading to writing and talking.
- Vary the center of focus for activities from the on-camera presenter to a receive site group or individual.
- Incorporate timely breaks as a respite from the television monitor.
- Alternate between instruction and interaction.
- Motivate peer learning and support by encouraging students to work together both in and out of class.
- Visualize callers' voices by displaying photographs of students.
- Encourage participation by fostering a team atmosphere.

Interaction

"The responsibility for effective interaction falls squarely on the shoulders of the instructor" (Winn, 1990, p. 62). *Interaction doesn't just happen*; it must be a clearly articulated component of the televised session's overall design. The instructor must employ purposeful strategies to initiate interaction. Failure to do so will inevitably result in an awkward, uncomfortable silence when distant students are asked to call in. Here are some techniques for ensuring that the telephone will ring when interaction is expected:

1. Pre-determine a block of time for interaction and advise students in advance when interaction is anticipated. Provide an advance organizer to enable students to prepare for the interactive segment.

2. Integrate on-air interaction with on-site activities or assignments prepared in advance of interaction.

3. Designate specific students or sites to call in with responses, comments, or questions. An unstructured invitation to call in will not ensure a response.

4. Motivate interaction with structured silence. Avoid "filling in time" with potentially distracting activities while waiting for calls.

5. Clearly define discussion topics or questions and allow time for distant students to prepare responses and conduct the mechanics of telephoning the studio.

6. Vary the timing of interactive segments: prior to, during, and following information presentation. Continued deferral of interaction until after information presentation may reinforce passive viewing.

7. Encourage student-to-student interaction and ensure opportunities for social affiliation. Ask an in-class student or a student from a different site to respond to a caller. Questions do not always have to be answered by the instructor.

8. Establish greeting protocols to facilitate social affiliation.

Ostendorf (1989) offers the following additional advice for achieving interaction:

1. Initiate interaction within the first 20 minutes. "Get the attendees talking early in the program" (p. 75). If this does not occur, distant learners may be lulled into *watching*, rather than *participating*.

2. Prime participants for interaction. Remind viewers ahead of time that an interactive segment is forthcoming. Tell participants that their responses to a particular topic are requested and desired. Also tell them how they can take part in the discussion.

3. Involving participants in discussion. Assign discussion questions in advance of the televised session so that learners come prepared for interaction. Build in opportunities for discussion at the receive site to stimulate on-air responses. Use written assignments like case studies and quizzes as a "jumping off point for discussion" (p. 76).

Questioning Strategies

Questioning stimulates thought processes and forms the basis for interactivity. However, "fear of embarrassment" and "fear of the technology" are potential barriers to two-way communication (Cyrs & Smith, 1990). Inexperience with questioning techniques and "clock pressure" may mitigate further against telephone interaction. Cyrs and Smith suggest the following approach:

> Begin your first few classes with a few probing or open questions possibly written on the blackboard or on a handout. Set the stage early and demonstrate that you want more than short responses to closed questions with fixed answers....Use simple wording that is clear and concise, and start with questions at the recall or understanding level, questions that you know many students can answer correctly. (p. 185)

The authors provide additional suggestions for facilitating both teacher and student initiated questions:

1. Establish the ground rules for questions during the first class.
2. Use the distant student's name when asking a question.
3. Ask a student by name to survey his or her group for questions.
4. Pre-plan instructor questions.
5. Ask questions that appear in writing on the television screen to enable students to both *see* and *hear* the questions.
6. Pre-determine the cognitive level of a question: recall, comprehension, application, or critical thinking. Rephrase the question at a lower cognitive level if students resist calling in with responses.
7. Match questions with the lecture's objectives.
8. "Articulate difficult questions slowly and repeat if needed" (p. 150).
9. Ask one question at a time and "after you ask a question, wait for the answer" (p. 186). Endure the silence, wait patiently, and project complete confidence that someone will call with a response.

Well-prepared, clearly articulated questions will contribute to the effective utilization of the interactive capability of the medium. Planned interactive segments will help to achieve instructional goals and active participation by distant learners.

Summary

A plethora of video-based technologies is available to the distance educator and trainer. However, technology selection and utilization must be considered within the context of a holistic instructional system. The mediated classroom model poses that the televised instructional process is contingent upon four antecedent phases: instructional design, system design, administration, and media and print production. Communication and interaction among instructors and students separated by distance is influenced by situational variables and the technological filter.

"Visual thinking" is a primary consideration in designing effective televised instruction. Photographs, slides, graphics, roll-ins, video clips, and print materials are devices that will enrich the visually-mediated instructional process. The instructor's knowledge of basic television production techniques, the medium's codes and conventions, and hands-on experience in the studio's environment will assist in the adaptation of classroom teaching strategies to a telecommunications-based venue. Teacher immediacy behaviors that compensate for distance and intervening technologies will enhance mediated communication. A participatory learning experience for students at a distance relies on purposeful instructional strategies and questioning techniques intended to maximize interaction. Lastly, a well-established support infrastructure for students, in concert with a receive site environment conducive to learning, will influence learner satisfaction and the quality of distance delivered instruction.

Case Study

Saskatchewan is one of ten Canadian provinces situated in western Canada, north of Montana and North Dakota. Fewer than one million residents are scattered across 252,000 square miles, a land mass equivalent to the state of Texas. The province's geographic terrain, vast distances, and population distribution have created conditions highly conducive to the exploration of innovative solutions to communication problems. As a result, the province has become a testbed for experimentation in telecommunications and delivery of information to rural and northern residents. Distance education is an integral component of the educational experience in Saskatchewan.

During the early 1980s a spate of satellite trials conducted by the University of Saskatchewan (U of S) spawned the creation of a consortium called the Saskatchewan Tele-learning Association (STELLA). The pioneering efforts of STELLA members demonstrated that video-based distance education was indeed an effective method of instruction; however, a lack of systemic administrative and technical support hampered the delivery mechanism, and at times, the learning experience. The STELLA experience revealed that a reliable, transparent telecommunications system requires a formal operational infrastructure; a commitment to on-going technical training, site support, and hardware maintenance; and a dedicated administrative unit to coordinate network activity.

STELLA's fledgling satellite network laid the foundation for the development and implementation of the Saskatchewan Communications Network (SCN), a telecommunications network designed to provide the operational scaffolding to support and facilitate distance education in the province. This case study will examine SCN's role in video-based distance education and provide a sampling of delivery models and presentational strategies employed by network programmers.

Saskatchewan Communications Network (SCN)

Network Architecture

SCN comprises two interrelated networks: the SCN Cable Network, an educational television channel distributed to cable subscribers, and the SCN Training Network, a narrowcast network dedicated to the delivery of live interactive credit courses and training programs.

The network maintains a hybrid telecommunications infrastructure that melds terrestrial and satellite delivery strategies. The terrestrial component employs the fiber optic and microwave distribution system of SaskTel, the provincial telephone company. A full-time satellite transponder leased from Telesat Canada provides the satellite component and point-to-multipoint distribution capability.

Narrowcast Network System Design

The narrowcast network is a one-way video, two-way audio configuration. A combined video and audio signal, originating from any one of seven studio facilities, is transmitted by fiber optic and microwave links to either of the province's two uplinks. SaskTel's Television Operating Center (TOC) routes signal traffic to the appropriate uplink and programs each receive site to capture and process a pre-determined signal (see Figure 2). Students registered in an English course, for example, attend class at sites receiving the signal originating from the U of S. Sites where Geography students are gathered may receive, at the same time, the University of Regina (U of R) signal. There are 54 SCN receive sites located across the province, housed in regional colleges and the four campuses of the Saskatchewan Institute of Applied Science and Technology (SIAST). Each center is equipped with a Ku-band satellite receive dish, signal receiver, decoder device, television monitor, video cassette recorder, telephone and facsimile machine.

Network Management

The province's nine regional colleges are the delivery agents for SCN and the post-secondary institutions. The colleges provide a myriad of local support services, from counseling and registering students to issuing textbooks. Site Coordinators are appointed by the colleges and SIAST under

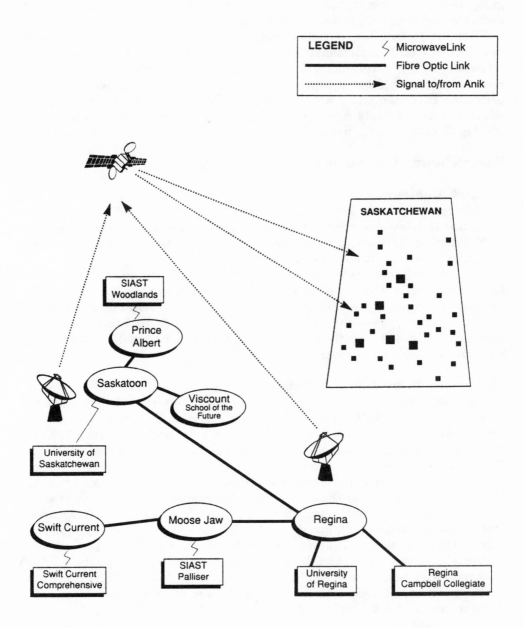

Figure 2. *Saskatchewan Communications Network configuration.*

contractual arrangements with SCN. The coordinators supervise the receive sites and administer the distance delivered programs. Most locations employ a Site Attendant who manages the technical operation of the site. The SCN Network Manager coordinates the province-wide team and provides the vital inter-institutional information link.

SCN is the interface between the technical infrastructure and the network client—the "programmer." SCN's primary function is to coordinate and facilitate access to network services, bridging the gap between program content and telecommunications technology. The network management role consists of the following key functions:

- coordinates network activity, including allocation of satellite transmission time, scheduling of the network, and monitoring of daily operations;
- coordinates information dissemination among programmers, administrators, technical engineers, studio production personnel, regional college program coordinators, and SCN Site Coordinators and Attendants;
- provides on-going technical training and system orientation; and
- coordinates and monitors hardware installation, repair, and maintenance.

Hardware Management and On-Site Support

Site Attendants prepare the receive site for distant learners, tuning in the appropriate satellite channel and audio signal and ensuring that the hardware is in working order. Ten minutes prior to the delivery of each class, the originating studio generates color bars and an audible tone. It is during this test period that attendants identify transmission problems. A telephone "Help Line," staffed by SaskTel's TOC, is available 24 hours a day should technical problems occur. Attendants simply telephone the Help Line, explain the transmission problem, and follow step-by-step instructions for correcting the problem.

The Help Line support system has proven highly effective. While most technical problems are attributable to operator error rather than equipment failure, the majority of problems can be "talked through" and resolved during these brief telephone calls. If technical difficulties persist, an on-site service call is conducted and a back-up videotape is dispatched to the site the following day.

Videoconference Applications

Although credit course delivery is the primary activity on the network, a number of organizations use the SCN Training Network to conduct videoconferences. Seminars and workshops designed for televised delivery provide professional development and training to a dispersed clientele. Videoconference organizers note three primary advantages of the delivery method:

1. Increased access to human resources. Time, distance, and travel expense frequently preclude face-to-face training. Videoconferencing provides increased access to content experts and professional development opportunities that may not otherwise be available.

2. *Timely dissemination of information.* A videoconference enables workshop leaders and content experts to be in multiple locations at the same time. Although separated by distance, participants acquire the same information collectively.

3. *Convenience and cost effectiveness.* Access to professional development resources in or near one's own community is convenient. The alternative is often a lengthy road trip or costly airline flight to a centralized location. Reduced expenditures for travel, meals, accommodations, and instructor time saves money.

Videoconference Planning and Delivery

A videoconference demands the same careful planning and organization as a face-to-face conference with the added challenges of mediated distance. Typically, network clients conduct the following pre-conference organizational activities:

1. *Instructional Design.* Audience analysis and message design lay the foundation for the videoconference. A preliminary meeting with studio production personnel activates "visual thinking" and early planning provides the necessary lead time to pre-produce and acquire visual resources.

2. *Scheduling.* Four components require advance scheduling: human resources, the videoconference date and transmission times, the desired receive sites, and the appropriate studio facility. Identifying and reserving workshop leaders, content experts, and site facilitators are early planning requirements. The instructional design phase determines the amount of on-air satellite transmission time required and the total time needed in receive site classrooms. Early site identification ensures availability and facilitates advance distribution of support materials. Studio selection is determined by budget and the production requirements of the videoconference.

3. *Staging the event.* The logistics of planning, organizing, and promoting a videoconference are more complex than a face-to-face event because of the involvement of multiple locations. Effective promotion of the event at the local level has proven essential to ensure participation from the targeted audience. Brochures and posters designed to provide relevant program information and logistical details such as site identification and registration procedures have been effective marketing tools for network programmers.

Methods of Delivery and Presentational Strategies

While SCN's technological menu is constant, each network programmer applies the creative energy and instructional design ingenuity to adapt the technology to both the subject matter and the needs of the learner. Effective programmers assume a holistic approach to video-based distance education. Successful strategies have evolved from extensive experience in mediated instruction and communication.

The following is a sampling of video-based models and presentational strategies used by network programmers in the delivery of credit courses and videoconferences.

Delivery Models

Tutor/proctor model. The University of Saskatchewan's network delivered courses are developed by an instructional design team led by the Division of Extension and Community Relations. Instructional designers develop and guide delivery of courses within a teaching/learning conceptual framework comprising the following steps:

1. The teacher disseminates information to the learner.
2. The teacher helps the learner contextualize and understand the information.
3. The information is incorporated into the learner's own reality. (Wong, 1988)

In distant-delivered courses, this process is facilitated by the instructor, on-site tutors or proctors, and learning peers. A tutor, who holds a master's degree in the subject area, or a proctor, with a relevant bachelor's degree, is employed at sites where six or more students are registered. The role of the tutor/proctor in the teaching/learning process includes three primary functions:

- assists students in contextualizing course content;
- stimulates and focuses on-site group discussions; and
- provides feedback to both the instructor and the student.

The tutor/proctor can lessen the anxiety of a distant learner and reduce the remoteness of a far-away institution. As an advocate for the learner and as both an intellectual and logistical guide to the learning experience, the tutor/proctor is a valued link in the supportive chain.

Multi-mode delivery. The U of S and SIAST employ a multi-mode delivery strategy designed for optimum flexibility. Each course consists of modular components that can be reconfigured depending on enrollment, budget, instructor availability, and network capacity.

A multi-mode course is constructed from an extensive print foundation. During the first year of delivery, print is combined with live televised transmission, on-site activities and discussion, and on-air telephone interaction. The weekly broadcasts are taped as they are transmitted and subsequently edited. The edited version becomes a video component for an alternative delivery strategy. The U of S History course, for example, uses pre-recorded lectures which are distributed to receive sites. Students gather in groups to watch the tapes and participate in site and on-air discussions. In SIAST's Business Administration diploma program, lectures delivered live in the first year become video components of independent study courses, supplemented by audioconferencing and periodic face-to-face tutorials.

Multi-mode courses are an efficient and cost-effective method of reconstituting instructional resource materials. The courses are highly adaptable to differing local circumstances and are not solely reliant on prime time live transmission on the network. A variety of live and multi-mode courses, amenable to the varied needs of adult learners, ensures a rich selection of post-secondary opportunities.

Secondary team teaching model. Satellite delivery of secondary courses is an option available to the small rural high school struggling to provide its students with a complete selection of academic credits. In experiments with a satellite-based delivery method, a team teaching model serving small clusters of students has shown promise. Similar in function to the U of S tutor/proctor model, the team teaching approach links a television teacher or "tele-teacher" with receive site facilitating teachers. The tele-teacher provides the subject matter expertise and regular televised instruction while facilitating teachers manage the learning process at each remote site. The on-site facilitating teacher, while not necessarily a subject matter expert, bridges the distance between tele-teacher and student and conducts the following activities:

- monitors each student's progress;
- manages logistical tasks such as assignment and exam distribution and collection;
- facilitates discussion and encourages interaction with the tele-teacher and other learners;
- compiles supplementary instructional resources;
- consults with the tele-teacher and assists in student evaluation; and
- provides supervision and manages the group process.

A larger task, of particular importance at the secondary level, is the nurturing of independent study and research skills inherent in both distance education and lifelong learning.

The facilitating teacher helps reduce the isolation of the high school distant learner and provides the necessary pacing and tracking mechanism often missing in independent correspondence study. The team teaching model and interaction with other distant learners has been instrumental in providing a sense of community and a shared learning experience, contributing factors in the continued perseverance and eventual success of distant learners in the secondary sector.

Presentational Strategies

Panel format. A panel of presenters hosted by a moderator has been an effective videoconference delivery strategy. Panelists provide the vocal, visual, and presentational variety that holds the attention of the viewer. The moderator provides the structure and continuity that enables presenters to concentrate on content rather than the mechanics of the studio production.

An effective moderator is unobtrusive, gently imposing structure on the proceedings without impeding discussion or detracting from guest presentations. The moderator's role includes the following tasks:

- interprets and relays the instructions of the floor director;
- provides opening and closing remarks, procedural instructions, and continuity commentary;
- attends to the script and clock, keeping participants on track and on time;
- facilitates discussion;

- responds to telephone calls and directs questions to the appropriate panelist; and
- ensures optimum usage of the time and resources available.

Use of Drama. Drama was the focal point of "The Instructor Road Test," a videoconference delivered by the Saskatchewan Association for Lifelong Learning (SALL). It featured pre-produced roll-ins that dramatized the foibles of the ineffective instructor. With a liberal injection of humor, the dramatic segments gained instant viewer attention and sparked discussion at the sites. Following each dramatized example, viewers completed a check list, rating their own instructional attributes. Following on-site discussion of the exercise, participants were invited to telephone the studio and acquire advice from award-winning teachers.

In a further use of drama during the U of S televised History course, actors in full costume often arrived on set from the past to "interrupt" the professor and enact events from the pages of history. These historical vignettes, scripted and acted by on-campus students, used drama and the visual impact of television to stimulate interest, assist comprehension and understanding, motivate discussion, and provide multi-sensory reinforcement of concepts, events, and ideas.

Illustration and demonstration. In a Gerontological Nursing class, delivered by SIAST's Wascana Campus, the instructor effectively used the medium of television to "show" rather than "tell" nurses how a patient assessment was conducted. With a few simple props, the studio was transformed into an examining room. A real physician and his volunteer patient demonstrated each step of a patient assessment while nurses observed the procedure on their receive site monitors. Following the demonstration, the physician joined the instructor on set and students called in to ask questions and discuss the patient assessment with the physician. Through illustration and demonstration, subject matter is transformed into visual images, providing the distant student with an alternative form of learning and comprehension.

Site facilitators and off-air activity. The Saskatchewan Alcohol and Drug Abuse Commission (SADAC) is a provincial government agency whose mandate includes the professional development of those involved in substance abuse counseling. Through regular videoconferences, SADAC provides increased access to human resources, particularly in the north of the province where distance and the expense of travel preclude regular access to continuing education opportunities.

SADAC is particularly effective in utilizing the videoconference medium as a stimulus for on-site discussion, activity, and community action. Because the nature of the subject matter requires group discussion and group-oriented instructional strategies, the role of the site facilitator is an essential ingredient in a successful videoconference.

As part of a carefully articulated instructional design process, SADAC provides site facilitator training and a pre-conference orientation to each videoconference. Facilitators are equipped with an understanding of adult education principles, group process management skills, and videoconference procedures and protocols. Support materials and a facilitator's manual are distributed prior to each videoconference. During the videoconference the site facilitator becomes an extension of the studio presenter, managing the group process and encouraging active participation.

In a typical four- to six-hour videoconference, less than half the time is devoted to on-air transmission. This is a purposeful design strategy intended to balance the videoconference's focal point. In a richly varied visual and oral format, each videoconference integrates on-air information presentation from subject matter specialists with off-air discussion and information assimilation. Telephone interaction provides the capstone of a participatory learning experience.

In conclusion, the Saskatchewan Communications Network coordinates access to telecommunications services and maintains an infrastructure supportive of point-to-multipoint satellite communication. The model supports the premise that distance education is grounded in a symbiotic relationship: people and technology working in tandem, each contributing to the nature of the communication process. The most sophisticated telecommunications network will be rendered ineffective without a well-developed human infrastructure and firmly established communication strategy. The responsiveness of the network's foundational strata and the cooperation among its many players influences ease of access, operational efficiency, information dissemination, and fundamentally, the quality of the educational experience for distant learners.

A number of effective delivery models and presentational strategies have emerged from the experiences of network programmers including a post-secondary tutor/proctor model, a team teaching model for high school course delivery, and a multi-mode course development and delivery strategy. The panel format; the use of drama, illustration, and demonstration as stimuli for discussion; and facilitator-led site activities are some of the video-based strategies that facilitate two-way communication. Each strategy contributes to a telecommunications environment that fosters active, participatory learning.

Summary

Instructional media continue to evolve, moving ever closer to technological fusion. Hybrid systems that meld data, audio, and video persistently erode the barrier of distance and enrich the learner's environment with multi-sensory stimuli. Distant learners, once resigned to isolation, are increasingly capable of venturing boldly into interconnecting spheres of communication.

Digital technology is propelling video into multiple technological configurations. The instructional applications of compressed video are beginning to break free of the commercially viable traditions of broadcast television, creating video forged in distance education rather than entertainment television. Video at its most effective is one communication tool among many, each applied according to a finely crafted holistic design.

References

Anderson, J. F. (1979). Teacher immediacy as a predictor of teaching effectiveness. In D. Nimmo (Ed.), *Communication Yearbook 3* (pp. 543–559). New Brunswick, NJ: Transaction Books.

Barker, B. O., Frisbie, A. G. & Patrick, K. R. (1989). Broadening the definition of distance education in light of the new telecommunications technologies. *The American Journal of Distance Education, 3*(1), 20–29.

Bates, A. W. (Ed.) (1984). *The role of technology in distance education.* New York: St. Martin's Press.

Bates, A. W. (1991). Third generation distance education: The challenge of new technology. *Research in Distance Education, 3*(2), 10–15.

Bates, A. W., Harrington, R., Gilmore, D. & van Soest, C. (1992). *Compressed video and video-conferencing in open and distance learning: A guide to current developments.* Unpublished manuscript, The Open Learning Agency, Burnaby, B.C.

Brown, S. (1984). Video cassettes. In A. W. Bates (Ed.), *The role of technology in distance education* (pp. 43–55). New York: St. Martin's Press.

Brown, B. & Fortosky, D. (1986). Use of television. In I. Mugridge & D. Kaufman (Eds.), *Distance education in Canada* (pp. 260–282). London, England: Croom Helm.

Burrows, T. D. & Wood, D. N. (1986). *Television production. Disciplines and techniques* (3rd ed.). Dubuque, IA: Wm. C. Brown Publishers.

Carl, D. R. (1986). Developing faculty to use videoconferencing to deliver university course credit over cable and satellite. *Canadian Journal of Educational Communication, 15*(4), 235–250.

Cyrs, T. E. & Smith, F. A. (1990). *Teleclass teaching: A resource guide* (2nd ed.). Las Cruces, NM: New Mexico State University, Center for Educational Development.

Dick, W. & Carey, L. (1985). *The systematic design of instruction* (2nd ed.). Glenview, IL: Scott, Foresman and Company.

Donis, D. A. (1973). *A primer of visual literacy.* Boston, MA: M.I.T. Press.

Florini, B. M. (1989). Teaching styles and technology. In E. R. Hayes (Ed.), *Effective teaching styles. New Directions for Continuing Education, 43,* 41–53. San Francisco, CA: Jossey-Bass Publishers.

Forster, A. (Ed.) (1992). *Satellite technology: A versatile ingredient in distance education programs.* Gloucester, ON: Telesat Canada.

Gagné, R. M., Briggs, L. J. & Wager, W. W. (1988). *Principles of instructional design* (3rd ed.). New York: Holt, Rinehart, and Winston.

Garrison, D. R. (1990). Communications technology. In D. R. Garrison & D. Shale (Eds.), *Education at a distance: From issues to practice* (pp. 41–52). Malabar, FL: Robert E. Krieger publishing Company.

Garrison, D. R. & Shale, D. (1990). *Education at a distance: From issues to practice.* Malabar, FL: Robert E. Krieger Publishing Company.

Gehlauf, D. N., Shatz, M. A. & Frye, T. W. (1991). Faculty perceptions of interactive television instructional strategies: Implications for training. *The American Journal of Distance Education, 5*(3), 20–28.

Gunawardena, C. (1989). Current approaches to using communications technologies for delivering adult continuing/professional education. In C. Campbell Coggins (Ed.), *Proceedings of the 30th Annual Adult Education Research Conference* (pp. 171–176). Madison, WI: University of Wisconsin, Madison.

Gunawardena, C. (1990). The integration of video-based instruction. In D.R. Garrison and D. Shale (Eds.), *Education at a distance: From issues to practice* (pp. 109–122). Malabar, FL: Robert E. Krieger Publishing Company.

Hackman, M. & Walker, K. (1990). The impact of systems design and instructional style on student reactions to distance education. *Research in Distance Education, 2*(2), 7–8.

Heinich, R., Molenda, M. & Russell, J. D. (1989). *Instructional media and the new technologies of instruction* (3rd ed.). New York: Macmillan Publishing Company.

Kemp, J. E. & Smellie, D. C. (1989). *Planning, producing, and using instructional media* (6th ed.). New York: Harper & Row Publishers.

Leshin, C. B., Pollock, J. & Reigeluth, C. M. (1992). *Instructional design strategies and tactics.* Englewood Cliffs, NJ: Educational Technology Publications.

Lochte, R. H. (1993). *Interactive television and instruction.* Englewood Cliffs, NJ: Educational Technology Publications.

Massoumian, B. (1989). Successful teaching via two-way interactive video. *TechTrends, 34*(2), 16–19.

Meyrowitz, J. (1986). Television and interpersonal behavior: Codes of perception and response. In G. Gumpert & R. Cathcart (Eds.), *Intermedia. Interpersonal communication in a media world* (3rd ed.) (pp. 253–272). New York: Oxford University Press.

Millerson, G. (1990). *The technique of television production* (12th ed.). Boston, MA: Focal Press.

Noll, A. M. (1988). *Television technology: Fundamentals and future prospects.* Norwood, MA: Artech House, Inc.

Oliver, E. L. (1993). *Interaction at a distance: Mediated communication in televised post-secondary courses.* Unpublished doctoral dissertation, Northern Illinois University, DeKalb, Illinois.

Ostendorf, V. A. (1989). *Teaching through interactive television.* Littleton, CO: Virginia A. Ostendorf, Inc.

Rowntree, D. (1990). *Teaching through self-instruction. How to develop open learning materials* (2nd ed.). New York: Nichols Publishing.

Schwier, R. A., Brown, F. B., Misanchuk, E. R. & Proctor, L. F. (1992). *Interactive media and distance education for Saskatchewan schools.* Unpublished manuscript, University of Saskatchewan, Department of Communications, Continuing, and Vocational Education.

Stahmer, A. & Green, L. (1992). *The satellite event management guide.* Oakville, ON: Canadian Satellite Learning Services, Inc.

Telesat Canada (1991). *The Canadian education market survey.* Gloucester, ON: Author.

Wagner, E. D. (1991, January). Assisting educational users of telecom delivery systems: The instructional design process. A workshop presentation at the Pacific Telecommunications Council conference, Honolulu, HA.

Weinstein, S. B. (1986). *Getting the picture. A guide to CATV and the new electronic media.* New York: IEEE Press.

Wileman, R. (1993). *Visual communicating.* Englewood Cliffs, NJ: Educational Technology Publications.

Willis, B. (1992). *Effective distance education. A primer for faculty and administrators* (Monograph Series in Distance Education No. 2). Fairbanks, AK: University of Alaska Center for Cross-Cultural Studies.

Willis, B. (1993). *Distance education: A practical guide.* Englewood Cliffs, NJ: Educational Technology Publications.

Winn, B. (1990). Media and instructional methods. In D. R. Garrison & D. Shale (Eds.), *Education at a distance: From issues to practice* (pp. 53–66). Malabar, FL: Robert E. Krieger Publishing Company.

Wong, A. T. (1987). Media as agents of interaction in distance learning. *Canadian Journal of University Continuing Education, 13*(2), 6–11.

Wong, A. T. (1988). *An experiment in televised university courses: Evaluation of English 110.6 and History 112.6.* Unpublished manuscript, University of Saskatchewan, Division of Extension and Community Relations, Saskatoon, SK.

Zigerell, J. J. (1986). *A guide to telecourses and their uses.* Fountain Valley, CA: Coast Community College District.

Chapter Eight

Computer Tools for Distance Education

Richard A. Markwood

Computers are rapidly becoming the preferred long-distance communication tool, and computer networks are evolving as a major resource in distance education. The increasing communications capability of computers is being stimulated by networking research and development in universities and in the computing and telecommunications industries, and also by government initiatives such as the National Research and Education Network (NREN). These developments are taking place at such a rapid pace that it is difficult to say anything that is timely for more than a few weeks or months; nevertheless, educators in both public and private settings are making decisions daily to employ computers in distance education, and the broad outlines of trends for the future are becoming clear.

Computers and Curricula

The discussion of the role of computers in curricula has been ongoing since the 1970s and logically followed work on programmed instruction in the 1960s. Computerized instruction falls into two broad categories—computer assisted instruction (or learning) (CAI or CAL), and computer managed instruction (or learning) (CMI or CML). Computer assisted instruction generally includes discrete lessons to achieve specific but limited educational objectives, such as mastery of a narrowly defined specific concept, a spelling list, or a mathematical process. Computer managed instruction incorporates broader objectives and utilizes the computer's branching, storage, and retrieval capabilities to manage students as they progress through an entire sequence of learning processes, individualized tutorials, evaluations, and guidance. Within elementary and secondary school environments, today's CMI systems are referred to as integrated learning systems (ILSs). One significant difference in these two models is the role of the teacher: in CAI the teacher uses the computer as an additional tool as he/she manages the classroom processes; in CML the teacher or staff of teachers become program developers. The computer replaces the teacher in carrying out many management and teaching tasks (Rushby, 1979, pp. 34–35). Practice of both CAI and CML can be found in distance education.

One notable example of the extent to which computer managed education may be utilized in distance education is a project in the United Kingdom. The Home Computing Program of the Open University is a national effort to deliver university education to homes. The primary technology in this program is the stand-alone personal computer. This program commenced in 1988 with the decision by the Open University to switch from a university-supported terminal network (the computer terminals were located in education centers throughout the country) to the home-based stand-alone personal computer. In 1990 alone the program enrolled 13,000 students. The curriculum on floppy disks is delivered to students by mail. Students can earn a baccalaureate degree in this program. Part of the decision to base the home-school delivery on the personal computer was the assumption that personal computers are as available as televisions, radios, and audio cassette systems in homes. The university makes available alternative modes of acquisition to those students who do not have computers—e.g., rental agreements and subsidies—but their assumption that personal computers are widely available appears to be valid (Berry & Burrows, 1990).

The Home Computing Program demonstrates the extent to which computers as stand-alone devices can be used in distance education, but the most exciting opportunities are being created by the ability to link computers through *networks*. Networks combine the efficiency of a digital signal with the ubiquity of the worldwide telephone system to make possible the connection of desktop computers all over the world. Personal computers put production of course materials in the hands of the teacher, and networks tie the teacher and students to each other, to libraries, to data bases, and to other information resources of the education enterprise, opening up entirely new opportunities. Stephen Wolff, Director of the National Science Foundation Division of Networking and Communications Research and Infrastructure (quoted in *The Chronicle of Higher Education*), believes that because of the emergence of the National Science Foundation Internet, "It's now conceivable that the U.S. can implement a network connecting every student and teacher in the country—from kindergarten to post-college—before the end of the century, revolutionizing education and research" (*Technological Progress*, 1992, December 16, p. A12).

Networks

Networks make computerized distance education increasingly attractive. Two or more computers connected to each other are, in effect, a network. If the computers are within a building or close enough to have a permanent wire or radio circuit between them, the network is called a LAN (local area network); if two or more computers rely on telephone circuits to connect them over long distances, the network is called a WAN (wide-area network). Most universities in the United States, many colleges, and a growing number of high schools and elementary schools have computers or LANs which are connected to WANs, in turn interconnected through a network of networks called the "Internet." The term "internet" is generally used to refer to two or more networks connected together. "Internet" (with a capital "I") normally refers to the government sponsored network of networks called NSFnet developed by the National Science Foundation. It is sometimes also called the Interim NREN, anticipating the establishment of a National Research and Education Network. The Internet, to be described in more detail later in this chapter, reaches into essentially every country in the world.

Tanenbaum (1981) identifies four major reasons for networking computers: (1) resource sharing, (2) reliability through redundance, (3) decentralization of the computing operation, and (4) providing powerful communication tools among widely separated people. Each of these goals has direct relevance to the task of distance education, but perhaps none more than providing powerful communication tools among widely separated people. One of the reasons for bringing students to a school is to enable them to engage in dialogue with teachers and the collective scholarship embodied in all the resources of the institution. Networks are increasingly making it feasible for this dialogue to take place via computer networks without the students being physically present in a central location.

In its simplest form a network connects a computer and its unique applications (e.g., word processor, spreadsheet, utilities, games, user files, and so forth) to another computer and its unique set of applications. The two computers may be connected by an actual cable which runs from one to the other, or they may be connected temporarily (as are two telephones at opposite ends of a long distance telephone call) by a series of cables, telephone wires, and microwave radio circuits, many of which may be owned by several different commercial telephone companies.

Tanenbaum (1981) points out that one way to imagine a network which would connect all of the world's telephones is to envision several hundred million wires running from each telephone, one wire to each of the other telephones. Every house would become a massive cable terminal. A much less costly alternative to this ludicrous situation is to run a single wire from each telephone to a single central switchboard capable of connecting every other telephone. In reality the telephone network (and the emerging computer networks) are combinations of these two approaches which minimize both cost and complexity by deploying interconnected and strategically well-placed switches in a few well-dispersed high-traffic areas.

On the Internet, individual computers or LANs (networks of computers) connect to routers (specialized computers) whose function is to identify and open the best circuit path (through cables, telephone circuits, and other routers), and to use that circuit path for communication between two distant computers. Under ideal conditions, the speed at which this process takes place is very close to the speed of light plus processing time for the routers and computers to handle their tasks.

Commonly used bandwidths on WANs are determined primarily by services and tariff structures of the telephone companies. The backbone circuits of the current Internet are called "T3" circuits (44.7 million bits per second). A gigabit network (1 billion bits per second) is a vision for the year 2000 set forward in *Grand Challenges*, a supplement to the President's Fiscal Year 1992 Budget (Committee on Physical, Mathematical, and Engineering Sciences, 1992). A gigabit is approximately enough bandwidth or capacity to transmit the entire contents of the *Encyclopaedia Britannica* in one second. While these vast numbers are essentially meaningless to users in the field, increased bandwidth is of importance because it means increased networking capability. More persons will be able to simultaneously engage in more complex computing activities if the network is larger.

The simplest form of WAN is a central computer, commonly called a "host," with the ability to receive telephone calls. A specialized computer called a "server" performs the function of responding to and connecting telephone calls to the host. This simplest form of WAN can be very useful. An example of a well developed implementation of this type network is Big Sky Telegraph, operated in rural Montana by Western Montana University. Big Sky Telegraph supports a wide variety of services, including bulletin boards, on-line courses, electronic newsletters, and access to many other resources. This system is based on relatively inexpensive equipment, a very small staff, and low operating costs. The low costs are partially maintained by users paying their own circuit costs by dialing the server via regular long-distance telephone calls. Big Sky maintains a very large data bank of lesson plans available to all its members. It operates several discussion groups where participants can post questions and get answers from other participants or cooperating experts. It delivers courses to Montana teachers. It supports electronic mail among participants.

At the other extreme of complexity and functionality, the network of most significance to distance educators is the Internet. Most universities in the United States, many colleges, and a growing number of high schools and elementary schools are connected to WANs, which are in turn interconnected through this network of networks. The major U.S. component of the Internet, NSFnet, was initially funded by National Science Foundation grants to several regional or mid-level networks, who in the grant process assumed responsibility for distributing network connections and services to universities, Federal research laboratories, and research facilities of private industry. NSFnet, over time, has incorporated BITNET, an earlier network which interconnected universities. Later, NSFnet included colleges, community colleges, and K–12 institutions in its service community. These government-sponsored mid-level networks act like utilities supporting technical aspects of the operating network, but they also promote development of the national network through education, training, and support services.

Institutions that wish to connect to the Internet may join the network through various network organizations. The regional networks (like NorthWestNet, MidNet, or West Net), some state networks (like Colorado SuperNet or OARnet—Ohio Academic Resources Network), local networks (like Cleveland FreeNet or its spin-off the National Public Telecomputing Network), and other special purpose networks (like FrEDmail or KIDSnet) make opportunities for qualified organizations to become active.

Each mid-level network or network access provider establishes its own criteria and costs for connecting organizations to the network and provides different functionality and services. The organizational structure of each differs: some are independent not-for-profit corporations; some are informal cooperative associations; some are university-based services. Nearly all of the mid-level networks recover operating costs through some type of member fee structure. Most of the mid-level networks are actively encouraging connection by all levels of education including K–12. Two factors which normally inhibit connection for those who are interested are cost and technical expertise. Operating wide area networks is a complex process requiring a sound working understanding of computing and computer networking operations. The staffs of the mid-level networks have only limited resources to train and support organizations that wish to connect; they normally expect members to have the capability to commit human and financial resources to maintaining their end of the connection.

All networks have bandwidth to support e-mail and file transfers (these and other network tools will be discussed in the next section). To support highly interactive communication with a large program on a remote computer requires significantly greater bandwidth. For example, the number of bits involved in transmitting a color image is enormous, and the cost of bandwidth for transmitting such images is formidable. Realistically, most networks in today's world are limited to text transmission. The cost of bandwidth is not subject to the same forces that have made computers so readily available. Circuit costs are more clearly tied to the telecommunications infrastructure and the commercial carriers who must bear initial cost for expanding the telephone system. The cost of bandwidth will continue to be a major hurdle in the effort to develop educational telecommunications networks.

Network-Specific Tools

The earlier example of the Open University's Home Computing Program demonstrates that networks are not essential to distance education (the OU relies on the mail system); however, networks provide the opportunity to utilize resources which enhance curriculum, and networks encourage interactivity and interpersonal collaboration.

E-mail (electronic mail)

E-mail (electronic mail) is an easy way to communicate with persons all over the world. Many distance learning providers depend on e-mail for routine communication between teachers and students and among students.

Bulletin boards are a type of e-mail conference. Their analogy to the bulletin board in the office or hall is apt. Anyone with access to the bulletin board can post something; there is no particular organization; there are large differences in the quality of the information which might appear; and the items displayed may be quite interesting if one has the time to sort out the information. Moderated bulletin boards have an editor who determines what may be posted. Bulletin boards are often topical as a means of focusing content. In their best form, bulletin boards can provide useful, long-distance, ongoing discussion. Two common public bulletin boards on the Internet are USENET and LISTSERV.

USENET is the most widely-used system of bulletin board discussions on the Internet. Files in the USENET system are stored on network host machines throughout the Internet. Discussions, called USENET news groups, can be accessed by individuals connected to the Internet (Kochmer, 1991, pp. 72–73). LISTSERV is a system set up originally by BITNET to support discussion groups. It differs from USENET in that an individual may "subscribe" to a list (though no fees are involved). Once the user subscribes to a discussion, items posted to that discussion are automatically directed to his/her unique Internet address by LISTSERV software somewhere within the network (Kochmer, 1991, pp. 88–89). For practical purposes, both USENET and LISTSERV are available to any persons with access to the Internet. The amount of information available through these systems is virtually limitless. The quality and usefulness of the information varies. The usefulness of these information resources to the task of distance education depends on the educator's creativity, imagination, and knowledge of the resources.

Computer Conferencing

A computer conference is a bulletin board type of system used exclusively by a teacher and an individual group of students. The computer conference can be used to support and organize all the computer communication of a class. Separate groups of files, easily retrieved and searched, may be used for teacher-to-class communication, teacher-to-individual-student communication, class discussion including both teacher and students, student-to-teacher communication, classroom management information, and so forth. The students need not be located in proximity to each other. If they have access to the Internet, students worldwide could participate in such a discussion.

TELNET

TELNET is the Internet tool for logging on to distant computers. The network allows your desktop computer to function as a terminal for a remote computer. Resources on the Internet grow at such a pace that it is difficult to grasp the amount of information available to the desktop computers of students, teachers, and schools. But the function of TELNET allows Internet users to access computers which maintain current directories of these resources. One notable example is WAIS (Wide Area Information Server) at Thinking Machines Corporation, Cambridge, MA. WAIS allows the user to have access to a user-friendly Macintosh computer programmed to find and use many different resources on the Internet (Kochmer, 1991, pp. 150–160). Another specific example of the use of TELNET is to gain access to any of the libraries attached to the Internet.

Most universities and many public libraries are automated and have their card catalogs and other resources available to users on some type of network. Many are available to the Internet community. These are commonly called OPACs (On-line Public Access Catalogs). The information commonly found in the card catalogue can be browsed. Some library systems allow you to perform searches to generate topic-related lists of books. Some provide access to abstracts. Some provide assistance in locating the books nearest you and assistance with inter-library loan (Kochmer, 1991, pp. 104–106). While lists and descriptions of books and resources have some utility in education, the content of those resources are of primary importance. Thus, several efforts in the networking community are designed to deliver the *content* of books and articles to users.

Teachers and Networks

Speaking from their own experiences as humans, as students, and as scholars, teachers enter into dialogue with their students—informal conversations, formal lectures, and the whole range between. Some dialogue involves evaluation: teachers correct students' thinking, their grammar, their behavior. Formal evaluation of papers and performances of all kinds, including summary evaluations of a student's semester or year is one type of dialogue. Teachers create or recreate experiences and expect students to reflect on and understand those experiences. These may be immediate experiences, such as events in the classroom, on the playground, or in the laboratory, or experiences distant in time or place—current events, history, or complex phenomena like social problems or environmental issues. Some experiences are vicarious: stories, artificial laboratory experiments, simulations. Then, too, in helping students understand these experiences teachers introduce them to methods and procedures—students are made to think about how we know and learn. These might include methods of science, or adaptations of the scientific method for specific disciplines, as in literary criticism, history, or mathematics. Every discipline has a different approach to understanding and interpreting experience. Finally, students eventually understand that knowledge is incomplete and that truth is always fragile and subject to reexamination and revision. Teachers introduce students to the community of scholars where the discussion of truth and knowledge takes places. Libraries are the most common place to interact with the community of scholars: scholars speak in books and in scholarly research published in journals or reported in magazines. Sooner or later most students engage in direct dialogue with members of the community of scholars, in classrooms, in professional meetings, and through correspondence. So, all of these things— student/teacher dialogue, reflecting on and understanding experiences, learning and using methodologies, and participating in the community of scholars—summarize the major ways in which teachers relate to students.

How do networks enable us to conduct distance education? The brief answer is that networks allow teachers to perform all of the above functions. Networks have the potential of enabling teachers to do many of these things easily and perhaps more effectively. This section will illustrate how teachers in distance education have at their disposal through networks the ability to perform each of the teacher's functions. This section is not a "how-to" on using networks, but is rather intended to increase awareness of how teachers might use the tools which networks put at their disposal.

Networks make it possible to conduct classroom activities free from the constraints of time and place. Individuals in the networked "class" may be anywhere. The schedule of networked "classroom" activities may be very flexible. Individuals may participate in "class" activities at times convenient to them and not dictated by the teacher or other members of the "class." Other than these freedoms from time and place, these network-enhanced teaching methods are not different from using computers as teaching/learning tools in the regular classroom. Within limits imposed by equipment and network functionality, what teachers do with computers in the classroom, they can also do on networks in a virtual classroom. Networking capabilities are evolving rapidly. All of the things mentioned in the following sections are possible, and they will become increasingly easy as networking technologies and networking tools develop.

Networks and Dialogue

Electronic mail (e-mail) and bulletin boards are the primary network tools for distance educators to use in carrying on dialogue with students. Informal e-mail—one-to-one correspondence—is in many ways more effective than even telephone conversations. Frequently e-mail is spontaneous like conversation, but unlike a person-to-person conversation or a telephone call, one is not actually in the presence of the person or the person's voice. This tends to have a leveling effect. Correspondents address each other more as peers. Good teachers always strive to create this atmosphere, but it is difficult: students in the classroom seldom forget that the teacher represents authority. E-mail seems to create the peer-to-peer discussion more easily. Bulletin boards are similarly spontaneous. The major difference is that a bulletin board allows the discussion to be one to many; an individual posts his/her comments to the class, and every other individual is free to respond, one to many. The bulletin board becomes an ongoing record of an entire class conversation. The bulletin board also has a built-in mechanism for structuring the content so that if a given topic stimulates a large amount of conversation, or if the conversation is of interest to only a subset of the class, it is easy to subdivide the file space and create a separate discussion for that subtopic, thus giving added structure to the ongoing discussion.

A more formal use of e-mail is in the submission and evaluation of assignments. A networked student may submit assignments by e-mail. Because the teacher then has a computer file rather than a paper, the teacher may use all the tools of his/her word processor. For example, he/she can insert text, and the paper will automatically be reformatted. The inserted text is adjacent to the problem and is readable (unlike many scribbled marginal notes or cryptic codes, e.g., "See text, Para. 5.a," which teachers handwrite on hard-copy papers). The teacher can move blocks of text to improve the word order or the structure of the entire composition. The instructor can attach summary comments. He/she can use "macros" to efficiently insert frequently-used comments, and track whether or not the student continues to make the same errors over time. When the work of evaluation is completed, the teacher can return the assignment and comments as e-mail, and the student then has a computer file with which he/she can utilize all the tools of his/her own word processor in making revisions. The teacher can "publish" model papers by distributing them to the entire class on the bulletin board. The bulletin board system can be used for a group-editing process or critique.

Teachers can lecture by e-mail or make other kinds of formal presentations. Most networks are capable of delivering large text files via e-mail. Most e-mail is in a text file format, but more and more desktop computers are being equipped to handle video and sound. Understand that even if a computer file includes video and sound, it is still a digital file and can be distributed over a network. The major difference between a text file and a multimedia file is its size. The two major limiting factors are the equipment required for multimedia and the capacity of the network. If the network has multimedia capabilities and the receiving computers are properly equipped, a teacher using a network for distance education can have the advantages of text enhanced by sound and graphics.

Experiences

Networks provide many resources teachers can use to create educational experiences for students. Networked students in elementary schools commonly correspond with distant schoolmates via e-mail. Instead of reading about children in Japan, Europe, or Russia, they are "talking" with them. E-mail between school children gives the global community a dimension unique to this medium. There are many resources available on the Internet for experiences through news services, e.g., *USA Today*, or NPTN's (National Public Telecomputing Network) "Student News Network."

Literature, folk tales, short stories, novels, and so forth, are a common means of creating experiences for students. Several projects on the Internet are involved in making standard literary texts available on the network, i.e., Project Gutenberg at the University of Illinois. Having the text of these books on line makes possible many approaches that having them in print does not permit.

Teaching Methodology

Teachers use a variety of strategies; lecture, demonstration, critiques of scholarly work, and so forth, but gathering information and data and analyzing them are at the heart of most teaching approaches. Unfortunately, much pedagogy is based on pre-existing information or data in secondary sources. Data of all kinds are available on computer networks. These data can be used effectively in teaching. Various branches of the Federal government are making available access to data which they collect. Some data are being made available expressly for elementary and secondary school teachers and children, designed to be useful in school curricula. One example is SPACELINK made available by NASA, which has a great deal of information about NASA and its activities in space. Vice President Gore (1992), one of the sponsors of the National Research and Education Network legislation, has proposed in his book, *Earth in the Balance: Ecology and the Human Spirit*, that school children through the Internet and by means of national data bases currently being built by nationally sponsored research laboratories could actually become involved in the task of science by monitoring environmental systems (p. 356).

Community of Scholars

Networks are an invaluable tool for accessing published works in libraries. The large majority of university libraries in the United States have made their collections accessible through the Internet. The degree of access usually includes, at a minimum, knowing what works the library has in its collections. In some of the more advanced systems, the user can do subject searches by topic and can combine topics to reduce the number of works identified. The "UnCover" program of CARL (Colorado Association of Research Libraries) is an innovative approach for making text of scholarly and popular magazines available on the Internet. CARL has dealt effectively with the copyright issues so that a student on the network can request a document online and for a small fee have the text of that article delivered by fax. The community of network managers, publishers, and librarians has committed enormous energies over the past several years to solving the problems of copyright and to cooperatively addressing the unique special interests of publishers and of scholars to make materials available to students and scholars on the network. Slowly, more material is becoming available.

In addition to library access, networks are making it possible for students to correspond directly with working scholars. One innovative approach is a school science project at Montana State University in which students convene for a summer science camp and after a period of on-campus work return home with a computer and a modem. With this desktop system they are able to correspond with their science professor throughout the school year on issues that arise in their science projects. In this way school children have an ongoing dialogue with a working scholar, made possible by computer networking and its ability to connect one desktop computer to another.

The Future of Computers in Distance Education

In the relatively near future the information revolution will make possible the pinnacle of individualized education. Students will have access via networks to interactive curriculum materials which will tutor them in all the basic content of the curriculum. Students will be free from the tyranny of classrooms, where the best students are often bored "wasting time," while slower students in their group work to master the material. Students will be challenged to the limits of their abilities by systems which recognize and address their individual knowledge levels. The teacher in this setting will become an information specialist, guide, and advisor. The teacher will be "connected" to national data bases of curriculum resources, which will include the major national and university libraries, scientific data bases, and consulting services to address questions about both curricula and academic disciplines. There will be an abundance of equipment. Manufacturing efficiencies and continuous progress in chip and software design will make tools more and more accessible. Students and teachers will have access to school networks through desktop workstations in classrooms and homes so that distance education will be common. School networks will be connected to national networks as an extension of the National Research and Education Network. The computers themselves will become increasingly useful so that teachers will spend less time learning about technology and more time using it. The primary difference between "then" and "now" will be the user interfaces. Students will not have to learn how to use systems because the systems they will use will be immediately intuitive. The speed and efficiency with which they will be able to find the resources they need and with which they can get to the task of learning will be greatly increased. Economies of scale, collaboration made possible by networks, and advances in computer managed instruction will ensure that the best materials developed by the most capable teachers will be available on the desks of all students.

Two Brief Examples

Two brief examples illustrate many of the most attractive aspects of computers in distance learning. Both illustrate uses of the Internet. Both consist of teacher-driven courses, using readily available technologies. Both accomplish educational objectives that would be difficult to accomplish in the conventional classroom. The costs (excluding the network access, which is institution-wide) are nominal.

Professor Norman Coombs of Rochester Institute of Technology (RIT) uses the Internet to teach "Black History" to students who are blind or deaf. Students register at RIT in Rochester, New York, or at Gallaudet University in Washington, DC. The students participate in class discussions and student-teacher dialogue every week. Coombs regularly communicates with them, one-to-one and one-to many. The technology makes it possible for some deaf students to participate in class discussions for the first time in their lives. Coombs points out that this medium strips students of status symbols which in face-to-face settings sometimes inhibit real exchanges between students of different social skills, ethnic origins, or social-group identities. The mechanisms for these classes are relatively straightforward—PCs equipped with voice synthesizers (for blind students, to replace the normal visual feedback of a monitor); a LAN to connect the computers of students to their campuses, RIT or Gallaudet; the Internet to connect the two campuses together; and database software, which makes the files of the entire class accessible to every member of the class. This "class," which never actually "meets" in the same room, or even the same state, carries on a rich exchange of ideas and information. This case illustrates that the computer is providing access to hearing- and sight-impaired students and utilizing the knowledge, experience, and training of a sight-impaired professor (Coombs, 1991).

Joyce Kaufman of Whittier College in California teaches a course in international affairs via a computer network. This course involves campus-based students from several schools throughout the world in a large international problem-solving simulation. The students from each site assume the roles of diplomatic authorities for their countries. The professor/coaches create simulated international problems for the diplomatic teams to address. This mechanism provides the opportunity for students who are naturally expert in their own cultures to engage in normal, disciplined dialogue with students from other cultures to address problems and find solutions. In most cases the simulated problem is a very small step from reality. The computer in this case is nothing more than a communication device and a means of storing and making available the files which comprise the discussion. The profound effects of this kind of international discussion on cultural awareness is difficult to estimate (Kaufman, 1991).

Summary

The rapidly declining cost of computing equipment and the emergence of worldwide computing networks as a common mode of communication are creating enormous opportunities for educators. Computing provides an ideal mode for individualizing education and delivering it to students in remote locations. Networks are making it possible to get immediate access to resources formerly available only in select university libraries. These combined developments create unprecedented opportunities for students and for providers of distance education.

References and Suggested Readings

Azarmsa, R. (1991). *Educational computing: Principles and applications.* Englewood Cliffs, NJ: Educational Technology Publications.

Berry, S. L. & Burrows, D. J. A. (1990). Computers in education: A distance learning model. In A. McDougall & C. Dowling (Eds.), *Computers in education: Proceedings of the IFIP TC 3 Fifth World Conference on Computers in Education—WCCE 90, Sydney, Australia, July 9–13, 1990,* 945-950. New York: Elsevier.

Coombs, N. (1991, October). *Internet applications—Real people doing real work.* Panel presentation at NorthWestNet Annual Meeting, Pasco, WA.

Committee on Physical, Mathematical, and Engineering Sciences of the Federal Coordinating Council for Science, Engineering, and Technology. (1992). *Grand challenges: High performance computing and communications (FY 1992 U.S. research and development program).* Washington, DC: National Science Foundation.

Gayeski, D. (Ed.) (1993). *Multimedia for learning: Development, application, evaluation.* Englewood Cliffs, NJ: Educational Technology Publications.

Gore, A., Jr. (1992). *Earth in the balance: Ecology and the human spirit.* New York: Houghton Mifflin.

Kaufman, J. (1991, October). *Internet applications—Real people doing real work.* Panel presentation at NorthWestNet Annual Meeting, Pasco, WA.

Kochmer, J. (1991). *NorthWestNet user services Internet resource guide (NUSIRG).* (3rd ed.) Bellevue, WA: Northwest Academic Computing Consortium.

Longworth, N. (1990). From computing to information technology to distance education—What do we do when teacher isn't there? In A. McDougall & C. Dowling (Eds.), *Computers in education: Proceedings of the IFIP TC 3 Fifth World Conference on Computers in Education—WCCE 90, Sydney, Australia, July 9–13, 1990,* 931–936. New York: Elsevier.

Markwood, R. A. & Johnstone, S. M. (Eds.) (1992). *New Pathways to a Degree—project evaluation: First year report.* Boulder, CO: Western Cooperative for Educational Telecommunications.

Maurer, H. & Tomek, I. (1990). Hypermedia in Teleteaching. In A. McDougall & C. Dowling (Eds.), *Computers in education: Proceedings of the IFIP TC 3 Fifth World Conference on Computers in Education—WCCE 90, Sydney, Australia, July 9–13, 1990,* 1009–1015. New York: Elsevier.

Moore, G. E. (1992, October 12). Streamlined EPA rules crucial for high-tech success. *San Francisco Chronicle*, p. B3.

Quarterman, J. S. (1990). *The matrix: Computer networks and conferencing systems worldwide.* Bedford, MA: Digital Press.

Rosch, W. L. (1989). *The Winn Rosch hardware bible.* New York: Brady.

Rushby, N. J. (1979). *Computers in the teaching process.* New York: John Wiley & Son.

Tanenbaum, A. S. (1981). *Computer networks.* Englewood Cliffs: Prentice-Hall.

Technological progress has claimed another victim. (1992, December 16). *Chronicle of higher education*, p. A12.

Waggoner, M. (Ed.) (1992). *Empowering networks: Computer conferencing in education.* Englewood Cliffs, NJ: Educational Technology Publications.

Watkins, B. T. (1992, November 11). Electronic service offers libraries computer access to 12,000 journals. *Chronicle of Higher Education*, A19–A21.

Chapter Nine

Contemporary and Emerging Interactive Technologies for Distance Education

Richard A. Schwier

When we think of technology in distance education, we often think of large-scale carrier systems such as direct broadcast satellites and fiber optic networks. When media are considered as part of instruction at a distance, we think of using media as audiovisual aids to support traditional instruction. Newer interactive technologies expand these notions and challenge us to think of powerful, non-conventional ways to construct learning environments for learners—sometimes removing the instructor from the media mix entirely.

This chapter reviews the roles interactive technologies can play in distance education; examines some recent developments in interactive media technologies; and speculates about future directions interactive media may take.

Most of the media we have come to know and use in instructional settings are singular and linear, not interactive. Films or videos are typically shown from beginning to end, with an introduction and follow-up by an instructor. Filmstrips and slides are shown in sequence. Interactive media, by contrast, ask the user or viewer to make choices. Some amount of control is turned over to the learner to construct the nature of content. Therefore, the media discussed in this chapter are characterized by their capacity for interactivity; that is, they can be used to actively engage the learner while learning.

Interactive media usually include, but are not necessarily limited to, computer, videodisc, and compact disc–read only memory (CD-ROM). Each medium has unique features, advantages, and disadvantages; however, the power of these instructional systems lies in the way instruction is constructed and delivered—not in the technological components. Our only fascination with technology is with its potential to assist learning, and research suggests effective learning in distance education, as with various media we discuss here, can be attributed to preparation more than innovation (Willis, 1993).

Emerging technologies also challenge us to look beyond the attributes and differences of individual media components, and instead extend attributes across developing technologies. Emerging technologies focus on an ability to manage, deliver, and control a wide range of educational activities (Hannafin, 1992), and educators are challenged to reexamine the assumptions, models, and strategies we employ in instructional design (Cognition and Technology Group at Vanderbilt, 1992; Jonassen, 1991; Osman & Hannafin, 1992; Rieber, 1992; Schott, 1992; Spector, Muraida, & Marlino, 1992; Tennyson, Elmore, & Snyder, 1992).

In this chapter, interactive media meet several criteria:

- They are instructional.
- Interactive media programs are broken into segments—not presented linearly.
- The viewer may follow an array of paths through a presentation.
- To "navigate" through material, interactive media require periodic and structured input from the user.
- Interactive media relinquish partial or complete control of the instruction, placing it in the hands of the user.
- Interactive media are the resources—not the equipment on which the resources run. They usually require, however, that the educator or learner use computers, videodisc players, CD–ROM players, or other related technology.

One big disclaimer on the frailty of prognostication: This chapter speculates about some of the trends and technologies which are only emerging in distance education circles. The trends suggested here will probably be more robust than the specific technologies used to illustrate the trends. For instance, some form of video capability will be available on computers, and distance educators will likely make use of it, but there is no way of knowing how the process of harboring video in a computer system will change, or which of several competing approaches today will win out over others.

Why Interactive Media?

Print-based correspondence courses are successful. Why adopt newer technologies if the old ones can accomplish everything we want? Here are some of the reasons why interactive multimedia can benefit distance learning, and also a few disadvantages associated with them.

What Interactive Media Do Well

Interactive media offer several advantages to educators:

- Different paths can be taken through interactive media, thereby satisfying individual learner needs and preferences.
- Careful development leads to scrutiny of the content and delivery. Interactive media products, much like other distance education courseware, are subjected to greater scrutiny than traditional, day-in and day-out lessons.

- When several media are combined into interactive multimedia systems, they capitalize on the individual strengths of other media— animation, drama, realism, and control of time and space.
- In well designed interactive media, the learner is constantly active, and this activity can result in increased cognitive investment in the content to be learned.
- When interactive media are used for independent study, they allow flexible scheduling and pacing.
- Interactive media used for independent study can provide a low-threat environment. Learners can determine how much time to spend on various lessons, and can review material privately.
- Interactive media can be designed to provide immediate and relevant feedback to learners. This can go beyond traditional question-answer formats. "Learner advisement" is the term used to describe systems which serve as wise companions, advising students about choices they make during instruction.
- Computers can automate the process of recordkeeping within an instructional program. Everything from performance data to time-on-task and complete audit trails can be invisibly tracked as the learner works on instruction.
- Generally speaking, after they are produced, interactive media formats are cost-effective to reproduce and convenient to distribute. Copies of computer programs, CDs and videodiscs can be made easily and inexpensively, and they can be packaged and sent to learners easily.

Challenges Facing Interactive Media

Interactive media, as most are designed today, exhibit several limitations. Many of these limitations may be overcome by ingenious instructional designs, future improvements in technology, and the inclusion of communications technologies in the learning systems.

- Interactive media can only simulate human interaction between a learner and teacher. Media do not, and probably will not, successfully duplicate the power, flexibility, and immediacy of face-to-face instruction.
- Interactive media cannot adapt to undefined or unexpected needs and characteristics of students.
- Most interactive media programs require some level of print literacy for students to succeed. While this may be a function of inadequate instructional designs more than the media themselves, it is nevertheless characteristic of most instructional programs.
- Accommodation of individuals with specific learning or physical disabilities often requires elaborate technological intervention, such as custom interfacing.
- Although there is promising research which suggests small groups of students can work together successfully on a computer, student-to-student interaction is not a typical by-product of interactive media programs.

- As a rule, interactive media support independent study more than foster communities of learning, although work in collaborative and cooperative learning should be watched carefully.
- Generally speaking, interactive media are more expensive than many other formats to design and produce. While most interactive media are inexpensive to reproduce and distribute, they must also amortize high front-end costs. This means that they are most cost-effective when distributed in large quantities.
- Instruction requiring specific equipment configurations is not necessarily portable to different settings. As of yet, there is little standardization among multimedia computers and programs.

Roles Interactive Media Play in Distance Learning

There is a shift in sentiment toward greater learner autonomy and control, and newer technologies can lead to bold changes in how we approach learning in distance education systems. But until educators adopt interactive media resources to support what they already do successfully, educators will resist other, more innovative, purposes. It is more likely, though, that once teachers adopt interactive media resources to support traditional teaching approaches, they will progress to more innovative instructional approaches.

Traditional Instructional Support

Media have always played an important part in instruction, and those traditional roles will continue to be important in the future.

- **Illustrate Presentations.** Interactive media, can be used to support lectures by providing visual and aural illustrations. Collections, almanacs, and databases of materials are available on videodisc, CD–ROM, and computer software. These collections are often quite comprehensive and inexpensive.
- **Supplement Lessons.** In a traditional distance education setting, supplementary instruction is needed to support the primary instruction delivered by an instructor. This support can be provided by the teacher or assistant to smaller groups or individuals, by peers to other students, or by well-designed instructional materials.
- **Provide Learning Resources and Reference Material.** Currently, many people think of learning resources as books—and only books. On the contrary, learning resources can include any collections of materials which can be used to promote learning.

Independent Study

Interactive media can also carry the primary responsibility for content, and can be used to deliver partial or complete courses to learners. Such media can employ several approaches to the content, some of which are described below. Some are prescriptive, in which lesson content is determined and structured by an "instructor"; others emphasize the development of learning environments in which individual learners can pursue knowledge in their own, unique ways. Hannafin (1992) calls on instructional designers to embrace learning environments which promote individual constructions of knowledge, rather than prescribing and controlling lesson content to be learned.

- **Drill and Practice.** Drill and practice usually takes the form of a string of question-answer-feedback sequences. For drill-and-practice, interactive media instruction can be used to increase the types, amounts, and layers of stimuli and feedback presented.

- **Tutorials.** Tutorials are used to teach new information. Information is usually presented, learners are given opportunities to practice using the information, and learning is reinforced. A well designed tutorial will motivate the learner to enter the instruction enthusiastically, guide or coax the learner to complete the instruction, provide ample opportunities for meaningful interaction, correct errors or misinterpretations, and applaud successes. In mediated tutorial instruction, the challenge is to provide a rich vicarious experience which approximates genuine human interaction.

- **Games/Simulations.** Games are usually directed at a specific goal and involve some measure of competition. Simulations provide an abstraction or simplification of reality, some level of mimicry, in which the learner encounters circumstances and tries to respond to them. In interactive media instruction, features of games and simulations are often combined, as both approaches offer highly motivational, and potentially relevant environments. Interactive media systems are ideally suited for gaming and simulation. In order to provide an interesting, robust environment, huge amounts of information must be available to the learner in realistic representations of reality.

- **Collaborative and Generative Study.** Collaborative and generative study shifts some measure of control over instruction to the user. For interactive media resources used for collaborative and generative study, the emphasis shifts from constructing and controlling instructional events to providing easy access to instructional support. These types of interactive learning resources emphasize navigation, motivation, and access, and typically downplay objectives and evaluation. They take the form of resources which are easy to use by the learner.

- **Hypermedia.** Hypermedia refers to a programming approach which allows the user to link pieces of information together in a theoretically unlimited number of ways, meaning the user could then move in an unrestricted fashion through a forest of information. The movement through the forest would not be restricted to moving from one tree to another in any direction, but it would allow you to be transported to another tree in another part of the forest, or indeed be transported to an entirely different forest. Theoretical limits have not even been approached in practice, as most hypermedia merely expand the number of directions an individual can move through data.

- **Cybernetic Learning.** Some educators, in questioning the limited approaches employed in most computer-based instruction suggest we should be developing learning environments which interact intelligently and mutually with the learner. The ultimate goal of such artificial intelligence is to create "thinking" systems. Such systems will be able to respond to novel situations, create and implement strategies for solving problems—in effect, learn from experience and introspection. Understanding how people think and learn, and applying that to a computer program is a difficult, and some suggest, impossible task. Using the "human thought" metaphor and current technology, we might think of a videodisc or CD–ROM as housing fixed thought, such as vivid memories, conclusions drawn from experience, or stable components of knowledge. As the storage capacity of digital media increases dramatically, so does the potential warehouse of thoughts. The computer adopts the functions of flexible thought, including mental activities such as comparison, inference, deduction, analysis, and insight. In "intelligent" systems, the program is often also capable of expanding its knowledge base from the types of user responses encountered, and adapt its performance (learn from experience).

Educational Technologies in the Future

This section describes some current and promised technologies and discuss their possible impact on distance learning.

Optical Media—Two Old Friends

The most prevalent types of interactive media at present, excluding computers, are videodiscs and CD-ROMs (Compact Disk-Read Only Memory). Some speculate that these media represent only intermediate technological steps toward full digitization of information, but they will probably exist for a long time to come, and continue to offer valuable resources to distance educators.

Videodisc[1]

Videodiscs look like silver LP (Long-Playing) records, covered with a durable, mar-resistant plastic coating, and they are used almost exclusively for video and audio information. Information is embedded within the disc and protected by plastic, so the product is extremely rugged. Unlike videotape, a videodisc can suffer considerable abuse and still reproduce an unblemished image. A 30 cm CAV (Constant Angular Velocity) disc has two sides, each of which houses 54,000 spiral tracks, each of which can be devoted to a single frame of video. If recorded in a different format (CLV-Constant Linear Velocity), videodiscs can house twice as many frames. Unfortunately, this format also sacrifices several of the interactive features of videodisc with most players.

---

[1] For additional information on videodisc design and production, see Katz (1992), Katz & Keet (1990), Lynch (1991), Sales (1989), Schwartz (1987), Schwier (1987), and Schwier & Misanchuk (1993).

Videodiscs permit a user (either an educator or learner) many functions and advantages for using video for learning:

- **Random Access.** Any of the 54,000 frames can be accessed in less than one second.
- **Two Audio Channels.** Either or both of two audio channels can be used to accompany visuals or play without visuals. This permits options such as two languages, alternative treatments of the same material, or full stereo.
- **Still or Motion Images.** Still pictures are crisp, and use very little of the space on the disc. Full motion segments can be contained on the same disc, and they occupy 30 frames per second. An instructor or learner can select from a collection of still and motion segments housed on a videodisc data base.
- **Various Programming Options.** Videodiscs can be controlled with hand-held devices (e.g., remote control unit, barcode reader, light pen, voice recognition interface), by a "hidden" computer program recorded on the disc itself, or by an external computer.
- **Various Instructional Options.** Videodiscs can support any approach to instruction which would benefit from databases of still and motion visuals—from self-guided study by individual learners to broadcast lectures to large groups.

CD–ROM[2]

CD–ROM (Compact Disc–Read Only Memory) is a digital recording on a 12 cm plastic disc, with a silver finish and a spiral tracks, just like a videodisc. Except for the difference in size and the fact that CD–ROMs are recorded on one side only, the two media are virtually identical. However, rather than converting analog video and audio for playback, the information recorded on CD–ROM is designed to remain in digital form, and therefore can only be interpreted by computers. To use CD–ROM, a computer system must include a CD–ROM player, which looks and functions much like a floppy disk drive.

Any type of information which can be represented digitally (i.e., almost anything) can be contained on CD–ROM. This includes computer programs, data, any type of audio, and compressed video (discussed later). There are several characteristics of CD–ROMs which are important to distance educators. CD–ROMS:

- hold large amounts of data (up to 660 Mb of data—more than 800 double-sided floppy disks).
- are an economical format for purchasing and distributing software if produced in large quantities.
- can hold a variety of kinds of information on a single disc. Audio, video, and computer data can coexist on one disc.

---

[2] For additional information on CD-ROM and related technologies, see Bechtel (1989), Brandon (1988), Harvey & Corbett (1991), Schwier & Misanchuk (1993), and Tisdall (1990).

- offer a rich variety of information to illuminate many types of instruction, from independent study to instructor-guided discussions.
- provide a robust, stable storage medium: they cannot be erased and re-used, and they do not deteriorate with age or usage. This makes them attractive for distribution in distance education systems.
- provide a standardized format. Any CD–ROM will play back on any CD–ROM player (although a program written specifically for one type of computer and recorded onto a CD–ROM will not play on a different type of computer).
- provide random access to information stored on the disc. Access times for very large programs and files, such as those containing compressed video images, are somewhat slow at the time of this writing, but improvements in compression technology and hardware are coming quickly.

As attractive as optical media are for storing and distributing a variety of information, they also have a few limitations at present. Videodiscs and CD–ROMs are not convenient or economical production media, unless you are producing many copies of your own material. For this reason, they are not suitable media for content which is volatile; changes are difficult or expensive to make. They also require additional equipment to use.

Digital Media—Two New Friends

Digitizing and Compressing Video[3]

Video images can be changed from their common analog formats (as they exist on videotapes and videodiscs) to digital formats (computer files). Once the signals are digitized, they can be manipulated very easily by a computer. One advantage this gives distance educators is the ability to combine several media into a single package for distribution—it is not necessary to put an awkward collection of different materials together for the learners, and the learners do not need to assemble many different types of media equipment to play the material. In addition, digital video can be passed efficiently from one place to another over telephone lines, fibre optic cable, or single satellite transponder in much the same way fax and electronic mail are handled. An example of this is fractional T1, a telephone network service that permits users to purchase 56 Kbps or 64 Kbps increments of a T1 bandwidth for videoconferencing. In order to send video signals over the telephone lines, it is first necessary to convert the signals from analog to digital data.

The main problem with digitizing video is that resulting data files are huge. Approximately 1000 Megabytes of data are needed to store only 30 seconds of motion color video, and this is obviously well beyond the capacity of microcomputers or telephone lines to handle.

The solution is to compress the huge files into smaller packages for storage and transmission, and decompress the packages for playback. There are

---

[3] For additional information on digital video, see for example Arnett (1990), Schwier & Misanchuk (1993), and Seiter (1991).

currently two leading standards for video compression: Digital Video Interactive (DVI) from Intel for the PC market; and Compact Disc Interactive (CD–I) from Philips, Sony, and Matsushita for the Apple Macintosh, Commodore Amiga, and NeXT. The Moving Pictures Experts Group (MPEG) is developing standards for compressing motion video which may become an international standard for DVI, CD-I, and other emerging approaches.

Files are compressed by sampling video signals and eliminating unimportant or redundant parts of images. For example, if video is compressed of a bird flying across a static skyline of a city, the parts of the picture which do not change from one frame to the next would not be saved as part of the file. Also, any large areas of a single color can be reduced to smaller amounts of data.

One drawback of these types of compression is that, generally, compressed video is expensive, and because it must be carried out at a production house, it does not offer real time compression and decompression for easy local production or live broadcast. This is being remedied by compression software (e.g., Apple's QuickTime™) which allows producers to digitize analog video with their own computers and use it in computer programs. Programs essentially "pack" and "unpack" compressed files rapidly as they are used. Similar "On-the fly" compression/decompression of digital video has been around distance education circles for a long time in the form of slow scan videoconferencing. The signals are sampled and compressed by a codec at an originating site, sent over telephone lines, and decompressed by a codec at a receiving site. Given the current state of compression technology, these approaches share similar quality problems. Compressed digital video appears increasingly blurry and choppy the closer it approaches full motion playback. This is because the higher the quality of the compressed image, the larger the amount of data required for the image, and full-motion video images require 30 frames per second. The choice has been to live with higher quality still or slow-scanned images, or lower quality images as the video approaches full motion. There is a great deal of development activity in compression technology right now, and it is likely that these problems will be short-lived.

Digitizing and Compressing Audio[4]

In order to efficiently create and use audio in computers, it is necessary to first record audio signals on a computer and then compress the recordings into manageable sizes of files. At present there are two primary methods for recording sound on a computer:

- **Digitizing sound.** A small electronic device (commonly called a sound recorder) is attached directly at one end to a computer which is running a sound editing program, and either a microphone or line source of audio at the other end. As the sound source is played, the sound recorder samples the sound waves, converts the samples to bits of data, and passes the data on to the sound editing program on the computer. The resultant files of data can be manipulated, stored, and

---

[4] For a more complete discussion of digital audio see Schwier & Misanchuk (1993).

replayed by the computer. It is a very simple procedure, much like duplicating a cassette tape. Some newer models of computers come with built-in sound digitizers and microphones, eliminating the need for the external sound recorder.

- **MIDI recording.** MIDI (Musical Instrument Digital Interface) is essentially a common protocol for communication between electronic musical instruments, such as synthesizers, and computers manufactured by various companies. Sounds originating from a synthesizer are converted by a MIDI interface and stored on a computer by using a specialized program called a sequencer. The sequencer represents the sounds as (you guessed it) a sequence of numbers which describe the pitch, volume, timbre, tempo, attack, and other attributes of any particular sound. To play back the sounds, the streams of numbers are sent from the computer, back through the MIDI interface, and back to a synthesizer. The numbers, like other digital data, can be edited or composed on a computer.

As with digital video, digital audio results in large files, and the same quality principles apply. The higher the sampling rate used, and consequently the higher the quality of the sound reproduction, the larger the digital file created. The procedure for compressing audio files is the same as for video. Audio is sampled, redundancies and less essential data are removed, and smaller files are stored for playback. The same software which can be used for on-the-fly video compression and decompression (e.g., Apple Computer's QuickTime™) works for audio.

Improvements in digital video and audio have potential for improving any distance learning system which can benefit from graphic, illustrative, or aural material. Audiographic teleconferencing, such as that being used by Optel and Bell Canada, is a good example. Currently, teachers and learners have simultaneous voice and computer communication using narrow band telecommunications channels and a telephone bridge. Along with the two-way voice communication, pictures, graphics, and any other information which can be delivered digitally from the instructor's station can be received by learners on their computer screens. Given current technology, this is limited to data, graphics, and still video images. As digital compression technology improves, so will the quality of visual material available for transmission, and it is possible to dream of full motion, real-time broadcast (and perhaps three-dimensional) video accompanied by concert quality sound in audiographic settings.

Multimedia Systems

Multimedia systems refer to a combination of media housed in a single system (typically a multimedia computer). Classically, multimedia systems include computer programs, still and motion video, audio, graphics, text, and animation. In the near future, they may include virtual reality systems, holographics, and an array of other exciting possibilities. When these media are combined into powerful instructional systems, commonly called interactive multimedia instruction (IMI), the particular strengths and limitations of individual media can be magnified or mitigated. IMI systems can be quite modest, restricted to some computer assisted instruction and print materials, or extremely elaborate, including videodisc, CD–ROM, hypermedia, and virtual reality interfacing.

Because IMI is really a hybrid of existing interactive media, this chapter will not reiterate the particular strengths and weaknesses of its contributing parts, but focus briefly on the advantages and potential of the concept. The real advantage of IMI over its components is centralization—pulling motion and still images, audio, computer programs, perhaps even some interaction with a "live" instructor, and increasingly engaging, realistic and functional ways to work with all of these items into a single place. Centralization is convenient, and convenience will inevitably lead to increased usage.

Centralization seems to be emerging through several stages:

Stage 1: Component Media. If I want to make a presentation this afternoon to a group of people and use a variety of contemporary media (let's not even think about films, overheads, flip charts, and similar useful, yet archaic media), I will need to assemble a videodisc player, monitor, computer with a CD–ROM, and software to play on these pieces of equipment. I will use them independently of each other.

Stage 2: Multimedia Component System. Given the same mandate, I assemble the same equipment and software into a system by adding the correct cables, connections, extensions, and a program which can operate each of these components. At this point, the component media become a multimedia *system* because they are tied together.

Stage 3: Multimedia Computing. Discard all of the equipment, save the computer, and digitize all of the software so it can be played by the computer. At this point, the component media are hidden inside a *multimedia computer*.

Stage 4: Emerging Technology. The multimedia computer system becomes increasingly translucent and ultimately transparent. Because natural interfaces make the multimedia computer so easy to operate, an individual using the system sees less and less of the system, and becomes more of a participant in the system, rather than one who merely interacts. Multimedia technologies will also handle multiple tasks, including the administration, management, delivery, support, control, and communication systems.

Perhaps the ultimate glory of interactive multimedia instruction, if its potential is realized, will be the lost fascination with hardware technology, and the emergence of sophisticated learning material and environments.

Two-Way Multimedia Stations

Bi-directional video is not new to distance education, but it typically requires elaborate production and carrier technology, as well as on-site technical and logistical support. Desktop multimedia stations with two-way live interactive video are currently being introduced, making it feasible to link individuals and their computers in several locations to an instructor—or each other— in real time. VISIT video, a product of Northern Telecom, is an example of this technology. It is a desktop system designed to be attached to Macintosh or IBM PCs and compatible computers. It includes a proprietary card, camera, and application software, and the system works over telephone, voice, and 56 or 64Kbps ISDN (Integrated Services Digital Network) lines. The integrated system includes:

- Desktop videoconferencing. A camera mounted atop your computer sends your image, and a video window on the screen receives remote video transmissions.
- Screen sharing. Pairs of individuals on the system can simultaneously alter common screen data. In other words, two people can work on the same file at the same time, and see the changes in both locations.
- Data transfer among stations.
- Desktop control of telephone and electronic voice mail functions.

This does indeed offer exciting possibilities for distance learning, particularly because it promotes the social interaction and community learning features so often missing from interactive media. At this time, the systems are expensive, and for distance education applications, they require extensive use of toll lines or networks. Nevertheless, as the technology becomes more affordable and commonplace, these types of systems will have a profound effect on distance learning. Two-way multimedia stations may evolve into many-way multimedia stations, permitting clusters of learners to interact commonly in real time.

Interfaces

The trend in interfaces is toward "transparency," that is, attempting to provide natural and unimpeded interactions with learning materials. This is beneficial for all users of interactive media. In addition innovations in interfaces make instruction readily available to individuals often ill-served by technology—those with physical and intellectual disabilities, and individuals from an aging population. This, in turn, is challenging us to redefine the composition of markets for distance learning and the intellectual communities we serve. With the passage of the Americans with Disabilities Act in 1990, and a powerful human rights movement in Canada and other countries, educators are challenged to facilitate learning opportunities for individuals with challenging needs, often requiring the introduction of specialized interfaces. The following are very few examples of interfaces which may have an impact on distance education in the future. Relatively familiar and mundane interfaces—keyboards, mice, touch screens, and the like—are not discussed here, in favor of technologies whose impact has not been as widely felt.

Barcode

Barcode technology has been adapted to videodisc systems. A barcode interface for videodisc allows an instructor or learner to create barcode strips which contain commands to control the player (Zollman, 1991). When a user sweeps over the barcode with a special scanning pen, commands are executed.

Barcodes offer some very useful options for distance educators and learners. For independent study, the barcode reader offers easy access to a wide range of material without dedicating a computer to a particular learning station, and without spending a great deal of time training learners how to use it.

For group instruction, barcode strips can be placed in the margins of lecture notes or pasted onto a reference index. During a class, an instructor can select from a planned set of video illustrations without having to look up frame numbers and enter them with a remote control unit.

Another version of this is the illustrated guidebook for learners (a modest print and video multimedia system). In the margins of the learner's guide, or in the body of text, barcodes can offer illustrated sojourns for students through related video pictures and segments. This is indeed a useful application, and it couples a newer instructional technology with one of the oldest ones, resulting in a familiar, yet potentially highly interactive multimedia resource for learners.

Voice Recognition

Voice recognition interfaces permit the user to give verbal instructions, commands, and responses to programs. Obviously, this is a desirable (almost transparent) interface; the user does not need to learn how to operate any external device or even make the effort to point. Voice recognition is growing in significance for distance education, most noticeably for distance learners with physical disabilities which hamper the fine motor activity necessary to manipulate a keyboard or mouse efficiently (Shuping, 1991). Others dream of the day we can speak in natural language with a computer ("Good morning, Hal"), and have it interpret our instructions conversationally.

Voice recognition systems require a user to speak into a microphone. Vocal patterns are compared to pre-recorded command patterns. For example, if you said, "Save the file I am using," a numerical representation of that speech would be constructed. A user, anticipating this request, would enter the phrase ahead of time and save it for comparison. The input phrase would be compared to all pre-recorded phrases, and if a match occurred, the command would be carried out. In distance learning systems voice recognition systems might be used over telephone lines to request electronic resources which could be subsequently transmitted over the same lines to the user's computer.

For now, the vocabulary of voice recognition remains small, but development is brisk in this area, and it is not unreasonable to expect free-form natural language interfaces to be available at some time in the not-distant future.

Speech Synthesis

For individuals who have difficulty communicating verbally, speech synthesis is the flip side of voice recognition. A computer containing an internal voice synthesizer permits a user to type a message and the computer "speaks" the phrases. In effect, the software provides an audio interpretation of anything on the computer screen, including pre-recorded text. This allows blind learners to listen to printed material, or individuals who have difficulty typing to select phrases from pre-typed menus of material to construct speech. There are numerous potential applications of speech synthesis for distance learning. For example, a learner who has severe speech difficulties could create a synthetic recording of a poem, and send a recitation of the poem to an instructor located elsewhere. Another distance learner who is blind could download resources from a database to a local computer, and then use a speech synthesizer to "read" the material.

Virtual Reality

Virtual reality is a complete environment which is assembled and managed by a computer program, one in which the user physically enters and interacts with the program. Instead of sitting at a keyboard and viewing the "playing field," you wear a special interface which puts you on the playing field, and makes you a player. For example, if you wanted to learn about restaurant design you could enter and walk around an empty building to be renovated. You could walk around kitchen work spaces, pick up virtual images of equipment and carry them to new locations, decorate the dining and reception areas, install lights, and move tables from one location to another. With your design in place, you could walk through the restaurant and view it from a number of perspectives and make changes. Finally, you might open for business, and participate in opening night as a waiter, manager, chef, or bus person. Absurd? Perhaps out of the reach of most users at this moment, but certainly not absurd. In fact, systems already exist which can accomplish many of these tasks, and their sophistication is growing rapidly (Stewart, 1991).

The reason virtual reality is discussed under this section on interfaces, is because the most dramatic external evidence of a virtual reality system is its interface. The interface to accomplish this type of interaction is specialized and usually specific to a particular treatment, although most interfaces include some combination of goggles and gloves or data suits. The interfaces can give the user the sensation of touch, and the ability to pick up virtual objects, move, and manipulate them. A great deal is written in popular, electronic, and computer publications about prototypes and visions of virtual reality, but commercial applications are beginning to emerge.

A virtual reality system also requires a presentation system, just like any other type of multimedia. The trick is to make the presentation system so complete, so absorbing, that the user can treat the simulated "world" as if it were real. Typically, this is accomplished by wearing a pair of goggles which places a small television in front of each eye, thus giving the wearer binocular, three dimensional vision. The goggles sense the position of the head and communicate with a computer, which changes the perspective on the screen as you change the position of your head. When you want to see what is behind you, you turn and look. As part of the presentation system, the user also wears earphones of some sort, in order to introduce stereo sound into the system.

The potential learning applications are staggering. A surgeon who can practice an appendectomy on a virtual patient, a plumber who can try out various systems in a virtual building, a novice archaeologist who can explore exotic sites—these are exciting notions.

This area of development, as exciting as it is, is also very highly specialized, and is unlikely to significantly influence classrooms in the immediate future. Nevertheless, I mention it because of its potential and vitality. Also, a caution: Virtual reality is reductionistic in that it samples reality, and by that selective process, alters it. While there is wonderful potential for creating rich tapestries of instruction, there is also the possibility of misrepresenting reality if the actual system being mimicked is too complex to represent fully or accurately. Take for example an historical event such as the 1962 Cuban Missile Crisis. An individual who participates in a virtual re-enactment of those events, and who participates in decisions, would get a limited and distorted experience—limited by the decisions already made by the programmer as well as our confined knowledge of actual events.

Case Study

Although it is folly to paint a precise picture of an interactive multimedia distance learning environment, a humble bit of speculation may help solidify some of the ideas presented above. Please note that this scenario is only illustrative, and it does not represent the varied forms interactive media could take in distance learning in the future.

The technology highlighted in this example is a sophisticated multimedia computer network. A host computer is maintained at a central location, and it houses all institutional and administrative data, courseware, and a digital library of audio, video, and 'print resources. In addition, it manages communication among any users logged onto the system and handles electronic and voice mail. Distance learners, instructors, and tutors have access to multimedia computer stations which are connected to the host computer via telephone lines or fiber optic cable. Each multimedia station can be used to communicate with the host, or with anyone else on the system— omni-directional video among stations is also possible. With this system, learners and instructors can conduct video conferences in real time.

For this example, a learner (Erin) works in apparent isolation at a multimedia computer station. It resembles a typical laptop computer with a small camera mounted to the corner of the screen, and it is connected to a phone line in Erin's home. The phone line provides access to multimedia courseware, an instructor or tutor, and every other student taking the same courses as Erin.

Erin logs onto a course, and requests a status report on material completed to date. A summary is given, but one of the marks causes concern. The project, a one-page critique of a research article on the topic of global warming, is called onto the screen, and Erin reviews the comments on the paper given by her instructor. Some of the comments are confusing, so she pages her instructor on the system. The instructor isn't available, so Erin leaves a voice-mail request for the instructor to make contact as soon as possible.

Still concerned, she pages other students in the course who are currently logged on the system. Two appear in small windows in the upper-left hand side of the screen. They are at systems similar to Erin's, and the cameras allow them to have a video conference (everyone appears on each others' screens). Erin asks her classmates to look at her critique and the instructor's comments. Their systems allow them to share the document in real time, and they collectively review the instructor's comments and try to apply the instructor's suggestions to the critique. One learner rewrites the lead paragraph to the paper and another changes the wording in three places. They call up a video help-file on global warming and consult a National Science Foundation (NSF) data base for South American data. A holographic image of the earth appears to all three, they apply the NSF data to the holograph, and watch the climatic changes over South America.

In the meantime, the instructor receives the voice-mail message, and pages Erin. The instructor then joins the other two students on Erin's screen, and reviews the changes made by all three students. The four individuals hold a brief discussion of different ways to approach the problem, and then log off the system.

This glib example, I hope, illustrates a few key points. It may indeed be a conservative view of the future, and it will certainly be flawed, but it contains features which are easily within the grasp of distance education.

- This simple, yet sophisticated technology is already, for the most part, available in the marketplace (with the exception of omni-directional video and holographic media).
- The learning needs were defined by the learner. Erin chose the agenda, and elected to collaborate with other learners to examine her problem.
- This was a rather typical instructional problem which could cause difficulty for a student working in isolation.
- This distance learning system nurtured a community of learners within autonomous settings. These learners might have been separated by continents, and yet they were able to join each other in real time to address a common problem. Although distance education is often criticized for inhibiting group problem solving, Erin arrived at solutions she might not have found alone, and the learners were able to manipulate a common document.
- Simple, human scale interactions, rather than bold "Brave New World" changes characterized this scenario. There was nothing particularly exceptional about the nature of interaction among the learners and the instructor—it was fairly normal and routine.
- The learners had seamless access to a wide range of human and media resources from one location. Erin was able to pull together classmates, a database of information, and interactive software.
- There was harmony among learning needs, learning systems, and educational media, primarily because the system fostered the immediacy and flexibility of interpersonal communication.

As this example attempted to demonstrate, many of the limitations typically ascribed to interactive media may be minimized by careful instructional systems design. Rather than consider the advantages and limitations associated with specific media, we should concentrate on developing a tapestry of powerful instructional systems which together contribute to the development of learning environments.

Summary

This chapter outlined some of the advantages and limitations of interactive media and discussed the roles they can play in distance learning systems. Specific technologies of optical media, digital media and multimedia systems were described along with some potential applications to distance learning.

It is apparent that many of the improvements in technology discussed above are offering opportunities to distance educators and instructional designers. At the same time there appears to be a persistent shift away from prescriptive instruction and toward approaches which encourage learners to use their own strategies with resources to derive their own, unique constructions of learning. What are some trends we can anticipate for interactive media and distance education?

- **Face-to-face.** Regardless of the approach employed in distance learning, human contact is, and will continue to be, vital. Independent learning approaches will permit us to alter roles played by instructors in larger learning systems, but they will not replace instructors. On the other hand, humans are expensive, unpredictable, and bound by schedules, unions, conventions and personalities. Interactive media can compensate for some human frailties.
- **Philosophical cohabitation.** Prescriptive and learner-controlled strategies (what some call *instructional* systems versus *learning* systems) will coexist in distance education and interactive media. We seem to be on a healthy progression toward increased learner autonomy. At the same time, there is increasing pressure for accountability in education generally. I suspect that there will be significant attention given to democratic models of learning in the design of interactive media, but there will also continue to be a persistent need for prescriptive, objective-driven instruction.
- **Digital everything.** Most interactive media are digital, and this trend will continue. Eventually, all media will be in digital form, and multimedia computers will be able to combine all sources and deliver them on a single platform. Multimedia computing will provide the foundation for communication, resource acquisition, and learning management in distance education. Analog media such as videodiscs and audio cassettes will be replaced by fully digital systems.
- **Increased power per dollar.** The unit cost of computing power has dramatically and steadily decreased. This trend will continue, and while the cost of interactive multimedia systems will probably plateau or rise, the capabilities of the systems will continue to increase.
- **Compatibility among systems.** Market pressure will increase for manufacturers to impose industry standards and develop compatible

products. This is already true for many media such as CD–ROM and videodisc, but remains a stumbling block for multimedia platforms. Until interactive multimedia can be moved smoothly from one system to another, there will be significant resistance to its adoption.

- **Turbulence and blind alleys.** Changes will accelerate, and educators will make some unproductive decisions about technology. This is expected in a robust system, and if philosophical and technological shifts in education are to survive, the system will have to be tolerant of stumbles. Also, educators cannot wait for developments in technology to stabilize; the wait will be long, indeed.
- **Development precedes utility.** Improvements in instructional strategies will probably continue to lag behind technological advancements. In the past, seed money for research and development often came from the military and corporate sectors. This will probably continue, as there is not any evidence as yet of a major shift in resources to the academic sectors.

References

Arnett, N. (1990). Digital video arrives. *PC Magazine, July,* 152–153.

Bechtel, B. (1989). *CD–ROM and the Macintosh computer.* Cupertino, CA: Apple Computer Advanced Technology Group.

Brandon, P. R. (1988). Recent developments in instructional hardware and software. *Educational Technology, 28*(10), 7–12.

Cognition and Technology Group at Vanderbilt (1992). The Jasper experiment: An exploration of issues in learning and instructional design. *Educational Technology Research and Development,40*(1), 65–80.

Hannafin, M. J. (1992). Emerging technologies, ISD, and learning environments: Critical perspectives, *Educational Technology Research and Development,40*(1), 49–63.

Harvey, D. A. & Corbett, J. (1991). Unlimited desktop storage: Optical drives that blow away the competition. *Computer Shopper, 11*(11), 230ff.

Jonassen, D. H. (1991). Objectivism versus constructivism: Do we need a new philosophical paradigm? *Educational Technology Research and Development, 39*(3), 5–14.

Katz, L. (1992). Essentially multimedia: An explanation of interactive laserdisc and optical technology. *The Canadian Multi Media Magazine, 1*(1), 18–20.

Katz, L. & Keet, C. (1990). *Innovations in laser and optical disc technology.* Calgary, Alberta: Alberta Laserdisc Committee.

Lynch, P. (1991). *Multimedia: Getting started.* Sunnyvale, CA: PUBLIX Information Products, Inc. for Apple Computer, Inc.

Osman, M. & Hannafin, M. J. (1992). Metacognition research and theory: Analysis and implications for instructional design. *Educational Technology Research and Development,40*(2), 83–99.

Rieber, L. P. (1992). Computer-based microworlds: A bridge between constructivism and direct instruction. *Educational Technology Research and Development,40*(1), 93–106.

Ross, S., Sullivan, H. & Tennyson, R. (1992). Educational technology: Four decades of research and theory. *Educational Technology Research and Development,40*(2), 5–7.

Sales, G. (1989). An introduction to videodiscs III: Videodisc hardware. *Computing Teacher, 16*(7), 50–51.

Schott, F. (1992). The contributions of cognitive science and educational technology to the advancement of instructional design theory. *Educational Technology Research and Development, 40*(2), 55–57.

Schwartz, E. (1987). *The educators' handbook to interactive videodisc* (2nd ed.). Washington: Association for Educational Communications and Technology.

Schwier, R. A. (1987). *Interactive video.* Englewood Cliffs, NJ: Educational Technology Publications.

Schwier, R. A. & Misanchuk, E. R. (1993). *Interactive multimedia instruction.* Englewood Cliffs: Educational Technology Publications.

Seiter, C. (1991). Optical outlook. *Macworld, 8*(6), 139–145.

Shuping, M. B. (1991). Assistive and adaptive instructional technologies. In G. J. Anglin (Ed.), *Instructional technology: Past, present, and future,* pp. 292–301. Denver, CO: Libraries Unlimited.

Spector, J. M., Muraida, D. & Marlino, M. (1992). Cognitively-based models of courseware development. *Educational Technology Research and Development, 40*(2), 45–54.

Stewart, D. (1991). Interview: Jaron Lanier. *Omni,* January, 45–46, 113–117.

Tennyson, R., Elmore, R. & Snyder, L. (1992). Advancements in instructional design theory: Contextual module analysis and integrated instructional strategies. *Educational Technology Research and Development,40*(2), 9–22.

Tisdall, B. (1990). Buyer's guide: Optical disk [*sic*] drives. *PC User,* July 18, 74ff.

Willis, B. (1993). *Distance education: A practical guide.* Englewood Cliffs, NJ: Educational Technology Publications.

Zollman, D. (1991). What's m-ss-ng? *EBUG, 1*(1), 1–2.

Chapter Ten

Distance Education: Copyright Issues

Janis H. Bruwelheide

Copyright Quiz

Which of the following statements are true?

1. Distance educators have no need to be concerned about copyright violations because educators have complete protection from prosecution under the Copyright Act.

2. All visual material may be broadcast over a distance education network and copied at remote sites for reuse.

3. Individuals' images, course content, and instructional materials may be freely used over a distance education network without concern for ownership.

4. The Copyright Act is explicit, clear, and understandable for all distance education program applications.

5. Legal penalties for copyright infringement are very light.

6. Absence of a copyright notice on material means that it is in the public domain and therefore may be freely used by anyone, including distance educators.

If readers answered "true" to *any* of these statements, this chapter will provide much needed insights into copyright, since *all* these statements are **false**. Finding one's way through the copyright maze is not easy, and even attorneys disagree concerning interpretations. This chapter will highlight specific areas of the United States Copyright Act and accompanying guidelines relevant to distance educators. Chapter contents include: overview of the Copyright Act and accompanying guidelines, public performance vs. classroom application, photocopy issues, new technology and video concerns, copyright policy and personnel training, tips for avoiding difficulty, and sources of information. Technical legal language and references were avoided as much as possible. It is important to remember that the copyright owner has the authority to grant permission to use works beyond parameters specified in the law and its guidelines.

Reasons for Concern

The area of copyright is of concern to all distance educators, since they want to comply with the law and legal interpretations, while providing quality instructional programming and materials for their consumers. However, at this time, distance educators find themselves increasingly confused as well as vulnerable to copyright violations.

There is a lack of legal interpretation and case law for distance education applications. Distance education programming is often much more visible by its technical nature than is traditional classroom instruction, carried out behind closed doors, and thus opportunity for "detection" of violators is increased.

Before producing or distributing any programming incorporating copyrighted works, telecommunications organizations must obtain *written clearances* from owners, which allow the performance, display, distribution, and reproduction of these materials. In addition, rights should also be obtained to create, reproduce, and distribute derivative works prepared from the original materials. Rights for printed materials to be distributed to telecourse students should also be obtained. Therefore, copyright matters must be considered prior to program delivery. Otherwise, a controversy may occur after a program is produced and distributed, which might become an expensive legal nightmare. The potential exists for "test" legal cases, and no distance educator wants to be selected for such a distinction.

The Fair Use Dilemma and Distance Education

A great deal of misunderstanding exists at this time, even though the Copyright Act was first implemented back in 1978 (it was passed by the U. S. Congress in 1976). The new technologies now proliferating rapidly make it easy for distance educators to perform tasks which are not always considered to be fair use, and this ease contributes to the confusion. It is difficult sometimes to understand why an act made so easy by technology is not considered legal for classroom use. Examples of such nonpermissible applications for distance educators include creating a new videotape using clips from copyrighted materials and broadcasting it without permission over a satellite system, or using music from a popular CD to accompany a presentation, or as a transition between program segments, which is then broadcast to students.

Fair use is a provision in the copyright law which "limits the copyright owner's monopoly by reserving to others the right to make reasonable uses of copyrighted materials without specific consent of the author" (Hutchings-Reed, 1987, p. 5). It is tempting to stretch this statement to encompass all distance education application of copyrighted materials. Technology makes it very easy, however, to abuse copyright privileges. One must stop to consider that an act considered to be fair use in a classroom setting may change into something else, i.e., a public performance, when removed from that setting making such usage "unreasonable" and "not fair."

The perception, then, that anything copied for educational application is considered to be fair use and thus legal is *not* correct. However, there are many situations which are legal or where permission may be obtained by request or license. Educators must decide where "fair use" begins and ends and how to approach protecting the needs of their students as well as the rights of copyright owners. The task is not easy, since technology continues to become more sophisticated. A general rule for distance educators to apply when deciding if an act would be considered fair use is simply to ask this question: "Is copying being done to escape purchasing, renting, or licensing use of a legal copy?" An affirmative answer indicates that the use probably will not fall within fair use guidelines.

Copyright Concerns Which Need Clarification

The current Copyright Act and Guidelines provide guidance for using copyrighted materials in nonprofit educational institutions. However, several areas now exist which need to be clarified in light of new technologies. One issue is that of face-to-face instructional activities. Now that we have technologies (e.g., compressed video) which allow instructors to be electronically face-to-face with students in several sites, it would seem that the old, literal definition, where the teacher and class shared the same physical location, no longer applies. Another issue is the transmission of copyrighted material over such a network. Is the problem one of transmission, or is it the possibility of illegal copying at a site? At the present time, those questions are unresolved as applied to the context of distance education.

What Is Copyright and Why Is It Important to the Distance Educator?

Copyright is the legal right to exclusive ownership and distribution extended to creators of works, fixed in a tangible means of expression, such as literary, musical, artistic, or dramatic works, for a specified amount of time. Ideas as such are not copyrightable—only their specific expression in an article, a book, a film, a video, etc. An owner of a copyright is granted certain exclusive rights and privileges. Protection is extended to both published and unpublished works. Congress has been granted the authority to regulate copyrights by the U.S. Constitution: "The Congress shall have Power ... To Promote the Progress of Science and the useful Arts, by securing for limited Times to Authors and Inventors the exclusive Right to their respective Writings and Discoveries."

Protection begins at the moment of creation, whether registered with the government or not. For published or unpublished works created on or after January 1, 1978, copyright protection begins at creation and lasts for fifty years after the author's death. Different time limits apply for works created prior to 1978. Works for hire, pseudonymous works, and anonymous works have copyright protection for seventy-five years from first publication or 100 years from the year of creation. Copyright notice is optional for works first published on or after March 1, 1989. Unfortunately, this means that it can be difficult to track down the owner of a copyright when permission is needed to use material. On expiration of copyright, the work passes into the public domain, where it may then be freely used. Registration is filed with the Copyright Office in Washington, DC, although the failure to register does not mean that a work is not copyrighted. The chief purpose for registration is to formally establish the date(s) of ownership. Since a copyright owner is granted exclusive rights by the law, user violations may result in legal action for copyright infringement, and penalties can be severe.

Salomon (1993) suggests that telecommunications organizations should affix copyright notices at the beginning and end of all telecourse transmissions and on all copies in all media distributed to the public. Such notice informs the public that the work is protected, by whom, and shows the first year of publication. Also, it is difficult for infringers to claim innocence if they have used a properly labelled, copyrighted work improperly.

Related Legislation

Two additional pieces of legislation are relevant to distance education and copyright. The first is often called "the computer amendment." In 1980 the Copyright law was amended in order to allow the owner of a copyrighted computer program to make or authorize creation of a backup copy to be stored in case of damage to the original. However, the individual copyright holder, according to rights, may state that one should store the original and use the copy, or may even provide additional rights to the purchasers. This amendment to the Copyright law allows limited copying for creation of a backup copy, addition of features to a program if the program is for one's own use, and the making of adaptations for the owner to use the program correctly. The copy is to be destroyed if the original is sold or given away. The backup is not a "second copy" and cannot be used as such.

Another important piece of legislation for distance educators is called the Copyright Remedy Clarification Act, passed in 1990. This Act effectively overruled the Constitution's 11th Amendment dealing with sovereign immunity, which had been used by some states to escape copyright liability for infringements. In essence, the act stated that governmental agencies can be sued for copyright violations. In other words, a state university or telecommunications organization supplying a distance education program can be sued, and individuals involved with production and design of the program can be named in the lawsuit as well. This Act illustrates the importance of having a copyright policy in place which delineates organizational stance on copyright.

Authors of the Copyright Act used language to include forms of expression then known or later to be developed. This was not an easy task considering new technological developments. The language used reads: "works ... fixed in any tangible means of expression, now known or later developed, from which they can be perceived, reproduced, or otherwise communicated, either directly, or with the aid of a machine or device." This clause is the one always cited and argued by attorneys to encompass new technologies. Designated works of authorship are:

1. literary works;
2. musical works, including accompanying words;
3. dramatic works, including accompanying music;
4. pantomimes and choreographic works;
5. pictorial, graphic, and sculptural works;

6. motion pictures and other audiovisual works; and
7. sound recordings.

Many of the newer forms of technology, such as CD-ROMs, video cassettes, computer databases, and other computer programs, fall into these protected areas. The *medium* or technological format of the material is not the issue; *copying* of the material is the issue. Illegal copying can deprive the copyright owner of revenue, and thus discourages creation of new works.

Under the law, absence of a copyright notice does *not* mean that the work is automatically in the public domain. Copyright notice information generally appears on the title page or general media designated substitute, such as title frame or credit frame on a videocassette recording. It is also possible that illustrations in a work, such as photographs, are individually copyrighted, thus requiring that the photograph copyright owner also be contacted for permission.

Exclusive Rights of Copyright Holder

According to the current Act, the copyright owner has certain exclusive rights. These rights may be exercised by the copyright owner, sold, or given away in whole or part. Unless the copyright holder grants permission, though, other uses of copyrighted materials will be an infringement. These rights include:

1. to reproduce the copyrighted work in copies or phonorecords (or any format);
2. to prepare derivative works ... (such as a videotape of a script or an anthology);
3. to distribute copies or recordings of the copyrighted work to the public by sale or other transfer of ownership, or by rental or lease;
4. in the case of literary, musical, dramatic, and choreographic works, pantomimes, motion pictures, and other audiovisual works, to perform the copyrighted works publicly;
5. in the case of literary, musical, dramatic, and choreographic works, pantomimes, and pictorial, graphic, or sculptural works, including the individual images of a motion picture or other audiovisual work, to display the copyrighted work publicly.

Definition of Fair Use and Factors
Used to Determine Eligibility

Copyright law contains provisions for limited use of a copyrighted work without obtaining the copyright holder's permission. This use includes reproduction of portions of the work. This concept is called "fair use," and is defined as the privilege to use copyrighted materials, for the purposes of criticism, comment, news reporting, teaching, scholarship, or research. Four factors are applied to determine whether use of a copyrighted work is a fair use. It is reasonable to apply these guidelines to various forms of multimedia materials until told otherwise. The factors are:

1. the purpose and character of the use, including spontaneity and whether such use is of a commercial nature or is for nonprofit educational purposes;
2. the nature of a copyrighted work;
3. the amount and substantiality of the portion used in relation to the copyrighted work as a whole; and
4. the effect of the use upon the potential market for or value of the copyrighted work.

The first factor means that nonprofit educational use, done in a manner that is relatively spontaneous (the teacher simply does not have enough time to reasonably obtain permission), will have more leeway than a commercial use. In number two, nature of the work refers to the fact that the type of work copied may have inherent limitations, such as the difference between a CD recording and a sheet of paper. A factor which is a continual source of friction is number three: the amount and substantiality of the work. This concept refers to how much of the work is being used and how important the excerpt is to the whole. Guidelines for classroom copying and music suggest that copying 10% or less of the total work is "fair use." However, if the 10% amount is a "substantial portion" or the essence of the work, which might affect sales if copied and distributed, then such use does **not** constitute "fair use." For example, making a transparency of one chart from a book or computer screen to use on an overhead projector is certainly less damaging from a sales standpoint than copying the contents of an entire compact disc onto an audiocassette. Another example is copying the emergence of a butterfly from a cocoon onto videotape. Even if the "emergence" sequence is less than 10% of the entire video, its use could be prohibited, if it is considered the centerpiece of the video production.

Since copyright owners hold the exclusive rights to reproduction, they alone may give permission to use a work which exceeds the fair use limits. The guidelines for classroom copying provide minimum guidance for using print copyrighted materials in an educational setting. Users are expected to affix appropriate copyright identification to the copies. It is assumed that these print guidelines could also apply to multimedia formats, at least until further clarification is provided. When in doubt, the distance educator should always ask the copyright owner for permission and explain the purpose. The use may be granted or negotiated subject to specific limitations and perhaps a fee payment.

Photocopies, digitizers, scanners, and facsimile machines offer ease of copying. For copyright purposes all copying technologies are viewed in the same way as photocopiers. In other words, a fax copy of an article would be viewed the same as a photocopy of the article. One of the most prevalent abuses of copying by distance educators has been the illegal creation of print and nonprint anthologies.

The term "face-to-face" teaching activities is a part of the Copyright Act which exempts instructors and pupils involved in "face-to-face" instruction in a *nonprofit* educational institution from copyright liability so that any part of a work may be displayed or performed in class. Copies of audiovisual works used in such a fashion must be lawfully made copies or originals. Profit-making institutions are then excluded from using copyrighted materials under this exemption in most cases. The students and teacher must be present simultaneously in the same general area, although not necessarily in sight of each other. This situation has been interpreted by some authorities to mean at the same physical plant. The term "teaching activities" does not include entertainment or recreation applications. The instruction must take place "in a classroom or similar place devoted to instruction which is being used as a classroom for systematic instructional activities," and not for entertainment (see Appendix A). Under these conditions, authorization is given to students and instructors engaged in face-to-face instructional activities to use copyrighted works such as slides, videos, print media, and computer software. When in doubt, an instructor should ask permission. However, permission is not extended to transmitting these materials via networks, such as compressed video or satellite, without the copyright holder's approval.

Penalties for copyright infringement are steep and may include damages ($20,000 to $100,000 per work involved), legal fees, and court costs *per* infringement. The Copyright Clarification Remedy Act illustrates the vulnerability of distance education organizations and employees.

Performance Versus Classroom Use

Confusion concerning fair use in an educational setting often occurs concerning classroom use and how this differs from a "performance." Often a use which is legitimate in a classroom is not permissible in another setting without permission or licensing. An example would be an instructor using background music to accompany a computer-aided presentation. Such use in class might fall under fair use provisions. But a project beginning as an in-class presentation could then be changed into a public performance when shown outside the classroom, say, for an audience of parents. The same principle would apply to creating "anthologies" from scanned images, videodisc, CD-ROM, and videotapes. The problem is compounded when the classroom presentation is copied for distribution (free or not) or placed into a media center collection. A classroom use often changes into a performance for entertainment when it is removed from the classroom. For example, showing the movie "Romeo and Juliet" in a classroom could be defensible if the instructor has written the movie into a lesson concerning Shakespeare. However, showing the same movie after school or in a student residence hall would change the use into a public performance and require the copyright owner's permission and possible payment of a fee for usage.

Copyright Policy, Training, and Implementation

Case law and the Copyright Act have certainly demonstrated that individuals can and will be held liable for copyright infringements. Thus, a way for an institution to install protection is to design and implement copyright policies accompanied by manuals and to provide subsequent training concerning copyright policy. Without such agreements, distance education providers may be liable for copyright infringements. There is no need to develop a policy from scratch, since sample copyright policies are available (see Sources of Information).

Pisacreta (1993) states that institutions should develop guidelines specifying which activities can be undertaken without the advice of counsel; situations which automatically require legal review; and activities prohibited without consent of the copyright owner. Vlcek (1992) offers information and sample policies. His article (1993) provides a brief overview of policy content.

The following section presents an overview of what a policy should contain. A policy need not be lengthy. Rather, the policy should be concise and be accompanied by a manual and appendices containing applications information.

Policy Content

1. A statement that the board intends to abide by the Copyright laws, the Patent laws, and accompanying guidelines. This statement makes it clear that the institution and employees will work within the required parameters.

2. A statement prohibiting copying not specifically allowed by the law, fair use, license agreement, or the permission of the copyright holder.

3. A statement which places liability for willful infringement upon the person requesting the work. This statement must make clear that no institutional support will be provided to an employee who violates policy parameters.

4. A statement naming a copyright officer for the institution. This individual should have the authority to provide enforcement as well as education and advice concerning copyright. All relevant copyright paperwork should be centralized with this person, who serves as the copyright liaison to the institution's counsel.

5. A statement mandating development of a manual detailing what copying can and cannot be done by employees. Though optional, the manual can be extremely helpful in detailing the proper and improper application of copyright principles. Employees must know what is legal. The manual should contain examples, institutional procedures, and sample forms such as permissions letters and licensing agreements. All employees likely to use or duplicate copyrighted materials should receive copies. Training and information workshops should also be conducted concerning copyright. Several legal settlements have required this step, as it is not sufficient simply to *have* a policy—if no one knows about it. The policy and manual should be reviewed often for currency.

6. Intent to place appropriate notices on/near all equipment capable of making copies. This act is mandated in the Copyright law. Included would be self-service photocopy machines as well as university copying services. Vlcek (1992) suggests that video recorders, audio recorders, and other such copying equipment be labeled. Copyright notices should be affixed on all copies, regardless of format.

7. A statement which mandates that adequate records will be maintained regarding permissions, response to requests, and license agreements. It is easier to consolidate all of this activity in one office.

Policy Implementation

1. Have the policy reviewed by counsel and adopted by the governing body of the organization.

2. Develop a manual which will explain in detail the policy and illustrate with good examples and sample forms for permission and licensing.

3. Designate a copyright contact person who will be responsible for training and monitoring.

4. Place warning notices on/near copying equipment.

5. Widely distribute policy and manual and provide employee training.

Training of Personnel

1. Consider having someone from outside the organization conduct training sessions. Presentation length depends on need but consider two to four hours in a workshop format. Individuals who perform this activity as consultants are used to handling all sorts of questions concerning the various media formats and situations. A good presenter can also keep the session positive and businesslike.

2. Briefly review the policy emphasizing the importance of copyright, but don't overload the attendees with technical aspects of laws and guidelines.

3. Review the penalties for infringement and the importance of following the policy and documenting the permissions procedures and monitoring process. Emphasize employee responsibilities.

4. Review the manual or present issues pertinent to different types of media: print, television taping, music, computer software, broadcast concerns, and others deemed relevant to the group.

Suggestions for Distance Educators

In order to avoid problems and confusion, distance educators who are concerned about copyright should consider the following suggestions:

1. Enlist support of the governing body to develop a copyright policy with a manual and make sure it is adopted by the governing body. Work with a small team comprised of representatives from various factions. Have the policy and manual reviewed by counsel prior to implementation, and update it often.

2. Provide employee training concerning copyright in order to develop awareness and explain the policy. Consider having employees sign a statement that they will abide by the policy.

3. One should never hesitate to request permission. When in doubt, ask.

4. Be aware of the copyright provisions but realize that there is a great deal of educational copying which is legitimate.

5. Ask oneself the question, "am I copying this media in order to escape purchasing a copy or paying reprint, leasing, renting, or licensing costs?" If the answer is yes, then the use is probably not within fair use parameters.

6. Give copyright credit on legally made copies and uses. For example, if a company provides permission to broadcast a videotape over a satellite network, acknowledge this act on the credits and perhaps verbally as well by having the instructor make a statement prior to showing the videotape.

7. Be aware of the setting in which the use will occur. Classroom use has more leeway than a public performance. Remember that a legitimate classroom use of copyrighted material may change into a public performance when it leaves the classroom.

8. Know how to help instructors locate alternatives which are legitimate (i.e., selection aids, sources of clearing services, clip art clearinghouses).

9. Develop a form letter for requesting permission from copyright holders which applies to the various media forms, and develop a good, centralized tracking system.

10. Label equipment with restriction notices that could be used for improper copying.

11. Consider and anticipate controversies before distributing distance education programming. It is much easier than dealing with consequences after an incident.

12. Retain a paper trail of the permissions route followed when trying to obtain permission to use a copyrighted work. Store in a central location for easy access.

13. When requesting permission to use a copyrighted work, include two copies of the request letter and a self-addressed envelope to expedite return.

14. Develop procedures for monitoring taping and use of the distance education network.

Summary

Distance educators at all levels are vulnerable to misperceptions concerning copyright. Because of the wide "reach" of distance delivered material, they are also more likely to make errors than are traditional classroom teachers. This is not to say that distance educators are more cavalier about copyright than other educators. However, the mixture of combining a variety of pre-existing materials with new materials and then *transmitting* this information over a distance education network can lead to a variety of potential copyright problems. Thus, one may need to request permission from the copyright owner to incorporate the pre-existing material into a new course as well as secure permission (or license) to transmit it. The use of copyrighted materials for broadcast or transmittal may require special permission not required of a traditional classroom application. Distance education providers must consider all aspects and obtain all relevant clearances prior to releasing and distributing a program.

The current Copyright law and various interpretations can seem confusing to distance educators who are unsure about compliance in an environment which has changed technologically since 1978. A basic understanding of copyright is important in order to ensure that compliance is accomplished. A copyright owner has certain exclusive rights but the law provides some exemptions for educational use of copyrighted materials. The copyright owner, if asked, can also extend permission beyond the law.

Copyright policies and implementation procedures adopted by the appropriate governing body are mandatory for distance education program providers in order to ensure that appropriate measures are taken in order to comply with copyrights. Employee training concerning copyright and the institutional policy is also mandatory.

Sources of Information

Association for Educational Communications & Technology (AECT). Offers several books; 1025 Vermont Avenue, NW Suite 820, Washington, DC 20005. Their monthly periodical, *Tech Trends*, has a regular column on copyright matters.

Association for Information Media and Equipment. AIME provides a packet of sample policies, miscellaneous information, and a video entitled, *Copyright: What Every School, College, and Public Library Should Know*. AIME may also be able to assist in locating information on specific formats if needed, P.O. Box 865, Elkader, IA 52043.

Cable in the Classroom. Produces a magazine and maintains information concerning copyright for cable programming; 190 North Beauregard St., Suite 108, Alexandria, VA 22311.

Copyright Clearance Center. This agency has the right to grant permission for photocopying of articles from a group of publications. It serves as a central clearinghouse for users to pay fees and acquire the duplication rights to certain information; 27 Congress St., Salem, MA 01907.

Independent Media Distributors Association. IMDA may be able to assist in locating a video producer for a specific title; P.O. Box 2154, St. Paul, MN 55102.

Motion Picture Association of America. MPAA is a source of information for theatrical motion pictures; 14144 Ventura Blvd., Sherman Oaks, CA 91423.

Music Publishers Association of the United States. Offers booklet on music rights for educators; 152 W. 57th St., 31st Floor, New York, NY 10019.

National School Boards Association. NSBA has several publications of interest concerning schools and law. *Copyright Law: A Guide for Public Schools* provides copyright information; 1680 Duke St., Alexandria, VA 22314.

Software Publishers Association (SPA). Provides literature, a self-audit kit, and a videotape concerning computer software theft; 1730 M St., NW, Suite 700, Washington, DC 20036.

U.S. Copyright Office; Washington, DC 20559. Has several publications available which are free:
Circular 1   Copyright Basics
Circular 2   Publications on Copyright
Circular 21   Reproduction of Copyrighted Works by Educators & Librarians
Circular 22   How to Investigate the Copyright Status of a Work

Video Software Dealers Association. The VSDA may be able to help with location of a video producer, if one needs to obtain permission concerning a specific title; 303 Harper Dr., Moorestown, NJ 08057.

References and Suggested Readings

Association of American Publishers. (1991). *Questions and answers on copyright for the campus association community.* Oberlin, OH: National Association of College Stores.

Becker, G. H. (1992). *Copyright: A guide to information and resources.* Lake Mary, FL: Gary H. Becker.

Bruwelheide, J. H. (1994). *The copyright primer* (2nd ed.). Chicago, IL: American Library Association.

Dukelow, R. H. (1992). *The library copyright guide.* Washington, DC: Association for Educational Communications and Technology.

DuBoff, L. D. (1991). *High-tech law (in plain English).* Washington, DC: Association for Educational Communications and Technology.

House Report, Act of 1976, 94th Congress, 2d Session, Report No. 94-1476.

Hutchings-Reed, M. (1987). *The copyright primer.* Chicago: American Library Association.

Miller, J. (1988). *Using copyrighted videocassettes in classrooms, libraries, and training centers* (2nd ed.). Washington, DC: Association of Educational Communications and Technology.

Pisacreta, E. A. (1993). Distance learning and intellectual property protection. *Educational Technology, 33*(4), 42–44.

Salomon, K. D. (1993). Copyright issues and distance learning. *Teleconference, 12*(1), 18–21.

Saltpeter, J. (1991). Are you obeying copyright law? *Technology & Learning, 12*(8), 14–23.

Sinofsky, E. R. (1988). *A copyright primer for educational and industrial media producers.* Washington, DC: Association for Educational Communications and Technology.

Strong, W. S. (1984). *The copyright book: A practical guide.* Cambridge, MA: MIT Press.

Talab, R. (1989). *Copyright and instructional technologies: A guide to fair use and permissions procedures* (2nd ed.). Washington, DC: Association for Educational Communications and Technology.

United States Code, Public Law 94-553, 90 Stat. 2541.

United States Code, Public Law 96-517

United States Code, Public Law 101-553.

Vlcek, C. (1992). *Adoptable copyright policy: Manuals designed for adoption by schools, colleges, and universities.* Washington, DC: Association for Educational Communications and Technology.

Vlcek, C. (1993). Copyright policy development. *Tech Trends, 38*(2), 13–14, 46.

Appendix A

Guidelines for Classroom Copying: Books and Periodicals
(H. R. 1476, Section 107)

I. Single Copying for Teachers

A single copy may be made of any of the following by or for a teacher at his or her individual request for his or her scholarly research or use in teaching or preparation to teach a class:

A. A chapter from a book;
B. An article from a periodical or newspaper;
C. A short story, short essay or short poem, whether or not from a collective work;
D. A chart, graph, diagram, drawing, cartoon or picture from a book, periodical, or newspaper.

II. Multiple Copies for Classroom Use

Multiple copies (not to exceed in any event more than one copy per pupil in a course) may be made by or for the teacher giving the course for classroom use or discussion; provided that:

A. The copying meets the test of brevity and spontaneity as defined below; and,
B. Meets the cumulative effect test as defined below; and,
C. Each copy includes a notice of copyright.

   Definitions.

Brevity

(i) *Poetry:* (a) A complete poem if less than 250 words and if printed on not more than two pages or, (b) from a longer poem, an excerpt of not more than 250 words.

(ii) *Prose:* (a) Either a complete article, story or essay of less than 2,500 words, or (b) an excerpt from any prose work of not more than 1,000 words or 10% of the work, whichever is less, but in any event a minimum of 500 words.

(iii) *Illustration:* One chart, graph, diagram, drawing, cartoon or picture per book or per periodical issue.

(iv) *"Special" works:* certain works in poetry, prose or in "poetic prose" which often combine language with illustrations and which are intended sometimes for children and at other times for a more general audience fall short of 2,500 words in their entirety. Paragraph "ii" above notwithstanding such "special works" may not be reproduced in their entirety; however, an excerpt comprising not more than 10% of the words found in the text, thereof, may be reproduced.

Spontaneity

(i) The copying is at the instance and inspiration of the individual teacher, and

(ii) The inspiration and decision to use the work and the moment of its use for maximum teaching effectiveness are so close in time that it would be unreasonable to expect a timely reply to a request for permission.

Cumulative Effect

(i) The copying of the material is for only one course in the school in which the copies are made.

(ii) Not more than one short poem, article, story, essay, or two excerpts may be copied from the same author, nor more than three from the same collective work or periodical volume during one class term.

(iii) There shall not be more than nine instances of such multiple copying for one course during one class term.

(Note: The limitations stated in "ii" and "iii" above shall not apply to current news periodicals and newspapers and current news sections of other periodicals.)

III. Prohibitions as to I and II above

Notwithstanding any of the above, the following shall be prohibited:

(A) Copying shall not be used to create or to replace or substitute for anthologies, compilations or collective works. Such replacement or substitution may occur whether copies of various works or excerpts therefrom are accumulated or reproduced and used separately.

(B) There shall be no copying of or from works intended to be "consumable" in the course of study or of teaching. These include workbooks, exercises, standardized tests and test booklets and answer sheets and like consumable material.

(C) Copying shall not:

    (a) substitute for the purchase of books, publishers' reprints or periodicals;
    (b) be directed by higher authority;
    (c) be repeated with respect to the same item by the same teacher from term to term;

(D) No charge shall be made to the student beyond the actual cost of the photocopying.

Appendix B

Guidelines for Off-Air Recording of Broadcast Programming for Educational Purposes (Congressional Record, October 14, 1981, vol. 127, no. 145)

The following guidelines reflect the Negotiating Committee's consensus as to the application of "fair-use" to the recording, retention, and use of television broadcast programs for educational purposes. They specify periods of retention and use of such off-air recording in classrooms and similar places devoted to instruction and for homebound instruction. The purpose of establishing these guidelines is to provide standards for both owners and users of copyrighted television programs.

1. The guidelines were developed to apply only to off-air recording by non-profit educational institutions.
2. A broadcast program may be recorded off-air simultaneously with broadcast transmission (including simultaneous cable retransmission) and retained by a nonprofit educational institution for a period not to exceed the first forty-five (45) consecutive calendar days after date of recording. Upon conclusion of retention period, all off-air recordings must be erased or destroyed immediately. "Broadcast programs" are television programs transmitted by television stations for reception by the general public without charge.
3. Off-air recordings may be used once by individual teachers in the course of relevant teaching activities, and repeated once only when instructional reinforcement is necessary, in classrooms and similar places devoted to instruction within a single building, cluster or campus, as well as in the homes of students receiving formalized home instruction, during the first ten (10) consecutive school days in the forty-five calendar day retention period. "School days" are school session—not counting weekends, holidays, vacations, examination periods, or other scheduled interruptions within the forty-five calendar day retention period.
4. Off-air recordings may be made only at the request of and used by individual teachers, and may not be regularly recorded in anticipation of requests. No broadcast program may be recorded off-air more than once at the request of the same teacher, regardless of the number of times the program may be broadcast.
5. A limited number of copies [guidelines do not provide the number] may be reproduced from each off-air recording to meet the legitimate needs of teachers under these guidelines. Each such additional copy shall be subject to all provisions governing the original recording.
6. After the first ten consecutive schools days, off-air recordings may be used up to the end of the forty-five calendar day retention period only for teacher evaluation purposes, i.e., to determine whether or not to include the broadcast program in the teaching curriculum, and may not be used in the recording institution for student exhibition or any other non-evaluation purpose without authorization.
7. Off-air recordings need not be used in their entirety, but the recorded programs may not be altered from their original content. Off-air recordings may not be physically or electronically combined or merged to constitute teaching anthologies or compilations.
8. All copies of off-air recordings must include the copyright notice on the broadcast program as recorded.
9. Educational institutions are expected to establish appropriate control procedures to maintain the integrity of these guidelines.

Chapter Eleven

Regulatory Issues in Distance Education

Ellen D. Wagner

During the past decade, interactive electronic distance education has become a viable means of distributing courses and programs to geographically dispersed audiences. Distance educators and trainers have become increasingly proficient at using audio, data, and video telecommunications transmission systems. They have modified their classroom strategies to work with distant students, and are adapting instructional methods and materials to deal with distance-specific conditions and circumstances. They are confirming the quality of the learning which takes place when electronically mediated communications occur in lieu of, or in conjunction with, face-to-face instructional exchanges. They are providing widely distributed library services, and are accommodating copyrights for print, video and electronic resources. They are beginning to grapple with the complex inter-institutional negotiations required to equitably share a common telecommunications infrastructure, to cross traditional institutional service boundaries, and to address state certification and professional accreditation requirements.

To date, however, educators and trainers have NOT been notably active in telecommunications regulatory and related public policy arenas. Perceived by many as the realm of attorneys, bureaucrats, and politicians, regulatory and public policy environments are places where far-reaching decisions occur which both direct and manipulate the rapidly-evolving field of telecommunications. The limited degree of participation by educators is certainly understandable—regulatory decisions may not appear to have as direct an impact upon schools, colleges, universities, or training enterprises as they do upon telephone, cable, satellite, and broadcast industries' ability to conduct their primary lines of business. Telecommunications industries are directly affected by regulatory decisions, whereas educational and training institutions simply use telecommunications as they do any other utility. For educators and trainers, telecommunications are a means to an end since it improves access to programs and resources, provides a mechanism for communications, and serves as a vehicle for distributing information.

While it may appear to be more appropriate to relegate political negotiation and legal discussions to those whose expertise lies in those areas, there are two reasons why the education and training community may be well served by taking a more active role in regulatory debates and discussions. First, there is the matter of establishing a "distance education presence" in the places where regulations are forthcoming. Regulations are the result of legislative, judicial, and executive decisions. They determine the features of the telecommunications landscape. Distance education is simply one of many telecommunications applications which make up that landscape, so it is increasingly important that the views of distance educators and trainers be clearly articulated.

Secondly, a basic understanding of telecommunications regulations will enable educators and trainers to better leverage purchasing power, better negotiate service contracts, and better exercise political influence to create favorable conditions under which to pursue distance educational activities. As educational and training organizations consume increasing volumes and varieties of telecommunications services, it is increasingly important that they are quite clear about the instructional and organizational objectives they expect to meet through expanded telecommunications services. Identifying the types of telecommunications services needed, the parameters of service provision, and the price one is willing to pay for those services to meet those objectives are all activities which are directly affected by telecommunications regulations.

To better accomplish these ends, this chapter has been written with the following goals in mind:

- First, it provides educators, trainers, and decision-makers with an overview of what the telecommunications regulatory environment is, and describes the impact of regulations upon telecommunications, in general, and distance education, in particular.
- It describes the relationship which exists between regulations and public policy. If a law exists which impedes the utilization of educational telecommunications, it IS possible to change that law. This can be more easily accomplished if one is aware of how regulatory and public policy interests interact, and understands the enabling and restraining variables which will affect the enactment of regulatory change.
- It identifies some of the key activities from the three primary contexts of the telecommunications regulatory environment and considers regulatory impact upon distance educational systems and practices.

The following discussion has been undertaken based upon four basic caveats:

- *The telecommunications application shaping this discussion is that of distance education and training*: Distance education and training consists of the transmission of educational or instructional programming to geographically dispersed individuals and groups

(OTA, 1989). Distance education is a subset of the broader field of educational telecommunications, which represents a wide variety of technology applications. Data services, telephone services, academic research and administrative computing, television, and radio are examples of educational telecommunications which may or may not involve the delivery of interactive instructional programming. Other telecommunications applications include security, banking, communications, transportation, and commerce, none of which have anything (directly) to do with education.

• *This discussion addresses telecommunications regulatory issues within the context of telephone services.* Telecommunications regulatory agencies are currently structured along technological lines. For example, broadcast, cable television and radio, and telephone and satellite industries respond to specific regulatory bureaus which dictate accessibility of telecommunications services and pricing for those services.

The anti-trust activities which led to the break-up of AT&T resulted in a dramatic reorganization of the telephone industry in the United States. The availability and cost of a wide array of telephone-based telecommunications technologies and services (which include digital signal transmissions, compression technologies, information services and integrated audio, video and data services transmitted over twisted pair copper telephone wire) has affected distance education in profound and significant ways. Given the complexity of the regulatory environment, selecting one technological context which has profoundly affected the evolution of distance education will give readers a solid foundation for pursuing future regulatory investigations.

• *This discussion is oriented toward decision-makers who either work in educational and training environments, or who represent the interest of an education and training constituency.* Information describing both regulatory and public policy perspectives of telecommunications is abundant. However, it tends to address telecommunications as the end of the discussion rather than as the means to the end of improving educational services. This discussion has been undertaken to improve *educators'* understanding of how the availability and cost of telecommunications services and equipment is determined through regulatory means. Parker (1991) has noted that telephone carriers need to help education prepare the workforce to cope with the new telecommunications environment. The education and training community must take on some of the responsibility for preparing themselves to be more effective consumers of telecommunications services.

Regulations and Public Policy

Any discussion of regulations must be framed by an understanding of the relationship between regulations and public policy. Regulations consist of laws, executive orders and judicial decision. They come from legislative actions at the local, state and federal levels, from decisions made by government officials empowered to make such decisions, or from municipal, state, or district level court decisions. In the telecommunications arena, regulations have evolved to address the conditions, circumstances and provision of equitable service access, which ultimately deals with issues of cost and pricing of those services.

Public policy, on the other hand, deals with determination of societal value. It defines the social climate in which public opinion will prevail in the form of laws, executive orders, and judicial decrees. For example, public policy operationally describes such intellectual abstractions as social responsibility, competitiveness, diversity, privacy and freedom of speech. Governmental positions taken with the "good of the people" in mind can elevate an issue which promotes or encourages social responsibility, competitiveness and the like from obscurity to national priority.

Telecommunications public policy defines the context where access to and cost of telecommunications technologies (such as digital switching or fiber optics) and services (such as video telephone services or information services) will be determined. The national public policy of "universal telephone service" (which will be described in this chapter) resulted in pricing structures where certain telephone services subsidized other services. Some writers (e.g., U. S. Department of Commerce, 1988) have suggested that future access to "universal information services" may require a return to a telecommunications environment where the price of certain services includes incentives or subsidies to support specific telecommunications applications such as high-capacity data networks, ubiquitous information services, and "video dial tone." This may require changes to infrastructure amortization schedules by which telecommunications equipment is depreciated over time. Changing the legally mandated rates of return for telephone companies may be needed to encourage greater investment in telecommunications infrastructure for all users, including distance educators (Geeslin, 1989). These regulatory changes will be more likely to be forthcoming if a strong case can be made for the value of making such changes. A public policy endorsing distance education gives testimony to distance education's perceived value to society; it creates a rationale for creating an environment through which public support of telecommunications systems, services and users may be forthcoming. If distance educators and trainers succeed in demonstrating the value of improving access to educational opportunities for dispersed populations by means of telecommunications technologies, it will create the climate to encourage pricing conditions favorable for encouraging systems growth, and social conditions for greater acceptance of distance education at local, state and national levels.

Universal Service and Competition: Public Policies at the Crossroads

A brief examination of two policies historically associated with telephone services—universal service and competition—will demonstrate how public policy shapes the environment in which telephone-based telecommunications service provision takes place.

Universal telephone service—that is, having telephone service available in every home and business in the United States—is an example of a telecommunications public policy. Universal service has shaped the development of the telecommunications industry since 1910, when Theodore Vail noted:

> The Bell System was founded on broad lines of "One System," "One Policy," "Universal Service," on the idea that no aggregation of isolated independent (telephone) systems not under common control, no matter how well equipped, could give the country the service. One system with a common policy, common purpose and common action; comprehensive, universal, interdependent, intercommunicating like the highway system of the country, extending from every door to every other door, affording electrical communication of every kind, from everyone at every place to every one at every other place. (AT&T, 1910, cited in Dordick, 1990, p. 230)

The notion of universal telephone service was reiterated in broad terms in the Communications Act of 1934, which reflected the government's consensus that telephone service should be available to all citizens. The Communications Act created a mechanism, the Federal Communications Commission, to ensure that the goal of universal service would be attained. Over the years, universal telephone service has been described as necessary for economic development and essential for ensuring delivery of adequate public services including emergency health and public safety. Through such descriptions, universal service's value to the country was made explicit.

Universal service was closely associated with a government-supervised pricing policy that allowed a telephone company to charge some customers more, so that other customers may be charged less (Lenert, 1991). This practice was known as *cross-subsidy*. To pay for universal service, long distance tolls were inflated to a level greater than actual cost to provide a funding source to pay for local access for less than actual cost. This helped to ensure local telephone access services for the greatest number of people, regardless of socio-economic status or geographic location.

According to U. S. government statistics, 93% of American households have access to telephones at home, thus achieving the pragmatic intent of universal service (U. S. Department of Commerce, 1988, 1991). However, access to a simple voice grade copper telephone wire and switching facilities, which may have been sufficient in the universal telephone service era, may no longer be adequate for providing access to the "universal information services" which are currently available, given recent technological developments (U. S. Congress, 1991; Parker, 1991; Hudson and Parker, 1990). Multiple party telephone lines are no longer sufficient, even for residential services—private telephone lines are required for using enhanced services such as voice messaging and facsimile. "Touch tone" capacity is needed to access remote messaging services or to "direct dial" using a telephone credit card. Digital telephone lines permit the use of high-speed facsimile and compressed video telephones; the higher the line's capacity, the more audio, video, and data information can be carried. Even as telephone users are adjusting to the services available over twisted pair copper lines, developments featuring optical fiber promise to increase capacity and services many times over current levels.

Changes in the U.S communications infrastructure appear to have widened the gap between those who can access emerging communications services and those (including the poor, the educationally disadvantaged and the geographically isolated) who cannot. The cost of enhanced telecommunications service may be an increasing barrier to access, particularly in an era which is no longer served by a single completely integrated telephone service provider. Rapid development of new telecommunications technologies that can deliver new services to the home, and deregulation and divestiture (two outcomes of a public policy supporting competition) have fostered increased efficiency and innovation at some expense to equitable distribution of the new telecommunications services (Hadden & Williams, 1991).

Like universal service, the public policy of *competitiveness* has had dramatic impact upon the evolution of the telecommunications industry. *Competition,* a basic construct shaping "supply and demand" economics, was a driving force in bringing about the divestiture of AT&T. Divestiture resulted in forcing the price of telephone service toward actual cost; this means that the sources of cross-subsidy are reduced or eliminated.

From the 1950s to the early 1980s, when technological progress made it possible for entrepreneurs, such as MCI, to challenge the AT&T monopoly in the long distance service market (ACIR, 1990), there had been an increasing number of challenges to AT&T's protected, monopolistic status. One particularly notable challenge was the 1956 Consent Decree, which separated long distance (inter-exchange) and local access (local exchange) services, and limited the activities of AT&T to the provision of common-carrier communications services (as opposed to computer or information related services). This was done to ensure that other companies attempting to compete in the telecommunications marketplace would, indeed, be able to compete against AT&T. The Modification of Final Judgment (ACIR, 1990; US WEST, 1990), went even further toward the creation of a competitive telecommunications marketplace. This is the consent degree which the U. S. District Court for the District of Columbia entered on August 24, 1982, in **United States vs. Western Electric et al.**, Civil Action Number 82-0192. Simply stated, the Modification of Final Judgment, generally referred to as the MFJ, led to the complete reorganization of the telephone industry in the United States:

- It created a competitive long distance market, while retaining the monopolistic, protected status of local exchange carriage. Local exchange carriers (LECs) provided the connections needed to address local telephone service as well as long distance service within the boundaries of a Local Access and Transport Area, or LATA. Inter-LATA services were to be provided by any number of long distance, or interexchange (IXC) carriers. This separation of services altered the subsidy basis upon which universal service, particularly for rural telephone subscribers, was funded. It has led to changing the telephone rate structures where residual rate of return regulation, approved by a state's legislature and managed by its public utilities commission, has determined pricing for telephone service.

- It stipulated that the regulated regional Bell Operating Companies (the former AT&T local exchange carriers responsible for providing local telephone service) must provide equal access to their local exchange facilities on an unbundled, tariffed basis to all long-distance/interexchange service providers. This has led to a dramatically expanded number of interexchange carriers providing long distance service at rates which are generally lower than what was being charged in pre-divestiture days (U. S. Department of Commerce, 1991).

- It forbade the regional Bell Operating Companies from engaging in the provision of information services: that is, generating, acquiring, storing, transforming, processing, retrieving, utilizing or making available information which may be conveyed via telecommunications (except what is required for network operation and maintenance). This has led to the growth of over 4000 information service provider companies in the ten years beyond the MFJ decree (U. S. Department of Commerce, 1991).

- It restricted regional Bell Operating companies from engaging in the manufacturing of telecommunications equipment. This has resulted in the development of a number of equipment manufacturers competing with one another in the highly-competitive telecommunications marketplace, which has led to the more rapid deployment of such innovations as video compression and voice recognition systems.

For almost 60 years, universal telephone service was an important tenet of governmental social responsibility. The entire regulatory structure for pricing telephone service in the "AT&T era" was established to ensure its support. It continues to be important enough that regulators are looking toward alternative forms of regulation to establish appropriate means of cross-subsidizing "universal information service" in an otherwise competitive telecommunications marketplace.

At the same time, competition is an essential component of a free-market economy. It is valued so highly in this country that the entire telecommunications industry has been restructured to encourage competition. The benefits of competition—increased service options, cost-based service provision and market-sensitive pricing structures—are off-set to some degree by the access and cost incongruities encountered when combining regulated local access services, unregulated competitive long distance service, and enhanced telecommunications services. These enhanced services include but are not limited to the digital transmission capacity required for "video dial tone," Integrated Signal Digital Network (ISDN) services, and signal conversion services (e.g., converting voice-mail or electronic mail messages to facsimile). Until a market for enhanced telecommunications services has been created, the cost of providing such services to a limited number of "early adopters," such as distance educators and trainers, is significant. Ironically, it is the high initial cost associated with construction, switching, and multiplexing which tends to keep the number of early telecommunication service subscribers low, even when subscribers see the benefits of the enhanced services for applications like education and training. Furthermore, the regulatory complexities associated with telephone service access and provision present additional challenges, especially for educators who have not spent a lot of time working in this arena. Under current conditions, an educational institution interested in creating a state-wide distance learning network carried over T-1 telephone lines must, for all intents and purposes, create its own dedicated telephone network.

One strategy which promotes greater use of enhanced telecommunications services is the introduction of public policies which support and encourage their use. Clearly, the determination of relative socio-economic worth of a service defines the degree to which marketplace conditions are allowed to affect the supply of and demand for goods and services OR the degree to which government intervention is likely to structure pricing and access options. If telephone services for schools are valued as a necessary element of serving the needs of students, it may, for example, be possible to develop pricing structures for lowering rates charged to schools for telecommunications services, or for providing "bandwidth on demand" through the public switched network for compressed video, data services, and other big capacity transmissions, just as is currently provided for regular telephone calls.

The Telecommunications Regulatory Environment

Telecommunications regulations provide the means of ensuring access to non-competitive services for the broadest number of subscribers, and establish pricing parameters, or tariffs, for non-competitive services. In their simplest sense, regulations specifically deal with the variable of cost. They are designed to substitute for "free market" conditions when dealing with essential services such as communications, transportation, or electrical power. Rather than dealing with a situation where customers pay what the market will bear, price structures in a regulated industry provide parameters to establish reasonable expense compensation and fair profit to those who provide essential services, while ensuring that those essential services are available to the broadest distribution of a population for a reasonable cost. This is especially important in an environment where the true market value of an essential service, like telecommunications, has not yet been determined.

The regulatory environment (see Figure 1) is defined by three dimensions: *governmental context, source of governmental control, and technology:*

* *Governmental context:* This first dimension identifies the branch of government from which regulations come forth. Telecommunications regulations are generally the consequence of legislative actions, executive orders or judicial decisions, or the interaction between and among them. In other words, the system of checks and balances that drives governmental processes in this country is very much in evidence when looking at the regulatory environment.

    Generally speaking, the regulatory process begins when legislation is passed which creates the authority to establish oversight responsibility. For example, the Communications Act of 1934, passed

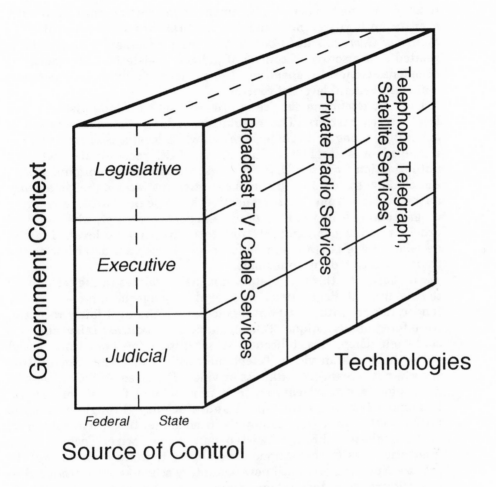

Federal   State

Source of Control

Figure 1. *Dimensions of the telecommunications regulatory environment.*

by the U. S. Congress, called for the creation of the Federal Communications Commission (FCC) to oversee the entire array of this country's communications concerns. The FCC was established for the expressed purpose of regulating interstate and foreign commerce in communications. (Intra-state oversight is coordinated through state Public Utilities Commissions (PUCs) which are empowered through legislation passed at the state level.) While created by legislative degree, the FCC functions within the executive branch of government; decisions made by the FCC are executive orders. While these orders are not laws in and of themselves, their authority is protected by law. Judicial decisions address the legality of the interpretations of legislation and of executive orders in actual practice. The interaction among legislation, executive orders, and judicial decisions is designed to keep any one branch of government from exerting undue influence over the authority of the remaining two branches of government.

- *Source of Governmental Control:* The second regulatory dimension is related to the source of control of judicial, legislative, and executive decisions. Generally speaking, the primary distinction is between state and Federal levels of control.

Current telephone service is provided by both long distance and local access carriers. The regulation of long distance services is generally managed through the FCC, while local access concerns are managed by state PUCs. Just as the FCC received its statutory authorization from the U. S. Congress through the Communications Act of 1934, state public utilities commissions receive their statutory authorization from their respective state legislatures. Executive orders coming from the FCC provide Federal oversight, whereas PUC orders provide oversight at the state government level. Judicial decisions made at state and Federal levels also vary according to the court in which a decision is made.

- *Technology:* The third regulatory dimension relates to the technology to be employed. Regulations, and regulatory agencies, have typically tended to deal with specific technologies which, until fairly recently, were functionally unique. Television meant *broadcast* television, not cable television, direct broadcast satellite television, compressed video, or slow-scan video. Telephone services involved transmitting speech, not streams of data bits or video. Digitized audio, video, and data signals can be carried in a narrowband format, or can be transmitted with greater speed and efficiency through fiber optic lines, whether they were originally intended for broadcast, cablecast, or transmission through twisted pair copper wire. Technological innovation has far outstripped the ability to manage or control its growth. Nevertheless, until new regulatory schemas are introduced to reconfigure this technology dimension, the current functional structures are likely to be maintained.

Key Telecommunications Regulatory Activities Affecting Distance Education

As users of telecommunications services, distance educators are directly affected by decisions made in the regulatory arena. After divestiture, for example, when local access calls were no longer subsidized by long distance toll charges, the basic rate charged for local telephone services increased for schools along with every other consumer group. Furthermore, when divestiture effectively did away with the mechanisms for maintaining universal service, it eliminated many of the opportunities for "social responsibility" on the part of telephone service providers. In the post-divestiture world, educators were nonplussed to discover that telephone service providers were unable to provide schools with telecommunications equipment, funding for projects to pay for telecommunications services, or service contracts based upon special "educational" service rates; it was increasingly difficult to forge school/business "partnerships" as had been done in the past.

The following examples provide a look at activities that have occurred in the various dimensions of the telecommunications regulatory arena which have had direct impact upon the provision of telecommunications services for all users, including distance educators.

Judicial Decisions: Two judicial decisions which have direct impact of national scope upon developments in the telecommunications industry are the 1982 U. S. District Court/AT&T anti-trust settlement which divested AT&T of its local service providing Bell Operating Companies, and the 1991 decision by the U. S. District Court to overturn its earlier decision restricting regional Bell Operating Companies from providing information services.

In 1982 the United States District Court approved a consent decree settling the United States vs. AT&T antitrust litigation which had been pending since 1974. As mentioned earlier in this chapter, AT&T was required to divest itself of all of its regional Bell operating companies (RBOCs) but was permitted to keep its manufacturing subsidiary (Western Electric), its research division (Bell Laboratories), and its international and domestic long distance service divisions. Under the terms of this agreement, the regional Bell operating companies were required to provide all interexchange (long distance) carriers equal access to local exchange subscribers. Additionally, AT&T was given permission to enter lines of business other than the provision of common carrier communications services, including computer equipment manufacture. Restrictions were imposed upon regional Bell operating companies regarding their provision of enhanced services/ information services. Furthermore, the RBOCs were denied access into non-telecommunications businesses such as equipment manufacturing.

Judge Harold Greene overturned his earlier restriction on the information services provision in July, 1991, through the U. S. District Court's Civil Action Number 82-0192. He noted that there was no direct evidence to show that the entry of the regional Bell operating companies into information services markets (such as electronic "yellow pages," fax/electronic mail conversion services, messaging services, integrated audio, video, and data services through the Integrated Signal Digital Network, or *ISDN*) would lessen competition, even though he warned that "the most probable consequence will be the elimination of competition from that market and the concentration of the sources of information of the American people in just a few dominant, collaborative conglomerates with the captive local telephone monopolies as their base" (Carnevale, 1991, B1).

Legislative Decisions: Salomon (1992) has noted that during the 102nd Congress, members of the House of Representatives and the Senate introduced 108 bills dealing with telecommunications. Some of the diverse concerns included among these proposed statutes addressed infrastructure developments, "video dial tone," information services, local telephone exchange service provisions, and funding for educational programs which make use of telecommunications technologies for course delivery. Many of these bills have been introduced as a way of changing some of restrictions imposed upon regional Bell operating companies by the "Modification of Final

Judgment." The bills noted are recent examples of legislation having direct impact upon distance education:

- House of Representatives (H.R.) Bill 3553 addressed guidelines for financial aid for distance education programs.
- H.R. Bill 656/Senate Bill (S.B.) 272 called for the development of a national high-speed research and education network.
- Senate Bill 1200/ H.R. 2546 recommended the creation of a national integrated telecommunications network to be available to all people, businesses and households by 2015.
- Senate Bill 173/H.R. 1527 called for elimination of restrictions on telecommunications equipment manufacturing by regional Bell operating companies which are currently imposed by the U. S. District Court's "Modification of Final Judgment" (Wagner, 1992).
- A decision by the U. S. District Court in 1991 to relax the Final Judgment's restrictions on provision of information services by the Bell operating companies has resulted in H.R. Bill 3515, which would reimpose competition to local exchange carriage in exchange for offering information service. Senate Bill 2112 presents a more moderate view of restrictions on information services provision by regional Bell Operating Companies.

State legislatures have also been actively engaged in changing their current regulatory structures. From January 1, 1983 to July 1, 1990, legislatures in thirty-one states enacted forty-one statutes to deregulate telecommunications services or companies (Stoffregen, 1990). The nature of deregulation varied from state to state. For example, in 1986, the Nebraska legislature completely removed all telecommunications companies from rate regulation by its PUC. On the other hand, in 1987 the Colorado legislature divided telecommunications services into three categories for regulatory purposes: regulated services, which included non-competitive basic local exchange services and new services necessary for providing basic exchange services; emerging competitive services, which included inter- and intra-LATA long distance calls; and deregulated services, which included highly-competitive services like cellular service, mobile radio, radio paging and operator services.

Thirty of the states' deregulation statutes gave their Public Utilities Commission greater power to determine the nature of deregulation activities for competitive services. In other cases, "deregulation" was limited to modifying tariff structures for regulated services. In all cases, state legislatures looked to adapt the regulation of telecommunications services to conform to local needs and conditions (Stoffregen, 1990).

Executive Decisions: The two Federal agencies having primary oversight responsibilities in the telecommunications arena are the Federal Communications Commission (FCC) and the National Telecommunications and Information Administration (NTIA) of the U. S. Department of Commerce. Generally speaking, the NTIA functions as a public policy organization while setting technical standards by which regulations can be enforced, while the FCC provide direct regulatory oversight of the entire telecommunications industry through its four Bureaus and addresses the policy implications of its regulatory decisions.

The *Common Carrier Bureau* is responsible for FCC rules governing wire and radio common carriers such as telephone, telegraph and satellite companies. The *Mass Media Bureau* is responsible for FCC rules governing television and radio broadcasting services, direct broadcast satellites, and cable television systems, while the *Private Radio Bureau* is responsible for radio stations that serve the communications needs of businesses, state and local governments, non-profit organizations and individuals. The *Field Operations Bureau* is responsible for inspecting radio stations, detection of violations of radio regulations and investigation of radio interference complaints (FCC, 1986).

The NTIA is actively involved in telecommunications from the perspective of establishing telecommunications public policy through technical standards. It provides engineering reports (e.g., Linfield, 1990; Nesenbergs, 1989) as well as reports (e.g., U. S. Department of Commerce, 1988, 1991) dealing with technological developments and implications of those developments to the telecommunications industry. The NTIA is not directly involved in regulatory oversight per se, but instead sets the standards by which regulations can be established.

At the state level, telecommunications regulatory decisions are managed by a Public Utilities Commission or other comparably named board. As noted in the legislative discussion, PUCs are given their oversight authority from their respective state legislatures. They are primarily concerned with intra-state or intra-locality telecommunications. PUCs are involved in determining the rate of return allowed to public utilities such as local access carriers, and can establish enhanced service rates and other forms of alternative regulations for setting telecommunications rate structures within states.

Establishing Distance Education Public Policy to Call for Regulatory Change

An example of how public policy is being used to support calls for regulatory change in support of distance education comes from a position paper distributed by the United States Distance Learning Association (USDLA) in 1991. Noting that today's education, communication, and information policies were developed long before the advent of contemporary distance educational capability, the USDLA declared that new technologies, particularly computers and digitally processed and transmitted information, have blurred or eliminated institutional, technological, and functional boundaries in the once discrete world of audio, data, and video (USDLA, 1991). Given these changing technological conditions, their policy recommendations call for:

- the development of a national infrastructure vision recognizing the critical importance and interdependence of systemic educational reform and advanced telecommunications services;
- bringing coherence to educational technology and distance learning funding, and focusing financial resources upon educational restructuring projects;

- the development of national demonstration sites for educational technology and distance learning that disseminate research results, educational applications, and effective teaching strategies;
- the provision of incentives for teacher training institutions to restructure pre-service and in-service programs recognizing the importance of communication and information technologies;
- the provision of incentives for regional and professional accreditation associations to recognize and encourage appropriate uses of distance learning technologies;
- ensuring that financial aid programs recognize distance learning as a peer to traditional course delivery;
- revising copyright laws to address educational use via distance learning technologies;
- providing incentives for states to remove barriers to distance learning around teacher certification, textbook adoption, and accreditation practices; and
- providing incentives for faculty who maximize resources and achieve quality instruction through use of appropriate educational technologies. (USDLA, 1991, pp. 3–4)

The purpose of articulating a "wish list" such as this is to *identify* issues of importance to distance educators, to *inform* decision-makers working outside the realm of distance education that these are the goals toward which distance educators strive, and to *focus attention* upon common activities of distance educators and trainers which may be better served if approached in a comprehensive, collaborative fashion. The process of articulation determines the operational parameters for ongoing discussion, and provides strategic direction to create conditions to more easily attain those ends.

To accomplish what they believe to be highly desirable policy ends, the USDLA suggested a series of specific regulatory reforms. Recognizing that advanced telecommunications services are critical to supporting distance learning and educational reform, they called upon federal, state, and local government to:

- encourage the development of a publicly switched broadband network for educational users;
- provide incentives for telecommunications carriers to develop cost-based pricing for educational applications;
- provide incentives for telecommunications carriers to provide dynamically allocated ("bandwidth on demand") links on a common carrier basis to schools, libraries and other learning sites;
- lift line of business restrictions on telephone companies for distance learning and educational applications;
- maintain "set-asides" for educational applications in radio frequency allocations; and
- provide incentives to ensure adequate cost-effective access to satellite transponders for educational applications. (USDLA, 1991, p.4)

What is interesting about these proposed regulatory reforms is that even though they tend to call for relaxing existing restrictions to make telecommunications services more accessible as well as more competitive, they were proposed only after being framed by the larger concern for educational restructuring, research and development, user incentives, and improved access to information resources. The logic behind this approach is if one believes that the broad policy goals are worthy, then the proposed regulatory solutions will be reasonable and appropriate. It presents a rationale for making changes to the status quo. Considering USDLA's proposed policy reforms, it is somewhat ironic that a majority of the policy recommendations proposed (specifically those dealing with incentives, copyright and research/dissemination efforts) are not directly related to relaxing existing restrictions on telephone regulations. Nevertheless, this provides a good example of how distance educators are beginning to make use of strategies which have long been used by the telecommunications industries to create favorable conditions for conducting their lines of business.

Summary

While it is important for distance educators to remember that they represent a small piece of the telecommunications landscape, it is also important to remember that distance education serves a potentially huge constituency—every school child, every college student, every business person, every adult is part of the national audiences whose informational and educational needs can be accommodated by means of distance educational systems, methods and practices. The views of distance educators and trainers need to be clearly articulated and need to be accompanied by strategies for creating the environment in which to effectively meet the informational and educational needs of that constituency. Our collective ability to move from the vision to the reality of providing cost-effective, quality information sources, courses, and programs via telecommunications may be dramatically compromised if these perspectives are not directly nor adequately represented in regulatory and public policy decision-making.

References

Carnevale, M. L. (1991). Bells close in on information services. *Wall Street Journal*, July 26, 1991, B1.

Dordick, H. S. (1990). The origins of universal service: History as a determinant of telecommunications policy. *Telecommunications Policy*, June, 1990, 223–231.

Federal Communications Commission (1986). *Telecommunications Policy*. Washington, DC: Federal Communications Commission.

Geeslin, B. M. (1989). Funding the future telecommunications infrastructure. *IEEE Communications Magazine*, August, 1989, 24–27.

Gilder, G. (1991). Into the Telecosm. *Harvard Business Review*, March–April, 150–161.

Hadden, S. G. & Williams, F. (1991). *Considerations for a redefinition of universal service: Results of a policy research project*. Austin: University of Texas.

Hudson, H. E. & Parker, E. B. (1990). Information gaps in rural America: Telecommunications policies for rural development. *Telecommunications Policy*, June 1990. 193–205.

Lenert, E. M. (1991). Paying for universal service: An examination of depreciation, cross-subsidy and bypass. A working paper of the Policy Research Project: Universal service for the twenty-first century. Austin: University of Texas.

Linfield, R. L. (1990). *Telecommunications networks: Services, architectures, and implementations.* U. S. Department of Commerce, National Telecommunications and Information Administration, Report Number 90–270.

Nesenbergs, M. (1989). *Stand-alone terrestrial and satellite networks for national interoperation of broadband networks.* U. S. Department of Commerce, National Telecommunications and Information Administration. Report Number 89–253.

Parker, E. B. (1991). State telecommunications policy recommendations. Unpublished paper, supported by the Ford Foundation and the Aspen Institute.

Salomon, K. D. (1992). The regulatory environment and distance education: The role of Congress. A presentation at the 4th Annual Meeting of the Western Cooperative for Educational Telecommunications, Albuquerque, NM.

Stoffregen, P. E. (1990). State telephone regulation report. Unpublished report distributed by Dickinson, Throckmorton, Parker, Mannheimer, and Raife, P.C., Des Moines, IA.

United States Congress Advisory Commission on Intergovernmental Relations (1990). *Intergovernmental regulation of telecommunications.* Washington, DC: U. S. Government Printing Office.

United States Congress Office of Technology Assessment (1989). *Linking for learning: A new course for education.* OTA-SET-430. Washington, DC: U. S. Government Printing Office.

United States Congress Office of Technology Assessment (1991). *Rural America at the crossroads: Networking for the future.* OTA-TCT-471. Washington, DC: U. S. Government Printing Office.

U. S. Department of Commerce, National Telecommunications and Information Administration (1988). *NTIA Telecom 2000: Charting the course for a new century.* Washington, DC: U. S. Government Printing Office.

U. S. Department of Commerce, National Telecommunications and Information Administration (1991). *NTIA Infrastructure Report: Telecommunications in the Age of Information.* Washington, DC: U. S. Government Printing Office.

United States Distance Learning Association (1991). National policy recommendations. Unpublished paper.

U. S. District Court for the District of Columbia, United States of America vs. Western Electric Company, Civil Action Number 82–0192. Judge Harold H. Greene, presiding.

U S WEST Communications (1990). *The winning edge: Modification of final judgment/civil enforcement consent order compliance process.* Denver, CO: US WEST Communications, Inc.

Wagner, E. D. (1992). Keeping Watch on Public Policy. *TechTrends, 36*(6), 9–11.

Williams, F. (1991). *The new telecommunications: Infrastructure for the information age.* New York: The Free Press.

Chapter Twelve

Distance Education: An Opportunity for Cooperation and Resource Sharing

Mollie A. McGill and Sally M. Johnstone

The preceding chapters have described how the field of educational telecommunication and distance education have undergone incredible growth in recent years. The impetus for this growth has not been *exclusively* the availability of new technologies. Indeed many of the most effective applications involve technologies that are not new at all, such as the telephone. Instead more educational institutions have recognized how technology can effectively extend their educational programs and services to students and teachers in rural as well as urban settings.

In 1989, the U. S. Office of Technology Assessment (OTA) conducted an extensive study for the U. S. Congress on how schools were using technology for distance education. They found a dramatic increase among elementary and secondary schools over the previous five-year period and attributed this growth to two factors: (1) the ability of telecommunications technology to meet specific educational needs and expand access to scarce resources, and (2) the advancements in the technology itself that make it more flexible, more powerful, and more affordable (U. S. Congress, 1989). A third factor fueling comparable growth among postsecondary institutions is the rise in the nontraditional student population. This group of older, working adults, who are frequently restricted in their ability to attend on-campus classes, is a major market for distance education providers. In fact, it was the continuing education needs of working professionals in high-technology businesses that spurred the initial development of many university distance education programs.

Quite possibly the future of distance education and technology will be in their ability to help institutions continue to meet new demands in an environment of tight fiscal resources. The California State University (CSU) System, for example, recently initiated Project DELTA to explore how the system will be able to accommodate a projected increase of over 150,000 students by the year 2005. CSU estimates that 50,000 of those students will not be able to be accommodated by existing facilities, and technology is expected to play a major role in serving these students off the campus (California State University System, 1992).

The transition from traditional classroom delivery to one involving multiple remote sites, switches, and black boxes is not a simple one for teachers, faculty, administrators, or students. Not only are there myriad technical issues, but also schools and colleges must address a host of policy, instructional, and attitudinal issues which can hinder effective and efficient uses of the technology. The fact that every distance education provider, at elementary/secondary through graduate education levels, is wrestling with this same set of problems is one of the reasons that today we can find several examples of formal organizations whose goal is to cooperatively find solutions to these issues.

Webster's dictionary defines the word "cooperate" as "to associate with another or others for mutual, often economic, benefit" (Webster's, 1972). The economic payoffs that can be realized from cooperation do indeed provide a strong argument in support of cooperation. In the field of distance education, however, equally compelling are the potential improvements in efficiency and effectiveness in dealing with all of the above policy, program, and training issues.

This chapter will discuss how cooperative organizations of schools, colleges, agencies, and states can work together and share information, resources, expertise, even hardware, to the benefit of their individual distance education efforts.

Distance Education: An Opportunity for Cooperation

Clearly cooperation can take place with or without a formal organizational structure. In this chapter, however, we are talking about formal agreements among a group of entities, such as schools, colleges, and state agencies, to work together toward a set of common goals or problems. The "members" of these cooperatives typically are the organizations themselves, not *individuals* within those organizations. The particular label given to these partnerships is not significant. Whether the partnership is called a cooperative, consortium, compact, or cluster, they all rely heavily on the time, effort, guidance, and expertise of the groups that comprise their constituency.

It is not always easy to persuade schools, states, and others to cooperate and keep them committed to the overall goals of the group as a whole. A study on regional resource sharing in higher education examined what prerequisites needed to exist to ensure successful cooperation and found the following conditions critical:

- incentives for participation,
- legal authority,
- information and communication,
- time and timeliness, and

- a locus for initiating action and sustaining it (Western Interstate Commission for Higher Education, 1983).

In distance education, the incentives for cooperation are many; they may include the desire to expand network connections, negotiate group discounts for satellite time or telecourse licenses, or simply to share information about innovative uses of the technology. In very broad terms, the major incentives address the areas of programming, teacher and administrator development, equipment and network development, policy development, and advocacy.

Programming. This may well be one of the more important yet tougher areas for cooperative action because of the high costs to produce and, with some technologies, to transmit programs, and also because of myriad state and campus policies related to course credits, quality standards, and out-of-state providers that impede efforts for resource sharing.

Still, many examples of cooperation exist where joint program planning and development are the primary objectives. One example is the International University Consortium (IUC) which began in 1980 as a consortium of colleges and universities to produce media-assisted courses at the upper division level. IUC now has about 40 members in the United States, Canada, Europe, and the Pacific Rim and coordinates among its members the production of video, print, and audio courses.

Special programming for targeted markets is another area that can be addressed effectively as a cooperative venture. One successful model is the National Technological University (NTU) which utilizes faculty from many of the country's top engineering schools to offer completely articulated graduate programs in engineering specialties. This model of pooling faculty and resources to offer a distance education program in a specialized field has been adopted in the fields of graduate teacher education by the Northwest Satellite Consortium for Graduate Teacher Education and in agricultural education by the AG*SAT network.

Teacher and administrator development. Teacher and administrator development is an important area in distance education that can be met quite effectively through a cooperative organization, although seldom is this the driving need behind the establishment of a formal organization. Still, whether dealing with teachers and administrators at the elementary/secondary or postsecondary education level, a cooperative approach to this problem is oftentimes easier and usually more effective than going it alone. In the neutral environment of a cooperative, teachers and administrators are more at ease in sharing information with their peers and learning from one another.

As with programming, a cooperative can effectively draw on expertise of its members to conduct training for faculty and administrators. For example, a group of administrators from schools across the state might engage in an electronic mail discussion of how distance education programs are funded at their respective schools. Or, for on-site workshops, faculty from a specific discipline and experienced with a particular technology may be brought in via audioconferencing to share their interaction techniques with faculty attending a face-to-face workshop.

Equipment and network development. The genesis of many statewide cooperatives has been the planning and construction of a telecommunications delivery network. One of the most successful examples in this area is the state of Utah, which created a cooperative organization of schools, colleges, and state agencies to work together to secure state and federal funds for equipment and network development. In Washington, a consortium of public community colleges merged their plans for data and video networks into a single organization which contributed to their success in securing state funds for a satellite system. In Colorado, Kansas, Minnesota, North Dakota, and other states, there are a growing number of public school and college "cluster" arrangements whose goals are to expand networking capabilities within a community.

Policy development. Many policies at the local, state, and federal levels can impede efforts to offer a quality distance education program, and eventually will have to be changed. A worthwhile and effective role for a cooperative organization is sharing information about each other's current and proposed stance on a particular policy issue. A more proactive posture, of course, is to identify those policy areas shared by all members and to work as a group to revise and implement them. The Utah cooperative was able to negotiate among its public universities and state department of education solutions to some tough policy areas that have resulted in increased programming and enrollments over the state's instructional television networks.

Advocacy. Cooperative organizations, especially ones that have a broadly represented membership, can be very effective in promoting distance education issues at the policy level. They are able to draw on the expertise of their diverse constituency and thus able to present a powerful unified position on matters before state legislatures, educational governing boards, governors' associations, and the U. S. Congress.

A subset of the advocacy role is serving as a neutral convener. Cooperatives whose members represent a single interest group, such as a community college consortium or a single state, may not be able to perform this role as effectively as an organization with a more diverse membership. Broad-based cooperatives can very effectively serve this role by bringing together key players on a given issue and facilitating discussions.

Some Examples of Distance Education Cooperatives

Single State Cooperatives

Utah. Utah's higher education institutions and state agencies for postsecondary and public education formed a cooperative in the early 1980s to work together in planning and funding a statewide network for the delivery of education. From the start, the Utah cooperative has been a voluntary association involving the senior level administrators from each of the participating universities, schools, and state agencies. This model of cooperation has resulted in the construction and ongoing expansion of several networks for the delivery of education programs and courses statewide. By being able to present a single plan to their state legislature, they have been very successful in securing state as well as federal funding to construct a microwave network that now reaches nearly every part of the state. In addition to planning and operating the microwave network, this group has been highly effective in recommending and effecting the adoption of new policies that support the cooperative use of the state networks, such as articulation agreements, criteria for course selection, and reciprocal agreements enabling students to obtain full degree programs via distance education (Western Cooperative for Educational Telecommunications, 1991).

Arizona. Planners of the Arizona Education Telecommunications Cooperative (AETC), organized in 1989, looked very closely at the Utah model and its successful funding record with its state legislature and the federal government. As in Utah, the Arizona cooperative also is a voluntary organization and also is represented by top-level administrators from the participating institutions. One difference between the Utah and the Arizona initiatives is the emphasis on network development. Due in part to pre-existing telecommunications facilities at several Arizona institutions, AETC has placed more emphasis on information sharing and policy development versus the major thrust in Utah during the early years on network planning and expansion. The major focuses of the AETC are information sharing, joint legislative proposals, and cooperative policy development.

Oregon. Whereas educators were the prime instigators of the Utah and the Arizona cooperatives, in Oregon it was private business, particularly the electronics industry, that drove the initial concept, the planning, and the political processes that led to the creation of Oregon ED-NET. The ED-NET designers also looked closely at the Utah model of voluntary cooperation but recommended a significantly different approach. With the goal in mind of building a sophisticated network that would serve all of the diverse needs of business, schools, hospitals, libraries, and higher education, the planners of Oregon ED-NET developed a long-range business plan approach for selling the concept to the state legislature. ED-NET is not a voluntary organization; instead it is a not-for-profit state agency and requires dues from its broad membership of schools, colleges, hospitals, libraries, state government, and private business.

The structure and the mission of each of these examples of single state cooperatives were shaped by the unique circumstances and pressures that were present at the time in each state. In the case of Oregon, for example, the proponents of ED-NET took advantage of the particular financial and political climate that created a window of opportunity for passage of the legislation and an $8 million appropriation. Whether creating networks or an environment for program sharing and policy development, funding is one area where state cooperatives may find their strength. In a time of limited financial resources, statewide partnerships or cooperatives, as opposed to an individual institution, stand a much better chance of success in terms of securing financial support, producing a full menu of quality instructional programs, and attracting sufficient enrollments to make the delivery system work.

Local or Single Constituent Consortia

The preceding models of statewide cooperatives may not be feasible in other states that have multiple educational governing bodies or competing plans for network development. Moreover, such a broadly represented group may not be appropriate for achieving the particular goals of the group. The following examples illustrate how a more local and more targeted cooperative arrangement can be effective.

K–12 distance education cooperatives. Local level cooperatives representing K–12 schools and agencies are found in many states serving both urban and rural communities. Typically, the primary goal of these cooperatives has been to expand access to specialized courses in foreign language, math and science, and the arts by interconnecting the schools to form an "electronic cluster." Since these groups focus on specific local needs, they can be quite successful in securing local funding and resolving academic and political issues that get more complex with larger broad-based cooperatives. Many of these public school clusters have in place enviable state-of-the-art telecommunications delivery systems.

One such network is the High Southwest Plains Network (HSPN) in Kansas. In 1989 a group of nine school districts along with their regional service center entered into a partnership arrangement with two local independent phone companies and one of the regional Bell operating companies to interconnect the schools via 160 miles of fiber optic cable, giving the schools the capability of two-way, full-motion video transmission. Critical to the success of the HSPN has been the commitment from school superintendents and the local school boards to fund the initial network construction and to enter into a long-term lease agreement with the telecommunications providers. One of the network's more significant achievements was its successful petition to the public utilities commission to authorize, on a pilot basis, a reduced incremental rate for use of the fiber network. The HSPN continues to add additional sites to its local network, including a connection to the region's four-year state college, which now is serving the continuing education needs of bankers and engineers in the area.

Community college consortia. Another type of cooperative arrangement that has emerged with the growth of distance education is the community college-based consortium, established principally to coordinate group licensing or purchasing of nationally distributed telecourses. Depending on the number of telecourses and the number of college sites, the potential savings from this kind of cooperative purchase can be significant, up to 95 percent savings on licensing fees. Typically, the leadership of these consortia tend to represent more of the practitioner's perspective, with less involvement from senior level administration.

Several of these consortia, found in California, Colorado, Oregon, Washington, and other states, have progressed well beyond their original mission and now collaborate in a number of areas, including the development of distance education policies, user handbooks, and program production. The Texas Consortium for Educational Telecommunications, for example, began in 1982 as a consortium of seven two-year colleges in northern Texas and now has 22 institutional members throughout the state, including one public university. Although the coordination of telecourse licensing and purchase agreements continues to be its primary goal, the consortium is recognized within the state as a major player in distance education, and as such serves as an advisor on a variety of distance learning and telecommunications issues brought forward by the state's higher education and telecommunications governing agencies.

The Texas consortium is run as a volunteer operation, directed by a three-person executive committee elected from the membership. Each member college pays a minimal annual fee to cover incidental costs, such as postage and printing; plus a small percentage of each telecourse contract goes to the Dallas Community College District as compensation for the accounting and contract negotiation services it provides to the consortium.

Some states are actively promoting the concept of regional distance education clusters within their states. Some advantages to the smaller cluster arrangement include (1) fewer special interests that may side track or complicate the larger agenda, (2) more opportunities for innovation and experimentation, and (3) more direct involvement among teachers, librarians, media technicians, and other users who may have a lesser role in larger organizations.

Multi-state Cooperatives

Western Cooperative for Educational Telecommunications. The Utah telecommunications cooperative served as the model for yet another cooperative, this one created to serve a broad audience of primary and secondary education, higher education, state agencies, and other providers and users of educational telecommunications, yet on a multi-state basis. The Western Cooperative for Educational Telecommunications, established in 1989, is a membership organization among 15 states—Alaska, Arizona, California, Colorado, Hawaii, Idaho, Montana, Nevada, New Mexico, North Dakota, Oregon, South Dakota, Utah, Washington, and Wyoming. Although one of the early visions for the Western Cooperative was to work with states to physically interconnect and/or ensure technical compatibility among the growing number of educational telecommunications delivery systems, the Western Cooperative is not involved in the construction or operation of a technical network. The members quickly recognized that the most important function of such a comprehensive and diverse cooperative was the construction and maintenance of a "people" network. They use this network of veteran and novice distance education practitioners and administrators to address those barriers mentioned earlier in this discussion—faculty development, policy development, and program development. In the West, 150 schools, colleges, state agencies, nonprofit groups and corporations now work together to address these issues under the umbrella of the Western Cooperative.

The Western Cooperative is a membership-based organization where (1) member dues represent 50 percent of the operating budget, and (2) members appoint an advisory board from among their peers. The membership, quite diverse in terms of geographic spread, expertise with technology and distance education, and educational markets served, is directly involved in determining the organization's specific activities and in carrying out these activities. It is this level of direct involvement in agenda-setting that helps to solidify the "cooperative" nature of the organization. It is also through this direct involvement that members often realize the greatest benefits, through the personal networking and increased awareness that result from active cooperation with colleagues throughout the region. The range of activities sponsored by the Western Cooperative covers information brokering, people networking, faculty and administrator training, regional matching of needs and resources, and advocacy with institutional, state, and federal leaders. This external advocacy rule is one that is not easily replicated by single-state cooperatives.

Regional Educational Compacts. One of the reasons that the Western Cooperative can be particularly effective in the role of external advocate is its connection with the Western Interstate Commission for Higher Education (WICHE). WICHE is one of four regional, higher education compacts in the United States. To date, WICHE, through its Western Cooperative, is the only compact that supports regional resource sharing and cooperation in the field of educational telecommunications.

Nearly every state in the country participates in one of the four existing educational compacts. (Delaware, New Jersey, New York, and Pennsylvania are not eligible for membership in any of the compacts.) Central to the mission of each is recognition that not every state needs to support costly programs in all professional fields, and through agreements among the states, students could still be assured affordable access to these fields. The four compacts and their member states include:

- The Midwestern Higher Education Compact (MHEC), established in 1991, encompasses seven states: Michigan, Minnesota, Kansas, Illinois, Ohio, Nebraska, and Missouri. (Iowa, Indiana, North Dakota, South Dakota, and Wisconsin are eligible for membership but have not yet joined.)
- The New England Board of Higher Education (NEBHE), created in 1955 serves Connecticut, Maine, Massachusetts, New Hampshire, Rhode Island, and Vermont.
- The Southern Regional Education Board (SREB), created in 1948, serves 15 states: Alabama, Arkansas, Florida, Georgia, Kentucky, Louisiana, Maryland, Mississippi, North Carolina, Oklahoma, South Carolina, Tennessee, Texas, Virginia, and West Virginia.
- The Western Interstate Commission for Higher Education (WICHE), formed in 1953, originally served 13 states—Alaska, Arizona, California, Colorado, Hawaii, Idaho, Montana, Nevada, New Mexico, Oregon, Utah, Washington, and Wyoming. In the 1980s, North Dakota and South Dakota became affiliate members to gain access to the student exchange programs and to participate in WICHE's new educational telecommunications program.

The compacts have their own unique program emphases, but, by and large, each provides three central functions: (1) facilitate and negotiate regional contracts which allow states and their institutions to participate in various student exchange programs, (2) provide the region's legislative and executive leadership with timely information and research on key educational issues, and (3) promote regional planning.

These regional compacts represent more than just a geographic grouping of states. They are legal agreements among the states requiring legislative adoption and gubernatorial approval with ratification by the federal government. Although the language of the compacts precludes them from having any direct power or authority over their member states and institutions, their effectiveness stems from their direct ties with state executive and legislative officials and key educational decisionmakers.

There are many benefits in housing interstate cooperative programs under the umbrella of these regional compacts, the most powerful of which stems from the long history of cooperation among each compact's member institutions and states, and their direct ties with political and educational leaders.

Considerations for Successful Cooperation

Needs assessment. Determine what level of support and interest exists. It makes little sense to start a new organization if one already exists that fits your needs. Even if the cooperative will encompass only a limited geographic area, learn as much as possible from what other groups may already be doing in your state. A good place to start a search for existing distance education cooperatives is with your State Department of Education, university system office, and state higher education governing or coordinating agency. It is likely that each of these offices has an individual who is knowledgeable about telecommunications, technology, and distance education activities throughout the state.

Support from top level officials. A key next step is to secure the support and endorsement of select individuals who represent key positions of authority. These individuals can be extremely helpful in promoting the "vision" of the cooperative, in recruiting other organizations to participate, and in fundraising activities. Be able to provide them with a clear statement of the need and the proposed cooperative solution. In the case of WICHE's Western Cooperative, approximately two years were spent in documenting the region's needs and requesting input from top level people into the design of the proposed organization.

Consider membership in terms of achieving goals. In designing a formal framework for resource sharing and cooperation, it is important to consider who should participate in the cooperative. The membership is, of course, central to the overall mission but it also can affect issues of funding, staffing, political support, and feasibility of success. One of the particular strengths of the Western Cooperative, for example, is its broad-based constituency of both policy-level people and distance education practitioners. This enables the organization to draw on the subject expertise of the practitioners and the broader institutional and political perspectives of the policy group and sets it apart from professional associations with a more uniform membership and more limited agenda.

An important group to consider for membership in any distance education cooperative is the private sector, both as a source of funding and expertise on technical and organizational issues. In the Western Cooperative, corporate members are directly involved in planning and executing projects and oftentimes offer reality checks on implementation issues that can be overlooked by education groups. After several years of operation, the Utah consortium added representatives from private industry to have the advantage of their technical expertise.

It is useful to think about membership in terms of who can help achieve the specific objectives, and to match the two very carefully. For example, a diverse membership base can be quite effective in conducting policy and advocacy-related activities because they do not represent a single interest group. At the same time, a broadly represented membership also means that a number of different perspectives and needs will have to be served, requiring a fuller and more complex agenda.

Consider staffing needs. With a clear idea of mission and membership, the next issue relates to how the necessary work is going to get done. Keep in mind that at many schools and campuses, technology and distance education assignments are "added-on" responsibilities for teachers, faculty, and administrators to which they are already contributing extra time and effort. Having a small central staff assigned to coordinate the work should be carefully considered. The membership will likely involve very committed but also very busy people who are unable to contribute full-time attention to the cooperative's goals. A staff can move the tasks along to ensure that the overall objectives are met. In designing projects that may require some work from members, make sure that the final products not only benefit the group, but also have a direct payoff to their own school or organization.

Consider funding needs. Securing the funds to hire a staff is not an easy task with few funding sources available for administrative expenditures. A general yardstick used by some cooperative organizations is to have at least 50 percent of their expenses covered by the members, reinforcing the cooperative nature of the organization and members' sense of ownership in the organization and its goals. It also is critical to structure the membership fees so that those types of institutions/organizations that get the greatest benefit, pay the most.

Distance education is a funding priority for a growing number of foundations and federal programs, especially when the proposal addresses a specific educational need rather than the construction of a delivery system. Consider the development of one or two projects that will produce early on in some tangible and desired products. In an organization that relies on volunteered efforts, it is important to produce direct benefits to the members and thus reinforce their commitment to the cooperative.

Maintain and nurture member involvement. The essence of a cooperative organization is its membership and thus it is critical to continuously remind the membership of the agreed upon, common goal, reassess individual needs, revise the goal in light of members' needs, and develop projects and services that support the common goal. The larger the group, the more important this ongoing communication and needs assessment becomes. Even more challenging is the need to broaden the involvement and support from more than just a single person with a member institution. For instance, some cooperative ventures have failed because only a single individual within a school was committed to the cooperative concept. As critical as this step is, it may be difficult to accomplish since distance education and telecommunications issues typically are the responsibility of one office, or one person.

Test the political climate at your school and in your state, especially if funding will be sought from these groups. In the case of Oregon, the legislative coffers and climate were right in 1989 for moving forward with the ED-NET legislation. Members of Arizona's state cooperative, on the other hand, have not been as successful in selling to the legislature their vision for statewide access to quality education via telecommunications but they have succeeded in maintaining their commitment to cooperation and have benefitted in many tangible as well as intangible ways from their cooperative organization.

Summary

A variety of examples exist where schools, colleges, private business, and states have created formal organizations to deal with a common set of problems. In distance education, the incentives for cooperation may be to reduce costs for the purchase or production of quality educational programming, or share in the construction and operation of a telecommunications delivery system, or reduce institutional and state policy barriers, or simply to share information about distance education and the ever-changing field of educational telecommunications.

Cooperative relationships can be tough to get started and challenging to keep on track. They require the volunteered efforts of its members and their commitment to the larger goal of the whole group. Careful consideration should be given to the composition of the membership, setting an achievable goal, how the goal will be attained, and what staffing and funding levels are required.

Cooperatives can be incredibly powerful organizations when the right mix of interests and right level of support are involved. They can tap the information, resources, and expertise from a larger membership and represent a unified voice on important policy, funding, and academic issues at the local, state, and federal levels. And particularly in the field of distance education and technology, there are many windows for collaborative action on common problems and many opportunities for a whole host of unexpected benefits.

References

California State University System (1992). *Project DELTA: Planning phase.* Seal Beach, CA: California State University System.

U. S. Congress, Office of Technology Assessment (1989). *Linking for learning: A new course for education.* Washington, DC: U. S. Government Printing Office.

Webster's Seventh New Collegiate Dictionary (1972). New York: G. & C. Merriam Co.

Western Cooperative for Educational Telecommunications (1991). *Reports from western states: Educational telecommunications, plans, policies, and programs.* Boulder, CO: Western Cooperative for Educational Telecommunications.

Western Interstate Commission for Higher Education (1983). *Regional resource sharing: A strategy for improving western higher education in an era of limits.* Boulder, CO: Western Interstate Commission for Higher Education.

Chapter Thirteen

Enhancing Faculty Effectiveness in Distance Education

Barry Willis

Faculty training is critical to the success of any distance education program. In fact, designing, creating, and implementing effective in-service training is the most efficient pathway to the long-term success of distance education.

One need look no further than the contrasting challenges faced in the traditional classroom and those confronting the distance educator to see why faculty training and on-going support is critical. In a traditional classroom setting, teachers rely on a number of visual and unobtrusive cues from their students. A quick glance, for example, reveals those who are attentively taking notes, pondering difficult concepts, or enthusiastically preparing to respond to the teacher's questions. The same quick glance reveals those who are tense, frustrated, confused, tired, or bored.

Students entering class with organized class notes, well-worn texts, and obvious enthusiasm reveal something quite different from those who are withdrawn, and arrive without class materials, or receptive attitudes. Again, alert teachers factor these unobtrusive cues into class planning and delivery.

The effective teacher consciously and subconsciously receives and analyzes these visual cues with great subtlety and clarity. As a result, the delivery of information, and often the course content itself, is adapted to meet the unique mix of student moods, characteristics, and needs at any one time. This process of visually receiving information, processing it, and adapting teaching behavior is so rapid and automatic that few teachers spend time thinking about it. To them, having an instinctive feel for their students is just "good teaching."

In reality, however, while natural instinct may help, it is the dynamics at play in and around the traditional classroom setting that increase teacher effectiveness. For example, a traditional classroom setting offers both teacher and students many spontaneous opportunities for interaction outside of class. Perhaps they talk between classes, meet informally on an assignment over lunch, or share mutual interests. Merely living in the same community provides a common frame of reference leading to broader understanding and a sense of shared experience.

Finally, face-to-face interaction takes place without any technological link. Communication is spontaneous and free-flowing, without the distraction of manipulating switches, anticipating potential technical difficulties, or relying on equipment to link teacher and students for purposes of communication and feedback.

Faculty Changes

In contrast, the challenges faced by the distant teacher are imposing. The instructor must, for example:

1. Look at the course in a new way. Few with distant teaching experience would downplay the importance of adapting traditionally-delivered courses to the unique instructional environment confronted in distance education. In many cases, the more comfortable the instructor is in teaching in a traditional setting, the more difficult it is to face the reality that significant re-thinking and adaptation will be required for effective distant course delivery.

2. Shift from the role of content provider to content facilitator. To use a concert analogy, the traditional instructor serves as lead soloist, while the distance educator is the conductor and concert master. Proficiency here requires undisputed mastery of the subject being taught as well as an ability to draw on the varied backgrounds and hidden talents of the students.

3. Gain comfort and proficiency in using technology as the primary teacher-student link. In most distance education contexts, technology is the critical link between the teacher and students. Effective use of this link requires a working understanding of delivery system strengths and weaknesses, as well as related utilization strategies. This understanding, in turn, leads to the technical competence and confidence needed to effectively teach at a distance.

4. Learn to teach effectively without the visual control provided by direct eye contact. Distant teachers have few, if any, visual cues. Even the visual cues that do exist are filtered through technological devices such as video monitors. The effortless flow of stimulating teacher-class conversation can feel contrived and lacking in dynamism when spontaneity is altered by technical requirements and distance.

Unless one uses a real-time visual medium such as television, the teacher receives no visual information from the distant sites. The teacher never really knows if, for example, students are asleep, talking among themselves, or even in the room. Separation by distance also affects the general rapport among students.

5. Develop an understanding and appreciation for the distant students' lifestyle. Living in different communities, geographic regions, states, or even countries deprives the teacher and students of a common community link or reference point. Often, the students' realm of experience, living conditions, and culture are foreign to the instructor, or even other class participants. To be effective, the instructor must gain an understanding of the students, either through first-hand observation or discussion with colleagues experienced with the target learner group.

Faculty Development Underpinnings

By any measure, teachers face a new world of challenge in transferring their traditional teaching skills to the distance education context (Beaudoin, 1990). Enter faculty development and the need for systematic in-service training and continuing faculty support.

The concept of faculty effectiveness training dates back to the early 1960s when McKeachie (1964) published a report suggesting that college and university teaching needed improvement. This effort was followed by other studies analyzing the teacher's role in higher education and offering suggestions for instructional improvement or, as the term gradually evolved, *faculty development* (Astin, Comstock, Epperson, Greeley & Kauffman, 1974; Axelrod, 1973; Eble, 1972; Lovell-Troy & Eickmann, 1992).

Although the idea of faculty development appears in various contexts, it typically focuses on enhancing the talents, expanding the interests, improving the competence, and facilitating the professional and personal growth of faculty members, primarily in their role as instructors (Gaff, 1975).

Evolutionary changes have occurred in the field of faculty development in the past 15 years. Early approaches addressed the symptoms of the problem (i.e., disenchanted students, falling enrollments, etc.) in contrast to the problem itself: the lack of training designed to improve teacher effectiveness. For this reason, early efforts in the field focused on curriculum change, the recruitment of brighter students and new doctoral faculty, reducing the student-faculty ratio, and the development of instructional resource centers.

In recent years, faculty development strategies have taken a different approach by addressing instructional improvement through skill development, enhancing support services, and ensuring that institutional reward structures reflect the rigorous challenges confronting the effective distance educator.

By any measure, the goal of faculty development is *change*, and it must occur not only in the way instruction is delivered, but in the way instructors view learners. Regardless of the need, change in complex educational environments is difficult to accept, let alone promote.

An additional and perplexing challenge relates to the technical and administrative infrastructure in place at many institutions. For many years, and with few exceptions, technical managers have played a more dominant role than educators in distance education planning and implementation. Although much time is spent convincing funding agencies, governing boards, politicians, and fellow administrators that distance education technology is the solution, faculty are seldom consulted as to the nature of the problem. In fact, subtle and obvious attempts are often made to keep faculty out of the process of identifying instructional problems and selecting potential solutions. Unfortunately, a poorly-defined problem has an infinite number of vague solutions, most of which lack merit. As a result, faculty are often expected to make a system function that they had little input in planning and that may or may not be instructionally appropriate.

Too often, administrators and technical managers stumble on this conundrum after the technological system is in place. The academic reality dawns slowly that the interest, support, and enthusiasm of the faculty is required if a distance education program is to be successful, regardless of its technological sophistication.

Faculty acceptance of distance education is seldom automatic, even when they are included in the planning process. This hesitancy is primarily due to an educational environment that inhibits, rather than promotes, change and innovation. The characteristics often associated with this academic culture are goal ambiguity, limited flexibility, low faculty interdependence, and high vulnerability (see Kurpius & Christie, 1978). More specifically:

Goal Ambiguity. Academic institutions and the faculty who staff them face a plethora of contrasting goals and expectations. In efforts to avoid scrutiny and appear responsive, many institutions rely on non-critical, but easily measured goals, lacking in specificity.

In contrast, due to the visibility and scrutiny it invites, distance education demands that goals be clear, concise, and measurable. Towards this end, institutions and departments participating in distance education must ensure that their involvement is related to specific institutional and departmental missions, goals, and objectives. If, for example, a program goal is to meet the needs of under-served students, the characteristics and expectations of those students must be understood in detail by the faculty and administration.

Limited Flexibility. Educational institutions are often static bureaucracies lacking in dynamic flexibility. As a result, emphasis is placed on changing students, staff, and faculty to best reflect the institution's often unrealistic view of itself, as defined by upper administration and governing agencies.

Applied to meeting student needs, for example, emphasis is placed on molding the individual to fit the offerings of the institution, as opposed to adapting the institution to meet student needs. Faculty often confront this same institutional rigidity. Rather than develop flexible delivery systems, for example, many institutional leaders intentionally make rigid technical decisions that defy creative adaptation by faculty.

To be effective, methods of instructional delivery must be responsive to the characteristics, needs, and styles of faculty and students alike. The degree to which this is accomplished will determine the success of the faculty development enterprise, as well as the educational institution itself.

Low Faculty Interdependence. The rigid departmental structure of many academic institutions provides few opportunities for faculty to receive advice, trade ideas, and solve problems collaboratively. This isolation leads to faculty insecurity regarding their own effectiveness in the classroom and tends to protect those lacking the motivation and desire to improve teaching skills.

To overcome this problem, collaborative strategies that join faculty in the improvement of instruction and the attainment of commonly agreed upon goals should be pursued.

High Vulnerability. Because of decreased education funding and ever-changing societal demands, academic programs are extremely vulnerable. As a result, academic administrations and faculty often avoid programs or approaches to problem solving that appear innovative.

The distance delivery of instruction is often considered a new approach to education. As a result, it is especially open to criticism. In truth, however, the novelty of distance education is more perception than reality. In one form or another and under various labels (e.g., correspondence study, independent learning), distance education has been an accepted educational approach for decades.

Studies have shown that the method of delivery, whether face-to-face or technology assisted, has little to do with student performance, if delivery methods are appropriate to the content being delivered and the characteristics of the learners. To overcome faculty perception of vulnerability, distance delivery methods must be

- appropriate to the requirements of the content,
- insightful in their incorporation of relevant content examples, and
- unobtrusive and easy to use by faculty and students.

Once these conditions are met, in-service training can reduce the uncertainty that faculty may feel as they get involved in distant teaching.

Organizing for Success

Garnering the overall interest and support of the faculty is typically a two-step process. As previously discussed, the first step entails including them in the planning effort. The second step requires training opportunities and on-going support in their distant teaching efforts.

On a national level, training opportunities for distant faculty have historically been limited, sporadic, and seldom pursued until faculty morale problems have developed. By this time, however, influential faculty have typically spread the word that distant teaching is a frustrating and stressful assignment to be avoided at all costs.

Although enlightenment has come slowly, the importance of in-service training in distance education has recently gained acceptance (see Graham & Wedman, 1989). Moore *et al.* (1990), for example, report a number of content-specific areas in which telecommunication is used for in-service training. They include adult and early childhood education (Downing, 1984), as well as science, career guidance, and math training (Elliott, 1989).

Effective faculty training programs take many forms and are seeing wider use both nationally (see Self, 1983) and internationally (see Robinson, 1991; Scriven, 1989). Some focus on the delivery medium, such as audio (see Shaeffer, 1990) or television (see Carl, 1986; Kromholz & Johnstone, 1988; Nevins & Wright, 1984; Tresman, 1988), while others focus on general principles of effective teaching, adapted to the context of distance education (see Batey & Cowell, 1986; Scriven, 1986; Willis, 1990, 1992, 1993).

At some institutions, one-to-one sessions are emphasized, typically at the faculty member's initiation. Others rely on campus-wide faculty development workshops (Brzoska, 1991), or self-paced instructional materials. Depending on the circumstances and available resources, each has its strengths:

One-to-One Sessions typically remain focused and cater to the unique needs of specific faculty and individual courses. Participants tend to be more open and willing to consider suggestions and ideas that could make them defensive in group settings. These focused efforts, however, are time-consuming and relatively expensive. In addition, one-to-one sessions might be impractical if faculty-wide training efforts are required.

Campus-wide workshops are a cost-effective way of drawing faculty together. These workshops are typically most effective for generating initial enthusiasm, answering general questions, and establishing direction for an institution's distance education efforts (see Weaver, 1982). Logistically, however, they are sometimes difficult to schedule. In addition, some participants are typically frustrated by their emphasis on "breadth" not "depth."

Self-paced instructional print materials are relatively inexpensive to produce and allow faculty to review and use them at their convenience. They typically focus on overview material, however, and may lack the depth needed for detailed exploration of the issues facing the distant educator.

An integrated approach is often the most effective path in which distance education training is combined with institutional efforts to improve on-campus instruction. A well publicized school or campus-wide faculty development workshop, for example, could be used to discuss overall instructional challenges as a pretext to addressing distance education issues. During this session, faculty interest and background knowledge can be judged. If only a few have immediate needs, one-to-one sessions with instructional developers or experienced distant faculty can be planned. Self-paced materials should be made available to those who have yet to decide if distance education is an appropriate solution to the instructional challenges they face.

Regardless of format, support personnel will be needed to work with teachers, organize and staff workshops, develop instructional materials, and implement the training effort. Several short- and long-term options are possible for staffing the faculty development effort. Some schools, for example, use external consultants and content experts while others rely on internal staff, department faculty, and student assistants. Still others blend outside expertise with internal support to create an atmosphere of mutual support and group problem solving.

Although available staff and funding constraints will likely determine the selected approach, an integrated strategy is typically the most functional. A national leader, for example, might be invited to keynote a workshop series and energize faculty. In addition to a general presentation, invited speakers should be available for individual and small group consultations with faculty. The institutional administration should also take advantage of this outside expertise to get fresh perspectives on planning and policy issues. An unbiased view can sometimes provide the spark needed to resolve difficult issues.

Still, outside expertise should not be relied on as the sole solution to institutional challenges. An over-dependence on outside expertise can lead, for example, to simplistic solutions to complex institutional problems. While outside experts provide a unique perspective, they often have difficulty understanding the internal complexities and political realities that determine the institutional culture. It is the institution that "owns" its distance education-related challenges and opportunities, and it is the institution itself that must take the lead in resolving the complex issues it faces.

Faculty, staff, and administration are uniquely positioned to understand the subtle complexities, realities, and obstacles to be overcome in their own institutional context. Too often, however, their expertise is taken for granted or too narrowly focused.

In most situations, a combined approach is best. Institutions should consider blending outside expertise with on-going internal support and focused effort. This combined approach can add validity and momentum to the faculty development effort.

Successful Program Characteristics

Regardless of the format or mix of local and outside expertise, faculty in-service training experiences should be on-going, upbeat, and incorporate the following characteristics:

• Faculty should be encouraged to share concerns and constructively question the administrative expectations of the technical system. Equally important is the honesty with which their concerns are addressed. Administrators should avoid making excuses for not involving faculty earlier in the planning process. They should frankly discuss the evolution of the distance education effort and the institutional role that it will likely play in the future.

• Administrative and academic leaders should articulate the institution's "vision" or plan for incorporating distance education. It should be shared with enthusiasm and reality. Ideally, this plan will be firmly grounded in a formalized needs assessment. This assessment should be widely available and serve as a combined rationale for change and blueprint for action.

• The strengths and weaknesses of the distance education program and planned delivery systems should be discussed, focusing on the opportunities, challenges, and potential difficulties to be faced.

While academic administrators might facilitate these discussions, their primary role should be "listening" not "talking."

• Technical systems should be described in the language of the user, not the technician, and incorporate easily understood and jargon-free language and related visuals.

"Techno-babble" has no place in effective faculty development programs. It is the job of technical staff to speak in terms that are understood by educators. It is not the job of educators to become versed in the technical language of system managers, although new terminology will gradually add to the educator's technical vocabulary.

• Technical assistance should be available when needed, with advice offered in a supportive manner using commonly understood terminology and straightforward suggestions for improvement.

• Academic administrators should work closely with technical managers to establish technical standards and procedures that accommodate a faculty members' schedule and teaching style, while maintaining production quality. This is sometimes easier said than done. When there are conflicts, emphasis should be placed on meeting academic standards and faculty preferences, not showcasing features of the technical delivery system.

• The goal of adapting traditional instruction to a non-traditional environment, not making "bad" instruction "good," should be emphasized throughout all in-service training programs and experiences.

• Faculty should be provided with handbooks and other "take home" materials that clearly and concisely detail a step-by-step process for developing distance delivered instruction. Other sections should cover the technology of delivery, utilization strategies, and support issues.

• Faculty "ownership" of distance-delivered instruction should be emphasized in word and deed. The role of in-service training consultants and instructional developers is to provide support, instructional options, and well-grounded recommendations, without wresting project control and decision-making from the instructor.

• If an in-service workshop is planned, it should be a hands-on experience, with faculty receiving practical training using the technologies they'll be using in the classroom. At the same time, faculty should get a "behind the scenes" look at the role of technical support staff. In addition, and perhaps most importantly, faculty should see what it's like to be a distant student at a receiving site.

In a workshop setting, getting a feel for these multiple roles is easy to accomplish. Faculty participants, for example, might be divided into three groups. While one group "teaches" over the system, a second views the presentation from the control booth, and the third participates from an adjacent classroom serving as a student site. Participants cycle through each station until they've experienced the distance education process from all perspectives.

• Emphasis should be placed on providing useful information and strategies that can be immediately applied. Areas of practical discussion should include techniques for managing distance education, tracking student participation, increasing student motivation, understanding unique student needs, enhancing group cohesion, fostering student-student interaction, adapting traditional instruction for non-traditional delivery, and evaluating instructional effectiveness.

• Current research in the field of distance learning should be widely discussed, even debated. Emphasis should be on both quantitative and qualitative studies exploring teaching methods, technical delivery systems, and comparative student performance.

• The development and adaptation of instructional strategies should be a major focus of in-service training efforts. Suggestions for increasing the relevance of content examples and adapting them to the unique experiential backgrounds of distant students should be emphasized.

At the same time, special emphasis should be placed on increasing faculty sensitivity to the social, cultural, educational, and economic backgrounds of the intended audience.

• Alternative roles played by faculty, students, and support staff should be explored. For example, distant students should be encouraged to take more responsibility for researching and presenting information to other class participants. In addition, faculty roles should expand beyond that of content provider. In many distance education settings, for example, the faculty member facilitates the involvement and interaction among outside speakers and distant students.

• Communication patterns that transcend traditional teacher-student and student-content interaction should be discussed. The role of student-student interaction, for example, should be explored, including practical techniques for enhancing it, such as joint presentations and out of class assignments.

• Networks of faculty involved in distance education should be created and nurtured on local, regional, and national levels. These relationships, once developed, offer many opportunities for issue identification and group problem solving.

• Efforts should be made to target interested, enthusiastic, and committed faculty. Some teachers will have little interest in teaching at a distance. Rather than spend time and resources attempting to convince the intractable, energy and resources should be focused on those who are receptive, or at least open to the potential benefits provided by distance education. In addition, highlighting the efforts of the "early adopters" will often lead to the interest and eventual participation of those who were initially skeptical.

• Administrators must proactively address the relationship of distance education to the institutional reward structure, including promotion and tenure, and the integration of distance education research, teaching, and service.

Faculty Incentives and Support Issues

Because of the options and opportunities it affords, distance education poses unique challenges to the traditional culture of higher education. To a great extent, the future success of distance education rests in the degree to which it is embraced by the faculty. If the continued support and success of distance education is to be ensured, educational institutions must consistently address traditional issues with fresh ideas and innovative approaches. Towards this end, there are a number of critical faculty development issues to be confronted. They include:

1. *Promotion and Tenure.* Institutions and the academic administrators leading them expect teachers in distance education programs to take their responsibilities seriously, devoting the time and effort needed for success. In return, it is appropriate that educational bureaucracies recognize the legitimacy of distant teaching and reward this effort as they do more traditional forms of instructional delivery (see Parker, 1988).

When traditional indicators are used, however, this is often difficult. Providing teacher performance feedback, for example, is challenging because distant students are seldom integrated into day-to-day campus life and often have limited contact with on-campus faculty and administration. In addition, campus-based distance education programs are relatively *invisible* because courses are often taught during evening hours or from off-campus locations.

For these reasons, academic administrators, as well as promotion and tenure committees, must gain a better understanding of the important educational role filled by distant faculty. Towards this end, an important step is to improve the faculty and course evaluation process in efforts to better assess the instructional impact and effectiveness of distant courses and faculty. Rather than rely solely on paper and pencil evaluation measures, for example, faculty review committees should consider using qualitative indicators such as interviews with distant students and observations of the distant teacher at work (see Seldin, 1981).

At the same time, it is equally important that the quality of distance delivered instruction meet or surpass that of traditionally delivered programs. These same review committees must ensure that appropriate course design and rigorous academic review takes place before instructional programs are delivered at a distance.

2. *Released Time.* Adapting traditional instruction for distance delivery demands concerted and time-consuming effort. Just understanding the unique characteristics and needs of distant students, for example, requires hours of research, phone calls, and potential on-site visits. Still, this background work is critical to the success of the distance education enterprise. While initial interest and enthusiasm might fuel early participation, sustained faculty interest and involvement will require released time.

Progressive institutions with a commitment to maintaining the quality of distance delivered courses typically provide two to five credit hour releases, or equivalent monetary "overloads" to instructors charged with distant course adaptation. In addition, some institutions offer teachers released time to visit participating sites. Gilcher and Johnstone (1988), for example, described an in-service training program in Pennsylvania that included substitute teacher coverage while satellite sites were visited, adequate travel funds for regional visits, and opportunities for distant teachers to meet together each semester to share instructional concerns and delivery strategies.

In many respects, it is easier to develop a new distance delivered course than it is to adapt an already existing one in which instructional patterns and expectations have previously been set. Once again, however, course development is time-consuming, especially when the course will be delivered to distant audiences with whom the instructor may have little first-hand contact and knowledge. As a general guideline, it takes about twice the time to develop a distance delivered course as it does to develop and organize a course for traditional delivery.

Institutions can help ensure the continuing interest of the faculty and reward their distant course development, adaptation, and revision efforts by granting adequate released time or providing equivalent financial compensation.

3. *Course "Load."* In a traditional single-site course, a class size of 15 to 25 students is not unusual. What happens, however, if these 25 students are split among two or more sites, each with unique characteristics and needs? Or, what if the instructor teaches a "live" class that is simultaneously delivered to a remote site? For purposes of load, should this be considered one or two distinct courses?

Rather than wait until a faculty uprising or waning instructor interest, academic administrators should proactively address this issue. While generalizations will likely prove inaccurate, one can easily imagine how an instructor's workload and time commitment might be multiplied in meeting the varied needs of students in multi-site courses. One strategy is to establish a distant teaching practices committee or faculty senate sub-committee to deal with this issue on a course-by-course basis.

4. Course Updating and Revision. In some cases course components, or even entire classes, are videotaped or otherwise preserved for future use. In these instances, what are the faculty members' rights for approval before recorded segments are used in the future with or without revisions? Again, generalizations will likely prove problematic, although the faculty member typically has the final say before pre-recorded class segments are used in future courses. Regardless of the institution's policy, however, academic administrators are well served by developing explicit procedures to address course revision issues, before problems develop.

5. Publishing. It is no secret that publishing is a critical requirement in the academic progression of most faculty. Publishing traditionally focuses on the development, review, and distribution of printed material, through refereed journals and general interest publications. As in other areas, distance education has blurred these traditional publishing boundaries.

What if, for example, a faculty member develops a videotape that is widely distributed, after critical review, for use in an academic discipline? For purposes of recognition and advancement, should this be considered a "publication"? If not, why not? While some disregard the media of distribution in their publishing criteria, others hold to more traditional standards and disregard or discount non-print work. Again, institutions should progressively consider review criteria before faculty interest fades in non-traditional methods of publishing.

6. Faculty Mentoring. It is easy to feel alone when teaching a distance delivered course for the first time. This feeling of isolation is accentuated by the fact that in many campus settings, the vast majority of faculty have had little if any exposure to distant teaching. One strategy for addressing this problem is through the establishment of a faculty mentoring network, similar to the teaching education support groups recently developed on a national level (Hackworth, 1987; Nicklin, 1991).

The central premise in the establishment of a mentoring network is the matching of "veteran" faculty with distant teaching experience, with those new to distant course delivery. When developing or teaching a distance delivered course for the first time, many faculty prefer to consult with colleagues in their own academic discipline, not instructional developers who are often content generalists or specialists in the technology of delivery. Other faculty feel comfortable grappling with their course content, but wish to consult colleagues on questions related to the technology of delivery or strategies for providing feedback and encouraging student interaction.

Faculty mentoring networks can be formal or informal, depending on the needs of teachers, the commitment of the academic administration, and the resources available to develop and maintain collaborative support systems. Small, institution-wide gatherings of new and veteran faculty can prove beneficial in developing informal partnerships and a shared sense of purpose. If resources are available, computer-accessible networks and regional databases can be established, providing faculty with phone contacts, resource directories, content-specific teaching techniques, and strategies to improve the effectiveness of different delivery systems.

Once initiated, mentoring programs typically expand and take on a life of their own. This is because small and informal clusters of distance educators frequently exist and it takes little effort to link these already functioning networks. They are proving to be invaluable to those who teach at distance for the first time and enjoyable, as well, for veteran faculty who are granted a forum for sharing their innovative ideas and expertise.

7. *Consistency across departments.* One of the greatest faculty development challenges confronting educational institutions is the consistency with which policies and procedures are applied. Unfortunately, many schools have unintentionally created a system of "haves" and "have nots." While some departments encourage and fully support faculty involved in distance teaching through "over loads," released time, and increased funding, others provide little in the way of incentives and recognition.

Academic administrators should take a holistic approach to developing and implementing consistent distance education policies that ensure fair and equitable distribution of resources and rewards on an institution-wide basis.

Summary

Although it is true that distance education provides many institutional opportunities, its inherent fluidity tends to create numerous challenges in the process. Nowhere are these challenges more pivotal than in the area of faculty development and support. Teachers and administrators must work together in identifying and resolving the issues, policies, and biases that inhibit systematic use of distance education in meeting academic goals.

When training is needed, effort should be made to identify required program components and provide creative, flexible, and "hands on" in-service experiences. If the institutional reward structure lacks the flexibility to recognize the role played by distance educators, it should be modified before faculty interest and enthusiasm wanes.

There can be no denying that the ultimate success or failure of the distance education enterprise is inextricably tied to the enthusiasm and continuing support of the faculty. Administrators and teachers alike are well served in actively identifying and resolving the faculty development issues that directly affect the success with which distance education programs are planned and implemented.

References

Astin, A. W., Comstock, C., Epperson, D. C., Greeley, A. M. & Kauffman, J. F. (1974). *Faculty development in a time of retrenchment.* Greenwich, CT: Change Publishing.

Axelrod, J. (1973). *The university teacher as artist.* San Francisco: Jossey-Bass.

Batey, A. & Cowell, R. N. (1986). *Distance education: An overview.* Portland, OR: Northwest Regional Educational Laboratory. (ERIC Document Reproduction Service No. ED 278 519)

Beaudoin, M. (1990). The instructor's changing role in distance education. *American Journal of Distance Education, 4*(2), 21–29. (ERIC Document Reproduction Service No. EJ 417 032)

Brzoska, K. L. (1991). *Faculty development in distance education.* Unpublished masters thesis. Pomona, CA: California State Polytechnic University.

Carl, D. R. (1986). Developing faculty to use teleconferencing to deliver university credit courses over cable and satellite. *Canadian Journal of Educational Communication, 15*(4), 235–250. (ERIC Document Reproduction Service No. EJ 345 879)

Downing, D. E. (1984). *Survey on the uses of distance learning in the U.S.* Austin, TX: Southwest Educational Development Laboratory. (ERIC Document Reproduction Service No. ED 246 874).

Eble, K. E. (1972). *Professors as teachers.* San Francisco: Jossey-Bass.

Elliott, G. P. (1989). Satellite delivery: What is going up for K–12? *The Distance Education Report, 3*(3), 7–18.

Gaff, J. G. (1975). *Toward faculty renewal.* San Francisco: Jossey-Bass.

Gilcher, K. W. & Johnstone, S. M. (1988). *A critical review of the use of audiographic conferencing systems by selected educational institutions.* College Park, MD: University of Maryland, College Office of Instructional Communications.

Graham, S. W. & Wedman, J. F. (1989). Enhancing the appeal of teletraining. *Journal of Instructional Psychology, 16*(4), 183–91. (ERIC Document Reproduction Service No. EJ 405 594)

Hackworth, R. (1987). This is telementoring: An interview with Rob Somers. *Journal of Developmental Education, 11*(1), 24–25, 27. (ERIC Document Reproduction Service No. EJ 358 379)

Kromholz, S. F. & Johnstone, S. M. (1988). A practical application to training instructional television faculty and students. *Lifelong-Learning, 11*(8), 15–16. (ERIC Document Reproduction Service No. EJ 372 993)

Kurpius, D. J. & Christie, G. S. (1978). A systematic and collaborative approach to problem solving. In D. J. Kurpius (Ed.), *Learning: Making learning environments more effective* (pp. 13–16). Muncie, IN: Accelerated Development.

Lovell-Troy, L. & Eickmann, P. (1992). *Course design for college teachers.* Englewood Cliffs, NJ: Educational Technology Publications.

Moore, M. G., Thompson, M. M., Quigley, B. A., Clark, G. C. & Goff, G. G. (1990). *The effect of distance learning: A summary of the literature.* University Park, PA: Center for the Study of Distance Education, The Pennsylvania State University.

McKeachie, W. J. (1964). Research on teaching at the college and university level. In N. L. Gage (Ed.), *Handbook of research on teaching.* Chicago: Rand-McNally.

Nevins, C. L. & Wright, L. J. (1984). *A handbook for ITFS teachers.* Chico, CA: California State University. (ERIC Document Reproduction Service No. ED 266 768)

Nicklin, J. L. (1991). For newly hired schoolteachers, an electronic lifeline: Harvard network helps fight feelings of isolation and failure. *Chronicle of Higher Education, 38*(11).

Parker, M. S. (1988). *Institutional support and rewards for academic staff involved in distance education.* Churchill, Australia: Centre for Distance Learning. (ERIC Document Reproduction Service No. ED 310 757)

Robinson, B. (1991). Distance education for inservice teacher education in the United Kingdom. *Action in teacher education, 13*(3), 60–61. (ERIC Document Reproduction Service No. EJ 436 830)

Scriven, B. (1986). *Teaching externally. A handbook for the guidance of staff* (2nd ed.). Brisbane, Australia: Brisbane College of Advanced Education. (ERIC Document Reproduction Service No. ED 311 864)

Scriven, B. (1989). *Distance education in Europe and Canada. A report on a professional experience program, August 6 to December 5, 1988.* Brisbane, Australia: Brisbane College of Advanced Education. (ERIC Document Reproduction Service No. ED 311 861)

Seldin, P. (1981). *Successful faculty evaluation programs: A practical guide to improve faculty performance and promotion/tenure decisions.* Crugers, NY: Coventry Press.

Self, C. C. (1983). *An overview of educational technologies and implications for staff development at the community college level.* Paper presented at the University of Massachusetts–Amherst, May 1983. (ERIC Document Reproduction Service No. ED 231 460)

Shaeffer, J. M. (1990). Preparing faculty and designing courses for delivery via audio teleconferencing. *Journal of Adult Education, 18*(2), 11–18. (ERIC Document Reproduction Service No. EJ 414 504)

Tresman, S. (1988). The potentiality of distance learning. *School Science Review, 69*(249), 687–691. (ERIC Document Reproduction Service No. EJ 379 194)

Weaver, G. (1982). The development of a workshop to train faculty to effectively use telecommunications. In L. Parker & C. Olgren (Eds.), *Teleconferencing and Electronic Communications*, Madison, WI: University of Wisconsin–Extension, Center for Interactive Programs.

Willis, B. (1990). Faculty development programs: Maximizing the potential. *Educational Technology, 30*(9), 39–42.

Willis, B. (1992). *Effective distance education: A primer for faculty and administrators.* (Monograph Series in Distance Education, No. 2). Fairbanks, AK: University of Alaska Center for Cross-Cultural Studies.

Willis, B. (1993). *Distance education: A practical guide.* Englewood Cliffs, NJ: Educational Technology Publications.

Glossary

Analog: Representations that bear some physical relationship to the original quantity, usually a continuous representation (electromagnetic wave) where information is encoded in direct relationship to the power of the original light or sound source, as compared to **digital** representations where information is presented as discrete numbers, steps, or time intervals. (see digital)

Analog transmission: Transmission of a continuously variable signal as opposed to a discretely variable signal. Physical quantities such as temperature are continuously variable and so are described as "analog."

Artificial Intelligence: Computer programs which perform functions, often by imitation, normally associated with human reasoning and learning.

Asynchronous: A term that refers to communication in which interaction between the sender and the receiver does not take place simultaneously.

Audio Bridge: A device used in audioconferencing that connects and controls multiple telephone lines to create a conference call.

Audiographic: A teleconference system that makes use of narrow band communication channels such as telephone lines to transmit audio, graphics, and computer text files.

Audio-only conference: A type of conference in which communication takes place by voice only.

Backbone: A primary communication path, usually a multi-conductor wire cable or multi-strand optic cable, from which other communication paths branch to customers.

Backup: A copy of an electronic file, retained in case the original is damaged or rendered unuseable.

Band: A range of frequencies between defined upper and lower limits. For example, the Medium Frequency (MF) band, as designated by the International Telecommunication Union (ITU), is 300-3,000 kHz.

Bandwidth: The width of an electronic transmission path or circuit, in terms of the range of frequencies it can pass without distortion. The wider or greater the bandwidth the more information can be carried by the medium of transmission. Typically measured in Hertz, but may be expressed in bits per second. A voice channel typically has a bandwidth of 3000 cycles per second; a TV channel requires about 6 megahertz.

Barcode: A type of code used on labels and read by a wand or bar-code scanner. The main application is in labeling retail products and documents in libraries. Also used to input programming code to devices such as videodisc players and CD-ROM players.

Barcode Reader: An infra-red scanning device that interprets barcoded commands for videodisc and CD-ROM players.

Binary: Language developed on two letter alphabets, e.g., "on," "off"; "X," "O"; "1," "2"; and so forth.

Bit: The abbreviation for a single binary digit. (see binary)

Byte: A single computer word, usually eight bits. (see bit)

Body Text: Text that forms the bulk (or body) of a document.

Bridge: (1) A device for interconnecting communication devices such as telephones and computers or two or more local area networks (LANS). (2) A telephone bridge is an electronic device that links three or more telephone lines together so that individuals can hold a teleconference. Advanced bridges automatically connect, announce those who join and those who leave a conference, and provide a constant volume for all conference participants.

Broadband: A communication system with a bandwidth greater than voice band. Broadbands are capable of high-speed data transmission and usually use coaxial, microwave, or optical transmission. Used to describe high-speed data channels, or one or more video channels. Used to describe digital technologies that provide integrated voice, data, video, and interactive communication services to businesses and households.

Broadcasting: A radio wave communication service in which the transmissions are intended for direct reception by a wide spectrum of receivers such as the general public. Broadcast service may include voice, television, or data transmissions.

Bullet: The character "•."

CAV (constant angular velocity): A CAV videodisc revolves continuously at 1800 rpm, one revolution per frame, making each frame of a CAV disc addressable, a basic requirement for interactive videodiscs.

C-band: A radio frequency band allocated to transmit satellite television or telephone signals. Signals on the C-band are transmitted at 6 Gigahertz and received at 4 Gigahertz.

CD (compact disc): A format that records digital data on 12 cm. optical discs.

CD-I (compact disc-interactive): A compact disc format that includes audio, video, and program data.

CD-ROM: Compact disc-read only memory. A format for recording data on compact discs, permitting virtual storage of a large amount of information in a small format.

CD-ROM XA: Compact disc-read only memory extended architecture. A format for integrating audio and data within a basic CD-ROM format.

CLV (constant linear velocity): A CLV or extended-play videodisc maintains a consistent length for each frame, thus enabling longer playing time per side, but sacrificing individual frame access in most players. Reference to locations on CLV discs is limited to time in minutes and seconds.

CPU (central processing unit): The component of a microcomputer in which the data processing takes place.

Cable Television: Broadband radio-frequency transmission of video signals over coaxial cable or optical fiber directly to television sets in the home as opposed to broadcast television. Video signals may be transmitted in one or two directions, thereby enabling viewers to input data. Cable television also makes possible pay services and video conferencing.

Carrier: (1) The frequency within a given bandwidth upon which an information-carrying signal can be impressed or modulated with another information carrying signal. (2) An organization, company, or business (vendor) authorized by a government regulatory agency to provide a specific communication service. (3) A carrier system using one of many modulation processes in order to derive more than one channel from a single path.

Channel: The segment of a bandwidth that provides a pathway or a communication link between sending and receiving points.

Coder-Decoder (CODEC): A coder-decoder (analog-to-digital and digital-to-analog converter) is used to convert analog signals, such as television, to digital form for transmission and back again to the original analog form for viewing.

Color Separations: Printing color pictures requires the preparation of four separate printing plates (one each for black, yellow, cyan, and magenta). The negatives for each plate, called separations, are made by photographing the original color picture through different-colored filters. Analogously, in computer-generated graphics, separations are those "pictures" which, when combined, provide a full-color representation.

Communications Satellite: An earth satellite designed to act as a telecommunications radio frequency relay that is positioned in geosynchronous orbit 22,300 miles above the equator so that it appears from earth to be stationary in space.

Compact: An agreement among a group of states, referred to in Article I of the U.S. Constitution, which limits the sovereign power of the states. In the U.S., interstate or regional compacts have been formed in the areas of higher education, water, energy, interstate parks, etc. Typically, interstate compacts require approval by the U.S. Congress and the President.

Compact Video: One of several devices used for storing large quantities of digital information for access by computers (about the size of an audio compact disc).

Compressed Video: A method of reducing the size of digital video files. It is often accomplished by removing redundant portions of frames and by saving only those portions of images that change from frame to frame.

Computer Assisted Instruction (CAI): Computer use designed to enable students to gain mastery of a discrete learning objective such as a spelling list as one part of a larger teacher-centered curriculum.

Computer Managed Instruction (CMI): Computer use encompassing broad management of curriculum including discrete learning objectives, but also administrative matters of guidance, evaluation, and referral to instructional aids.

Constraints: The limitations that must be taken as "given" in a planning situation, i.e., limits that are realistic within the current situation. These limitations include resources such as personnel time, money, energy, as well as time required to complete, cultural imperatives, and the like.

Courseware: Instructional materials in a completely mediated format. May refer to a single instructional component, such as a computer assisted instruction program, or a multiple instructional entity, such as guidebooks, videodiscs, and computer assisted instruction.

Cybernetics: (1) The science of communications and control in animals and machines. (2) A theory of communications and control that accounts for the operation of systems in terms of feedback effects.

DVI (digital video interactive): A proprietary format for placing digital video on a compact disc. Compressed files can provide full-motion video.

Database: The generic name for software designed to enter, manage, search, and retrieve information from multiple lists.

Design: Frequently used as an abbreviation for graphic design.

Digital: A method of processing, transmitting, and storing data that operates in discrete electronic or optical steps as contrasted to a continuous or analog method. Digital communications/switching is the transmission of information using discontinuous, discrete sequences of electrical or electromagnetic signals that change in frequency, polarity, or amplitude to represent or encode information. Analog information such as audio/video signals may be encoded for transmission on digital communications systems. (see analog)

Digital Video: Video signals that have been encoded as a series of binary digits. In this format they can be accessed and manipulated in a computer program.

Digitizer: A generic term for a scanner or video digitizer.

Direct Broadcast Satellite (DBS): A satellite system designed with sufficient power to transmit signals directly from orbit to small inexpensive earth stations for direct residential or community reception. This eliminates the need for a local cable loop by allowing use of receiving disks with a diameter of a meter or less mounted directly on a building.

Distance Education: The organizational framework and process of providing instruction at a distance. Distance education takes place when a teacher and student(s) are physically separated, and technology (i.e., audio, video, computers, print) is used to bridge the instructional gap. (see distance learning)

Distance Learning: The desired outcome of distance education, i.e., learning at a distance. (see distance education)

Double-page Layout: A format that involves printing on both sides of the page, so that most of the time the reader sees both a left-hand page and a right-hand page.

Dual Band: Used to denote equipment and antennas capable of using both C-band and Ku-band signals.

Electronic Blackboard: A pressure sensitive blackboard-like device through which writing is transmitted by telephone lines to distant sites and which can be annotated by participants at those sites.

Electronic Mail (E-mail): A general term referring to the electronic transmission, distribution, and delivery of messages. E-mail is characterized by storage of a message at an "electronic address" that can be received by the recipient via a telecommunication-equipped personal computer. Facsimile (FAX) transmission of messages operates in a similar manner, but is received directly rather than stored in a "host" computer until requested.

Evaluation: The process of determining the merit or worth or value of something; or the product of that process. The special features of evaluation, as a special form of investigation (distinguished, e.g., from traditional empirical research in the social sciences), include a characteristic concern with cost, comparisons, needs, ethics, and its own political, ethical, presentational, and cost dimensions; and with the supporting and making of sound value judgments, rather than hypothesis testing.

Extended syllabus: A collection of course materials intended for student use, usually several chapters long, providing course objectives, assignments, instructions, readings, etc., allowing students to work through the course as independently as possible.

Facsimile (FAX): A system used to transmit text and graphics over telecommunication channels. The original image is scanned at the transmitter, reconstructed at the receiving end, and duplicated on paper or stored on a personal computer. Facsimile transmission rates vary from analog Group 1, 2, and 3 faxes requiring five minutes, two minutes, and 20-40 seconds, respectively, to transmit a page, to digital Group 4 faxes, which transmit one page in three to six seconds.

Faculty Development: The process of improving the instructional effectiveness of faculty through training and an enhanced institutional support structure.

Fair Use: Fair use is a principle that provides for limited reproduction of copyrighted materials for purposes such as criticism, comment, news reporting, teaching, scholarship, and research. It is a limitation on the copyright owner's monopoly and may be applied only in certain circumstances.

Fiber Optic Cable: Thin filaments of glass or other transparent materials through which coded light pulses representing data, image, and sound can be transmitted for long distances by means of multiple internal reflections. Fiber optic transmission is characterized by extremely high transmission speeds and bandwidth.

Floppy disk: A thin plastic plate, commonly 3.5 inch or 5.25 inch in diameter, used for storing digital information to be read by a computer.

Floppy Drive: A device in a computer that reads information from a floppy disk. (see floppy disk)

Font: Strictly speaking, the collection of all characters making up a particular typeface, typestyle (e.g., roman, *italic*, **bold**, ***bold italic***), and size. Increasingly, in colloquial use, *font* is synonymous with typeface.

Footer: Information placed within the bottom margin of each page of a document (with the possible exception of the first page).

Formative Evaluation: Evaluation conducted during the development or improvement of a program or product (or person, etc.). It is an evaluation that is conducted for the in-house staff or the program and normally remains in-house; it may be done by an internal or external evaluator or (preferably) a combination.

Full-motion Video: A standard video signal capable of reproducing a full range of motion. (see compressed video)

Gateway: A specialized computer that connects two networks and translates addresses of one network so they can be read by the other network.

Glossary: (1) In a document, a list of new or unfamiliar terms (often technical), with their definitions. (2) In some word processing programs, a function that permits the storage and easy recall of frequently-used text or graphic material.

Header: Information placed within the top margin of each page of a document (with the possible exception of the first page).

High Sierra: A name for a popular data format for CD-ROM.

Host: A computer on a network that can receive information from another computer.

HyperCard: Course authoring software developed and distributed by Apple Computer, Inc.

Hypermedia: An approach to information storage and retrieval that provides multiple linkages among elements. In interactive multimedia instruction, it allows the learner to navigate easily from one piece of information to another.

ISO-9660: The most commonly used format for recording data on CD-ROM discs.

Icon: A small, simple graphic which is imbued with or assigned specific meaning.

Indention: Text laid out so that the first line of each paragraph begins to the right of the remainder of the lines in the paragraph; opposite of outdention.

Information Service: Generating, acquiring, storing, transforming, processing, retrieving, utilizing, or making available information in electromagnetic, digital, or optical form that may be conveyed via telecommunication technologies.

Instructional Television Fixed Service (ITFS): Microwave-based, very high frequency television used primarily in education. Receive sites must have a converter to change signals to those used by the television receiver. Capable of full-motion video and one-way audio over distances of up to 35 kilometers.

Integrated Services Digital Network (ISDN): Telecommunication networks that are capable of accepting all types of information (i.e., voice, data, facsimile, full-motion video, videotext) in a common digital code and transmitting it as if it were one signal. Provides end-to-end digital connectivity for simultaneous transmission of all types of information according to accepted international standards. Often referred to as a "universal network" able to support any device for transfer of information.

Interaction: The mutual reaction of the learner to the computer's actions and vice versa.

Interactivity: The property of requiring active participation by the learner for instruction to proceed.

Interface: A connection between a user and a piece of equipment or between two pieces of equipment.

Internet: The name for the network connecting education and research networks throughout the world.

Ku-band: The band of microwave uplink frequencies from 12 to 18 GHz. Band of satellite communication frequencies from 11.7 to 12.2 GHz. Ku-band transmission requires one meter satellite receiving dish whereas the C-band dish spans a minimum of three meters.

LATA (local access and transport area): A geographic region in which a regional Bell Operating company is allowed to provide long distance services. Long distance calls placed between two or more LATAs require the involvement of an inter-exchange, long distance carrier, such as Sprint, AT&T, MCI, or GTE.

LAN (local area network): Two or more computers connected by means of a physical connection (wire, line-of-sight radio signal, or fiber-optic cable).

Layout: The arrangement of text and non-text elements on a page.

Leading: (rhymes with wedding) The vertical space between lines of text. Typefaces are designed so that there is a certain amount of vertical space between adjacent lines. The amount of space between lines can be increased by increasing the leading (literally, in days of lead type, by inserting strips of lead between lines) to increase legibility when lines are long.

Logo: Computer language developed by Seymour Papert, described as a tool for developmental cognitive learning.

Loose-leaf Binding: A method of "binding" that involves placing pages into rings (often three) fastened between covers.

Low-earth Orbit Satellite (LEO): A non-geostationary satellite that orbits the earth at a height ranging between 400 to 800 miles. Termed a Smallsat, LEOs weigh from 75 to 400 lbs and due to their proximity to earth, their receive and transmit terminals require relatively little power. Since LEOs orbit close to the earth they cover only a small area of the earth's surface, and many satellites are required to provide global coverage. Present systems propose from 12 to 77 low-earth orbit satellites for seamless world-wide coverage.

Mainframe Computer: A large, relatively complex computer. Its capacity exceeds that of minicomputers and microcomputers.

Market Analysis: An essential part of the strategic planning process. It considers the basic assessment of the general educational market as well as a more specific course and curriculum market analysis. Demographic and social factors for each geographic area are gathered and analyzed as to their impact on the proposed distance education project.

Materials Evaluation (instructional products): Evaluations that assess the merit or worth of content-related physical items, including books, curricular guides, films, tapes, and other tangible instructional products.

MEU (Mind Extension University): A distance education offering of Jones Intercable, a cable television company. MEU provides courses offered by 24 participating universities and colleges via satellite to more than 600 cable networks.

Microcomputer: A computer based on a microprocessor (an integrated circuit or chip) and intended for one user; includes IBM and IBM clones, Apple and Macintosh, and Tandy products, among others.

Microprocessor: A silicon chip (integrated circuit) with a pattern of transistors and related devices that do the basic work of computing.

Mid-level Networks: Also called regional networks; network service providers (many created by the National Science Foundation) distribute network services to universities, research laboratories, colleges, and schools in their service areas.

Minicomputer: A computer designed to support multiple users like mainframes, but with less capacity.

Modem: A modulator/demodulator that translates a computer's digital information into analog for transmission on a telephone line.

Mouse: A hand-held input device electronically connected to an on-screen pointer used to communicate with a computer.

Mission Statement: A short, yet comprehensive statement of the purpose of the project. It allows all team members, customers, administrators, etc., to know what ultimate intent or result is intended. Normally, a mission statement is further explained and supported by goals and objectives that address specific areas of focus with time and qualitative achievement expectations. These anticipated accomplishments can then be compared with actual levels of achievement.

Narrowcast: Video signal delivery to a targeted audience at pre-determined receive sites, in contrast to open-air broadcast signal transmission to the general viewing public.

NTU (National Technology University): A graduate level and technical seminar program headquartered in Fort Collins, Colorado. NTU transmits engineering and technical courses from more than 45 colleges and universities via satellite facilities to more than 440 U.S. and international sites.

Needs Assessment: A need has been defined as "a gap between 'what is' and 'what should be' in terms of results." A needs assessment is a systematic inquiry into the most important needs to be met.

Megahertz (MHz): One million cycles per second.

Network: (1) A series of points connected by communication channels in different geographic locations. (2) The switched telephone network is the network of telephone lines normally used for dialed telephone calls. (3) A private network is a network of communication channels confined to the use of one customer.

Optical Disc: A videodisc or compact disc that reflects a light beam to read information from the surface of the disc.

Optical Scanner: An input device for reading a page or photographic image into a computer.

Originating Site: The location from which a teleconference originates.

Outdention: Text laid out so that the first line of each paragraph begins to the left of the remainder of the lines in the paragraph; opposite of indention.

300 *Distance Education: Strategies and Tools*

Packet: An "envelope" of digital information sent as a single unit on a wide area network (WAN).

Planning Models: Conceptual structures that provide a means for the comprehensive development and understanding of relationships associated with a distance education project. Such models often include a graphic depiction of key components and their interrelationships.

Picture Phone: Telephone equipment that can send and receive slow-scan pictures via standard voice grade telephone circuits.

Point: A measurement of length used in typography, equal to 1/72".

Point Form: A method of laying out lists of text items, such that items are below one another, in outdented form, usually preceded by a bullet (•).

Program Evaluations: Evaluations that assess educational activities that provide services on a continuing basis and often involve curricular offerings. Some examples are evaluations of a school district's reading program, a state's special education program, or a university's continuing education program.

Project Evaluations: Evaluations that assess activities that are funded for a defined period of time to perform a specific task. Some examples are a three-day workshop on behavioral objectives, or a three-year career educational demonstration project. A key distinction between a program and a project is that the former is expected to continue for an indefinite period of time, whereas the latter is usually expected to be short lived. Projects that become institutionalized in effect become programs.

Public Policy: Values that broadly define the social climate in which public opinion prevails in the form of laws, executive orders, and judicial decrees. It operationally describes such intellectual abstractions as social responsibility, competitiveness, diversity, privacy, and freedom of speech.

RAM (random access memory): Volatile memory used by a microprocessor.

Radio: Communication over a distance by converting sounds into electromagnetic waves and radiating them through space. In *Webster*'s dictionary: the wireless transmission and reception of electrical impulses or signals by means of electromagnetic waves.

RBOC: Regional Bell Operating Company.

Real Time: The condition in which communication is synchronous, i.e., live.

Receive Site: The location at which a teleconference is received.

Reflective Practitioner: Someone who is aware of the key issues in his or her professional area, who continues to inquire into the policies and practices that shape working experiences, and who recognizes that by reflecting on practice he or she can improve and develop professional competence.

Regulations: Laws, executive orders, and judicial decisions coming from legislative actions at the local, state, and federal levels, from decisions made by government officials empowered to make such decisions, or from municipal, state, or district level court decisions.

Router: A specialized computer used on a network for storing addresses of network hosts, communicating with other routers, and passing packets.

Runaround: Inserting a graphic (sometimes irregularly-shaped) in the midst of text, requiring that the lines of text be laid out around the graphic. Hence the graphic is called a runaround.

Sans-serif: Without serifs.

Scanner: A device that converts graphic or text material (on paper or similar medium) into an electronic equivalent suitable for manipulation by a computer.

Serif: Perpendicular finishing strokes on the ends of lines forming characters.

Server: A computer with a special service function on a network, for example, receiving and connecting incoming telephone calls, or managing traffic from more than one computer to a printer or modem.

Single-page layout: A format that involves printing on only one side of the page. The reader sees only a series of right-hand pages.

Slow-scan: A method of sending visual data, e.g., graphs of picture images over phone lines. Picture quality is adequate for some education uses but not comparable to commercial TV.

Slow-scan video: A method of capturing and transmitting a still video image through standard telephone lines. Also referred to as a freeze-frame and still-video.

Spreadsheet: The generic name for software designed to enter, edit, label, and manipulate arithmetic data in columns.

SME: Subject-matter expert.

Strategic Planning Process: A comprehensive and structure process for planning the design and accomplishment of a particular mission or project.

Style: An abbreviation for typestyle. Common typestyles include roman (or plain), *italic*, **bold**, ***bold italic***, outline, and shadow.

Style Sheet: (1) Originally, a sheet containing all specifications for type and layout of a given document. (2) An electronic equivalent of the original definition, incorporated as part of a word processing or page layout program on a computer.

Subordinate Heading: An inferior heading; one that comes below (is a subset of) a superior heading.

Superordinate Heading: A superior heading; one that comes above (is a superset of) an inferior heading.

Summative Evaluation: Evaluation conducted after project completion for the benefit of some external audience *or* decision-maker (e.g., funding agency, or future possible user), though it may be done by either internal or external evaluators or a mixture. For reasons of credibility, it is much more likely to involve external evaluators than is a formative evaluation. (see formative evaluation)

Supercomputer: The name for the largest and fastest computers.

Synchronous: A term that refers to communication in which interaction between the sender and the receiver is not delayed.

Transponder: A satellite's receiver and transmitter that receives and amplifies a signal prior to its re-transmission to an earth station.

Telecommunication: The art and science of communication at a distance.

Teleconferencing: Bringing people together by electronic means (audio, audiographics, video, computer). **Audio teleconferencing** permits different individuals in the conference to speak to one another. **Video teleconferencing** can be one-way video with two-way audio or fully interactive with two-way video and two-way audio. **Computer teleconferencing** connects individual computers to a host computer for asynchronous conferencing (not in real time) or synchronous conferencing that connects computers and users to each other in real time.

Telephony: The art and science of sound transmission over a distance by changing sounds into electrical signals for transmission through communication equipment.

Template (template document): An electronic document that is "empty" (devoid of content) or in which dummy content exists. In the former case, new information is placed into the document; in the latter case, the dummy content is replaced with new information.

Typeface: The characteristic, distinctive outline or shape of a collection of characters comprising all the letters of the alphabet, the numerals, and associated characters.

Typestyle: A variation of the basic, or roman, font. Common variants include *italic*, **bold**, ***bold italic***, outline, and shadow.

USENET: A service available on the Internet that supports ongoing discussions called news groups.

Universal Service: Having telephone service available in every home in the United States.

Uplink: The communication link from the transmitting earth station to the satellite. Consists of a large directional antenna and high power transmitters.

Video Digitizer: A device that converts a television picture into an electronic equivalent suitable for manipulation by a computer.

Videodisc: A reflective disc that contains video and audio information and is designed for playback on a television screen. Optical videodiscs are based on a system in which the tracks on the disc are monitored by an optical laser.

WAN (wide area network): Two or more computers connected over long-distances by means of telephone or radio circuits.

White Space: Space in which nothing is printed, in a deliberate attempt to unify continuous elements and separate them from disparate elements.

Word Processor: The generic name for software designed to enter, edit, and manage text documents.

Writing Tablet: An electronic device through which information that is written or drawn with a stylus or light pen is transmitted to and reproduced on a monitor. Also referred to as a graphics tablet or pad.

AUTHOR INDEX

Seiter, C., 220*n*
Seldin, P., 286
Self, C. C., 281
Sewart, D., 34
Shaeffer, J. M., 148, 154, 281
Shale, D., 149, 168, 173
Shapiro, J., 50
Shatz, M. A., 57, 180, 183
Sherow, S., 109
Shirley, R. C., 72
Shuping, M. B., 225
Simmons, C., 17
Smellie, D. C., 169, 176
Smeltzer, L. R., 156
Smith, F. A., 155, 177, 185
Snyder, L., 214
Soloman, G., 45
Sparkes, J. J., 143, 146
Spector, J. M., 214
Speth, C., 43, 47, 48, 49, 51, 52, 53, 54
Spiegelman, M., 121
Sponder, B. M., 92, 98, 103, 142, 146, 153
Spurlin, J. E., 112
Stahmer, A., 181, 183
Stark, J. S., 146
Stepich, D. A., 127
Stewart, D., 225
Stoffgren, P. E., 260
Stone, H., 47
Stowitschek, J., 59
Stroud, M. A., 5
Stubbs, J., 143
Stufflebeam, D. L., 100
Swain, P., 47

T

Tait, A., 18
Takemoto, P. A., 136
Tanenbaum, A. S., 201
Tavaggia, T., 43
Tennyson, R., 214
Thiagarajan, S., 145
Thompson, J. R., 5
Thompson, M. M., 135
Thorvaldsen, P., 3, 4
Threlkeld, R. M., 56, 156
Tinker, M. A., 119, 120, 121
Tisdall, B., 219*n*
Tresman, S., 281

Trollip, S. R., 121
Trueman, M., 112
Tucker, R. W., 101
Tyler, R. W., 100

V

Vail, T., 253
Vance, C. M., 156
Vandehaar, D., 152
Van Kekerix, M., 135
Van Monfrans, A., 92
van Soest, C., 169
Verduin, J. R., 136
Vivian, R., 57
Vlcek, C., 240

W

Wager, W. W., 173
Waggoner, M. D., 48
Wagner, E. D., 173, 260
Walker, K., 58, 183
Wallace, J., 16
Waller, R. H. W., 111, 125
Weaver, G., 282
Wedemeyer, C. A., 109
Wedman, J. F., 281
Weinstein, S. B., 20, 170
Weisenberg, M., 121
Wellens, R. A., 141, 142
Wells, R., 59
White, J. V., 120, 121
Whittington, N., 43
Widner, D., 139, 140
Wiesner, P., 143
Wileman, R., 156, 175
Wilkes, C., 50
Williams, D., 92
Williams, F., 254
Williams, R., 123
Willis, B., 23, 50, 55, 57, 97, 109, 110, 138, 150, 152, 166, 171, 183, 214, 281
Wilson, D., 26
Wilson, H., 18
Winn, B., 184
Witherspoon, J., 48
Witkin, B. R., 91, 92, 93
Wolcott, L. L., 143, 144, 154, 155
Wolff, S., 200
Wong, A. T., 173, 177, 181, 191

Wood, D. N., 178
Worthen, B. R., 100
Wright, L. J., 281
Wright, S., 55
Wydra, D., 59

Z

Zigerell, J. J., 168
Zollman, D., 225
Zvacek, S. M., 141

SUBJECT INDEX

H

Half-duplex systems for audio-only conferencing, 137
Hawaii, distance education in, 16
Hawaii Interactive Television System (HITS), 16
Headers and footers, 112
Headings
  explained in course introduction, 126
  number of levels of, 112
  placement of, 112
  Rule of X's for, 121
  tables of content reflecting structure of, 112
  white space used around, 121–122
Headings and titles, 112
High Southwest Plains Network (HSPN), 270
High vulnerability, characteristic of academic infrastructure, 280–281
Home Computing Program, 200
Hong Kong Open Learning Institute, 13
Hypermedia, 217
Hyphenation, interrupting reading, 120

I

ICDL (International Centre for Distance Learning), 9
Icons, 116–117, 125
IMI (interactive multimedia instruction), 222–223
Indention and lists, layout for, 114
Independent study, interactive technologies aiding, 216–218
Indexes, importance of, 115
India, distance education in, 7, 13
Indira Ghandi National Open University, India, 7
Individual interaction, 46. *See also* Interaction
Indonesia, distance education in, 7, 14–15
  Western model imposed on Asian culture, 15
Information explosion, 4
Information society, 4
Instructional design
  analysis phase of, 173
  basing on needs assessment results, 95

basing on technology to be used, 57
  design and development phase of, 175
  elements maximizing interactivity, 124–127
  evaluation phase of, 175
  for out-of-class work, 97–99
  student-centered approach to, 153–154
Instructional development, 95–97
  for out of class learning, 97–99
  individual approach to, 96
  steps in, 96–97
  system level, 96–97
  teacher level, 97
  team approach to, 96, 102–104
Instructional materials, writing for, 127–128
Instructional objectives, 126
Instructional products evaluation, 100
Instructional television
  See also Interactive television; Mediated classroom; Televised instruction; Television
  administration and coordination needed by, 175
  Business TV (BTV), 172
  camera making selections for students, 177–178
  effective for remedial courses, 53
  instructional design for, 173, 175
  Instructional Television Fixed Service (ITFS), 20, 22, 170
  instructor orientation for, 180
  media production and print support for, 175–177
  Midwest Program on Airborne Television Instruction (MPATI), 19
  North Dakota Educational Television Council (ETC), 24
  Oklahoma Televised Instruction System (TIS), 22
  production techniques suggested, 179–180
  Rural Alaska Television Network (RATNET), 22
  studio considerations, 177–179
  system design for, 175
  Television Northern Canada (TVNC), 28
Instructional Television Fixed Service (ITFS), 20, 22
  as a low cost alternative, 170

Telecommunications *(Continued)*
  public policy affecting, 251–256
  regulations affecting distance
    education, 249–251
  regulatory activities affecting
    distance education, 258–261
  regulatory environment of, 256–258
Teleconferencing, 171–172
  See also Audioconference teaching;
    Audioconferencing technologies;
    Videoconferencing
  changing teachers' role, 141
  effective teacher behaviors for, 58
Telephone-based instruction, 44–46
  equally effective with traditional
    instruction, 44–46
  not preferred over traditional
    instruction, 45
  widely used for distance education,
    44
Telephone services
  antitrust action against AT&T,
    254–255, 259
  benefits of competition offset by
    access and cost problems, 255–256
  cost of enhanced services barrier to
    access, 254
  cross-subsidy charges, 253
  effects of divestiture, 258–259
  encouraging pricing favorable to
    distance education, 252
  executive decisions affecting, 260–261
  growth of information service
    providers, 255
  high initial cost of enhanced services,
    255–256
  impact of competition on, 254–256
  Local Access and Transport Area, 254
  local exchange carriers, 254
  long distance and local service
    separated, 254–255
  Modification of Final Judgment
    leading to complete reorganization
    of telephone industry, 254–255
  need for public policies encouraging
    use of enhanced services, 256
  pricing structures, 252
  regulations ensuring access, 256–258
  restrictions on Bell Operating
    Companies, 255
  role of Federal Communications
    Commission (FCC), 253, 257–258

role of state Public Utilities
    Commissions, 260, 261
  telecommunications regulatory
    environment, 256–258
  universal service policy in conflict
    with competition, 252–256
  universal service policy shaping
    industry development, 253–254
  universal telephone service policy,
    252
Telephone technologies
  analog and digital, 137
  augmented by computer technology,
    136
  used for audioconferencing, 137
  used for audio-only conferencing,
    138
  used for distance education, 136
Televised instruction
  See also Instructional television
  defined, 165–166
  effective for remedial courses, 53
  reasons for choosing, 50
  useful for at-risk students, 53
Television. *See also* Instructional
    television; Televised instruction
  asynchronous interaction
    characteristic of, 169
  broadcast television, 168
  cable television, 170
  encouraging passive viewing, 168
  integrating ancillary media to
    alleviate weaknesses, 168
  mass media approach a problem, 168
  production techniques suggested for,
    179–180
  visual imagery essence of, 181
Television Northern Canada (TVNC)
  owned and operated by aboriginal
    people and northern residents, 28
  spanning five time zones, 28
Television Receive Only (TVRO) earth
    station, 170
Television studio, 177–179
  camera angle, 178
  camera making selections for
    students, 177–178
  camera movement, 179
  field of view of camera, 178
  lens movement, 179
  points of view of camera, 178
TELNET, 204–205

W

WAIS (Wide Area Information Server), 204

Warrnambool Institute of Advanced Education, Australia, 15

Western Cooperative for Educational Telecommunications, 271–272

Western Interstate Commission for Higher Education (WICHE), 272, 272

White space
  around headings, 121–122
  used to separate disparate items, 119

Wide Area Information Server (WAIS), 204

Wide area networks (WANs), 200–202
  bandwidths for, 201–202
  Big Sky Telegraph, 202
  simplest form of, 202

World communications net, technologies making possible, 4

WYSIWYG, 122

Z

Zambia, distance education in, 10–11

Zambian National Correspondence College, 10–11